THE
CORPORATION

Making Bessener Steel in Pittsburgh, 1886.

THE CORPORATION

A Centennial Biography of

United States Steel Corporation,

1901–2001

Brian Apelt

Warren Hull, Editor

CATHEDRAL PUBLISHING
UNIVERSITY OF PITTSBURGH

Written by Brian Apelt
Edited by Warren Hull

Designed by Einhorn Design
Pittsburgh, Pennsylvania

Published by Cathedral Publishing,
University of Pittsburgh,
Pittsburgh, Pennsylvania 15260

ISBN 1-887969-12-8

Printed by Hoechstetter Printing Company, Inc.,
Pittsburgh, Pennsylvania

Contents

Thomas J. Usher
Chairman, USX Corporation

Foreword

The business world had never seen anything like it: United States Steel Corporation, incorporated February 25, 1901, and capitalized for $1.4 billion, an amalgam of 10 major steel producers and manufacturing companies. The company opened for business on April 1. Some called it a colossal combine, others a behemoth trust. By any measure, it was a giant.

In 1901, life moved at a slower pace for the 76 million souls who populated this country. William McKinley was our president. Americans earned an average annual wage of $438. There was no income tax. To most folks at the time, $1.4 billion was an incomprehensible sum, a figure vast as the nation itself. A good thing, then, that *United States* was part of the corporation's name.

Almost from the moment the company burst on the scene, Wall Streeters gave it a nickname: **The Corporation**, with emphasis on THE. The financial and daily media took up the name; it fit well on the tongue and in the headlines. For nearly three decades, it was the spoken and printed name by which the world's first billion-dollar business enterprise was known. Only after the era of Judge Elbert Gary, U. S. Steel's first chairman, did the name begin to fade from use. By then, 1927, the company which was born to be Big Steel was no longer such a novelty. General Motors and Ford had made their corporate appearances. Big was getting bigger.

However one considers it, U. S. Steel was a very big deal. Writing in *Barron's* in 1996, Hofstra University Professor Robert Sobel explained just how big. "Adjusted for inflation, that $1.4 billion probably is the equivalent to around $75 billion-$80 billion today." He pointed out that in 1901 the country's gross national product was $20.7 billion and that U. S. Steel's capitalization was 7 percent of it. In today's terms, he concluded, when the gross domestic product is $7 trillion, "an IPO (an enterprise involved in an initial public offering of stock) would have to raise close to $490 billion." Almost unfathomable, isn't it?

The Corporation, *a Centennial Biography of United States Steel Corporation, 1901-2001* is not intended to be an academic study. Although it reflects scholarship, this book is meant to be easily accessible to the reader, a fond recollection of stories about people, processes—from Bessemers to BOPs to casters and beyond—and about products. It is a biography of an enormously successful business venture which in the year 2001 celebrates its 100th birthday. *The Corporation* is a tribute to those who shaped the enterprise a century ago—Andrew Carnegie, Henry Clay Frick, J. P. Morgan, Judge Elbert Gary, Charles Schwab. It is also a tribute to the million or more employees who have earned their livelihoods from U. S. Steel during those hundred years.

If I were to choose one attribute which, above all others, influenced the development of our corporate character, I would pick Judge Gary's moral compass. With it, he chartered an ethical course we strive to follow still, an integrity in conducting business evident today in the air of strength and power we continue to exude as a corporation.

Ours is a history of firsts. U. S. Steel was the first corporation to publish an annual report, the first to hold an annual meeting for its shareholders. It was the first corporation to create and apply a code of business ethics (the Gary Principles), the first to introduce benefit programs for its workers, including medical and pensions plans (called in the early years worker "welfare" programs). It was the first to adopt the eight-hour day. It was the nation's first steel company to invite the United Steel Workers (USW) to organize its workers. And the contract that followed ended a festering mistrust between labor and management stretching back into the nineteenth century, erupting in 1892 in the Homestead Strike.

It is also the history of the fascination Uncle Sam has often held for U. S. Steel. Within a few years of its founding, the corporation was the target of two major attempts to dismantle it on antitrust grounds. Both attempts failed, and we escaped the fate of Standard Oil and American Tobacco, dismembered earlier in the decade. In effect, U. S. Steel had finally been accepted as a "good trust."

Harry Truman was to meddle in our affairs more than once. As senator, he hauled U. S. Steel before his investigative committee near the end of World War II to answer charges that our Irvin Works had sent inferior plate to the war effort. Although some of our employees had fudged chemistry and test data—an embarrassment, surely—they knew the plate would meet or exceed government specifications. And it did.

As President, Truman seized steel plants in 1952 during the Korean War while a steel strike was in progress. The seizure occurred in April and lasted only three days. The Supreme Court ruled that Truman's use of muscle was unconstitutional.

Almost immediately, the President summoned U. S. Steel's Ben Fairless and USW's Philip Murray, chief industry and union negotiators, to the White House for talks. Fairless and Murray eventually reached an agreement. And later, we had a much-needed price increase.

In April 1962 came the most celebrated industry-government clash, and it was over a price increase, or, at least, an attempted one. President John F. Kennedy took on the industry, U. S. Steel in particular and Chairman Roger Blough. Never before had the government exerted such power to enforce its will, except in wartime against a military adversary.

President Lyndon Johnson weighed in with his presidential persuasion, as well. In 1965, he jawboned another pair of negotiators—U. S. Steel's Conrad Cooper and USW's I. W. Abel— into a White House settlement that avoided a strike

U. S. Steel and the government were locked in combat in the early days of the environmental movement. The issue produced such heat—and media attention—that it took years for U. S. Steel and the U.S. Environmental Protection Agency to reach an amicable relationship and workable air and water standards and compliance timetables.

The Corporation is a history, too, of the times the government and U. S. Steel were allies, working toward a shared objective. In 1907, panic swept Wall Street. Brokerage firms failed. J. P Morgan, his brother bankers in New York and the U.S. Treasury pumped money into banks and financial houses to keep the economy afloat. Nothing helped until Morgan called in U. S. Steel. What happened next would need the approval of President Theodore Roosevelt. But it would bail out Wall Street and make U. S. Steel a significant player in the steel business of the South.

Before we entered World War II, the Secretary of War convinced U. S. Steel to buy shiploads of government guns and munitions and trans-ship them to Britain. These armaments replaced arms lost in its defeat at Dunkirk and helped save England from collapse.

At the request of President Franklin D. Roosevelt, who feared Germany and Japan could attack steel mills on either coast, we built a plant from the ground up in Utah, a safe 700 miles from the Pacific. We ran the plant for the government, and at war's end, it became our Geneva Works.

U. S. Steel-U.S. government relations were never closer than during the two world wars. In both conflicts, we shipped prodigious amounts of steel, including armor plate. We built tanks and ships, made bombs and munitions, fabricated airplane parts, even invented portable steel panels which could be locked together to form landing mats. Of the 467 million tons of steel and armaments produced by America's steel mills during World War II, more than one-third came from the mills of U. S. Steel.

Examples such as these suggest that the history of U. S. Steel is, in large measure, the history of the twentieth century. It is. And the relationship between this company and the government—rancorous some of the time, cordial most of the time—shows clearly that our fortunes and those of the United States were often inextricably intertwined.

Eighty-one years after its founding, U. S. Steel redefined itself by buying an oil company—Marathon. The aquisition sheltered the company from a severe downturn in steel that dashed the life out of many of its competitors. U. S. Steel finally owned a business, unrelated to steel, which would respond to its own market forces while being immune to steel's cyclical ups and downs. Marathon could be expected to add significant revenues to U. S. Steel's corporate treasury.

The Corporation tells how we got a new corporate name—USX Corporation—and about the separation of the corporation's stock into two classes, one representing steel, the other, oil and gas.

It tells of our battle with corporate raider Carl Icahn who tried to spin off the steel business as a dividend to shareholders.

In these pages you will read, as well, about one of the most painful times in our history—the closure during the Seventies and Eighties of steel mills long past their productive and profitable lives, the layoff of employees, the early retirement of thousands of others and the decline of steel towns across the country.

The Corporation also tells about revival, the slow but determined turnaround which U. S. Steel made toward the end of the last century. And about recognition, especially during the Nineties. It was a time when U. S. Steel was succeeding on many fronts, and the company was winning praise—*and* awards—from its customers, from the EPA, even from the news media. It was recognition for our employees who had been invited into the decision-making process, who had been encouraged to help us set and meet new standards of product quality and service to customers, who had helped us achieve environmental excellence, who had helped to improve our corporate citizenship. Their success is recounted in the very last section of this book which also describes U. S. Steel's *Vision* program, a solid foundation on which we can build in the new century which lies before us.

(Mr. Usher's comments are concluded in the Afterword which ends this book.)

Chapter 1

Carnegie Creates
His One Big Basket

New Yorkers strolling past their city's exclusive University Club on the crisp evening of December 11, 1900, may have slowed their stride to study the top-hatted gentlemen parading into the opulent establishment. The passersby might even have recognized some of them as giants of banking and industry, and wondered what business these notables had here this night.

Or they may have been too preoccupied to notice, too busy mentally checking their holiday gift lists. Or lost in wonder about what the new year might bring.

After all, this was an incredible moment to be alive, exciting and unsettling at the same time. Think of it! In a few weeks the world would officially ring in the twentieth century—a new era that promised to heap fresh wonders on top of those bestowed during the post–Civil War age of invention.

Steel king Andrew Carnegie

The 80 moguls filing into their club couldn't know it, but they were about to witness an event that would help shape that soon-to-arrive century. They were here to attend a dinner honoring Charles M. Schwab, right-hand man of steel king Andrew Carnegie. The gathering would become a legend. But in the weeks ahead, some of the assembled would wonder whether it had been a carefully planned performance, a show staged to woo into an unthinkably huge business deal their most notable brother, hard-eyed J. Pierpont Morgan, the railroad magnate and the Gilded Age's foremost financier.

Schwab was president of the then-reigning steel giant, Carnegie Steel, and a superb manager of people. He also was a natural actor, a frustrated song-and-dance man who, as a boy in Loretto, Pennsylvania, won the attention of adults by performing stunts and magic tricks. Blessed with a photographic memory and a golden throat, he would scan a script and get it down cold. Then he would tear up the text, stride to the podium and flawlessly deliver a talk that sounded off-the-cuff.

Charles M. Schwab,
the dealmaker

He seemed to have a script stored in his formidable brain this night in New York. Called upon as guest of honor to give a short speech, he instead spun a half-hour oration: his vision of the steel industry for the twentieth century.

Schwab first reminded the group that the U.S. steel industry was ready to compete with foreign steelmakers head-on. But domestic steel companies were in no shape for hard battle, he said. They'd reached capacity and had wrung most of the excess costs out of their operations. That spelled hard times.

But Schwab had a solution. If several firms united, they could combine complementary operations while they slashed costs. The resulting, single, mighty, and mightily efficient trust would be a formidable competitor. Each of its plants would keep costs close to the bone by specializing in a single product—steel plate for ships' hulls, say, or rails for train track. Each would keep shipping costs low by operating in the same region as its customers.

Perhaps most important, all the plants would be run by executives who placed cooperation above cutting throats. The prevailing mindset was that the other guy was out to destroy you, so you had to get him first. It wasn't healthy competition. It was a free-for-all. End this destructive skirmishing, Schwab preached. If the bickering chieftains of steel would only consolidate and cooperate, they would share a glorious future. Calm would replace the competitive storm, encouraging investment in new technologies and products. Opportunities would blossom. So would profits.

Schwab accompanied his wonder-company sketch with powerful gestures and a calmly compelling voice. And he mesmerized his audience. J. P. Morgan sat through the entire speech staring at Schwab without so much as lighting the cigar dangling from his mouth.

Morgan was transfixed for good reason. He was the financial creator and chairman of Federal Steel, one of the only runners-up to Carnegie's formidable outfit. And he hated competition. Didn't it just add more disruption to an economy that was already in chaos? Didn't it waste precious energy and money, especially during depressions like the one from which the country had just emerged?

But instead of relief, Morgan foresaw only more trouble. Things had to be brought under control, and Schwab's supertrust, insulated from competition, could be his salvation. At evening's end, Morgan pulled Schwab aside and pumped him for details of his dream company. The next morning, as Schwab boarded a train to Pittsburgh and his office, Morgan mulled over how to weld together the mighty steel trust envisioned by the young Carnegie Steel executive.

It was a turning point for steel, and industry.

In the dance that followed, Morgan recruited Schwab to ask Carnegie how much money he wanted for his steel business. Schwab found the little Scotsman golfing in Westchester County and sounded him out. Carnegie pondered an asking price overnight. The next day he penciled "$480 million" on a slip of paper and handed it to Schwab, who relayed it to Morgan. It took the wily financier about two seconds to study the figure and accept it.

The way was clear for Morgan to assemble the largest steel corporation—the largest *corporation*—the world had seen, with Carnegie Steel as its keystone.

J. P. Morgan,
the moneyman

Legally born on February 25, 1901, the new United States Steel Corporation was really a holding company, a confederation of more than a dozen outfits. This was a behemoth, capitalized at an unheard-of 1.4 *billion* dollars. It would alter the way industry worked in the new century, imposing new efficiencies, new technologies, new ways even to think about making and using steel. It would influence the way business was conducted in other industries, too.

It also would make celebrities of some of the men who put it together. Charlie Schwab would soon fall because of personal failures, resigning after becoming one of the twentieth century's first media victims. He would bounce back. Now, though, he was riding high as the first president of an unprecedented company.

Andrew Carnegie? He'd stood in the spotlight for decades, and loved every minute of it—almost. He *was* steel. But selling to Morgan would set him free to slip into retirement, or at least the closest thing to it that he could abide. He could get busy giving away the money he had worked so hard to amass. Relieving himself of his riches would make good a pledge from his youth, and align his actions with a decree he had made before he achieved fame:

"The man who dies thus rich dies disgraced," he had written.

It was an odd creed for a Gilded-Age industrialist. But Carnegie always seemed to have a love-hate relationship with money. He appeared to fear wealth—or dying before he could share his. Robert L. Heilbroner, writing in *American Heritage* magazine, told how, late in life, Carnegie asked his private secretary, "How much did you say I had given away, Poynton?" At the answer, "$324,657,399," he would reply in bafflement: "Good heaven! Where did I ever get all that money?"

Was it an act? Of course. Carnegie followed every cent he made. But he liked to reinvent himself and his past when doing so made him look good. He fancied himself a social philosopher, moralizing for the good of others' souls when he should have been tending

Carnegie & Morgan—Steelman and Moneyman

to the devious side of his own. He was a brutal competitor, who spent much of his life creating industries and wealth, making himself the world's richest man. But then he worked almost as hard at giving most of his money away. With his white beard and plump cheeks, he looked like Santa Claus, and believed in playing the part.

This was a robber baron? Don't be fooled, warned his detractors. Carnegie's pious attitude and liberal ways were a front for greed. Typical opportunist.

They didn't understand him. Unlike some of his contemporaries who sucked their enterprises dry of cash and walked away, Carnegie really did see dollars as bricks, things to build with. And his roots were anything but old money. They were planted in radical soil.

Tile-roofed cottage in Dunfermline, Scotland, where Carnegie was born in 1835

Andrew Carnegie was born in 1835, in a tile-roofed cottage in Dunfermline, Scotland. The village was a hotbed of revolution where Carnegie's father and uncle made second careers of orating for working-class rights to vote and strike.

It was the kind of revolutionary fervor that put the villagers at dangerous odds with the British Crown. And it made a deep impression on young Carnegie. Seventy years later, Heilbroner wrote, Andy would recall being awakened one night by men who had come to tell his parents that his uncle, Bailie Morrison, had been thrown in jail:

"He dared to hold a meeting which had been forbidden. It is not to be wondered that, nursed amid such surroundings, I developed into a violent young Republican whose motto was 'death to privilege.'"

When Andrew's father, Will Carnegie, was not preaching revolution, he was at his hand loom weaving fine linens, a Dunfermline specialty. But linen had been losing ground against cheaper cotton. And while Will and his fellow handweavers tried to shrug off the Industrial Revolution, they were no match for the streams of cotton pouring off the new steam-powered looms. Andrew would never forget the day his despairing father pulled him aside and confessed, "Andra, I can get nae mair work."

Carnegie at age sixteen

Will considered laboring in a coal mine or factory to make ends meet. His wife said no, the family's hopes lie in leaving Scotland. But where would they go? While the family was making its plans, in 1848, revolutions were breeding chaos in Europe (an irony that could not have been lost on Will the firebrand). The family decided a better option was to undertake a "flitting" to America, and to Pittsburgh, the home of two of Andrew's aunts. Soon Will, his wife Margaret, and Andy and his brother and sister, were jammed with other emigrants into a ship and crossing the Atlantic.

Years later, after *he* had done so much to dethrone one material for another, turning himself into a rich celebrity, Andrew would return with his aged mother to Dunfermline for a victory visit. The family had chosen wisely. America was the right place for a boy as bright and bent on success as Andy Carnegie.

Still, getting to America was an ordeal. After the cramped sea voyage, the family took to slow-poke canal boats, drifting dreamily for hundreds of miles before reaching their destination. But after the Scottish Highlands, Pittsburgh was a painful letdown. It was smoky and dirty, and the family could afford only two modest rooms on Rebecca Street in Allegheny — "Slabtown."

Andrew had to forgo school to help support the family. He gamely stalked the sidewalks in search of work, and found it. In the spring of 1849, after a stint in a shop that made knitting bobbins (he fired the furnace and flirted with bookkeeping duties), Andy landed a job with the Ohio Telegraph Company. He was such a good study at telegraphy that he was soon translating the incoming clicks by ear rather than reading them as dots and dashes punched on a tape. The feat—Andy was one of few people who could do it—drew gawkers from the street.

One of them was Thomas A. Scott, local superintendent of the Pennsylvania Railroad. In *Andrew Carnegie* (Oxford University Press, 1970), Carnegie's biographer, Joseph Frazier Wall, traced young Andy's career with Scott. The railroad man, Wall wrote, could see that this bright lad would be a good catch, and, in early 1853, hired him as his own telegrapher and secretary. Carnegie proved his worth one day by defusing a crisis. Posing as his boss (who was absent) he flashed out telegraphed orders that untangled two wrecked freight trains. He was sticking his neck out, but his actions limited the injuries and damage.

Soon Scott was calling Andy "my white-haired Scotch devil." Impressed with Andy's talents, Scott advanced his demon, in 1859, to region superintendent. But he rewarded Andy in other ways, too—notably by persuading him to sink $500 into stock in a promising company, a sure thing. It was a staggering sum. Andy raised it by convincing his mother she should mortgage their home. Then came a revelation: the first dividend check, money made not by his own sweat, but with someone else's money. "Eureka!" Andy whooped. "Here's the goose that lays the golden eggs."

In a few years the stock was paying $1,400 in annual dividends, and Carnegie was hooked on breeding golden geese. He invested in railroad sleeping cars, oil, banks. According to Wall, he went in with friends to buy a farm out in oil country for $40,000. When that deal paid a million dollars in dividends in a single year, Andy exclaimed to a friend, "Oh, I'm rich! I'm rich!"

And he was. But the transaction that would open the gate to the kingdom of steel for him was his purchase of a share in a local iron works in the Pittsburgh area run by a hot-tempered German named Andrew Kloman.

Kloman and his milder brother, Anton, had hit on a technique to forge iron axles that were especially tough. With the Civil War demand for gun carriages, business skyrocketed. To finance their growth, the Klomans invited in new partners, and their money. But young Henry Phipps, Jr. and Tom Miller continually quarreled with the Klomans.

When discord put cracks in the association, Henry and Tom in 1863 turned to someone they truly respected: their longtime chum Andy Carnegie. Surely the wise Andy could restore order.

But everything Carnegie tried seemed only to stir up more bickering. After further wrangling, the team split up. In 1864, Andy, with his younger brother Tom in tow, started a competing iron mill just down the Allegheny River on a former cabbage farm. And as Andy lamented the loss of his friend Phipps' talents, the Klomans, Miller and Phipps kept glancing nervously at the plant run by the dangerously clever Carnegies.

Given the situation, it wasn't hard for Andy to convince his old associates that they and he should merge. The result: a new operation that Carnegie named the Union Iron Works. It was a fitting title, considering that much of the war-split nation was seeking a way to reunite.

Still, the elder Carnegie brother was skeptical of his and the Klomans' new enterprise. Given the tentative times, he considered investing in steel "most hazardous." As his later associate and biographer James Howard Bridge would write, "Carnegie found himself fortuitously and complainingly thrust upon a road which was to lead him to a 'fortune' of 250 million dollars."

He needn't have worried. Events would soon remind him that, for a smart and shrewd young entrepreneur, this *was* the right place and time.

If you've studied the stiffly posed portraits that Matthew Brady and other nineteenth-century photographers left us, you might think of their era as sluggish and staid. In fact, it was wild and woolly, even after the Civil War.

The conflict created profits that were fed back into the economy. Labor was cheap, supplied by immigrants and folks off the farm. Others rushed off to find their fortunes in the West. It all triggered an explosion of invention, investment, growth, opportunity. But it was a wild ride, with the economy shooting up and down like one of the crazy roller coasters that would appear later in the century.

And in the last few decades of the century, the wonders kept coming: The electric light banished the early darkness of evening, postponing bedtime for quiet reading or a chat with the family—and the rest of the family could be miles away, thanks to the telephone. More than that, we did the impossible, taking to the air like the birds that owned it.

Technology was really something, and Tom Edison, Alexander Bell and the other wizards who gave the world these marvels were heroes. As for the bankers and business tycoons who put the fruits of science within reach—well, they were saviors, or scalawags. Or both. Your judgment depended on where you stood on the economic food chain.

Steel was obviously vital to the formula for the unfolding future. Back in 1852, Elisha Otis wowed the crowd at New York's Crystal Palace Exposition by daring gravity in *his* version of the "dangerous" elevator. He rode the rig's platform to a height well above the spectators' heads, then ordered an assistant to cut the rope with an ax. Instead of crashing to the floor, the platform and its inventor froze in their tracks. Elevators were safe! Supported by metal skeletons, buildings could take up less space on the ground by stretching even higher into the sky.

Meanwhile, the railroads were sprouting horizontally, growing faster after the war, and the prairie pioneers needed metal for farm tools. But iron wouldn't do. It was too heavy and not strong enough. It *worked* for railroad tracks, but it wore out much too quickly.

Steel was the answer. Yet making really good steel was too expensive. That problem was whisked away by an awesome new process.

We could quibble over who invented the "Bessemer" process. William Kelly of Eddyville, Kentucky, rightly claimed *he* fathered it several years before Sir Henry Bessemer—ignorant of Kelly's work—announced it in 1856. History gives the credit to Bessemer, who had perfected the equipment that would make the process work. (He started his career by inventing a super-sized military shell, and then had to figure out how to make a gun strong enough to fire the thing.) What's important here is the beauty of Bessemer conversion. By blowing cold air through molten iron, the process created heat so intense that it burned away the carbon and silicon that made iron too soft for rails, buildings and other high-end uses.

William Kelly

There's a story that Carnegie was sour on steel until, on a trip to England, he witnessed a Bessemer converter in action. He experienced himself a conversion that was almost spiritual, and spread hosannas to Bessemerized steel.

It didn't happen that way. True, with its mighty pear-shaped pot spewing smoke and flame, Bessemer conversion made one's jaw drop. But Carnegie had been experimenting with Bessemer conversion before he saw it at work in England. And he was a tenuous convert.

Sir Henry Bessemer and William Kelly were both involved in the development of the Bessemer steelmaking process at approximately the same time.

He knew there was a hitch, a serious one. The carbon- and silicon-banishing Bessemer process was fine for iron ores used in Britain—so fine, in fact, that the English were using it to take the rail business away from American mills. America's ore simply wasn't right for the process. It was loaded with another contaminant: phosphorous, which made even Bessemer-hardened steel crumble like stale crackers.

Fortune cooperated again when, in Michigan's Upper Peninsula, entrepreneurs opened fields of iron ore that were plentiful and virtually phosphorous-free. It was an unbelievably rich trove. What's more, it was so shallow that it could practically be shoveled from the ground right into ships. Getting it to the East surely would put steel producers—Carnegie most of all—on top. The federal government and Eastern capitalists knitted a network of canals that would take the ore through the Great Lakes, to rail terminals in Ohio, Pennsylvania and New York. By the start of the 1870s, the work was done.

Sir Henry Bessemer

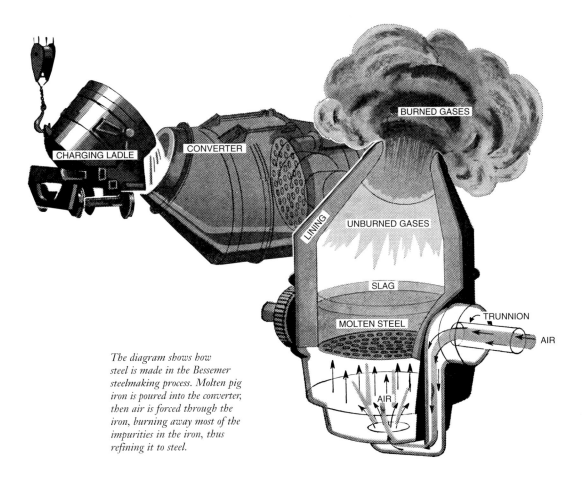

The diagram shows how steel is made in the Bessemer steelmaking process. Molten pig iron is poured into the converter, then air is forced through the iron, burning away most of the impurities in the iron, thus refining it to steel.

Now America had a bounty of rich iron ore, a cheap means of getting it to the steel centers, some amazing new technologies to cook up steel that was strong and durable, and a new generation of tinkerers, engineers and inventors to find ways to put the metal to work. The country was poised to become the ruler in steel. And the throne would belong to Andrew Carnegie.

The young man seemed to know he was bound for *some* throne. It was back in 1868 that he sat himself down at the desk in his room at the St. Nicholas Hotel in New York City, to draft the outline for the rest of his life. As Heilbroner describes the scene, Andy must have mentally replayed his up-from-poverty, Horatio Alger story as he sat down with his pen. "Thirty-three," he wrote, "and an income of 50,000$ [sic] per annum."

"By this time two years I can so arrange all my business as to secure at least 50,000 per annum. Beyond this never earn—make no effort to increase fortune, but spend the surplus each year for benevolent [sic] purposes. Cast aside business forever except for others.

"Man must have an idol—The amassing of wealth is one of the worst species of idolitary [sic]…Whatever I engage in I must push inordinately therefor [sic] should I be careful to choose that life which will be the most elevating in character."

In that letter to himself, Carnegie also vowed to resign business at the age of 35.

He couldn't hold himself to his pledge.

For the most part, though, Carnegie had an eerie ability to sense precisely the right thing to do at just the right time. As he sat at his desk in the iron works and pondered where to go next, he was well aware that steel—Bessemer steel—was getting set to soar.

He already had experience with the Bessemer process. In the late 1860s, he had installed a small Bessemer converter at his Freedom Iron Company in Lewiston, Pennsylvania. By 1868, the plant was turning out steel ribbons, which were bonded to the tops of iron rails. It was an early example of composites. Widely popular with the railroads at first, these hybrid rails eventually proved as unreliable and nearly as short-lived as standard iron rails. The Freedom mills, however, rolled a small quantity of rails made exclusively from Bessemer steel. But it was enough to convince Carnegie that it was time to commit himself to steel.

He would do so in a big way, establishing a full-scale steel mill devoted exclusively to the production of rails. It was a nice touch that the site selected was a tract called Braddock's Field. There, more than a hundred years earlier—in 1755—Edward Braddock, the British General

An early view of the Edgar Thomson Works. Ground-breaking took place in 1873.

who was the property's namesake, was routed by the French and Indians. The "Scotch" revolutionary in Carnegie must have felt an old score was at least partly settled when he plunked his new mill down on the old battlefield, adding insult to the injury of British defeat.

Built a dozen miles south of Pittsburgh on the Monongahela River, the new works was named after Edgar J. Thomson, the Pennsylvania Railroad president who had supported Carnegie in some of the budding tycoon's investments. (And whose company would be the works' biggest customer.) Ground for the works was broken in 1873. The country was deep in a depression, and that meant Carnegie could buy material cheap, about 25 percent less than in good times. And the plant opened for business in 1875, just in time for the steel revolution.

In its first full year of production—1876—Edgar Thompson produced 45,563 tons of steel and 32,228 tons of rail. Carnegie was overjoyed when his first order—2,000 steel rails in August 1875—came from the new mill's namesake at the Pennsylvania Railroad.

The works very likely accelerated the timetable for progress by getting the jump on another new process.

Besides two five-ton Bessemer converters, the Edgar Thomson Works—or "E.T.," as it was called—was equipped with two new Siemens open-hearth furnaces. Invented a decade earlier by a German mechanic, the open hearth was almost unknown in America in the 1870s. But Carnegie sensed that it, too, was promising. At several points in the process, crews could remove samples of molten metal from the furnace's belly. These could be quickly analyzed, and the "melt" adjusted as needed. Further, the open hearth was good for producing an especially high grade of steel for special orders. And the two open hearths at E.T. would allow Carnegie's people to experiment with the new process, which was eventually destined to supercede Bessemer steelmaking.

It was another example of Carnegie's knack for positioning enterprises in time and space, a talent which kept him far ahead of his competitors. And it was matched by his genius for spotting genius. He detected the faintest hint of extraordinary ability, enabling him to build up a stable of money-managers and idea men that arguably was second to none.

Carnegie, for instance, engaged Alexander Holley to oversee the building of the plant. Holley was the country's leading authority on the Bessemer process. So closely had he worked with Henry Bessemer that numerous improvements to the process had come from Holley's agile engineering mind.

Holley had already installed Bessemer converters for a number of Carnegie competitors, including the Cambria Iron Works in Johnstown, Pennsylvania. There he met a remarkable man who would loom large in the lore and fortunes of Carnegie Steel, Captain William Jones.

Jones was a true original. He accompanied Holley to E.T. He translated Holley's engineering plans into what then was the country's most advanced steel works. Jones also served as E.T.'s first superintendent. And his workers loved their Captain Jones. He always looked out for them, tending to details such as ventilation in the shops. He would even succeed in cutting the workday from the grueling standard of twelve hours to eight. James Howard Bridge quotes Jones' philosophy in *The Inside History of the Carnegie Steel Company* (Aldine Book Company, 1903; reprinted in 1991 by University of Pittsburgh Press):

Captain William Jones, first superintendent of the Edgar Thomson Works

"I have always found it best to treat men well, and I find that my men are anxious to retain my good will by working steadily and honestly…. All haughty and disdainful treatment of men has a very decided and bad effect on them."

Jones was a mechanical wizard, too. He collected patents like other people at the time collected antique reproductions. His inventions, such as his improved, railcar-sized steel mixer, saved the company millions of dollars every year. He was always on top of technology, never afraid to junk almost-new equipment in favor of new models, however costly, if they would fatten profits in the long run.

Carnegie had made sure his brother Tom stayed with him. It was a brotherly thing to do, especially when Tom proved himself to be among the sharpest of managers himself. (Sadly, he died young, before realizing his full capabilities.)

Henry Phipps, Carnegie's longtime pal, was once again at Andy's side. He was a bit timid, but he shared Jones' sixth sense for improvements. One day, an inventor suggested to Jones that a slight reshaping of Carnegie's famous Lucy blast furnace would produce more steel. It was a far-fetched idea, but Phipps sensed it could work. It did. The rebuilt Lucy (named after Tom Carnegie's wife) shot from an already impressive 550-tons-a-week capacity to more than 800 tons.

Phipps also discovered the virtues of recycling cinder, an abundant but annoying blast furnace waste. Putting the stuff back into the furnace made better steel and saved piles of money. Other steel operators would have loved that trick, but Phipps kept it under his hat.

The famous Lucy blast furnace of Carnegie's steelmaking operations

Of all his cohorts, Carnegie's hands-down favorite was a Captain Jones discovery, Charlie Schwab.

For one thing, Charlie made Carnegie laugh. For another, the affable, low-key Schwab charmed the steelworkers, cultivating camaraderie among them, smoothing their feathers when they voiced grievances. When he came across a worker smoking in the plant—against the rules—Schwab would quietly hand the offender an expensive cigar to light up after quitting time. He never smoked, himself, and rarely drank. But he did enjoy playing a little poker. Discreetly. The prudish Carnegie frowned on the sin of gambling.

Happily, the schoolboyish Schwab's agreeable disposition came with a first-class brain, and he never failed to salute Carnegie and do his bidding. The elder steelman took him under his wing and came to think of him as "my Charlie," perhaps reliving the bond he enjoyed with his mentor, Thomas Scott, years earlier.

Schwab was a prize, but in many ways the most formidable of Carnegie's associates was coke baron Henry Clay Frick.

THE IMPORTANCE OF BEING ANDY

While Andrew Carnegie was born in Scotland and spent much of his time there, it's fair to say that most Americans think of him as one of their own. Pop-artist Andy Warhol affirmed Carnegie's membership in America's gallery of icons when he painted the steelman in 1981.

The portrait, pure Warhol, depicts Carnegie in bright colors. Superimposed over the face and shoulders is a ghostly, duplicate image. A "second" Carnegie revealing itself? A glimpse of the "real" Andrew?

Carnegie at Skibo Castle in Scotland with his dog Lassie

How many Carnegies were there, anyway? In the popular version, Andrew Carnegie is about making lots of money, then giving it away. True enough. He became king of his hill and amassed a fortune through no-holds-barred competition, and through management innovations. For example, he was the first big boss to generate wealth by hiring the best brains and paying them handsomely to stay with him. But after retiring from industry, he tended to philanthropy with as much zeal and thought as he'd put into building his fortune.

Carnegie is most remembered for his specialty, donating his free public libraries, which he saw not only as institutions of education, but as community centers and primers of local economies. He and the trusts he fathered gave more than 2,800 libraries to communities in the United States, Great Britain, and countries as far as New Zealand and the British West Indies. Carnegie built Carnegie Hall in New York, established trusts and foundations to endow universities and in other ways plowed his wealth back into society.

But he did more. He dedicated his time and influence to an assortment of causes, from spelling reform (simplifying words—for example, cutting "thought" to "thot"—would make writing easier, save paper and ease writer's cramp), to the rights of African Americans (he contributed to black colleges and became a great friend and financial benefactor of educator–reformer Booker T. Washington),

Carnegie Free Library in Braddock, Pennsylvania, was the first of the endowed Carnegie libraries. It was dedicated March 30, 1889.

"If philanthropy is seen as the business of giving away money wisely, and social change the return on that investment, then knowledge —new ideas, discoveries, human achievements— is the currency."

to pacificism (he counseled world leaders on the urgency of creating a global peace-keeping organization, and was crushed when the doves failed to prevent the First World War). He supported extending the rights of women. And he shocked fellow industrialists by denying—in a 1908 article in The Century, and in later testimony before a federal commission—the need to continue a protective tariff on most products imported into the country. Reason: The "protected" industries, including steel, were on their feet, fit to compete in the world arena. A tariff merely taxed domestic consumers.

In short, Carnegie had entered the cocoon of retirement and emerged as a progressive.

He was worth $250 million at his retirement. American Heritage *magazine in 1998 calculated that the figure was the equivalent of $100.5 billion in 1998 dollars. Still, Carnegie was the second-richest American. John D. Rockefeller beat him, with $900 million ($189.6 billion in 1998 dollars) in 1913—20 years after he'd retired and was well into his second career, busily giving his fortune away.

"The man who dies thus rich dies disgraced," as Carnegie had written in his youth. And in 1919, at age 83, under his own terms, he died in a state of grace.

Chapter 2

Triumphs and Tragedy

I t would be hard to imagine two men more opposite than Andy Carnegie and Clay Frick. The Scotsman usually was bubbly and chatty, Frick silent and icily dignified. Phipps called Frick a machine, and Schwab said he was cold-blooded. But no one doubted Frick's mastery of business, or that the Carnegie outfit's stupendous success owed much to Frick's savvy and towering intellect.

Frick knew little about the technical end of steel. But he was a master of money and management, the ultimate capitalist. He'd proved it over and over, tending to the affairs of his hugely successful dealings in "coke," the term being a contraction of "coal cake." The black coke was essential to steelmaking.

Clay Frick was born on a farm in Pennsylvania's coal-rich Connellsville region. The fact that his grandfather was Henry Overholt, who made a fortune distilling the popular "Old Overholt" rye whiskey, probably made Carnegie's eyebrows shoot upward. Still, Carnegie would have endorsed young Henry Clay Frick's personal agenda: to amass one million dollars. "I propose," Frick put in writing, "to be worth that amount before I die."

After attending several colleges, Frick headed to Pittsburgh on a quest for business experience. In his book *Henry Clay Frick* (St. Martin's

Henry Clay Frick

Henry C. Frick Coke Company figured prominently in Carnegie's plans to integrate the various phases involved in the steelmaking process.

Press, 1995), Samuel A. Schreiner, Jr., reported that Frick clerked in a department store—and that the handsome youth was especially successful at selling buttons and bows to lady customers. He devoted evenings to business-school courses in accounting. But the city's coal-smoke clouds reminded him of the rich, shallow seams of coal over which, as a boy, he had walked barefoot. He knew the steel industry was about to boom, and that it would be hungry for coke. Someone would spin coke into gold, he figured, and it might as well be Henry Clay Frick.

He rushed back home and worked for Grandfather Abraham as a bookkeeper. But not for long. When a family friend who was struggling in the coal business wanted to bail out, Frick saw his chance. Acting on his faith in coke, Frick convinced his new associate that the future lay not in selling off his coal holdings, but in buying more. Together, they made a bold purchase of 123 additional acres for almost $53,000.

By 1871, Frick had parlayed the deal into the Henry C. Frick Coke Company, an enterprise boasting 300 acres of coal property and 50 of the beehive-shaped ovens that baked coal into coke. By 1880, his domain had grown to almost 3,000 acres with 1,000 ovens, and Frick was rubbing elbows with the likes of Pittsburgh's high priest of banking, Judge Thomas Mellon.

Frick was a natural at inspiring the confidence of creditors. He demonstrated that in 1871, when he concluded he should expand his operations, but exhausted his line of credit with local bankers. So he put on his best suit and took a train to Pittsburgh, bound for what would be a historic meeting with Judge Mellon. The old financier had a reputation for being tight-fisted and, as one grandson put it, "formidable as an eagle." But Judge Mellon did not intimidate the young Frick, who cooly laid out his plans for putting a loan to work—and walked out with a $10,000 loan to put to use building 50 new coke ovens. Frick also won the priceless respect of Mellon himself. When, several years later, Frick returned to Judge Mellon for another loan, the banker introduced him to Andrew, his son and associate.

"That young man has great promise," the elder Mellon told Andrew. "If he continues along his own line as he has begun, he will go far unless he overreaches. That is his only danger." This, according to Samuel A. Schreiner, Jr., in *Henry Clay Frick*.

Beehive coke ovens

Both quiet loners, both intrigued by art, Andrew Mellon and Clay became deep friends. Soon, permitting themselves a vacation, they were off on a "Grand Tour" of Europe, the highlights of which were the art treasures they ogled in Paris, Venice and London. Frick had long been interested in art. The experience elevated him to the rank of lifelong connoisseur.

The Mellon–Frick friendship had larger consequences. After Frick eyed Adelaide Childs at a party, Andy Mellon arranged an introduction. It took the decisive and persuasive Frick three months to convince Miss Childs, daughter of a prominent Pittsburgher, to marry him. Shortly, Frick and his new bride were honeymooning in New York City. There, the coke magnate would learn that, unbeknownst to him, he had entered into another union of solemn consequence.

Frick's greatest coke customer was Andrew Carnegie. So in 1881, while the newlywed Fricks were in New York, Carnegie invited them to dine at New York's posh Windsor Hotel. Frick probably took the gesture as a business courtesy. As the dinner progressed, Frick began to suspect something was up. But he retained his formal demeanor. Even when Carnegie stood and toasted the success of the newly formed Frick–Carnegie partnership.

It was news to Frick. To Carnegie, uniting Frick's coke company with the Carnegie steel interests was like buying a life-insurance policy. He had watched Frick increase his command to more than 80 percent of the coal and coking industry. He had felt Frick's breath on the back of his neck. So he had quietly bought up shares of Frick's company, and, during Frick's honeymoon, consummated a second marriage, between coke and steel.

He didn't realize it then, but, in the bargain, he wasn't just gaining a partner, he was gaining his topmost manager, a man he would come to call an "absolute genius."

The tragic irony is Frick would also become Carnegie's bitterest adversary. This would prove to be a partnership made in heaven *and* hell, and Carnegie could both credit and blame his own methods of handling business and his business associates.

Carnegie himself never attended a business school. Why should he? He was a natural at commerce and industry. He was unique among entrepreneurs for looking through the other end of the telescope—not at profits, but costs. He was a shark at slashing them, arguing that good profits followed naturally. And he regarded accounting as holy; it revealed to the beholder the unit cost, the talisman for exposing excessive spending.

Later in his career, he was asked about the secret to business success. "Put all your eggs into one basket—then watch the basket," he is said to have answered. Don't overextend yourself. It was perceptive, perhaps, for a veteran. But even as a young man, before he went into steel, Carnegie had distilled his work experiences down to several acute rules of thumb.

One of them was "Thou Shall Not Overcapitalize." He considered it a sin to strew about stock shares that were the equivalent of funny money, backed not by equipment or facilities, but by hope and warm air.

Second, he had a strong aversion to distributing profits to investors in the form of dividends. Better to hold them in reserve for hard times, like the depression of 1873, and use them to expand. Or to buy property or equipment at someone else's fire sale.

His partners argued hotly with him on this point. They preferred to skim the cream as it surfaced. The richer the cream, or heftier the dividends, the better. Short-sightedness, scoffed Carnegie.

His partners argued, too, that having their dividends constantly recycled into the business made them prisoners of the company. Making things more uncomfortable, though, was a policy which put trap doors under their feet. This was the infamous "ironclad agreement." It began innocently enough, as a method of buying out partners who were in debt to the company. But after several permutations were performed under Carnegie's influence, it emerged as a weapon. It required any partner to surrender his interest at the request of three-fourths of the voting partners, and three-quarters of the total voting shares. And it stipulated that the interest be surrendered at book value, grossly beneath its true worth.

According to the agreement's math, however, Andrew Carnegie could not be ejected in this manner. He held more than half the voting shares.

One of Carnegie's favorite ways of handling business was handling it from afar. He spent as much as half of each year as an absentee landlord—checking business deals, or summering in Cannes, or dedicating the libraries he liked so much to underwrite as centers of activity in dozens of American towns and in the British Isles. Or he sequestered himself at Skibo, his magnificent estate and castle in the Scottish Highlands. But he was never truly gone. He dashed off streams of letters and telegrams to associates, commenting on board decisions, making recommendations to sell this and buy that. His spirit always seemed to be floating around the offices and the boardroom back home. In a sense it was transported through the mails and telegraph wire.

John D. Rockefeller

Though he often pulled the levers from afar, he remained masterful at managing his men. His technique depended upon hand-picking the best people, giving them shares of the company (he pioneered in this method of motivation), then mixing his managers together in the heat of competition. The sparks flew, and out poured great insights.

Pressure was a byproduct. But Carnegie insisted that pressure was useful; it screened out all but the most energetic and determined among his men. Others pointed out that the internal competition seeded bitter rivalries, and needlessly intimidated Carnegie's managers. James Bridge tells us that Captain Jones, who rarely minced words, once drove the point home for Carnegie when the Scotsman told him how much getting away eased his strain.

"You cannot imagine," Carnegie said to the Captain, "the abounding sense of freedom and relief I experience as soon as I get on board a steamer and sail past Sandy Hook." Jones looked at Carnegie and replied with his usual bluntness: "My God, think of the relief to us!"

Arguably, Carnegie's greatest achievement was his vertical integration of his steel operations. One of the first steps was to induce the railroads to give him special rates, and special privileges, to ship ore in and product out.

Carnegie's deal with Rockefeller provided the steelman with vast amounts of iron ore from the Mesabi Mines in Northern Minnesota.

Carnegie wasn't the only industrialist experimenting with that concept. John D. Rockefeller was busily bolting together the pieces of his oil kingdom so everything ran in a continuous flow, from drilling for oil to delivering the final product, kerosene. In fact, "John D." and Carnegie were partners in vertical integration. The two sealed a complicated deal under which Carnegie acquired vast amounts of that "shovelable" ore from the Mesabi Range of northern Minnesota. Rockefeller the oil prince had, in 1894, acquired an ore-mining company, and a nice-sized chunk of ore properties to go with it. Naturally, his purchase set off rumors that he was going to create a steel monopoly to go along with his monopoly in oil. That didn't scare Carnegie into grabbing up his own share of ore properties. Not yet, anyway.

Joseph Frazier Wall quoted Carnegie as declaring that, "If there is any department of business which offers no inducement, it is ore." But Frick and other associates saw that their boss was the one being unrealistic this time. So Frick, in his capacity as his company's chairman, made a backdoor deal for rights to Mesabi ore.

Carnegie didn't like the arrangement at first, but he soon saw the light. It illuminated a multitude of cost savings, and therefore fatter profits, that Carnegie, for once, hadn't calculated in advance. He rushed off to meet with Rockefeller (whom, with uncharacteristic sarcasm, Carnegie called "Rockafellow"), and walked out with an agreement guaranteeing Carnegie's operations at least 600,000 tons of ore a year from Rockefeller's Mesabi Mines. The trade journal *Iron Age* saluted the deal as Carnegie's greatest triumph: "[It] completes the last link in a chain which gives Carnegie a position unequaled by any steel producer in the world."

Not quite the last link. Paying the railroads what he considered exorbitant rates had always gnawed at Carnegie. He managed to explain, patiently and quietly, to the railroad chiefs why they should lower the rates they charged his operations, and why they should buy a "fair" amount of their steel rail from him. As Carnegie smoothly signed off on one letter to the Pennsylvania Railroad:

> *"Hence we pray you, when distributing your patronage hereafter,*
>
> *not to wound our susceptibilities by treating us as in any way less*
>
> *important than smaller concerns upon your line; but kindly recognize*
>
> *the fact that no one should be given one ton more than…*
>
> *Your most obedient servants*
>
> *The Edgar Thomson Steel Co."*

Finally, after repeatedly trying to get what he thought was his fair share of the railroads' business, and freight rates as low as those his competitors got, Carnegie lost his patience. He would fix the arrogant railroads by buying or building his own line.

He joined William K. Vanderbilt of the New York Central Railroad in a venture to buy the South Pennsylvania Railroad and upgrade it, running it through the Allegheny Mountains, from Harrisburg, Pennsylvania, to Pittsburgh. The deal fell through for the

A cartoonist's view of the Rockefeller–Carnegie pact that insured Carnegie's mills a steady flow of iron ore from Rockefeller's Mesabi Mines. Courtesy of the Carnegie Library of Pittsburgh.

partners, but paid off nicely for Pennsylvania. In the 1940s, the state took over the roadbed for part of the Pennsylvania Turnpike. Today, drivers on the "pike" pass through some of the tunnels blasted through the mountains for the aborted Vanderbilt–Carnegie railroad.

Carnegie had more luck with a railroad project in the late 1890s. He bought and rejuvenated the Pittsburgh, Shenango and Lake Erie Line, which loaded up with ore from lake carriers at Conneaut, Ohio, and shuttled it down to his Pittsburgh-area operations. In 1899, Carnegie put the finishing touches on his transportation fiefdom by acquiring six ore carriers from the Lake Superior Iron Company and establishing his Pittsburgh Steamship Company.

He now controlled shipping on almost all the 1,500 miles his ore traveled from Duluth to his works in Pennsylvania. On the day the first vessel left Duluth for Conneaut, Wall related, Carnegie wrote the news to Frick in a grand statement:

> *"Today, Pittsburgh becomes a lake port."*

Carnegie was always a master of the written and spoken word, and he thrived on the role of sage. Encouraged by an ego several notches larger than his hat size, he could always be coaxed into philosophizing for the benefit of the public. In magazine articles and at the podium, he built up a reputation as wise man and prophet.

For some of his pronouncements, he slipped into his Horatio Alger mode. In 1885, for example, he delivered, for the benefit of students of Pittsburgh's Curry Commercial College, a speech entitled "The Road to Business Success," or "A Talk to Young Men." His advice: "Be King of Your Dreams." The message was wrapped in warnings about what Carnegie saw as the "gravest dangers" to the realization of the students' dreams. One was liquor. ("The destroyer of most young men.") Another was financial speculation. (Carnegie excluded himself when he told a group of students, "I have lived to see all of these speculators irreparably ruined men, bankrupt in money and bankrupt in character.")

Without a doubt, his most remembered piece of writing is his two-part work entitled *Wealth*, first published in the *North America Review* in 1889, and later reprinted in other publications as the "Gospel of Wealth." In the essay, Carnegie declared that it was the rich man's duty (and his escape hatch from disgrace after death) to spend his fortune

*a reputation for producing the best
is a sure foundation upon which to build.*

Andrew Carnegie

during his lifetime. Doing so also would short-circuit estate taxes by which "the state marks its condemnation of the selfish millionaire's unworthy life." It also would recycle profits, easing anguish over the uneven job capitalism did of sharing wealth.

Carnegie spoke to his workers, too, hailing the virtues of hard work, reminding them that, "It is all well enough for people to help others, but the grandest result is achieved when people prove able to help themselves."

That was part of his message when, in 1900, he spoke at the dedication of the library he donated to Braddock, Pennsylvania. Addressing the workingmen who called the steel town home, Carnegie proclaimed that "the interests of capital and labor are one. He is an enemy of labor who seeks to array labor against capital. He is an enemy of capital who seeks to array capital against labor."

It was a come-together message that the workers probably thought was delivered a bit late. Still vivid in their minds was the notorious Homestead strike, and its terrible toll in death, anger and remorse—and the fact that Carnegie wasn't seen or heard from too often in these parts since he and his men had retaken the Homestead Works from the strikers. Now here he was, posing as the workingman's friend. How could his words square with his deeds?

In truth, Carnegie did want to be their friend, and wished them better lives. But he was trapped in a dilemma.

This plant began operations in 1881 in the Homestead area. In 1883, it was bought by Carnegie Steel interests and renamed the Homestead Works. It was here where the bitter, bloody Homestead Strike took place in 1892. Courtesy of the Carnegie Library of Pittsburgh.

THE HOMESTEAD STRIKE: STEEL'S DAY OF INFAMY

The fuse that would set off the violent Homestead strike of 1892 was lit by a notice that appeared one day at the Homestead Works, upriver from Pittsburgh.

It read in part:

"These Works having been consolidated with the Edgar Thomson and Duquesne and other mills, there has been forced upon this firm whether its Works are to be run 'Union' or 'Non-Union.' As the vast majority of our employees are Non-Union, the firm has decided that the minority must give place to the majority. These Works therefore will be necessarily Non-Union after the expiration of the present agreements."

Andrew Carnegie and Henry Clay Frick had waited for this day. Now, they were sure, they could sweep away the powerful and persistent Amalgamated Association of Iron and Steel Workers.

The union's hand was weakened by several facts.

Its members were skilled craftsmen, paid on the basis of their output. But new, faster machines had raised their output dramatically, putting their wages through the roof. That couldn't go on, especially since prices were flat. So, as the notice pointed out, the company was introducing a new wage scale—one tied not to an individual worker's productivity, but to prices for products. The workers would be joining the company in taking on the market's risk and rewards.

On top of that, the new, more efficient machines could be run by unskilled, non-union workers. Even boys, right off the farm. Skilled workers were becoming obsolete. So was their union, in the eyes of Carnegie and Frick.

The company's actions, the notice declared, were not to be taken "in any spirit of hostility to labor organizations, but every man will see that the firm cannot run Union and Non-Union. It must be one or the other."

While Carnegie went off on his annual holiday in England and Scotland, Frick met with the union to talk turkey.

When the union refused to accept the new conditions, Frick locked them out— by means of a fence made of wooden planks, pierced with stockade-style gun holes, and topped with barbed wire. The fortress, Frick admitted afterwards, was "for the purpose of putting the property in a position that it could be defended against an assault."

The scene for the July 6 Homestead battle was set. Frick had arranged for 300 Pinkerton guards to be transported in barges up the Monongahela to Homestead, where they would occupy the wood-and-barbed-wire garrison—now called "Fort

Frick"—and defend the works against any attacks from strikers.

It didn't happen that way. Instead, workers and their families and friends (the whole town of Homestead supported the strikers) kept watch along the river. An alert Homestead lookout spotted two large, darkened barges gliding under Pittsburgh's Smithfield Street Bridge in the hot night air. He sent an alarm upriver. Sirens and factory whistles roused the town of Homestead at four o'clock in the morning, and thousands of men and boys grabbed rifles, fence staves and hoes and ran to the river to confront the invaders.

"Fort Frick" during the 1892 Homestead Strike

When the Pinkertons arrived, they found they were trapped in their barges by gunfire. They stayed inside, baking in stifling heat, during a series of skirmishes that went on until after five in the afternoon.

At times, the conflict took on the tone of a tragi-comedy. The workers pumped oil onto the river in an effort to run off the Pinkertons, but a breeze blew the flaming oil away from the barges. A homemade bomb, thrown onto the roof of one barge, rolled off, plunked into a pail of water and fizzled. The strikers fired rockets and sent a cart of burning oil rolling down an inclined track toward the barges. Nothing happened. But each barrage further lathered up the frenzied crowd.

"Each crack of a rifle made them more bloodthirsty, and each boom of the cannon more eager for the blood of the officers," said one eye witness.

"Finally," as Carnegie biographer Joseph Frazier Wall wrote, "in the last scene to be enacted on that tragic day, there was sheer horror mixed with a pathos which has haunted the memory of Homestead."

After lying in the cramped, hot barges, the Pinkertons managed to raise a white flag and get the strikers to stop firing. The guards dropped their guns and waded ashore. There they were forced to run a gauntlet of furious, screaming, cursing Homesteaders—men and women, elders and children. The crowd beat the "Pinks" with iron-filled stockings, jabbed at their eyes with the points of umbrellas, tore at their clothing, kicked and punched them.

Casualty figures vary. According to James Bridge in Inside History of the Carnegie Steel Company, "…10 men were killed and over 60 wounded." Of the dead, three were Pinkerton detectives and seven were steelworkers.

The strikers controlled the Homestead works for four days, until Governor Robert Pattison ordered in the state militia. For a while, the strikers enjoyed public support. But sympathy for their cause was greatly diluted by another, unrelated, act of violence that further heightened the Homestead melodrama.

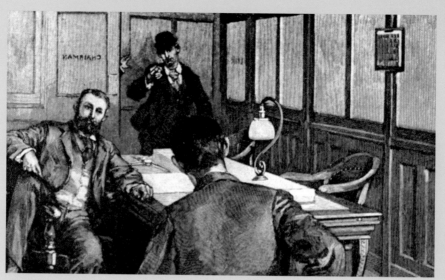

Assassination attempt on Henry Frick

Alexander Berkman

*O*n Saturday afternoon, July 23, 1892, Frick was seated in his office in downtown Pittsburgh, talking with his company's vice president, J. G. G. Leishman, when a nervous, pale, pistol-brandishing young man burst in and shot Frick twice at close range. One bullet entered Frick's neck and traveled to the middle of his back. Another lodged in the right side of his neck.

Just before the intruder squeezed off a third shot, Leishman struck his arm. The bullet bored into the ceiling. The injured Frick joined Leishman in grappling with the assailant. Then the would-be assassin pulled a handmade dagger from his pocket and stabbed Frick three times in the hip and legs. Office clerks rushed in to help. A deputy appeared and pointed his pistol at the intruder. Now Frick was leaning against his desk, staring at his assailant. "Don't shoot!" Frick cried. "Leave him to the law, but raise his head and let me see his face."

Frick saw the man was chewing something, and pointed to his jaw. The deputy forced the man's mouth open and pulled out a small but effective suicide device, a capsule of fulminate of mercury.

Frick remained unruffled through the entire ordeal. Soon he was coaching a surgeon who was probing for the bullets. This was too much for Leishman. He fainted. And as the doctor watched in awe, Frick calmly finished some correspondence, and paperwork for a loan.

The gunman, a Lithuanian anarchist named Alexander Berkman, was the lover of the notorious anarchist Emma Goldman, who had helped him plan Frick's assassination as an independent protest against the Homestead strike. The anarchists had no connection with the union. But much of the public thought the union was behind the attack, and the incident shifted public support from the union to the company. The brave Frick was seen as a hero.

Like other business leaders of his time, Carnegie was stuck between the rock of costs and the hard place of his workers' needs for shorter hours and higher wages.

Carnegie argued that if a firm were to prosper, all costs had to remain supple. The answer, he said, was to gear workers' pay to the firm's profitability. The potential for sharing the fruits of their own labor would encourage workers to hold costs down and keep production high. But they couldn't have it both ways. When the fruitbasket was almost empty, they would divide a smaller share, too.

"What we must seek," Carnegie told his workers, "is a plan by which men will receive high wages when their employers are receiving high prices for the product, and hence are making larger profits; and *per contra*, when the employers are receiving low prices for product, and therefore small if any profits, the men will receive low wages. If this plan can be found, employers and employed will be 'in the same boat,' rejoicing together in their prosperity and calling into play their fortitude together in adversity."

But the boats kept bouncing on a sea riled by economic winds. As a result, strikes became a trademark of the Gilded Age. During a severe depression that began in 1873, workers waged long and bitter strikes against wage cuts in New England's textile mills, in coal mines, and on the Pennsylvania Railroad. In 1877, a strike paralyzed railroads in the East and Midwest. The 1880s alone saw almost 10,000 strikes and lockouts.

Carnegie enjoyed positioning himself publicly as a true friend of the workingman. Sometimes he got carried away. In an 1886 article in the popular magazine *Forum*, he sympathized with striking workers who saw their jobs taken by substitutes and, as William Serrin reported in

Homestead: The Glory and Tragedy of an American Steel Town (Times Books division of Random House, 1992), Carnegie advised:

> *"... the employer of labor will find it much more to his interest, wherever possible, to allow his works to remain idle and await the result of a dispute than to employ a class of men that can be induced to take the place of other men who have stopped work. Neither the best men as men, nor the best men as workers, are thus to be obtained. There is an unwritten law among the best workmen: 'Thou shalt not take thy neighbor's job.'"*

The words would come back to haunt him during the steel industry's most notorious strike, the Homestead strike of 1892.

When labor strife grew at Carnegie's Homestead Works, upriver from Pittsburgh, Carnegie was already in Scotland, having left matters in the hands of Frick. The world was horrified by the terrible, and apparently unnecessary, battle between strikers and strikebreakers. After the gunsmoke, anger and tears, Frick came out the hero of the piece. The absent Carnegie ended up playing the cad. Why, the press wanted to know, was he hiding in Scotland? Had he run there after leaving his dirty work to Frick?

In fact, Carnegie was aghast when, from across the Atlantic, he first caught news of the Homestead battle. Conflict and bloodshed were the last things he wanted. He had instructed Frick to wait out a strike. But Frick remembered the previous anti-union actions that Carnegie had condoned by silence and was certain his absent boss endorsed his actions at Homestead. And when the conflict started, it was too late for Carnegie to step into the fray. He stayed in Europe, and remained quiet, as if he had not expected trouble and could not intercede, but could only wring his hands.

After returning from Europe, Carnegie maintained his distance from the Homestead tragedy. In a public statement, he reminded readers that he had retired four years earlier (he had, technically), and declared that he was not an officer, merely a shareholder, with no influence over the affairs of what was now the Carnegie Steel Company, Limited.

As for Frick, Carnegie wrote: "Of his ability, fairness and pluck no one has now the slightest question…I would not exchange him for any manager I know," Serrin points out in *Homestead*.

But the press and public saw Carnegie's attempts to distance himself from the Homestead violence as cowardice. As for Carnegie's pronounced faith in Frick, it wasn't quite genuine. The two men, of contrasting personalities, never really liked each other. Their disagreements over the handling of Homestead caused their bad feelings to fester. Over the next eight years, their dealings with each other lapsed into feuds and a final, bitter break.

I n 1894, Carnegie took steps to absorb another coke firm into the Frick Coke Company—without so much as telling Frick. Predictably, Frick was enraged. His coke business was his pride and joy, and W. J. Rainey, whom Carnegie was wooing, was one of Frick's oldest rivals. It was another case of Carnegie's disdain for Frick's coke business. Carnegie had always made Frick hold down the coke prices he passed along to the steel operations. The tactic made Carnegie's books look better, at Frick's expense.

But a behind-the-back merger was too much. It was humiliating, an obvious invitation to quit. Frick resigned. Carnegie, according to Serrin, accepted the resignation with a condescending wag of his finger: "You are not well, my friend. Go to Egypt. Take the cure."

Frick withdrew his resignation, but the hard feelings kept bubbling. They boiled over a few years later when Frick and Phipps, having heard Carnegie's frequent mumblings about selling out so he would have more time for leisure and philanthropy, called his bluff.

A syndicate of investors had approached Frick, offering to buy Carnegie's shares in the steel company and in the Frick Coke Company. Their offering price: $157 million. Frick and Phipps were to broker the deal with Carnegie. For their services, they would share a $5 million "bonus." Carnegie was willing to consider the offer, and demanded an option, or down payment, of $1.17 million. Sensing an opportunity to fatten their bonus, Frick and Phipps quietly, without informing their partners, put $170,000 of their own money into the option.

The deal looked good until the president of Wall Street's largest brokerage died, triggering a collapse of the money markets. One repercussion was that the syndicate could not exercise Carnegie's option before the deadline. But Frick and Phipps were confident the money crisis would blow over. They went to Scotland anyway, and asked Carnegie to extend the option deadline.

"Not an hour," Carnegie told them, in what must have been a tone dripping with self-righteousness. Then he sent them home without a sale. And he kept their $1,170,000 deposit.

It was his way of teaching Frick and Phipps a lesson. A lesson about what? About speculation, the ultimate sin. Carnegie had learned that Frick's and Phipps' syndicate consisted of the brothers William and James Moore, and John W. "Bet-a-Million" Gates—infamous speculators all.

The final rift came later the same year. Frick, tired of eating losses in the form of under-market prices for his coke, decided to break a verbal deal he had made with Carnegie the previous year. Instead of charging the agreed-upon $1.35 a ton, he began billing Carnegie at $1.45, then $1.60, then $1.75. Carnegie rejected the prices, then added insult to injury by spreading the story that Frick had acted unethically on a land deal. The clash escalated. Carnegie demanded Frick's resignation. Frick quit, but kept his interest in the company. Carnegie packed the board with his allies, who approved a contract requiring Frick to sell coke to Carnegie Steel at the previously agreed-upon $1.35 a ton, and to return the extra money he'd made selling at the higher prices. According to Samuel A. Schreiner, Frick was present at the contract-writing session, and marched out of the room in anger.

"You will see there are two sides to this matter," he warned over his shoulder.

The next morning, January 9, 1900, Carnegie called Frick into his office for a talk. He demanded Frick accept the new contract, with no lawsuits. "And," asked Frick, "if I am successful in enjoining the Frick Coke Company from making any deliveries to Carnegie Steel? What then?" Then, answered Carnegie, there would be nothing left but to invoke the ironclad agreement, forcing Frick out of the firm at book value, about a fifth of the real value of his stock.

Schreiner tells us that Charlie Schwab, in his office next door, heard Frick erupt. Leaping from his chair, he yelled at Carnegie: "For years I have been convinced that there is not an honest bone in your body! Now I know that you are a goddamned thief! We will have a judge and jury of Allegheny County decide what you are to pay me!"

And as Frick followed with his fists up, Carnegie bolted from the office and ran down to the board room. He hastily called the board together, told them what had just happened and demanded they act on the ironclad agreement. They agreed.

Frick made good on his threat in February by filing suit with the Allegheny County Court of Common Pleas. The nation was fascinated by the suit that followed, and by the huge sums of money tossed around by these men who lived and worked in the stratosphere of wealth. The steel industry was embarrassed by the accounts—especially by the media's revelation that these unimaginable profits and personal fortunes were made possible by the high tariffs that protected the steel industry.

The whole incident stirred up resentment of steel and trusts that, in the next century, would crystallize into attempts to break up "Big Steel." For now, though, the flap seemed to sputter out. Friends, and business leaders worried about repercussions against the industry, managed to cool down Phipps and Frick. They settled out of court by forming in March, 1900, a new company—the Carnegie Company, with Carnegie Steel and Frick Coke as separate divisions.

Frick was forced out of the company, but he walked away with $30.2 million in stock and bonds—a much tidier sum than the $4.9 million he would have gotten under the ironclad agreement.

Frick and Carnegie would never see each other again, even though they both kept houses in New York City. But there is a telling bit of steel lore that serves as postcript to the story:

Just before he died in 1919, Carnegie—never one to hold grudges—sent a note over to Frick. Wouldn't it be nice, he wrote, if, after all these years, the two could forget the past and meet again as friends?

Frick's response reveals a long-buried bitterness for Carnegie and, perhaps, second thoughts about how he had conducted his own life.

"Tell Mr. Carnegie," he instructed the messenger, "that I will meet him in hell, where we both are going."

Chapter 3

Birth of the Giant

Hell? Carnegie and Frick and the other steel chiefs figured they'd already been there, back in the waning days of the nineteenth century.

Competing hadn't been a subtle exercise in adjusting costs, prices and services. It was cutthroat and chaotic, and it wasted energy, time and money. Part of the problem was industry's adolescence. The prospect of wealth attracted high rollers and amateurs. Fly high today, go bust tomorrow. Confusion reigned over public financial and monetary policy, and there was no central bank to impose confidence and order on lending and investing. You couldn't plan. You could only react. But there wasn't much room left even for that; given the way the steel industry was structured, there were almost no places left to squeeze costs and profits. For a responsible and ambitious business executive, it was the perfect description of the Infernal Abyss.

All this was the heart of the message Charlie Schwab delivered to the assembled industrialists during his 1900 dinner address in New York. And it was Schwab's solution—create a steel company so large and diverse that it broke the cost barrier—that bewitched J. P. Morgan. The banker had been stewing a long time over this very dilemma.

If anyone could impose order and growth in steel, Morgan could.

Born into an old-money family in Hartford, Connecticut, John Pierpont Morgan was the son of a financier. In 1862, he opened his own financial firm and later joined forces with another. His methods worked like oil on the seething waters of finance. He tamed the fiscally unbridled American railroads that snaked across the country after the Civil War. He was aboard the post–Civil War gravy train of industrial growth, too, providing the money that launched General Electric and International Harvester.

Morgan was powerful, and often remembered as a "robber baron," but unfairly. He *looked* the part; in photographs, with his walrus mustache and top hat, scowling and waving his walking stick at an intruding photographer's camera, he makes a good stage villain. He was over six feet tall, and possessed a huge nose (bloated and reddened by skin disease) and piercing eyes that flashed when he was angry, or when he barked out orders. He scared people. Yet, as historian Paul Johnson pointed out in his *A History of the American People* (Harper Collins, 1997), Morgan's mannerisms and booming voice bespoke authority and wisdom. People trusted him.

Morgan deserved trust. He demonstrated this in 1895, when President Grover Cleveland summoned him to reverse a national run on gold. In that role, he held the country in his hand. And he orchestrated a buyback plan that replenished the gold supply and saved the country from bankruptcy. He would perform an encore during the Panic of 1907.

Faith in enterprise drove Morgan. He was a devoted churchman, an Episcopalian, and his religion influenced his business soul. While others insisted businesses should be chained, Morgan preached that restraints bred inefficiency. On the other hand, he argued, total economic freedom encouraged economic chaos. That was inefficiency, too. The answer, he insisted, was balance—creation of a business entity that largely had a free hand to create products, technology, jobs and wealth, yet was braked by just enough controls to keep it from running wild. The answer, he insisted, was to structure your business as a corporation. Or a trust; that word again. To Morgan, it meant what it said: confidence that an economic entity would do the right thing—create progress, and the wealth that perpetuates it.

Why was he so enthralled by Schwab's sermon on the potential for a mighty combine in steel? For the answer, we must bring into the story another larger-than-life figure, a man whose ideals and vision would leave an indelible mark on the steel business—in fact, on American business in general.

Elbert H. Gary was born in a log house near Wheaton, Illinois, in 1846, and was destined to become judge of DuPage County and the first chairman of the United States Steel Corporation. He was also destined to be called "Judge Gary" the rest of his life. More than a judge, he looked like a minister. He was a dapper dresser and a statesman, reserved and precise with his words. Some said he was haughty.

There's a whiff of irony surrounding the fact that Judge Gary's first business with the steel industry came in 1892, when he helped John W. Gates (the very "Bet-a-Million" Gates who sent Andrew Carnegie's blood pressure skyrocketing) with the legalities surrounding formation of Consolidated Steel and Wire Company of Illinois. DuPage County, Illinois—Gary's home—proudly relates, in information from its files, how Judge Gary took care of the legal end of Consolidated's launch, and became the company's general counsel. Five years later, Gates returned with another proposal, this time to fuse together 40 steel wire plants, including the Illinois Steel Company. (Gary was a director.) J. P. Morgan, heading the imperial-sounding House of Morgan in New York, was on board to supply the capital.

Judge Elbert Gary
as president of the new
Federal Steel Company

The deal dragged along, and was put on hold when, inconveniently, the American battleship Maine was blown up in Havana Harbor, setting off the Spanish-American War. But Morgan soon took the merger off the back burner. And he was so impressed by the way Gary handled it that he called the judge into his office for a congratulatory chat. Gary was about to catch a train for Chicago but stopped by. Morgan was there with the committee that helped him run the amalgamation. According to Jean Strouse, author of *Morgan: American Financier* (Random House, 1999), the banker quickly came to the point.

"Judge Gary, you have put this thing together in very good shape. We are all very well pleased. Now you must be president of the corporation."

But the judge hadn't expected the offer and told Morgan he couldn't think of taking it.

"Why not?" boomed the banker.

"Why, Mr. Morgan," Gary replied, "I have a law practice worth $75,000 a year and I cannot leave it."

"We'll take care of that," Morgan answered. "We must make it worth your while."

Gary said he'd think it over. Morgan persisted: "We want to know now. You can select the directors, name the executive committee, choose your officers and fix your salary."

The next day, Judge Gary said yes. Largely by virtue of Morgan's respect for his intellect, leadership and honesty, he became president of the new Federal Steel Company.

In an age of industrial consolidation, Federal Steel was a formidable combine. Capitalized at $100 million, it was the runner-up in might to Carnegie's outfit. But it wasn't big enough. Gary had thought through the economics and wanted an immense "Republic of Steel," an organization strong and agile enough to safely cruise the rugged seas of commerce, even go head-to-head with Britain, then the world's leader in steel. He wanted the market to be stable, and believed it would be if more people had a direct interest in how it worked. Ownership of industry should be spread among the people—especially the workers, who fed the furnaces and ran the machines and who really determined whether the products that came out at the end were of top quality or so-so.

He took his dream of a larger and more democratic enterprise to Morgan, but the banker kept putting him off. Meanwhile, Andrew

Officials from the Carnegie companies gathered on the evening of January 1, 1901, at the Schenley Hotel in Pittsburgh to celebrate the impending buyout of the Carnegie Company by financier J. P. Morgan. Courtesy of the Carnegie Library of Pittsburgh.

Carnegie finally admitted to himself it was time for him to sell out and concentrate on philanthropy. He had been shopping for a buyer for Carnegie Steel. He, too, settled on Morgan as the only person who could finance so large a merger. But Morgan kept hesitating over this deal, as well. So Carnegie switched his tactics to coercion. He knew Morgan owned a large piece of the National Tube Company. Carnegie made no tube or pipe, but he announced that he was going to build a huge tube mill on a site he'd bought on Lake Erie, in Conneaut, Ohio. *That* would give National Tube, and Morgan, a run for their money.

Morgan didn't flinch. Carnegie upped the ante, threatening to build a railroad that competed with the Pennsylvania Railroad. It would have hit Morgan's wallet even harder, considering his huge railroad holdings. Still the banker didn't bite. Carnegie went ahead and began building a competing railroad, but never completed it.

Carnegie's final, subtler strategy, steel lore tells us, was to contrive the December dinner in New York, with Charles Schwab cooing the blessings of a mega-steel company into the old banker's ear. The shrewd Scotsman bet the pieces would fall together in Morgan's brain.

He was right. Everyone knew Carnegie wanted to retire and give away his millions. Morgan saw the incredible opportunities in buying him out. And it wasn't long before he held the piece of paper on which Carnegie had penciled $480 million, his asking price for his empire.

But why stop there? By acquiring Carnegie Steel and adding it to Federal Steel, the second-largest producer, Morgan would command almost all the cogs in the steel-producing machine—iron mines, coke production, steel wire, plate and tube producers, a railroad, even a steel fabricator, American Bridge Co. Not quite soup to nuts. Missing was a fleet of iron ore ships. And Morgan and Gary knew where to get them.

Oddly enough, John D. Rockefeller's Standard Oil empire included a fleet of 56 mammoth ore boats. Not to mention most of the iron ore in Minnesota's rich Mesabi Range. They would nicely round out the almost-integrated trust Morgan was assembling.

There was a hitch. Morgan did not like Rockefeller. The banker considered him a pious outsider. After all, the oil king financed *his* trust with retained earnings. He was his own bank. Rockefeller, a down-to-earth Baptist at heart, returned the disfavor, as historian-writer Ron Chernow related in his award-winning *Titan: The Life of John D. Rockefeller, Sr.* (Random House, 1998). He shook his head over Morgan's high-and-mightiness. And, wrote Chernow, when Gary told Morgan he must go see Rockefeller about acquiring his mines and ships for "the Steel Corporation," the banker balked.

I wouldn't think of it, he told Gary.

Judge Gary asked why.

"I don't like him," Morgan answered.

Gary couldn't believe it: "Would you let a personal prejudice interfere with your success?"

Morgan relented, and agreed to see Rockefeller at his home on Manhattan's West 54th Street.

Rockefeller, who possessed sly humor, was ready for him. When Morgan asked the price he wanted for his ore properties, Rockefeller feigned an "oh-my-goodness" tone and reminded the banker that he, Rockefeller, was retired. Morgan, he regretted, would have to do business with his 27-year-old son, John D., Jr.—"Junior," to those who knew him.

Morgan must have bit halfway through his cigar at the insult, but he suggested that Junior should stop by his office. Junior let Morgan stew a while before paying a visit. Morgan, now ensconced on *his* turf, ignored Junior for an appropriately rude length of time. Then he looked at Junior and barked, "What's your price?"

A stock ownership plan enabled employees to own a piece of the corporation during its formative years. This certificate was issued on April 19, 1905, for 10 shares of preferred capital stock at $100 each.

Now it was Junior's turn. "Mr. Morgan," he said, "there must be some mistake. I did not come here to sell. I understood you wished to buy." The tone and reverse ploy didn't sit well with Morgan, but they wrapped up the conversation agreeing that Henry Frick would broker the deal. In the end, John D. and his son shared some snickers over the way they'd treated the mighty Morgan. And Morgan and Gary got their ore holdings and ships. The stock offering for this new colossus of steel moved forward.

The company was capitalized at an amount that exceeded the national debt: $1.4 billion. It was a mind-boggling figure, although it was said to hide a generous amount of "water." (Underlying assets were worth $880 million; the rest was "blue sky," or, more generously, confidence.) Besides setting a record, the offering signaled the end of an era in which entrepreneurs ran their own creations, and the beginning of the end of Wall Street's supremacy.

New-York Tribune reports on the formation of USS in its February 26, 1901, edition.

As Chernow put it in *American Heritage* magazine (July/August 1998), "By offering shares to the public, the financiers had paved the way, inadvertently, for a long-term demotion in their power. In time the shares of U. S. Steel and other companies would be widely dispersed among individual and institutional investors who would supersede the power of Wall Street investment houses."

United States Steel Corporation was incorporated February 25, 1901, and opened for business April 1 as a holding company. It derived tax benefits from incorporating in New Jersey, and management advantages from being headquartered in New York City, the nation's business capital. Pittsburgh, though, was its true home.

The corporation governed 10 companies, most of them combinations of smaller firms. All in all, the corporation at its founding controlled 213 steel mills and transportation companies, 41 iron ore mines, a fleet of 112 ore barges, 57,000 acres of coal and coke properties.

It was an amazing organization. And it inspired awe mixed with some fear.

Popular newspaper humorist Finley Peter Dunne, speaking through his creation, the rustic Irishman "Mr. Dooley," cartooned off the company's wealth:

Pierpont Morgan calls in wan iv his office boys, th' prisidint iv a

national bank, an' says he, "James," he says, "take some change out iv

the'damper an' r-run out an' buy Europe f'r me," he says. "I intind

to re-organize it an' put it on a paying basis," says he.

The press didn't think this huge new "steel trust" was funny. Papers in America and Europe rang the alarm by claiming the giant company was born of a conspiracy to crush competition at home, then move to dominate the world market. Smaller businesses joined consumers in crying "Trust!" as if it were a dirty word, and in worrying that this huge and powerful entity would squash them flat.

There was another crowd, the doomsayers. They fretted over the "watered" stock (they forgot to factor in the potential worth of the talent, experience and innovativeness behind the numbers), and predicted this behemoth would collapse of its own weight. How could Morgan have agreed to back an enterprise so large and clumsy?

Detractors who eagerly predicted failure or warned that the company would turn into a huge money-and-soul-eating ogre were in for a big disappointment. Instead of going up in smoke, the company proved it could prosper. Instead of engineering higher and higher prices, it acted to strengthen competition and maintain prices that were reasonable and fair. Instead of cracking the whip harder in the mines and mills, it was soon planning progressive employment policies. What kind of trust was this?

It was a trust as perceived by Morgan, whose motives lay not only in making money, but in creating a stable entity that would create

The (Original) United States Steel Corporation

Carnegie Steel Company
The largest of the ten companies that were merged. Included steel plants in the Pittsburgh area; H. C. Frick Coke Company holdings (40,000 acres of coking coal lands, 11,000 coke ovens and other property); controlling interest in Oliver Mining Co. and the Pittsburgh, Bessemer & Lake Erie Railroad.

Federal Steel Company
Formed in a merger of Illinois Steel Co., Minnesota Iron Co., Lorain Steel Co., Elgin, Joliet & Eastern Railway Co. and the Johnson Company of Pennsylvania. Second in size to the Carnegie Steel Company.

American Steel & Wire Company of New Jersey
A consolidation of the majority of the country's wire mills. Also owned extensive ore and coking coal properties.

American Tin Plate Company
A combine of 39 tin plate plants.

American Steel Hoop Company
A union of nine mills making hoops, bands, bars, "cotton ties" and "skelp."

American Sheet Steel Company
A combine of 164 sheet mills plus "puddling" and open-hearth furnaces, and bar mills.

National Tube Company
A combination of 13 steel pipe companies in the Pittsburgh District.

National Steel Company
A merger of various companies in the Midwest, most producing semi-finished products. Ore holdings in the Mesabi Range.

American Bridge Company
Uniting several companies which fabricated structural steel.

Lake Superior Iron Mines
An ore company owning or leasing almost 400 million tons. Also owned the Duluth, Missabe & Northern Railroad. Affiliated with the Bessemer Steamship Co., which United States Steel acquired later.

widespread wealth and stimulate progress. It was a trust that aligned with the beliefs of Judge Gary. The true father of United States Steel, he "raised" the firm according to his own high standards of fair play and decency. He knew his charge would have to make it in a world that was running out of patience with Gilded Age tyrants and 12-hour days.

Gary's biographer Arundel Cotter summed it up this way in his book *The Gary I Knew* (Stratford Company, 1928): "(Gary) believed… that business should be profitable not only to the parties concerned in any individual transaction but to the whole community. And he held that, as the sum of business affected the wealth and happiness of the entire community, each individual transaction should so far as possible contribute to the general good."

In her biography *The Life of Elbert H. Gary* (D. Appleton and Company, 1925), Ida Tarbell recorded for history one of Gary's standard responses to his associates' business proposals: "Is it right?" It wasn't the kind of question a business leader of the era would ask, unless he was making a joke. Gary wasn't joking.

Compared with the business tyrants who lurked in the popular imagination, Gary was a Boy Scout. His beliefs even found expression in what could be called Gary's version of the Boy Scout pledge: The Gary Principles, a formal code designed to inspire his associates to share his beliefs in honesty, fairness, lawfulness, competition, the need of openness in business operations and the supremacy of the public welfare.

He was a breath of fresh air.

Banquet program for Carnegie Steel Company operating officials in late 1901 following the formation of U. S. Steel Corporation earlier in the year

One of Gary's first acts was to open a few windows, letting a welcome breeze rush into the corporation and giving shareholders, legislators and the public a glimpse of what was going on inside.

First, Gary invited in the company's shareholders by inventing what is now a fixture of any corporation, the annual meeting. The 23 shareholders who attended the first meeting on February 17, 1902, in Hoboken, New Jersey, must have expected that, like shareholders in

The Gary Principles

Judge Elbert Gary voiced and acted on points of ethics that raised the eyebrows of managers who—in keeping with early-twentieth-century business beliefs—saw no place in industry for morality. Gary's principles undoubtedly raised the standards of business, as well. Although the date on which the principles were first introduced is unknown, they were generally recognized within U. S. Steel and elsewhere in the business community by 1909. Charlie Schwab referred to the rules in a dinner speech that year.

The principles undoubtedly comprised the first code of business ethics to be adopted by an American company. They have been passed along over the years, and appeared in the following version in 1951, in U. S. Steel's 50th anniversary book, *Steel Serves the Nation*.

- *I believe that when a thing is right, it will ultimately and permanently succeed.*

- *The highest rewards come from honest and proper practice. Bad results come in the long run from selfish, unfair and dishonest conduct.*

- *I believe in competition…that the race should be won by the swiftest, and that success should come to him who is most earnest and active and persevering.*

- *I believe that no industry can permanently succeed that does not treat its employees equitably and humanely.*

- *I believe thoroughly in publicity. The surest and wisest of all regulation is public opinion.*

- *If we succeed as businessmen we must do it on principles that are honest, fair, lawful and just.*

- *We must put and keep ourselves on a platform so fair, so high, so reasonable, that we will attract the attention and invite and secure the approval of all who know what we are doing.*

- *We do not advocate combinations or agreements in restraint of trade, nor action of any kind which is opposed to the laws or to the public welfare.*

- *We must never forget that our rights and interests are and should be subservient to the public welfare, that the rights and interests of the individual must always give way to those of the public.*

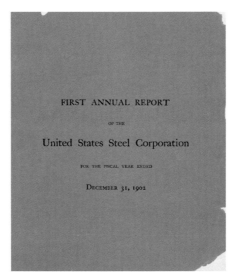
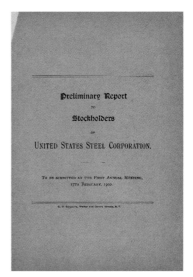

U. S. Steel's first annual report set the standard at the time for other companies to follow.
A Preliminary Report to Stockholders also set an industry precedent.

other companies, they were merely an audience to the rubber-stamping of policy by executives. They were in for a surprise. When a visiting stockholder stood to speak to a motion, one of the company's lawyers raised a point of order, challenging the shareholder's right to speak up. Judge Gary wouldn't have it, Tarbell wrote: "I cannot entertain [the point of order]," he said. "Stockholders have a right to talk in a stockholders' meeting. We have announced that [the meetings] shall be open and free, and I mean that they shall be."

The meeting itself was a novelty. But how else could shareholders truly understand and challenge the thinking and actions of the executives who were working for them if they could not meet them face-to-face, and hear and question policies and decisions?

That same insight drove another Gary innovation: In 1903, he issued from the company's 71 Broadway headquarters a publication considered to be the first corporate annual report. Its 40 pages covered fiscal year 1902 in charts and tables, and a narrative reporting revenues ($560,510,479.39) and earnings ($34,253,656). Down to the penny. It even reported equipment the company had bought during the year. It wrapped this up with a gallery of illustrations and photos of plants and other operations—some of them revealed in a light that was not so pretty, but honest. Accountants Price, Waterhouse & Co. blessed the facts and figures by certifying the document.

The financial community and other corporations were amazed. They'd seen other "annual reports" before, sketchy, obscure documents that really didn't reveal much. This United States Steel Corporation report was something else again. It took a little wind out of the sails of critics who claimed the company was secretive. It set an example for other companies to follow, and they did. (To the applause of paper companies and printers and the chagrin of some super-cost-conscious shareholders.)

The annual meeting and report were extensions of Judge Gary's psyche. He argued that people who had a stake in the company's success—which most everyone did, in one way or another—should know what that company was doing; shareholders, especially, since the company was using their money. His conviction was borne out by the political winds that were blowing when, at J. P. Morgan's request, he was organizing U. S. Steel. The gusts brought to his ears growing complaints against big business. He knew that companies which insisted on playing everything close to the vest were heading for trouble. He didn't want his company to be part of it.

For U. S. Steel watchers, there was plenty to keep up with in the corporation's formative years.

One potential danger foreseen by Gary (who officially became chairman in 1902) stemmed from the fact that U. S. Steel was not an operating company, with central authority over all its plants, mines and offices. It was a holding company, with each subsidiary under separate management. The bosses (and, for that matter, the workers) were motivated to tend to their business, but took no interest in the other subsidiaries or the corporation as a whole. It was not a formula for efficiency and tough competition.

The answer was to give employees a piece of the whole company. Let them be shareholders themselves. The company launched a stock ownership plan in which directors allotted a specific amount of stock each year to be offered to employees at prices slightly below the stock market's.

Employees could pay for the stock in small, monthly allotments. Besides dividends, employees who held stock and stayed with the corporation for five years got a bonus of $5 a year on each share of preferred stock they held and $3.50 a year on each share of their common stock. Now what they did really mattered.

The difference was illustrated in ore operations, when a group of engineers, thinking about advantages for them and their unit, started bickering over which ore concentrator to acquire. One of them spoke up, as reported by Cotter: "It is not a question of what is best for the Oliver Iron Mining Co. The whole question is, what is best for the United States Steel Corporation?" The argument stopped right there.

Oliver Iron Mining was one of a handful of outfits the company acquired during its first decade. Others included the Bessemer Steamship Co. (a Rockefeller company with 56 ships that plied the Great Lakes), a New Jersey steel tube company, and a Troy, New York, steel slab producer. There was a lot of attention to tightening operations and cutting costs.

Not that the leaders of United States Steel expected everything to go smoothly. There were problems and melodrama. Some incidents were serious. Others, viewed a century later, seem overblown. In the latter category was a scandal that proved the undoing—at United States Steel, at least—of Charles Schwab.

At Carnegie Steel, Charlie Schwab was Andy's fair-haired boy, a favorite with the workers, a great interview for the press, a brilliant manager, a superb steelman. At United States Steel, almost from his first day as president, Schwab seemed uninspired by his new administrative role, which cut him off from the steel plants and the workers he loved. His good ideas dried up. His earthiness drove the aristocratic Judge Gary to distraction. And when it came to interviews for the paper, he put his foot in his mouth. It all frustrated and confused him, and pushed him into a trap he should have seen coming: conviction in the press as a rogue and a gambler.

Not that anyone thought Charlie Schwab was a saint. His biographer, Robert Hessen, in *Steel Titan: The Life of Charles M. Schwab*, (University of Pittsburgh Press, 1975), characterized him as a man who liked to have fun. He enjoyed hanging around with celebrities like Mark Twain and Tom Edison. He loved music and travel. And he had episodes of wandering-eye. His wife Rana had been a good companion, but she contracted gout, gained weight (she reached more than 200 pounds) and grew so self-conscious about her appearance that she stopped going out with Charlie. She hid at home, instead.

Given this state of affairs, gregarious Charlie, while he was with Carnegie Steel, proved to be especially susceptible to the charms of the beautiful red-headed nurse brought into the Schwab home to tend to Rana's convalescing sister, Minnie. So susceptible was he that the nurse gave birth to a baby girl. Schwab dared not recognize the child as his. Doing so would have summoned the awful wrath of Andrew Carnegie, who would not abide straying sheep in his corporate fold.

Schwab found a good home for his daughter, supported her financially, and visited her and took her on trips as often as he could. He was far from heartless, but he had to protect his business life. Professionally, this had been a close call.

As the president of U. S. Steel, Schwab became a celebrity. He wrote for national magazines and addressed business groups and college classes. As his fame grew, his effectiveness as president of his company diminished. Hessen wrote how Schwab failed to take actions or make decisions that would have paid off the ideas he sketched out at the University Club. He seemed to be marching in place. He made careless statements to the press, and was too often misquoted in the papers, to his and the company's embarrassment.

It's difficult to say whether Schwab plummeted to mediocrity because he suffered an attack of creative paralysis, was distracted by fame or just didn't fit in with the Gary crowd. Certainly, he and Gary didn't get along. Charlie was a roll-up-the-sleeves operator, raucous as well as dashing. He smoked, drank and stayed out late. The judge avoided drink and cigars and went to bed early. He was dignified. He also saw in Schwab's views too much of Andrew Carnegie, whom he thoroughly disliked.

Worst of all, Schwab and Gary disagreed on policy, and took swipes at each other at meetings of the Executive Committee, which Gary chaired. Knowing Gary was inexperienced in the operations end of steel, Schwab made decisions without proper authorization from the committee. Gary overruled him, and tried to restrict his authority.

The whole ordeal humiliated and depressed Schwab. As Hessen reports in his book on the steelman, Schwab told an associate while Morgan was out of town:

"I am simply heartbroken.... I was so anxious to show that this company could be made a glorious success. And I am more enthusiastic today and surer of its success than I ever was before. I have suffered every torture on Mr. Morgan's account to make matters move smoothly until his return. I have been hampered, criticized and goaded by incompetent critics, who do not understand the whole steel situation."

He had to get away, and on December 26, 1901, he sailed for Europe, for Paris, the Riviera, Berlin, London. The press figured it was a business trip, but it was mainly for rest and renewal. It backfired almost right away.

In early January, Schwab picked up a speedy roadster in Paris and raced to Monte Carlo, where he joined a high-flying crowd in a casino. At the roulette table, at least, he had a run of fresh luck. A *New York Sun* reporter took care of that. Hearing secondhand about Schwab's fortune, he cabled to his paper a story whose headline screamed, SCHWAB BREAKS THE BANK. His winnings kept increasing in follow-up reports, and the papers crucified him. A rich and responsible executive wasn't supposed to behave this way.

Carnegie was infuriated, according to Hessen. "His boy" had misbehaved shockingly, so Carnegie cabled Schwab that he should retire. Then he confided to Morgan: "I feel as if a son had disgraced the family."

The man Schwab most admired had abandoned him. Schwab was crushed, and when he arrived back home, he confessed to Morgan: "I did gamble at Monte Carlo. But I didn't do it behind closed doors."

Morgan, surprised by Schwab's failure to be discreet, lectured him:

"Charlie! That's what doors are for!"

After walking out U. S. Steel's door in 1903, Charles Schwab saw fortune take another flip. During his presidency of U. S. Steel, he had acquired a controlling interest in the Cambria Steel Works, later to become Bethlehem Steel. He offered to sell the works to U. S. Steel, but Gary hesitated and the board showed no interest. After departing U. S. Steel, Schwab went on to head Bethlehem Steel, and was credited with building an enterprise that became U. S. Steel's chief rival.

Schwab's troubles in the steel corporation reinforced a lesson: Act responsibly. It was a good moral to begin with, but it was an absolute golden rule when the press was watching, and, too often, eager to blast across its pages—often without proper perspective—any sin of any size that the steel barons committed. It was good advice in any era. It was priceless advice during the Progressive Age.

For all practical purposes, the age began when Theodore Roosevelt assumed the presidency in 1901, the same year that U. S. Steel was born. It was an era known for "muckrakers," the critics who castigated industry and sounded the call for reform. It was an era in which the nation saw progress toward real reform, such as winning the vote for women. It was a time in which socialists won the ears of more people. In short, it was a period of confusion, debate, understanding, misunderstanding, hatred, violence—and progress—as America tried to figure out what it was about.

Business, of course, asserted great influence on the country's welfare, and the outcome could be good or bad. Given this reality and the nature of the time, influentials in industry and government often found themselves tiptoeing around each other, wary of each other's intentions.

The Panic of 1907 gave rise to some big-time tiptoeing as the next chapter will reveal.

Chapter 4

Opposing Forces

"There is just one place that can light my face ..."

"Gary, Indiana," from Meredith Wilson's *The Music Man*

"We have never intended to antagonize the laws of the country or the rights and interests of anyone."

Elbert Gary, chairman, United States Steel Corporation

Thomas E. Knotts knew a good thing when he saw it.

Knotts was a pudgy-faced policeman in Hammond, Indiana. And what he saw were the possibilities for enrichment in the big steel plant and city that United States Steel Chairman Elbert Gary announced his company would build on a stretch of almost barren land along Lake Michigan's southern shore. A made-to-order industrial town. Schools, churches, houses, hospitals, stores, streets, steel plant and all.

Knotts resigned from his city job, packed his family and belongings into a van, and trundled over to the still-undeveloped site of Gary's dream city. The family arrived on the afternoon of May 4, 1906, and pitched a tent for the night on the bank of the Grand Calumet River.

Soon they were ensconced in a makeshift house awaiting their destiny. They didn't have to wait long. They were the first settlers in a true boomtown, and, after claiming a slice of the action by running a tidy little real estate business, Tom Knotts got himself elected the first mayor of Judge Gary's kit-built city on the lake.

It helped that Tom Knotts' brother, Armanis F. Knotts, a former mayor of Hammond, was also an attorney and land surveyor and, as an employee of U. S. Steel, had been negotiating land purchases for that company. Judge Gary himself had summoned Armanis to New York to pick his brain for the best site for a new steel plant. As Armanis retold it later in the Gary, Indiana, *Post Tribune*, the judge called him into his office and said, "You know, we have several plants in the West, most of them built up from smaller plants, many of them old, some of them are not up to date. We want to build a modern plant which will be efficient, and meet the growing needs of the Middle West. And I would like for you to help us find a location for the plant we propose."

Knotts recommended the site that the company ultimately agreed on. And he filled in brother Tom about the judge's plans for their neighborhood. Other folks who were less imaginative than Tom—or who weren't in the loop—could be forgiven for not following him into the strip of wilderness along the southern shore of Lake Michigan. Because a wilderness it was.

The town of Gary was being staked out in the Midwest's version of a desert, a vast expanse of sand dunes sprinkled with scrub oak and spotted with ponds and marshes. The Potowatomi Indians once hunted here, and a few squatters managed to scrape a living out of the sand. Famed silent-film maker Francis X. Bushman thought the place looked like a good location for an adventure set in Mexico. During shooting, an actor dressed in a leopard skin and carrying a club got lost and wandered the dunes for a day and a night as reports circulated that a "wild man" was on the loose. He was found. Not so lucky was the gang of four bandits who made the dunes their hideout—until they had to come out with their hands up. They were hanged.

(Above and next page) In the beginning—Gary Works emerges from a strip of wilderness along the southern shores of Lake Michigan.

But the 1,500-acre site was almost perfect for the Steel Corporation. It was near abundant supplies of ore, coal and water, and it was its own port. Too long a commute for workers? Simply build them homes and a whole city right here.

It was a breathtaking plan, and Tom Knotts could have filled you in on it if you'd joined him on April 18, 1906, as he sank a stake at what would become the heart of Gary, Indiana: Broadway and Fifth Avenue.

"The Gary State Bank will be right over there," you might have learned. "Over there's the lake, and where the big steel plant will be built. And we'll have hotels, schools, churches, and some really fine houses."

And it happened. In a few years, this was a town of 12,000 people, with 15 miles of paved streets, 25 miles of cement sidewalks, a sewer system, water and gas plants, electric lighting, newspapers, shops and public schools that would be the envy of the nation. And, along the lake, the Gary Works was in place, covering about a square mile, equipped with a custom-made harbor serving great ore freighters.

THE MAGIC CITY

"Industry with its wand, as potent as Aladdin's lamp, has transformed this section of sand-driven desert into one of our most active and progressive manufacturing centers."

Charles Longenecker, managing editor of Blast Furnace and Steel Plant, had no qualms about resorting to magic-show imagery when he wrote about U. S. Steel's Gary Works for the show-me-the-numbers steelmen who read his trade journal. Why should he? People called Gary, Indiana, "the Magic City." Its miles of paved streets, hundreds upon hundreds of houses, and 1,250-acre steel works—the world's largest—seemed to materialize as if pulled from a huge hat. It was still quite a trick in 1937, when Longenecker wrote his Aladdin's-lamp tribute in an issue of his publication that commemorated Gary on its 30th anniversary.

Chicago had wanted the plant. Its citizens lobbied for a permit allowing U. S. Steel to build along their lakefront, on new fill land. But the city's public works commissioner forced a law preventing further construction on Lake Michigan. If it hadn't been for that "damn little cuss," groused one Chicago man, "the big plant would have been built here."

Not likely. U. S. Steel needed to hike output to satisfy customers in the western states. Its Chicago plant served the West, but couldn't fill the gap. And Chairman Elbert Gary, with further capacity on his mind, had his eye on a region farther east, where Indiana's Grand Calumet River flowed into the lake. The attractions?

Economics. Efficiency. For a reasonable investment, you could build a whole state-of-the-art mill from scratch, with plenty of working room, lots of space to grow and easy access to lake transportation. Even if you had to build an entire town for the people who ran the plant.

On March 12, 1906, civil engineers drove the first stakes and marked the lines for the Gary plant. Steam shovels and teams of horses excavated the sand dunes and prepared the ground. Workers moved or laid anew 51 miles of railroad track. An even bigger job: The Grand Calumet cut the plant site in two; crews moved the river more than 1,000 feet by digging a channel two miles long. A harbor slip was built. Mountains of topsoil were hauled in. When excavation was done, crews had moved about as much earth as was excavated for the Panama Canal.

By the end of 1907, the company (through its non-profit Gary Land Company) had built 500 houses, a restaurant, a 40-room hotel, churches, a hospital, a YMCA and a Carnegie library. In four years, the area had gone from wilderness to a city with a population of 17,000. The steel works was about the same size as the town.

As for spaciousness and efficiency: Gary's citizens enjoyed wide streets and did not have to put up with traffic-obstructing excavation of sewers and electrical lines; utility lines were run through alleyways behind houses and buildings. Forward *thinking extended to the school system. Its superintendent, William Wirt, was an enlightened educator who expanded the curriculum from traditional reading, writing, math and history, adding sheet-metal, pattern-making and other industrial courses.*

An example perhaps of backward thinking that was typical of the times was the region of town reserved for unskilled workers. This was the district that came to be infamous as "The Patch." It had more than its share of saloons and trouble, and its people lived in humble houses and enjoyed few amenities. If anyone cared to look, it offered a preview of hard times that Gary would experience later in the century.

*B*ut the world was admiring the tidy town of Gary, proper, and its steel works, where designing from scratch allowed for efficiencies greater than in older mills choked by chock-a-block growth. Mammoth ore boats could turn around in the spacious harbor; no need for the typical squadron of tugs to nudge them in a tight circle. Railroad sidings were laid out diagonally to the main tracks. The pattern optimized space, although space wasn't a worry; the company had acquired enough space to double the size of the steel works. Then there was the massive equipment for the making of steel and steel products— much of it proudly displayed in a black-and-white-photo booklet published five years after startup by U. S. Steel's subsidiary, Indiana Steel Company.*

Aerial view of the city of Gary, circa 1936

The Gary Works' plan called for eight blast furnaces (the first started operating at the end of 1908), 56 open-hearth furnaces , a rail mill, a billet mill, a plate mill, merchant bar mills, an axle plant, and more than 550 by-product coke ovens. Add to that machine shops, electric repair shops—even a blacksmith shop. In a system that prefigured the later age of recycling, the powerful engines that drove the blast furnaces were powered by waste gasses from those furnaces. In 1911, U. S. Steel subsidiaries, American Steel & Tin Plate Company and American Bridge Company, erected plants on the Gary grounds.

As Charles Longenecker wrote, industry had "waved its magic wand over the land upon which the vast steel mills of Gary now stand." In an age when people were as awestruck by giant machines as their descendants would be by computers and pocket phones almost a century later, this was magic.

Appropriately, on July 23, 1908, the freighter E. H. Gary arrived, its deck loaded with VIPs wearing bowlers and boaters, its hold loaded with 12,000 tons of ore. The ship unloaded the ore—the Gary Works' first delivery—to the accompaniment of a Navy gunboat's 21-gun salute. Five months after this grand event, Mary Louise Gleason, daughter of the Gary Works superintendent William P. Gleason, lit the fire in the work's first blast furnace. Unaccustomed to the red glare in the sky, some of the townsfolk called out the fire department—bonus excitement during the startup of a showpiece.

That's what Gary was. A show stopper. With 12 blast furnaces, 47 steelmaking furnaces, an assortment of mills and shops and a coke plant, the Gary works was the largest in the country, probably in the world. And it represented the latest in technology. The town was highly livable, with handsome homes in a range of prices. Sixty years later, global competitive forces, troubling and confusing to Gary and the rest of the nation, would drain the town of jobs and vitality. The Gary Works would lose some of its luster. Still, it would always be United States Steel's crown jewel. But for now, Gary was a gem, a symbol of the bright new century and the good things it seemed to promise.

Of course, U. S. Steel, itself, was a symbol of this new century. With Gary Works completed, The Corporation was riding high. That's what U. S. Steel was then called: *The Corporation* with emphasis on The. Wall Street bankers had given U. S. Steel the name soon after it was founded. The financial press then picked it up, followed by major daily newspapers across the country. It was the kind of name headline writers

Aerial view of Gary Works in the early 1900s

loved. And it was to be synonymous with the world's first billion-dollar enterprise until other companies just as grand came onto the business scene and until the era of Judge Gary ended with his death in 1927.

Elbert Gary liked to see other people get credit for good ideas, even when the good ideas were his. At least that's what Gary's biographer Arundel Cotter insisted. Cotter also asserted that, for the most part, Gary, Indiana, was the inspiration of its namesake. One thing was certain: the creation of the town and steel plant was the biggest deal since the creation of United States Steel itself.

Not that the company hadn't been busy with other matters since its birth in 1901. It spent a lot of time and money tightening up its operating units, and adding a few here and there. It also formed the Universal Portland Cement Company, the better to take advantage of blast-furnace ash, slag and cinder waste in manufacturing cement. (Taking over Illinois Steel Company's cement plants and adding new ones boosted production from 486,357 barrels in 1902 to more than two million in 1906.)

In 1903, the company looked across the oceans and created the United States Steel Products Export Co., which tailored products to the unique specifications of foreign markets: rust-resistant, varnished wire for tropical climes, for example, and light rails to South Africa, date-box nails to the Holy Land and, to Australia, the oval nails the Aussies liked to use. Structural steel and pipe went to a list of countries, and the company produced most of the steel and all of the cement for the Panama Canal—175,000 tons of steel and eight million barrels of cement.

The Panama Canal project demonstrates how political power can give an industry and a region a commanding edge over others. Historian David McCullough explained how in his book, *The Path Between the Seas* (Simon & Schuster, 1977). The canal, he points out, could more easily have been built in Nicaragua and at less cost. The route there would be at sea level, requiring less steel and cement. A Panama route, on the other hand, would require six double locks and massive steel gates, a prodigious amount of steel plate.

But there was a Pittsburgh connection to consider. Republican Senator Philander Knox, former attorney general under President Theodore Roosevelt, came from Pittsburgh. He'd made a considerable fortune by providing legal services to Pittsburgh's steel companies. It was payback time. So, a Panama route it became.

In 1906, United States Steel negotiated a lease of exceptionally rich ore properties owned by the Great Northern and Northern Pacific Railway Company.

By the end of 1906, the Steel Corporation had spent more than $200 million acquiring new properties, building new plants and increasing production capacities. It also closed down plants that were inefficient money-losers. The economy had helped, a little more than half the time, at least. A depression during 1903 and 1904 put a crimp in earnings. But, in late 1904, the economy rebounded, setting off a round of unparalleled commercial prosperity. The following year, U. S. Steel saw dramatic improvement in its earnings.

Then came 1907, when the autumn panic threatened to touch off an economic collapse.

In the last week of October, banks and trust companies big and small closed their doors. Thousands of people were ruined. Businesses fell into the hands of receivers or were wiped out. Stock exchanges were in such a state of hysteria that *they* closed. The panic threatened to derail the nation's economic engine. So J. P. Morgan rushed to the cab to commandeer the controls while Judge Gary and Clay Frick hurried to the White House to suggest to Teddy Roosevelt how U. S. Steel could help stabilize the financial markets. The nation avoided a total economic smashup, but not by much.

Industries including steel looked at all this and thought of banking their furnaces. Judge Gary ruminated over causes and effects. Gary believed the way to keep injecting sanity into the system was to end the old cut-your-losses-and-run mode of doing business. The answer was cooperation and conciliation. Share information with your competitors. Consider how decisions might affect the entire industry and economy. Look at the big picture. That way the members of the industry could wipe out the violent fluctuations in prices and earnings that had become so common in the industry.

Gary invited a group of the leading lights in iron and steel in the United States to join him for dinner at the posh Waldorf-Astoria in New York City, where they could explore what they could do to allay further pandemonium, and restore confidence in the economy. The first of the "Gary Dinners" took place November 20, 1907. The men around the tables listened to the judge as he told them what the meeting was about:

"Violent fluctuations resulting in abnormal, high prices when the demand exceeds the supply, and in unreasonably low prices when the reverse is true, are to be deplored. A friendly exchange of views rather than unreasonable and destructive competition is what our trade needs at the moment.

"This very meeting proves that there can be active, sharp competition in business without unfriendly and bitter warfare that, in the end, will be injurious to the manufacturer, the consumer, and to hundreds of thousands of employees, dependent as they are upon the success of the industry for work and fair wages."

The other steelmen weren't so sure. According to a summary written late the following year by the Independent Iron and Steel Manufacturers of the United States and Canada, the mood was one of depression. But the cloud lifted as the dinners, and committee work by the steelmen between the elegant affairs, progressed.

The dinners worked. Members reported back that cooperation really was benefiting buyers and sellers, and that the market was growing stronger.

The turnaround, Ida Tarbell added in what seemed to be a note of delight, even made the battle-scarred steelmen feel good about themselves:

"They had yielded to [Gary's] advice to their own surprise and, in 1909, when things began to revive, they were almost buoyantly exultant over their virtue. 'Who would have thought we could have been so decent?' was the gist of their talks at luncheons and dinners!"

In all, four Gary Dinners were held, the last December 10, 1908. But a fifth, "no-business-allowed," yet formal dinner was held at the Waldorf-Astoria on October 15 the following year. The only business at hand was honoring Judge Gary for taking so bold and insightful a step as saying "let's talk."

"If [a doctrine is good] for us, it is equally as good for others who are more or less affected by what we do. We should have it in mind in dealing with our employees, with our customers, and with the public. We must never forget that our rights and interests are, and should be, subservient to the public welfare, that the rights and interests of the individual must always give way to those of the public. We must not take undue advantage of the fact that great prosperity and increased demands for our products enable us to advance prices. They should always be maintained at a point within reason and justice."

The good feelings and amazed reformations were evident in comments from a lineup of speakers who praised the judge for his policy of cooperation. Of those who testified, Charlie Schwab probably made the most-telling, and—for Gary—the most-moving comments.

The one-time U. S. Steel executive, the old believer in "hit-'em-hard" competitiveness, did some fence mending. Part of his comments, preserved in a commemorative booklet of the evening's speeches, were addressed to Judge Gary:

> "*You and I have been associated in business—or we were—for some years. We have had many differences, and I am glad of this opportunity to say publicly that, with my bounding enthusiasm and optimism, I was wrong in most instances—indeed, in all instances—and you were right. The broad principles that you brought into this business were new to all of us who had been trained in a somewhat different school. Their effect was marvelous, their success unquestioned.*"

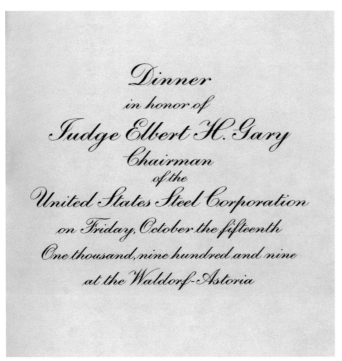

Invitation to a special dinner at New York City's Waldorf-Astoria Hotel, October 15, 1909, honoring Judge Gary

The touching address, Tarbell tells us, was followed by comments from Morgan that were moving, too, because of their brevity and spontaneity.

According to Tarbell, Mr. Morgan was at Gary's right. "They will want to hear you say something," the Judge told him. Mr. Morgan, as confused as a boy, replied, "I never could make a speech." But they called him out, and with one hand on Judge Gary's shoulder and another on his chair, he spoke fewer than two hundred words, the gist of which was in one sentence: "What I might say at another time would be pretty poor, but tonight I am very much overcome by all that I have heard said, for Judge Gary and I have been working together now for 10 years in a way perhaps none of you appreciate, or how much it has meant to me."

Then to Gary: "You know I never could have said a word if I had not had a chair and your shoulder to lean on."

What did the rest of the world make of these get-togethers by the chieftains of steel?

At the fourth dinner, Gary admitted before the assembled "that some, and perhaps many, of the leading thinkers and writers have misunderstood our action is probable…[But] we have never intended to antagonize the laws of the country or the rights and interests of anyone."

Still, U. S. Steel's success, and Gary's dinner sessions, drew suspicious stares from the trustbusters. In a series of investigations, they lined up to set things straight.

Actually, government investigations had become almost routine in the steel industry. Back in 1898, President McKinley and Congress created a 19-person industrial commission comprised of U.S. Congressmen and representatives of private businesses. It probed a host of issues in a variety of businesses, including subjects that would become familiar areas of investigation in steel. For example: What were the motives of steel operators in acquiring, and then sometimes closing, competitors' operations? Charles Schwab testified that the reasons were rooted in destructive economics—in the form of outdated equipment, for example, or disadvantageous location—and he made the case that the plant closings did, in fact, improve efficiencies.

Andrew Carnegie carved a small, second career out of testifying before government committees of one kind or another. Once he got rolling, he enjoyed the spotlight. As historian Page Smith related in *America Enters the World* (McGraw-Hill, 1985), the then-retired Carnegie was the inquisition's "star capitalist." He won over his interrogators with charm and war stories. When asked, "What is your business?" the industrialist-turned-philanthropist answered, "My business is to do as much good in the world as I can." During inquiries into protective tariffs, Carnegie so captivated questioners and spectators with his testimony opposing tariff protection that the lead attorney for the pro-tariff side regretted sending him a subpoena.

The mood grew heavier when Uncle Sam got around to launching investigations and lawsuits with the obvious end of busting up United States Steel.

The principal action here was the government's suit aimed at dissolving the company. This "dissolution" suit, filed against United States Steel in October 1911, came in the wake of the government's breakup of Rockefeller's Standard Oil trust, and it was the result of genuine concern about U. S. Steel's practices and its overall economic power, mixed with politics, and anti-business sentiment on the liberal left.

Historians opine that the suit never would have been filed had it not been for a fluke of history. This was the fatal, September 1901 shooting of President William McKinley. He had been a warm friend of big business. His successor, Teddy Roosevelt, was another breed of political animal, and he was soon taking mighty swipes at some of the trusts—including J. P. Morgan's own Northern Securities Company—and instigating breakups.

As Mark Sullivan pointed out in *Our Times*, his 1926 review of the twentieth century's first quarter, Teddy didn't swing his stick indiscriminately. While others saw the big business combines as angels or devils, Roosevelt had mixed feelings. In contrast to the "big-is-automatically-bad" sentiment that grew with the new century, Roosevelt's view was that the reigning kings of commerce should be judged on a case-by-case basis. He was willing to let some businesses grow as large as economics would permit. He was, after all, a Republican, and supposedly a friend of private enterprise. But he reserved the right of government to regulate businesses big and small as a means of helping them stay honest.

It was a position that caused some confusion. Perhaps most befuddled about Roosevelt's attitude against "big" business was his successor, President William H. Taft.

After Roosevelt carefully groomed Taft to follow in his political path, the 200-pound-plus heir to the presidency wandered off course. He gave the green light to the U. S. Steel dissolution suit. He thought that was what Teddy would do. But he misread his predecessor. One thing his actions did was revive doubts about Roosevelt's role in okaying U. S. Steel's purchase of the Tennessee Coal, Iron and Railroad Company. It sent Roosevelt off on another round of embarrassing rationalization— "I was not misled…. The representatives of the Steel Corporation did not deceive me." And it wrenched wide a chasm that had opened between him and Taft.

But Taft wasn't the only one who was perplexed. In looking back at the dissolution suit, it's useful to remember that it was part of a long process of refining the rules of the game business was supposed to follow. Those rules, and the lines across which business must not step, were never clear, even after the Sherman Anti-Trust Act of 1891 laid down the law forbidding "monopolistic behavior." What did that mean, really? Confusing things further was the suit's off-again, on-again course. When the First World War began, final judgments in the suit were put on hold. The government and U. S. Steel had other things to do for the time being.

The ambiguities of antitrust laws got a good, hard look from members assigned to one of the first of several overlapping waves of antitrust investigations aimed at U. S. Steel. This was the Stanley Committee, busy during 1911 and 1912, and chaired by Rep. Augustus Stanley, D-Kentucky.

Specifically, the Stanley Committee dissected the Supreme Court's decision in the Standard Oil antitrust case in 1911. That decision interpreted the Sherman Act in a way that failed to make clear what "restraint of trade" really was.

As recorded in the committee's report, Stanley Committee member Rep. Martin W. Littleton put the issue this way: "The immediate bewildering consequence was that a dense fog of uncertainty settled down upon and completely enveloped American enterprise."

Judge Gary, questioned by the committee, assured its members that U. S. Steel didn't want to transgress the law, and asked them to "tell us what we can and cannot do."

"All of us ought to be in favor of laws which will prevent injustice on the part of the Government and on the part of the governed, and which will protect the interests of both," he stated. "All I care for is to get out of this position of uncertainty, so that the business of this country may progress."

Andrew Carnegie was called in and made the same point this way: "You gentlemen should sit down and you should agree upon a law that will be so plain and simple that everybody will understand it. The Sherman law is all negative. 'You cannot do this.' 'You cannot do that.' What we want is positive action, telling [companies] what they can do and what they cannot do, and then punish them if they disobey it." It was a view expressed in other forums by a number of other political, academic and business leaders.

Over a two-year period—1911-1913—the Stanley Committee released more than 10,000 pages of reports. Then came another wave of investigation. The Stanley Committee had held hearings for five months when Uncle Sam, acting at the behest of President Taft and fresh from successful antitrust suits against American Tobacco and Standard Oil, filed its dissolution suit against U. S. Steel. The suit was filed in the District Court of New Jersey in October 1911, and its objective was to break up U. S. Steel as an unlawful monopoly. The principal actors in the drama appeared, plus 200 competitors. The printed record would dwarf Rep. Stanley's effort. It would take 189 days to interview these witnesses and the printed testimony filled 28 volumes covering 22,000 pages of testimony and exhibits.

Why should the corporation be broken up? What were the charges delved into by the Stanley Commission, the officials in the dissolution suit and, before them, a third investigative body, a government commission that investigated a number of U.S. industries?

The list of alleged sins was long. But if you boiled down the accusations and allegations as recorded in U. S. Steel legal documents, and translated them into charges that could be presented to a jury, they would read something like this:

Charge 1: The steel trust's founders conspired to create a monopoly...

Its creators intended U. S. Steel to be a monopoly, and it is. It dominates the steel industry, strangles competition, controls prices. One way is through "pooling"—agreements among competitors to hold at a specific price. And remember those famous industry get-togethers that Judge Gary liked to throw, the "Gary Dinners"? They weren't held, as advertised, so steelmen could simply share information that would let steelmen ride out a wild market. They were held to fix prices.

And what about the Tennessee Coal, Iron and Railroad acquisition? U. S. Steel pulled a fast one there, buying Tennessee Coal, Iron and Railroad—a dangerous competitor— at a bargain-basement price. And it pulled the wool over President Roosevelt's eyes in the bargain.

Charge 2: They plotted to 'get' Carnegie...

The main reason for organizing steel was to buy out Andrew Carnegie, eliminating him as a dreaded competitor by absorbing his company. J. P. Morgan put together the company as a stock-manipulation scheme, anyway. The main idea is not making steel, but profits on the stock exchange.

Charge 3: Their hatred of the union compounds their guilt...

U. S. Steel is so fanatically anti-union that American-born union men won't work there. The company has to hire immigrants, and it pays them wages too low for a decent living.

Joe Magarac

IMMIGRATION: NEW ROOTS IN THE GARDEN

Steelworkers have their own legendary hero, their own version of Paul Bunyan and John Henry. He's Joe Magarac. He had muscles and ribs of steel. He could stir molten steel and twist steel beams with his bare hands.

Magarac? The name sounds Eastern European. Appropriately.

A huge portion of the story of U. S. Steel—and of the American steel industry—is the story of the people who left their homes in other countries in the hope that they could build a better life in the States. Many of them, it turns out, claimed roots in Eastern Europe.

Immigration, of course, had always fed the country's growth. After the Civil War, America could be thought of as entering its adolescence, and it was experiencing a real growth spurt. As Bernard A. Weisberger wrote in a 1994 issue of American Heritage *magazine*, yearly immigration ranged from 318,568 in 1866 to 457,257 in 1880.

Then came the flood. In seven years between 1883 and 1903, annual immigration figures exceeded the half-million mark. "All told," Weisberger wrote, "some 14 million arrived at the gates between 1860 and 1900."

Immigrants fed the steel industry and the country's growth.

But things were changing. The traditional motherlands for immigrants had been eastern and northern Europe—Great Britain, Ireland, Scandinavia—as well as Germany. As the new century approached, more new Americans came from central Europe—the Austro-Hungarian Empire, Poland, Romania, Bulgaria, as well as impoverished southern Italy, and the pieces of the shattered Ottoman Turkish Empire. More were coming from Russia, too, and Greeks, Portuguese, Croats, Slovenes, Magyars.

Joining the Addams, O'Shannons and Graffs were the Capichonis, Pappases and Zyzneskis. These people talked and dressed differently, and belonged to different churches. Many were fleeing political upheaval or religious persecution. Most were running from poverty, and were poorer than those who had lined up at America's gates earlier. There was something else, too. The artisans were disappearing. The men among these new immigrants were peasants, by and large, and fit for labor jobs.

The differences disturbed a lot of the established Americans and prompted Congress in 1924 to enact the Johnson-Reed Act which, through quotas, closed the nation's doors much of the way to many "non-traditional" peoples. Still, for now, the newcomers were just what increasingly industrializing America needed; cheap labor. Andrew Carnegie and Charles Schwab, among others, had even recruited some of them from

By 1910, more than half of ironworkers and steelworkers were foreign-born.

Eastern Europe; there hadn't been enough already-settled Americans willing or able to fill the new jobs in the expanding factories, mines and mills. They were low-paying jobs with long hours, but many of the new immigrants who landed them would have told you that they were still better off than they'd been back home.

As the new arrivals sorted themselves out, members of each ethnic group and nationality tended to cluster in specific industries. And so, according to historian–author Page Smith, by 1910, more than half the workers in the iron and steel industry were foreign-born, and most of them were Poles and Slavs.

They were reshaping America and its cities. Pittsburgh, for one, became a classic "melting pot" (an apt label for an ethnically diverse steel center). In Stefan Lorant's analysis of the city, Pittsburgh: The Story of An American City (Doubleday and Co., Inc., 1964) we learn that the city's foreign-born population doubled between 1880 and 1900. In one chapter, Sylvester K. Stevens, then executive director of the Pennsylvania

Historical and Museum Commission, compared the old and new waves of immigrants: The majority of the newcomers were no longer Anglo-Saxons; they no longer came from Ireland, Scandinavia and Germany as in the past, but from Poland, Hungary, Slovakia, Italy and other European Countries. The immigrants, Stevens noted, posed thorny problems…

"There was a lack of housing for such large numbers of newcomers, not enough schools for their children, not enough funds for increased sanitation, fire and police protection…. Crowded in tenement houses without proper sanitation facilities, the immigrants started life at the bottom of the ladder."

Things would get better. The new Americans would climb the ladder, and help create cities, a country, an industry and a new world.

They were the children of Joe Magarac.

The litany of sins grew to become accepted wisdom. Long after the commissions had finished their work, the accusations were out there for the convenience of anyone who wanted to bash the Steel Corporation, or big business in general.

But what about these charges? The testimony and other evidence is far too lengthy and complicated to be fully summarized here. But let's touch on some key defenses.

Begin with the charge that U. S. Steel wanted to buy Carnegie out because he was so fearsome a competitor. As we've seen, steel, like other industries, was becoming more and more integrated in its operations as it sought advantages of scale. The ultimate was the huge, fully integrated operation that Gary, Schwab, Morgan and others dreamed about. And Carnegie had been open about his plans to sell out so he could turn to a life of philanthropy. It was about economics and a shot at a good opportunity.

As for the claim that Gary, Morgan and Frick duped President Roosevelt to grab the Tennessee Coal, Iron and Railroad Company, we've seen such an acquisition only made sense as a strategy to stabilize the panic-stricken market. (Admittedly, with long-term benefits to U. S. Steel—and to most everyone else.)

What about allegations that U. S. Steel was a monopoly, and acted like one?

Judge Gary repeatedly and patiently explained that the corporation knew that achieving a monopoly or in other ways restraining trade would invite trouble. Like an antitrust suit. And Gary repeatedly pointed out a fact he thought spoke for itself: U. S. Steel's market share had been shrinking. Company records trace it as starting at 67 percent and dipping to 50 percent at the time of the dissolution suit. Meanwhile, Gary noted, U. S. Steel's "oppressed" competitors were doing pretty well; several testified that they saw their production increase—from 200 percent to almost 4,000 percent. Some monopoly.

And as for price fixing: In the "bad old days," it was a fairly common practice. That was no secret. Steel executives would huddle in a meeting room and agree on common prices for products such as sheet steel, or rail or plate. The deals never held for long; the urge to compete (or get the best of the other guy) was too strong. There were even stories of steelmen, having just agreed to a fixed price, walking over to a window and signaling the price to comrades waiting outside, who ran off and undercut the other steel operators still in the meetings. The Gary Dinners, some claimed, were merely sophisticated versions of these backroom sessions.

Arundel Cotter dealt with the issue head-on in his 1916 book, *The Authentic History of The United States Steel Corporation* (The Moody Magazine and Book Company):

"Were prices fixed at the Gary dinners? … At the first of the Gary Dinners the host explained that the fixing of prices was forbidden by the laws concerning restraint of trade, and that nothing could or should be done which would not conform in all ways to the law. Yet it was plain that the effect of these dinners was to stabilize the price for steel. It does not appear that there was any definite agreement between the different interests represented as to what [prices] they should ask for their product, but it is obvious that the mere statement, between gentlemen, that one intended to adopt a certain course in regard to prices tended to influence his colleagues to follow a similar course.

"It must be suggested," Cotter continues, "that there was never any question of restraint, as all were free to act as they saw fit, and it seems that on some occasions there was not even absolute agreement. At worst, the participants at the Gary Dinners stretched the interpretation of the law a little to do a great right—the financial salvation of the steel industry."

Arguably the strongest piece of evidence in favor of Judge Gary's intentions, though, is this fact: Gary had written to U.S. Attorney General Charles J. Bonaparte for his opinion on the legality of the "Gary

Movement" right at the start. In her book on Gary, Ida Tarbell printed the Chairman's correspondence in part:

"We are perfectly satisfied to limit the amount of our business to our proportion of capacity and to do everything possible we can to promote the interests of our competitors; and by frequent meetings and the interchange of opinions we have thus far been able to accomplish this result without making any agreements of any kind."

The Attorney General, as well as President Roosevelt, noted Tarbell, "gave the Gary dinners what we may call a clean bill of health."

Not that Judge Gary or any of the others who attended his dinners expected price agreements to hold—especially prices that were hinted at. They didn't. By the last of the formal get-togethers, Judge Gary had learned that several of his competitors had, as Cotter put it, "departed from their intention to maintain for themselves…stability of business and prices."

Following the last dinner, Gary announced that the Steel Corporation would go it alone. It did. Gary sent orders to his sales managers that they should go after all the business they could get. "A vigorous campaign for orders followed," wrote Cotter, but U. S. Steel failed to cut into its competitors' businesses. In fact, it lost to them in some of its business lines.

On the record—the Stanley Commission's record, for one— Judge Gary denied trying to get around the Sherman law by entering into an agreement on prices. Witnesses backed him up.

Not all the members of all the bodies delving into U. S. Steel's books and practices were impressed by such arguments. The industrial commission and Stanley Commission recommended steps designed to curb corporate excess and bolster competitiveness. Superseding them were the findings and actions in the federal antitrust suit. And that suit had a long road yet to travel.

As we've seen, it was filed in the Circuit Court of the United States for the District of New Jersey on October 26, 1911. The answer was filed February 1, 1912. Hearings were held before a special examiner in New York from May 6, 1912, to March 27, 1914. On January 3, 1915, the District Court of New Jersey (where the case had been transferred) handed down a decision refusing to dissolve the corporation.

An appeal was entered in October 1916, and the case was argued before the United States Supreme Court over a week in March 1917. Then a re-argument was set for October of 1919.

In the end, on March 1, 1920, the Supreme Court affirmed the New Jersey district court's decision not to dissolve U. S. Steel.

The case was too complex for black-or-white decisions on activities that wandered into gray areas of the law. But, in its dismissal of the case, the Supreme Court was influenced by a number of factors as reported in a brief provided by the corporation's Law Department.

• No legal action had been taken until more than a decade after U. S. Steel was formed, and after the company had already ceased conduct that was "anti-competitive." (American Tobacco and Standard Oil continued their "crimes" even after suits were filed against them—a big factor in their dissolutions.)

• None of U. S. Steel's competitors had complained that the company was dominating the market.

• U. S. Steel had not been able to control prices unless its competitors cooperated—and even then finally dropped price-control machinations as futile.

• The government was inconsistent in its allegations that, on one hand, U. S. Steel had oppressed independent competitors by virtue of its size and market power, and, on the other hand, had sought their cooperation to set prices.

There was an important footnote:

• Supreme Court Justice Louis D. Brandeis, who had publicly denounced the "curse of bigness" in business, and Justice James C. McReynolds, who had prosecuted the U. S. Steel case as Attorney General between 1913 and

1915, did not take part in the final decision. Since these justices probably would have supported the government's bill to break up U. S. Steel, it is likely that the company narrowly escaped the earlier fate of Standard Oil and American Tobacco. What possibly motivated one of these justices to act as he did is discussed in the next chapter.

J. P. Morgan didn't live to hear the Court's final decision in the U. S. Steel case. In 1913, while on a trip to Egypt with his daughter Louisa and several friends, Morgan slipped into what his biographer Jean Strouse called a "delusional depression." He rejected food, suffered nightmares, asked constantly about conspiracies and, said his daughter, complained about "his whole life work going for naught!"

The group traveled on to Rome, and Morgan rallied enough to attend Easter services. But on March 31, at the age of 75, he died in his sleep. His body was returned to New York City, where funeral services were held April 14. One of his pallbearers was Judge Elbert Gary. Morgan's last official duty had been to testify at a government hearing, in Washington, D.C., on banking and finance. There, he impressed investigators and observers by contending that the most important thing a man can possess, before credit, money or property, is character. We can imagine his business associate and friend, Elbert Gary, nodding in solemn agreement.

As noted earlier, the final legal decision in the U. S. Steel dissolution suit had been postponed from 1917, the better to let the government and the Steel Corporation fight the ugliest war the world had yet seen.

THE PANIC OF 1907: USS TO THE RESCUE

What touched off the financial Panic of 1907? Conservatives and business leaders pointed at President Roosevelt, and his trustbusting policies, his suits against companies including Standard Oil and his enthusiasm for reviving legislative controls that had lain dormant for years. Confidence in business was being undermined, cried the critics, and now the ground was caving in.

Rubbish, countered Roosevelt. The blame should go to "certain malefactors of great wealth" who wanted to sow financial distress so they could discredit Roosevelt's policy, secure its reversal and "enjoy unmolested the fruits of their own evil-doing."

T. R. threw down the gauntlet: "I regard this contest as one to determine who shall rule this free country—the people through their governmental agents, or a few ruthless and domineering men whose wealth makes them peculiarly formidable because they hide behind the breastworks of corporate organization." (As quoted by H. W. Brands in his book, TR: The Last Romantic, *Basic Books, 1997.)*

It was not a statement to make investors feel better. They grew increasingly nervous about the security of business, and the money they'd put into it. In October their jitters gave way to a run on the Knickerbocker Trust Company of New York, which failed on the 22nd, drained of cash. Other banks toppled in a chain reaction.

J. P. Morgan came to the rescue. Arundel Cotter, in his United States Steel: a Corporation With a Soul *(1921), described how the financier dug in at his office and home library, commanding the financial forces that would save the markets. His strategy: Persuade the heads of the banks and trust companies to pool their resources and use them to help comrades in distress. A team effort.*

In effect, Morgan would be taking charge of the country's money supply. He was probably the only man who could rally for a rescue a group of independent bankers who had their own interests to look after. For two weeks, by virtue of his moral authority and reputation, Morgan administered a slow transfusion to the economy. The patient appeared to be improving.

Then Morgan got bad news on Friday, November 1: A prominent brokerage firm would go belly-up unless it received an injection of $25 million by the opening of the market Monday morning. If it didn't, it would probably topple, setting off another chain of failures.

At the root of the problem was now-worthless stock in the Tennessee Coal & Iron Company, which the brokerage was using as collateral for bank loans. Morgan was persuaded that U. S. Steel could save the patient, and the day, by exchanging shares of its good stock for the valueless shares of T. C. & I.—in effect, buying the company. He called Judge Gary and Clay Frick to his library to explain the proposition. They said no; they'd already been approach by T. C. & I., and it was a bad bargain. Morgan's

UNITED STATES STEEL CORPORATION
NEW YORK

November 7th, 1907.

CHAIRMAN'S OFFICE
Personal

MY DEAR MR. SECRETARY:

At the recent interview at the White House between the President, yourself, Mr. Frick and myself, I stated, in substance, that our Corporation had the opportunity of acquiring more than one-half of the capital stock of the Tennessee Coal, Iron and Railroad Company at a price somewhat in excess of what we believed to be its real value; and that it has been represented that if the purchase should be made it would be of great benefit to financial conditions, and would probably save from failure an important business concern; that under the circumstances Mr. Frick and I had decided to favor the proposed purchase unless the President objected to same. I further stated that the total productive capacity of our Companies would not be materially increased by the ownership of the properties of the Tennessee Company, and, after the purchase, would probably not amount to more than sixty per cent of the total steel production in this country, which was about the percentage of our Companies at the time of the organization of the U. S. Steel Corporation; that our policy was opposed to securing a monopoly in our lines or even a material increase of our relative capacity.

I understood the President to say that while he would not and could not legally make any binding promise or agreement, he did not hesitate to say from all the circumstances as presented he certainly would not advise against the proposed purchase.

If consistent, will you kindly write me if the above statement is in accordance with your understanding and recollection.

Sincerely yours,

[Signed]   E. H. GARY.

Hon. Elihu Root
    Secretary of State
        Washington, D. C.

DEPARTMENT OF STATE
WASHINGTON

Nov. 11, 1907.

MY DEAR MR. GARY:

I have your letter of November 7th.

It fully agrees with my recollection of the interview to which you refer, in which you stated to the President the circumstances under which the United States Steel Corporation had been asked to relieve the financial situation by purchasing a majority of the stock of the Tennessee Coal, Iron and Railroad Company. I have sent a copy of your letter with this answer to the President with a recommendation that it be transmitted to the Department of Justice for filing there.

Very sincerely yours,

[Signed]   ELIHU ROOT.

E. H. Gary, Esquire,
    United States Steel Corporation,
        New York, N. Y.

THE WHITE HOUSE
WASHINGTON

Nov. 19, 1907.

MY DEAR MR. SECRETARY:

I am in receipt of your letter of the 11th instant and enclosures, and have forwarded them to the Attorney General to be placed on the files of the Department of Justice, together with a copy of this letter. Mr. Gary states the facts as I remember them.

Very truly yours,

[Signed]   THEODORE ROOSEVELT.

Hon. Elihu Root
    Secretary of State.

response: "Unless someone furnishes immediate relief, no man on earth can say what the effect will be on the financial institutions of the country under these critical conditions."

Gary and Frick got the point. After further rounds of consultation and fact-checking about T. C. & I., Frick came back to Morgan and Gary and said he agreed to a bail-out. Gary said he would go along—if they could discuss the deal with the Justice Department or Roosevelt himself. "Why?!" snapped Morgan. To get the President's okay, answered Gary. The deal could look like a monopoly scheme. Always the lawyer, Gary wanted to head off antitrust suits.

What followed was a race against time that the budding movie industry would have been proud to film.

It was a Sunday night, November 3. The trio agreed that Frick and Gary must see the President and get his judgment before the opening bell of the market, at 10 a.m. the next morning. At 10 p.m., Gary got the President's secretary on the phone. Frick, a director of the Pennsylvania Railroad, commandeered a one-car train to whisk them to Washington. The two executives sneaked out the back door to give waiting reporters the slip, and, at midnight, in Jersey City, boarded a Pullman car that took off for the capital.

They arrived at the White House at 8 a.m., and were told Roosevelt couldn't see them until 10 a.m., the witching hour. Gary pressed the President's secretary to convey the urgency of their business to Roosevelt. Soon, an annoyed president walked into the room. What was going on?

The steel men explained. The Secretary of the Treasury could not be found, so Secretary of State Elihu Root was called in for the conference. He counseled Roosevelt: "You have no legal right to consent to this sale or purchase, but I should think it was a question of policy," Samuel A. Schreiner, Jr., quotes the secretary in his Frick biography. Roosevelt made an impulsive decision: He would not block the purchase. Gary phoned Morgan and relayed the good news. It was 10 minutes before the market opened—a Hollywood finale. The brokerage firm was saved, and the panic began to ease.

Some critics claimed that Roosevelt was in over his head in this affair, but his decision did take the wind out of the panic. Still, letting a huge corporation have its way was embarrassing for the famous trustbuster, and he was blasted by a wave of criticism. He never seemed to get over it, and justified his decision, over and over, the rest of his life.

"The action was emphatically for the general good," he wrote in his autobiography. "But I fully understood and expected that when there was no longer danger, when the fear had been forgotten, attack would be made upon me."

Chapter 5

'Over There,'
and Over Here

For most Americans, the First World War seemed like a family feud gone insane.

In a way which defied most people's understanding, old scores between a cluster of Balkan states and a collection of ethnic groups had piled up so high for so long that, by some kind of spontaneous combustion, they were on the verge of exploding. In the early summer of 1914 they *did* blow up, after a 19-year-old, gun-waving Serb conspirator named Gavrilo Princip fatally shot the nephew of the emperor of Austria-Hungary and his wife, the Duchess of Hohenberg, as they sat in their open car. The couple had been visiting Sarajevo, in Austria-Hungary's recently "acquired" province of Bosnia.

By killing Archduke Franz Ferdinand and Sophie, the young gunman touched off a firestorm that sucked in allied nations as distant and divergent as Russia and Brazil, France and Haiti.

And he hadn't even taken careful aim.

Out of the old animosities and alliances of Europe, two opposing sides took shape: the central powers (Germany, with Austria-Hungary, the Ottoman Empire, Bulgaria); and the Allied powers (Great Britain, France and Italy). And as Americans scanned news photos from Europe of soldiers marching into cities or lying dead in trenches, most of them probably agreed with the assessment of one of Chicago's daily newspapers: "Peace-loving citizens of this country will now rise up and tender a hearty vote of thanks to Columbus for having discovered America."

None of what was going on "over there" seemed to have much to do with the United States. It was all so distant. And as Neil Heyman wrote in *World War I*, an overview of the conflict published by Greenwood Press in 1997, President Woodrow Wilson, hoping he could, in time, negotiate a peace, asked Americans to remain disconnected, "impartial in actions as well as in name."

The USA, of course, had been more partial with the Allies. Great Britain, especially, had worked hard since the late nineteenth century to cultivate good Anglo-American relations. And since 1911, when he became president of U. S. Steel, James A. Farrell, a former salesman for American Steel & Wire, had been developing a brisk foreign steel trade. By the start of hostilities, the corporation's export business had grown significantly, topping $179 million by 1917. Clearly, Farrell's efforts had pushed U. S. Steel to the forefront of the war effort, and he succeeded in keeping it there.

By the end of 1916, American commerce with England and France had more than tripled in value. Along with much of industry in the United States, U. S. Steel found itself in the position of profiting from war. But not right away.

Back in 1913, Americans were mired in yet another depression. By the middle of 1914, industry seemed to be recovering, when—as Arundel Cotter put it in *The Authentic History of the United States Steel Corporation*—"the sudden clash of arms paralyzed world money markets, closed the stock and other exchanges, closed or restricted operations at hundreds of plants of one kind or another, and threw thousands of workers out of employment."

Demand for steel began to slump in mid-1913, and by the fourth quarter of 1914, U. S. Steel's earnings had dropped to the lowest point since the corporation was formed—$10.9 million. At the end of that year, the company recorded earnings of $71.7 million—considerably lower than the earnings of $141.4 million earlier in the decade.

Still, the company held wages where they were. Many of its plants helped workers in other ways, too—for example, by giving employees space for gardens where they could grow food for their families to stretch their incomes.

Victory Garden display during the war was turned into reality by many USS employees on land provided by the company.

Then the war's economic effects kicked in.

This was a war waged with steel, and the supply at the front was shrinking. So the Allies stepped up their orders from the United States and Canada for the guns, shells, trucks and other items they needed to crush the Kaiser. By the middle of 1915, said Cotter, the Corporation was running at 90-percent capacity. According to its annual report for the year, the company sent abroad more than 2.4 million tons, shipments valued at $95.2 million. As a result, earnings for 1915 totaled $130.4 million.

It was a remarkable turnaround, but the Allies called for more steel. The metal was still in short supply, and wartime demand kept driving up its price. It wasn't until U. S. Steel came into the war that the cost settled down, in part due to the industry's adherence to the U.S. government's price ceilings.

There was a nice domino effect: With the revival of steel and its associated industries, the domestic economy started getting its health back. Industry revived, and gloom was replaced by optimism. "A boom was on," said Cotter:

"As the trade balance of the United States for the first time in history reached and passed the billion-dollar mark, it became plain that the war, great evil as it was, was making America rich."

merica *was* getting richer from the war, but without any real sacrifice. It was standing on the sidelines while other nations sent their young men into the fray.

Could the United States stay off the field? Former President Teddy Roosevelt emerged from the wings and sounded a loud voice in favor of his country's participation. He worried that a German victory would throw the world off political balance and put the United States in jeopardy. President Wilson, the man who could give the green light for his country to rush into the war, insisted America should stay out of it, that this was not our fight.

Then, on May 7, 1915, a German sub sank the England-bound British liner *Lusitania*, suspected of carrying munitions to the Allies. (Some 60 years later, investigators would determine it was.) At least 130 American passengers died. Outraged, the United States pressured Germany into limiting its use of this new, "invisible" weapon of war. But it got harder and harder to defend a position of neutrality, and the world watched Wilson for almost two years before the Germans finally forced him to take his country to war. Germany was waging all-out submarine warfare again. More, it offered a secret deal to Mexico: In return for that country's military support against the United States, Berlin would help Mexico get back the territory it had lost to America in the War of 1848.

It was a pathetic proposition, but sinister. On March 1, 1917, Wilson revealed it to the American people. On April 2, he asked Congress for a declaration of war. He quickly got it. And a few weeks later, as David Brody wrote in *Steelworkers in America* (University of Illinois Press, 1998), Gary, Indiana, put on a gala, nighttime parade in support of the country's entry into the world conflict. Gary steel employees, many in uniform, joined town officials in a march down Broadway, to the cheers of thousands.

Then the town sent a telegram to President Wilson:

> *"Gary just now finished the greatest patriotic demonstration ever held in Indiana. Over 26,000 in line and all nationalities. Sentiment entirely with you."*

Patriotism was the order of the day.

So was steel. Now, with America signed on for the fight, U. S. Steel and its staff and steelworkers, and their brothers and sisters in other American steel companies, rolled their sleeves up even higher as they dug into the job they'd begun a few years before their country got into the action: making mountains of steel in the cause of peace.

And Judge Gary of U. S. Steel was running the show.

It has to be one of the neatest twists in the history of jurisprudence that the U.S. government assigned the task of mobilizing the iron and steel industry for war to the man—a judge, no less—who led the very steel company the government was trying to dismantle in its courts.

But the government knew steel was essential to victory, and Judge Gary was president of the American Iron & Steel Institute. (He had been instrumental in creating the association.) He went to work right away, forming a committee to make sure that the industry—already busy making war goods—was securely on wartime footing.

Besides acknowledging the judge's obvious managerial talents, his wartime appointment can be taken as an impressive vote of trust in his integrity—and of confidence in U. S. Steel's resources and ability to come through for the country.

Cotter gives us an example: tin plate. It was used to make cans for food, and it was declared an essential war material. But making tin required healthy supplies of "pig tin" and palm oil. The British controlled the sources of both. And the U.S. government entrusted to U. S. Steel the strategically vital job of importing both.

The corporation had already shown it was ready, willing and able for war duty. Even before America got into the action, the company was supplying shiploads of steel to the Allies. In order to do the job, it had to expand and modernize plants. It was an expensive proposition; the war had inflated the price tag of a major new or expanded plant to

$100 million. Some of those plants would never be profitable, not even during peacetime.

The company was even tapped by the Secretary of War to build a munitions plant to forge muscular cannons with 12- and 18-inch-diameter bores, and to produce ammunition for such guns. At its April 23, 1918, meeting, U. S. Steel's Finance Committee approved construction of the plant. It would be built on Neville Island, in the Ohio River, near Pittsburgh.

It was an ambitious project. The plant was to comprise an array of furnaces, mills, shops, forging equipment, machinery, tools, cranes, track and offices. Even housing. And in choosing U. S. Steel as its partner, the government got a bargain. Just how much of a bargain was revealed by the minutes of the company's Finance Committee:

"…as its profit for services rendered in and about the designing, supervising, constructing and operating said plant," U. S. Steel would charge Uncle Sam one dollar.

By early November, U. S. Steel had "contracted up to $50 million towards the undertaking," according to Gary biographer Ida Tarbell. Construction was well along when news broke about the armistice. The government had no further need of large guns and shells. Work at Neville Island stopped. The plant was dismantled, its equipment sent to other arsenals, and the government was out an initial $11 million.

The records don't show whether U. S. Steel ever got its dollar.

The company must have expected red tape and wheel-spinning from the start of the conflict, but these prospects didn't seem to drain its energy for the war effort.

Take the workers at the company's Homestead Works. U. S. Steel's 1917 annual report reveals that laborers there built a new 110-inch plate mill. According to author William Serrin, they completed it "in the astonishing time of six months" and set production records with it. It was called the Liberty Mill. When lots of steel was called for, Serrin wrote, "the men worked so hard and put in such long hours that they had to be admonished to stop working and were sent home."

Homestead Works' war effort was augmented by this 110-inch plate facility, which came to be known as the Liberty Mill.

Everyone knew there was a lot of work to be done. So the corporation increased its production capacity. During the war years, 1914 to 1918, it put $303 million into its plants. It used the money to expand and in other ways improve its plants, to build new housing for its burgeoning employee population, to develop its coal, iron-ore and limestone properties, and to enlarge its lake-shipping and ocean-going fleets.

It was an awesome investment, and it bought shipworks, gun-forging plants, electric furnaces and new facilities and equipment to turn out shells, cannons, torpedoes, barbed wire, the pie-pan helmets the soldiers wore at the front and a lot more.

The company didn't stop there. It turned over many of its ocean-going ships to the government for war duty. It also turned over the entire fleet of Great Lakes vessels to the U.S. Shipping Board. The board needed them to train naval reservists.

In California, U. S. Steel offered the Navy Department use of all its warehousing properties on San Francisco bay—buildings, equipment, docks and other installations. The Navy proved to be a good tenant. It revamped the property for construction of torpedo boat destroyers—the PT boats that prowled war-zone waters—and, in 1919, returned the properties in ship-shape condition.

Then there were literal investments in the war. The company bought $128 million in Liberty Loan Bonds, allotting $24 million of those bonds for subscription by employees. The corporation also bought nearly $100 million in bonds issued by the allies.

Employees, of course, made the greatest sacrifices by marching off to serve in the war.

In its 1918 annual report, U. S. Steel announced that 34,407 steelworkers from its plants had joined the army and navy. That was an eighth of the corporation's workforce, in an era that included the peak year of 1916, when employment reached 268,688.

The report also noted that "upwards of 200 officials…of the corporation and subsidiary companies were granted leave to connect themselves with various government departments, bureaus and commissions…executives, experienced operating officers, engineers, scientific and technical men, as well as office employees."

U. S. Steel enacted a liberal policy toward its employees who went to war.

In its June 20, 1916, meeting, the corporation's Finance Committee "unanimously voted to recommend to subsidiary companies that, upon request being made by an employee for leave to enter military service, he should be informed that he is at liberty to enter the service and that until otherwise determined by the company, payment of his salary would be continued and that the conditions apply to those who have already entered the service. Also, that it is expected to re-employ those who have been in such service if conditions justify."

David Brody in *Steelworkers in America* reports that many of the Slavic steelworkers enlisted in the Polish and Czecho-Slovak armies:

"There were many stars in the service flags of the immigrant churches

and societies of Homestead. The first death from the South Works

was Walter Stalmaszck, who had enlisted. John Manjikitis was the

first Homestead casualty."

Death reached up into U. S. Steel's higher offices, too. One of the first Americans of prestigious rank to be killed in action was Raynal C. Bolling, U. S. Steel's general solicitor. He was a favorite of Judge Gary. In fact, Gary was grooming Bolling to succeed him.

Gary's biographer Arundel Cotter told how "the judge more than once talked over with me the possibility of his retirement. If, he said, he could find available a man to whom he could hand over without a qualm the helm of United States Steel, he would immediately do so."

Later, Gary confided to Cotter that Bolling, skilled in business and brilliant in the law, was that man. But the judge would never see his young protégé follow him. Bolling, serving as an army colonel, was killed in action in March 1918 near Amiens, France.

Gary was devastated, Cotter says: "He admired not only Bolling's ability, but his high ideals."

At the April 30, 1918, board meeting in New York, Gary offered a tribute to Bolling for the minutes. It read, in part:

"He was an exceptionally able lawyer, a wise counselor, an industrious,

faithful member of the Law Department, and he was possessed of

unusual tact and discretion .... We mourn his death, and are

comforted only by the knowledge that voluntarily and cheerfully

he offered his life for his country."

In his message to stockholders in 1918, Chairman Gary summarized his gratitude for his workers' war efforts. "The demands upon the entire personnel of the organization in every department during the period of the war were extraordinary and exacting. All were zealous and loyal in the discharge of their respective duties under conditions which at times were trying, but were assumed from a desire to assist in an effort to 'win the war.' "

When victory came, the Allies were turning out more than four times as much steel as the enemy. They produced 66.5 million tons of steel—50 million of it from the United States.

From 1914 through 1918, U. S. Steel shipped nearly 75 million tons of steel. Of that amount, 19 million tons went directly to the war effort, sold to the U.S. government and exported to the allies.

And in the end, steel—and U. S. Steel—helped win the day.

But U. S. Steel did its part in other ways, too.

Foreseeing a shortage of manganese—crucial to steelmaking— the company stockpiled some 600,000 tons of the element. When the shortage came, U. S. Steel sold the product to its competitors—at the same price it had paid.

As we've seen, the company imported pig tin for the government. In another instance, when the supply of tin for food containers was all but exhausted, England desperately needed credit with its supplier in the Malay Strait. U. S. Steel advanced a million pounds sterling, and, on that insurance, the tin trade continued.

As much as the company made from the war, it could have made more without it. It was dealing with the government on the government's terms—which meant accepting prices that were lower than the free market would have set them. Steel plate, for instance. The government's price was $2.90 per hundred pounds. In the domestic, open market, that plate would have sold for $8 to $10 per hundred weight.

Similar terms applied to steel products across the board, and, as head of the industry's steel committee, Judge Gary faced a never-ending wartime job of keeping steel producers in line on prices. "Disparities" more than once caused some of the Iron and Steel Institute's war committeemen, hardcore wheeler-dealers, to walk away from war orders in disgust. They wanted more. Gary talked sense to them. They came back.

According to Tarbell, the judge even helped his competitors more than once. If they were low on billets or nuts or other material, the judge made sure U. S. Steel supplied them—"at a price below his own cost if the other concern stood to lose on the contract," said Tarbell. "They must be allowed to make a little money if they were to carry on."

"His work…was patient and tactful, but determined," concluded Tarbell, who cited the following lecture the judge gave to his fellow committeemen:

"The question of making money, while always important and necessary for the nation, is of no importance when compared to the immediate necessities of the government for the production and delivery of the things which it demands and finds necessary for military purposes."

War changed life in ways other than the sacrificing of it. War stirred the melting pot, too.

Enlistments created a labor shortage, and steel companies recruited African Americans to help fill it. Many southern African Americans migrated to industrial plants in the North; many of them were brought in as strike breakers. "At the Gary Works," Brody wrote, the number of African Americans "rose from 189 in 1915 to 407 in 1916, 1,071 in 1917, and 1,292 in 1918." By August 1917, 4,000 were laboring at the Carnegie plants in the Pittsburgh district. They'd found jobs, even if those jobs were almost always in hard labor. They also found a shortage in housing. At Homestead, U. S. Steel purchased a large structure to serve as a community center for the blacks.

The workers had to live in crowded, shabby flats for a time. But their role in steelmaking grew, and so did their worth in the eyes of their employers. One steel manager urged foremen to adopt a greater spirit of "helpfulness and cooperation" toward foreign-born workers. "Their loyal cooperation and their progress are good things for the company," he declared.

Another good thing happened: Steelworkers saw their pay climb to surprising levels, pumped up by the labor shortage, wartime demand for steel and the consequent game of leapfrog that prices began playing.

The corporation also gave a hefty chunk of its wartime earnings back in the form of excess profit taxes, which reached as high as $233 million on earnings of $487 million in 1917.

The company's earnings for the entire war—more than $1 billion—fed raises for the steelworkers, including common laborers. The first raise, of 10 percent, came February 1, 1916. It was followed over the next two years by eight pay raises ranging from nine to 13.6 percent. Cumulatively, the increases exceeded 150 percent. Calculated another way, the amount in workers' pay envelopes grew two-and-a-half times.

On paper, anyway. Food, fuel and rent had risen in cost during the war, and inflation nibbled the workers' real wage advances down to less than 25 percent from 1914. It was a lot better than nothing. But it still didn't elevate the lifestyles of the workers and their families to what most Americans would call a comfortable level.

But if the war did anything, it convinced steelworkers that their labor and skill were worth far more than they were being compensated. They'd helped win the war, *and* build the economy, and they deserved more than they were getting in return. Enough was enough.

Americans were in a wary and sullen mood in 1919, and their frustration and anger boiled over that year, one famous for strikes. They had just watched and fought the biggest, most death-dealing war imaginable. It had started among people they didn't understand. Many of those people seemed to have a taste for revolution—look what was going on in Russia alone, with the Bolshevik takeover. And their relatives and sympathizers were here, now. Were they spreading the same brand of poison?

It looked that way.

During the war, despite their employers' appeals for patriotism, American workers struck in many industries. Now that the war was over, they seemed to be upping the ante. From their viewpoint, they had worked hard to help win the war. Now they deserved a bigger piece of the American pie. If no one was going to serve it to them, they'd help themselves.

Their impatience grew. On January 19, 1919—only two months after the armistice—35,000 shipyard workers struck in Seattle. Then labor officials there called a general strike. In New England, 120,000 textile workers "went out" in towns in Massachusetts and Rhode Island, also in New Jersey. Telephone operators walked off their jobs. Police struck in Boston. In New York City, hotel workers, cigarmakers, shirtmakers, carpenters, bakers, teamsters, street sweepers, firemen, even actors, hit the bricks. Many quit their jobs. In Chicago, 16,000 carpenters and more than 7,500 International Harvester workers walked away from their hammers and tractors.

Business and government were sure they knew who was behind the wave of anarchy: the Bolsheviks. (They weren't called Communists until later.) True enough, anarchists and Bolshevists and their apologists were crooning into the workers' ears. How many of the workers' minds and souls the "Reds" really possessed is hard to say. But how do you stop an idea? Police, many employed by the companies that *were* under attack, resorted to beating strikers and their allies, and to mass arrests.

Still the strikes went on. Trains stopped. Elevators froze. Printing presses sat silent. Theaters closed. A lot of Americans were scared. The country seemed to be coming apart at the seams.

"The most extraordinary phenomenon of the present time," *The Nation* proclaimed in October 1919, "the most incalculable in its aftereffects, the most menacing in its threat of immediate consequence... is the unprecedented revolt of the rank and file...

> *"It is a world-wide movement much accelerated by the war. In Russia it has dethroned the Czar and for two years maintained Lenin in his stead.... In England it brought about the railway strike.... In Seattle and San Francisco it has resulted in the stevedores' recent refusal to handle arms or supplies destined for the overthrow of the Soviet government....*
>
> *"In Pittsburgh... it compelled the reluctant American Federation [of Labor] officers to call the steel strike, lest the control pass into the hands of the [Industrial Workers of the World—the 'Wobblies'] and other 'radicals.'"*

The steel companies must have seen the strike coming. As Jeremy Brecher reported in his 1997 South End Press book *Strike!*, one investigator of the labor situation reported during the war that "workmen of the most docile tendencies have been making demands.... Insignificant little rebellions, verging on strikes," had erupted here and there.

Labor unrest began even during the war years. In early 1916, a local strike by workers at a Youngstown, Ohio, plant run by one of U. S. Steel's competitors turned into a riot. Workers threw bricks at police. Police opened fire on workers. Workers threw more bricks, and an enraged mob burned buildings.

Local strikes broke out in Pittsburgh four months later. One newspaper, Brecher tells us, reported that a furious crowd "charged plant after plant, and many of the places were wrecked." At U. S. Steel's Edgar Thomson Works, guards opened fire, killing two people. Some plants shut down to avoid trouble.

The steelworkers' aggravations didn't end with the war, though. Pay had dropped and remained low, hours long. Unemployment spread. Now it was 1919, and the workers were watching to see what the American Federation of Labor and its chieftains, including the legendary Samuel Gompers, would do for them. Gompers was interested in negotiating the union's right to deal with company managers. A strike wouldn't help, he felt, and he didn't want one. Neither did President Wilson. So the union kept strategizing. It asked Judge Gary to meet with them, in his role as head of the Iron and Steel Institute, on behalf of the steel companies, to talk things over. Gary refused. Still no national strike.

The breaking point came in July, when a council of workers in Johnstown, Pennsylvania, wired the union heads, putting them on notice: If the union did not authorize a national strike vote immediately, the Johnstown workers would strike on their own. More meetings, more appeals to Gary, more talks with the President. But a more radical groundswell overcame the conservative elements, forcing the union's hand. The union called for a vote September 10. Members voted unanimously for a national strike to start September 22.

"The strike order was wired to the steel center," author David Brody wrote, "and the union officials scattered to their posts."

The national strike of 1919 was on.

There was the expected repression of strikers, and violence, much of it in the towns and mills of Western Pennsylvania. Strikers and mill guards scuffled at Homestead. At a Buffalo plant, two strikers were killed and several wounded. National Guard troops marched into Gary, Indiana, to keep the peace and stayed for the entire strike. In a number of mills, the steel companies battled back by hiring strikebreakers. It was not America's finest hour.

Then, in its sixth week, the strike began to falter. The fighting, the use of strikebreakers, the onset of winter, the workers' dwindling savings, had whittled away at the workers' morale.

In fact, only a minority of workers, the militant and aggressive ones, were enthusiastic about the strike from the start. Tarbell put it this way: "It was a strike which never fully believed in itself, which was saturated on the inside from the start with suspicion—suspicion of the radical for the conservative; of the conservative for the radical."

Reports conflict on the number of workers who struck throughout the industry. According to Brody, the union claimed 365,500 workers had gone out on September 30. The companies said it was fewer. Despite episodes of violence, most workers remained at their jobs in the industry's Pittsburgh mills. Most walked out in other towns, such as Chicago. But many came back a short while later.

When all was said and done, though, only a small percentage of the steelworkers took part in the strike. At U. S. Steel, which the union had picked as its prime target, participation was especially low. Judge Gary estimated about a quarter of the company's workers (some 70,000) went out, most temporarily.

Interestingly, among the strikers, the immigrants proved to be the most patient and resistant, the strongest holdouts. Did they lean farther left than the other workers? Perhaps, although a Polish striker, quoted by Brody, hardly sounded like a revolutionary:

> *"For why this war? For why we buy Liberty Bonds? For mills?*
>
> *No, for freedom and America—for everybody. No more [work like]*
>
> *horse and wagon. For eight-hour day."*

Why this "war"? It was a good question. The eight-hour day would come, of course, but not just yet.

But what did the steel companies want? Why was Judge Gary being so stubborn?

Why didn't he even talk to the union? Because he never strayed from his principles. And one of them was that the company should not deal with third parties who, in his eyes, did not speak for all the workers, or represent their true interests. And he was convinced that the union was such a third party.

"These men [the union leaders] are volunteers, outsiders entirely," Gary told Tarbell. "I don't think our men asked them to represent them.... Our 85 percent are working side by side with 15 percent who are members of the union. They [the "85 percent" of U. S. Steel workers] have no controversy over it, all they want is an open shop."

Why would so many workers support an open shop—the choice to join or not to join the union? Because, as Gary insisted, the company's already-in-place welfare programs were at least as good as any benefits the union could offer. The company's pension plans were as desirable as any the union could force on it. In places like Gary and Birmingham, the company maintained excellent hospitals. It built houses that its employees could buy at decent rates. In the plants, the company operated a safety program (U. S. Steel invented the slogan "Safety First") that won awards, and was admired and copied around the world. It worked.

The judge summed up his sentiments on the 1919 strike, and what he wanted for his employees, at the company's annual shareholders meeting in 1919. In part, he told shareholders:

"We never resent unfavorable criticism from any source concerning our attitude toward employees, if made in good faith, even though it may not be deserved. Whenever proper and practicable, we adopt measures to improve the living and working conditions of our workmen....

"We do not combat labor unions as such. We, of course, acknowledge the natural right of labor to organize. But we insist that a labor organization should be subjected to governmental control and regulation like other organizations."

In any case, several sources on labor history verify that the strike seemed doomed from the start for want of worker support. Probably the hardest evidence comes from Tarbell, who concluded that "the effort to unionize failed…"

"A most conclusive proof that the body of steel workers had not lost confidence in the Corporation is the fact that in this disturbed year of 1919, 61,324 subscribed for steel stock and 46,676 of these were men receiving from $800 to $2,500 a year. The year following, 1920, with the after effects of the strike hanging over the labor body, 66,311 workers subscribed to steel stock."

The strike was wearying. But it was relieved by a bright spot. On March 1, the U.S. Supreme Court's final decision in the dissolution case against U. S. Steel: Dissolution of the company was not warranted.

Remember that Justice Louis Brandeis, who had denounced the "curse of bigness" in business, sat out the final verdict. So did Justice James McReynolds, who had prosecuted the U. S. Steel case as Attorney General between 1913 and 1915. Both had advocated breaking up Standard Oil and American Tobacco. Why did they decline from recom-mending the same fate for U. S. Steel?

The Supreme Court rules in U. S. Steel's favor.

Had they taken to heart the insistence of U. S. Steel's competitors that "the Steel Trust" had never been a malicious or unfair competitor? That, in his dinners and discussions with his competitors, Judge Gary was not determined to strangle competition, but meant to keep it healthy? Could they decide against a company whose top boss had helped win the war without taking advantage of his position, and by keeping the other steel chiefs marching in step?

Did they withdraw from the final decision because they had come to realize that U. S. Steel was a "good" trust? That their peers might consider them inconsistent if they voted with the majority? That they ran the risk of making themselves look like hard-liners gone soft?

In the absence of other explanations, the answers to all these questions could be yes.

Or, in Brandeis' case, he might even have been making an apology.

In fact, the "good trust" had won. And shortly thereafter, Judge Gary was introduced to Samuel Clemens—"Mark Twain." Tarbell replayed the meeting:

"Judge Gary?" said Mark Twain, when the judge was first presented to him. "I know him. He is the good corporation."

"Mr. Clemens," retorted the judge, "the time will come when you and every one else will see that there is a difference in corporations."

"I believe it now, Judge Gary," the great humorist consoled him.

GUNS, SHIPS AND HORSESHOES

When the Allies went to war in 1914, they had to send to the United States—and to U. S. Steel and its fellow producers—a long shopping list of steel and steel war materials.

One of the first things on that list was barbed wire, strung around battlefields to snare attackers. It became a fixture of the First World War's new "trench warfare," and a symbol of the war itself. England may have been one of the world's principal steelmakers, but it didn't make much barbed wire. U. S. Steel's wire mills produced thousands and thousands of miles of the stuff for the war.

Orders poured in, too, for steel for Allied land mines, guns, shells, autos, trucks and a long list of other material and equipment for the highly mechanized, twentieth-century brand of battle. Russia needed locomotives and steel railway cars to transport its troops. Rails, too.

When America entered the war, the country stepped up its wartime steel production. The Allies' most urgent need was for ships. German subs were sinking ocean tonnage at a rate the Allies didn't dare make public. Munitions and food for the troops went to the bottom with the ships. So did steel in the form of riddled hulls. More than anything, victory depended on how fast Allied shipyards could replenish their shrinking fleets.

So U. S. Steel went into shipbuilding. According to Arundel Cotter, the U.S. government "placed contracts under which it stood the entire expense of plant construction with payment for the vessels on a cost-and-percentage basis."

The company didn't really want to go into the shipbuilding business. The yards—in Kearny, New Jersey, and near Mobile, Alabama—"were conceived and undertaken solely as war measures," Judge Gary explained in his 1918 report to shareholders. And it was a strange time to sink money into this kind of venture if you were merely interested in making money. Building costs were horrendous, and the future was a big question mark.

As it turned out, the yards did prove to be good business for the company after the war, when owning ships was cheaper than leasing them.

Together, the yards were designed to fabricate three dozen 10,000-ton vessels a year. Construction zipped along. Ground was broken for the New Jersey plant on August 1, 1917, and that yard's first ship—the Liberty—was launched 10 months later. By that time the war was almost over. All in all, the yards launched 30 ships for the government. Add to that the steel produced by other U. S. Steel plants for other shipyards—enough to produce about 70 mighty hulls.

To supply the yards, the corporation beefed up its plate-making mills in Pittsburgh and Lorain, Ohio, and built new plate mills—the 110-inch Liberty Mill at Homestead Works, the 160-inch mill at the Gary Works, the 90-inch mill at South Works, Chicago and the 110-inch mill at Fairfield Works in Alabama.

It was only the beginning.

The company built a 40-inch blooming mill at Gary to roll projectile steel for shells. It modified rolling mills at other plants so they, too, could produce projectile steel—and it dedicated the entire capacity of the new, fully integrated steel mill at Duluth to this kind of steel. In all, the company shipped more than 1.7 million gross tons of projectile steel to the government and to the Allies during the war.

A new gun-forging plant at Gary turned out 155-millimeter field weapons and 240-millimeter howitzers.

Production flowed from U. S. Steel mills around the clock.

From South Works' new electric furnaces came high-grade steel for gun forgings. From Homestead's armor plant came forgings for carriages for large guns. Shell forgings of nearly infinite variety rolled out of plants in Pennsylvania and Illinois. Torpedo and submarine "air flasks," steam pipes for war ships, gas bombs, trench mortars, and aircraft motor forgings spewed from the Christy Parks plant on the scenic Youghiogheny River south of Pittsburgh. American Sheet and Tin Plate contributed steel sheets for helmets, American Bridge turned out railway mounts for naval guns. American Steel & Wire sent out roll after roll of barbed wire, and geared up to weave steel rope for underwater mines and sub-snaring nets.

The new facilities had ravenous appetites for coal and coke used in making

A steady stream of steel and steel war products from U. S. Steel and other domestic producers helped to assure victory for Allied forces on the battlefield.

steel. At plants in Clairton, Pennsylvania, Cleveland, Lorain, Gary and Fairfield, 1,450 new coke batteries were installed. From them came coal-based chemicals that were in high demand by the government: toluol, benzol and sulfate of ammonia needed for making synthetic rubber, plastics, explosives and medicines.

From 1914 until the war's end in 1918, the Steel Corporation produced more than 74 million tons of steel, more than 10 million tons of it shipped to the Allies. Some of the war goods were hardly destructive; the company shipped to defense workers behind the lines such items as iron nails (500,000 kegs), and, to bureaucrats, book wire (200,000 tons of it) for binding government publications.

The company produced 75,000 kegs of horseshoes, too. Thoroughly modern as this war was, horses still served, towing supply wagons and transporting officers.

JUDGE GARY, FRONT AND CENTER

Elbert Gary and his wife liked to vacation in Europe. It was rejuvenating. And in the spring of 1914, the judge, especially, needed this brand of tonic. He'd just ended the long ordeal of testifying in the government's suit against U. S. Steel. It would be months before the court would announce its decision. The depression in the States was like a weight on everyone's shoulders. Gary was tired. Europe called.

In late June 1914, the Garys sailed for Europe, and Paris. They'd visited the City of Lights before, and now they used it as a base from which they launched motorcar excursions, visiting towns, talking with the people, visiting cathedrals, studying the "old world's" art. And Gary became a friend of Europe's leaders in iron and steel. Among them: Baron von Bodenhausen, a grandly named executive of Germany's mighty arms maker, Krupp.

On July 23, the Garys joined the Baron and his wife in Paris. Five days later, Austria declared war on Serbia. The horror that a saddened Baron von Bodenhausen had predicted to his American friend had come to pass.

Gary was sure the hostilities would engulf all of Europe, but not for a while. He stopped at a Paris bank to stock up on German and Austrian money for the next leg of his vacation trip. But the banks were not quoting exchange rates. The politically savvy judge recognized this warning sign and postponed his trip.

Then he watched history unfold. He wandered Paris, a city waiting for war. He

Judge Gary

saw thousands of soldiers mobilize. He saw the shops close, the lights go out every night at 8 p.m., the streets become empty. Paris, he wrote, had gone from bustling city to deserted village.

Thousands of other Americans, travelers throughout France and Eastern Europe, were eager to escape a continent at war and get back home. Many of them rushed to Paris, where they learned that the ships they'd booked for return passage had been commandeered for battle.

Myron Herrick, America's ambassador to France, stepped in. He asked Judge Gary to head a committee to arrange voyages home for the stranded Americans. "I don't know what I would have done without Gary," Herrick said later, repeatedly.

Gary stayed on, even after he'd finished his rescue mission. Just before he left France, he took a 100-mile auto tour along the battlefront—"Taking good care to keep within the safety zone," he modestly told Ida Tarbell and his friends later. Just ahead of the Germans, he retreated to his ship, and sailed September 6 from Havre, France.

When he got home, he told Tarbell that "proper publicity" would have prevented the war…

"It is not too much to demand that the people should know the reasons for the commencement and the continuance of pending wars and they should understand the awful consequences."

Publicity as a fail-safe device. Judge Gary often preached that it would save business from itself.

Chapter 6

Gains and Losses

Judge Gary must have felt good as he traveled between his elegant home on New York's Fifth Avenue and his 17th-floor office at 71 Broadway in the heart of the city's financial district.

It was spring of 1920. The "Great War" was history. After years of wartime production, America's industrial machine was set on "peacetime," cranking out farm implements, appliances and automobiles for a public whose long-restrained desire for consumer goods had been about to burst like an over-wound clock. The buildings outside the judge's window had been shooting up like spring grass. Gary knew that, on their vertical foundations of steel, they would rise even higher.

The world needed steel more than ever. Gary and his company had a lot of work to do. And they'd just gotten a bright green light with the Supreme Court's reaffirmation that U. S. Steel was no monopoly.

The court's proclamation was a victory for a man who insisted on playing the game straight. But if Gary thought it signaled a new era of faith in his methods of management-by-cooperation, he was wrong. He'd see soon enough that many of the men who ran the government really prized conflict over consensus. He'd never get over the disappointment.

The Twenties were like that. They gave and took. They roared in on a promise of good times, then whimpered out when the bottom gave way. In between was an age of craziness, when Americans shrugged off the ghost of the war by watching flagpole sitters, dancing in marathons, reading about the exploits of gangsters and drinking gin, which seemed to taste better now that it was forbidden. The national prohibition had taken effect in 1919. But not in a lot of America's hard-working towns.

As Stefan Lorant explained in *Pittsburgh: The Story of an American City*, the city pretty much shrugged off the ban. "The saloon," explained Lorant, "was the steelworkers' second home." It was the workingman's social club. You could stop there after your "turn," or shift, to rinse the dust from your throat and share the latest gossip about the plant.

Even more chat was being exchanged by telephone. Fifty million American homes had them. And you could clamp on a set of headphones and, in your living room, hear music sent through the air courtesy of Pittsburgh's KDKA, the country's first radio station. What really powered the economy, though, was the automobile. It was better and cheaper. More people could motor across town or miles out into the country in a matter of minutes.

It was all the bee's knees. Not for everyone, of course, but as Harold Evans summed things up in his 1998 book *The American Century* (Knopf), the typical factory worker had a third more real purchasing power than a decade before: "He could have him his automobile, radio, refrigerator and washing machine on the new installment plan."

And when people went shopping for cars and home appliances, they were shopping for steel by proxy.

Nowhere did the Twenties roar more exuberantly than in the steel industry. And U. S. Steel led the way. In the period from 1920 to 1929, the corporation's net income climbed from $109.7 million to $197.5 million, a total net income over the period of nearly $1 billion. Its employee rolls averaged almost 240,000 blue-collar and management workers a year. They earned wages and salaries of more than $4.3 billion. And the company paid its shareholders $627.60 million in dividends.

Gary was ever the optimist. His aboveboard way of doing his company's and the public's business was making him a larger figure on the world stage. He was named to New York City's Public Safety Committee. There were rumors he'd run for mayor. No one could blame him for any second thoughts about public office, though, after politicians double crossed him over a steel-pricing practice known as "Pittsburgh-plus."

"Pittsburgh-plus" was shorthand for a steel-industry billing method almost a century old. Its math was rooted in the era in which mills in Pittsburgh had an edge on their competitors. Because of easy access to ore and coal, and an abundance of rail and river routes, it was cheaper to make steel there than anywhere else. Pittsburgh steel's price, then, was used as a reference: steel's base price. To compete, a higher-cost producer quoted its own price for, say, plate or rail—*plus* the cost of freight from Pittsburgh.

Math aside, the system put independent mills at a competitive disadvantage against U. S. Steel. When the Western Association of Rolled Steel Manufacturers decided to contest the practice, it sent Chicago lawyer John Miller to have a little chat with the head of the iron and steel institute, Judge Gary.

To Miller's surprise, Gary admitted he'd been asking himself whether Pittsburgh-plus was ethical, and had been studying the issue and consulting with his institute colleagues. He told Miller that they should go to Washington to talk to the Federal Trade Commission (FTC) about the matter. They did. And on July 9, 1919, they sat down with members of the commission. Gary, being Gary, wanted the issue out in the open.

As *Daily Metal Trade* Editor J. F. Froggett described the scene in the October 28, 1919, issue of his trade paper, the judge looked around at the members and declared: "The whole iron and steel industry ought to be in here. You ought to have jurisdiction over the whole thing...."

"Now, I am not trying to bring work to this commission. But I am disposed to say that, from my standpoint, I would like to have this question fully heard on the evidence...and the whole thing settled.... If it is right to have this changed, I would like to have it done."

Gary could hardly have been more open and aboveboard. He told commissioners that he worried whether the pricing scheme was damaging the public interest. Imagine his shock and disappointment when, after thanking him and declaring the whole matter was outside its jurisdiction, the FTC turned around and prosecuted U. S. Steel for unfair business practices. Just U. S. Steel. And it happened almost a year after Gary had gone to the commission to ask its members whether his company was doing the right thing. It was not a good opening to the Twenties.

Ida Tarbell attributed the about-face to a changing of the guard in the commission. The new body of commissioners decided to act on the case, she added—"But they did not take it up as a cooperating and correcting body—they took it up as a prosecuting body...and they...centered the attack on the United States Steel Corporation."

Gary had practiced compromise and consensus, but the commissioners preferred confrontation. They'd gone gunning for U. S. Steel and the judge. And government adversity against business became the pattern for the rest of the century.

As Tarbell said in her Gary biography: "There is little political capital in cooperation. There is much, though it may be short-lived, in prosecution."

Extensive hearings were held from 1921 until 1924. On July 21 of that year, the Federal Trade Commission ruled. U. S. Steel and other steel producers could no longer sell steel products at Pittsburgh-plus prices. They couldn't set prices on any basing point other than the one where the products were manufactured or from where they were shipped. The companies could not sell any product without revealing the freight-on-board charges and the actual charges for transportation. And they could no longer discriminate among customers in pricing products when, to do so, would lessen competition.

Being blindsided by the Pittsburgh-plus decision didn't seem to undermine Gary's taste for political action. If anything, it strengthened his conviction that his business principles of openness and cooperation would make for better government, too. He spoke his mind in the fall of 1923, at the American Iron and Steel Institute's annual meeting in New York. Addressing the group as its president, Gary declared confidence that his principles could quell the world's persistent economic chaos.

The trouble went back to the end of the "Great War," and the Versailles Treaty, which inflicted upon Germany financial reparations the country couldn't hope to meet without being ruined.

In his history, *Modern Times: The World From the Twenties to the Nineties* (Harper Collins, 1991), Paul Johnson reminded us that astute public figures predicted the burden would bankrupt Germany, embitter the German people, and set the scene for a sequel to the war. "The damned treaty," seethed British economist John Maynard Keynes, "was an economic disaster and a formula for future bloodshed."

He was right. The compact split up countries, set nationalities at each others' throats, ruined and humiliated the German people, and pumped up the Nazis' power. Europe again was a bomb with a fizzing fuse. Its plight aggravated political and economic tensions elsewhere.

Gary used his American Iron and Steel Institute podium to recommend that representatives of the troubled nations gather in Washington for an international business conference. They could talk about their economic problems, maybe even agree on some solutions.

Nothing happened. In January 1922, tensions increased. Germany, strapped, wanted to postpone its war reparations payments a second year. In answer, the French government marched its army into

Germany's industrial Ruhr region to take over its factories. The fuse sputtered brighter, and it got *New York Times* journalist Rose Feld even more interested in Gary's peace ideas. She interviewed the chairman, who, she said, insisted that "world problems could be solved in the same manner as the problems of a nation, a corporation, a community, a business."

Alluding to the Gary Dinners, Gary told Feld, "There has, during the last few years, been a wonderful demonstration of the possibility of applying in matters of business the principles of what have been termed conciliation and cooperation....

> *"When the men representing the [steel] organizations were brought together, what did they talk about? About petty jealousies and quarrels between two organizations? Hardly. They were interested in the broad economic principles of costs and production and profit. Petty quarrels were shelved.*
>
> *"There is no reason why the representatives of the nations who are to meet cannot gather together in friendly and helpful conference and say, 'Come, let us forget political squabbles, boundaries, past epithets, past leaderships. Let us fairly and patiently consider the rights and interests of each other.' "*

If the prime ministers, kings and dictators squabbling over Europe rolled their eyes over this Sunday School talk, the old Gary Dinner crowd, the converts to Garyism, must have applauded.

Others detected hypocrisy. Fairly and patiently considering the rights and interests of each other? How did *that* square with Gary's persistent vetoes of shorter workdays for his employees?

It was the old argument that the steel companies must cut the hours and days for their workers—while keeping paychecks at or near the same levels.

After the war, the shouts to trim shifts from 12 to eight hours grew louder from the press and the pulpit. Gary was the chief tyrant, since he ran the biggest steel company and the steel institute. How could he talk about fairness and rights? The public heard all this and wanted to know why Gary and the other steel moguls didn't simply go to eight-hour turns. Why were they so greedy? Did they want to work their crews to death?

Gary noticed that the press and political figures usually didn't bother to ask the steelworkers what *they* thought about cutting hours. While these "experts" knew little about steel, they seemed to know what was best for the workers. But the hourly issue was far more complex than just setting back the time clock. Anyone who really thought about it would have realized that was the case. Why would the steel managers keep taking this abuse when they could "simply" do what their critics demanded?

"Probably no other big industry was ever so [unjustifiably] vilified and denounced by agitators in the press and sometimes in the pulpit as the steel men of this country," moaned the trade journal *Manufacturers Record* in June of 1923.

The opinions of the critics and the public rested on a foundation of falsehoods. First of all, people believed that steelmaking was absolutely backbreaking, grueling—and that all steelworkers were hard at it for a full 12 hours a day.

Manufacturers Record allowed as how this picture might have been true in the early days of steel, in the nineteenth century. But technology had changed it: "In those days among steelmaking companies and steel buyers and some steel employers it was 'every man for himself and the devil take the hindmost.' A mighty change has been wrought since then."

The paper rounded up people who explained the facts.

"It must be understood by the public that the labor is not continuous in these 12-hour shifts on blast furnaces and open-hearth furnaces," insisted James Bowron, chairman of Gulf States Steel Company of Birmingham, Alabama.

"On the contrary, there is not, on the average, more than six hours work for any of the men so engaged—it is a question of sometimes as much as two or three hours' work at a time, sometimes only 15 or 20 minutes at a time, and then a rest, where a man can sit down, smoke a pipe, read a newspaper or anything else that he has with him, or in many cases even take a doze while his comrades watch the condition of the heat."

And the labor was not nearly as severe as it was in the old days. Gary insisted that the work "uses up comparatively little of the steel men's energies, because most of it is mechanical. The actual labor is confined to the machines."

Another false assumption was that converting two 12-hour shifts into three eight-hour shifts was a simple task that no steel producer had even tried to make work. The facts? The technology and economics of steelmaking demanded a kind of perpetual motion.

Bowron explained it this way: "Blast furnaces and open-hearth furnaces must have constant attention, night and day, week in and week out, running for … weeks, or months, or years, according to the character of the plant and the process."

Those furnaces could not be turned off at the end of each eight-hour shift. That would damage their heat-containing linings of "refractory" brick. But leaving the furnaces burning and handing them off to the next shift raised other complexities. For one thing, it tempted crews to postpone the most demanding part of their day—pouring the hot metal into molds—until the following shift had to do the work for them.

The whole idea of converting 12-hour shifts into shorter ones— three "turns" of eight hours, for example, or two six-hour shifts a day for each man—would bring on all kinds of headaches, mainly for the men themselves. The steel companies knew this because they had tried it. As Willis King of Jones & Laughlin Steel Corporation's American Iron and Steel Works in Pittsburgh explained in *Manufacturers Record*, "The steel manufacturers, within the last 10 years, have voluntarily reduced the number of men working 12 hours from about 75 percent of the total to 20 to 25 percent, and did this in spite of some opposition by the men."

Other companies tried the switch but had to go back to 12-hour turns. Lukens Steel Company of Coatesville, Pennsylvania, went to three eight-hour shifts for three months in 1919, then dropped the whole idea. It had to hire more workers, and trim wages to pay for changes. "The result," reported President A. F. Huston, was "very unsatisfactory in the efficiency of the plant, in the disturbed spirit of the men, disturbed condition and dissatisfaction in the homes, and in the unsatisfactory earnings."

The economics of eight-hour turns would backfire. More workers would have to be hired—half again as many to man the furnaces in days of three eight-hour shifts. The American Iron and Steel Institute issued a report that concluded the eight-hour day was impossible because it would require too many additional men. Judge Gary estimated the shorter day would call for 60,000 more workers at a time when labor was still tight. That would short-circuit the country's prosperity. Producers couldn't afford to increase payroll by 50 percent. They would go out of business. There would be *no* shifts. Any way you cut it, an eight-hour day meant workers would bring home less pay. Gary, for one, was sure they wouldn't be happy about that.

Lost in the whole debate was this fact: The traps in shortening the shifts applied only to the crews who tended the furnaces. That was because of the need to keep the furnaces roaring away. Other tasks such as maintenance *could* be handled in shifts of less than 12 hours—and were. U. S. Steel employed 10-hour-a-day workers. There were no reasons other than higher payroll costs and lower wages that the hours *they* worked each day couldn't be cut to eight.

Trying to drive those points home for politicians and the man on the street seemed futile to the judge. No matter. The demands among the populace for the eight-hour day had grown big enough to roll right over Gary's arguments, and those of his peers.

Whether or not it was a good idea, the shorter day was an idea whose time had come. The final nudge, in early August of 1923, came from President Warren Harding.

The President read the iron and steel institute report. Disappointed, he sent Gary a note, a masterpiece of gentle persuasion:

> *"I am wondering if it would not be possible for the steel industry to consider giving an undertaking that before there shall be any reduction in the staff of employees of the industry through any recession of demand for steel products, or at any time when there is a surplus of labor available, that then the change should be made from the two shifts to the three shift basis. I cannot but believe that such an undertaking would give great satisfaction to the American people as a whole and would, indeed, establish pride and confidence in the ability of our industries themselves to solve matters which are so conclusively advocated by the public."*

The words carried enough political pressure to prod Gary into surrender. After conferring with his iron and steel institute directors, Gary wrote Harding: "We are determined to exert every effort at our command to secure in the iron and steel industry of this country a total abolition of the 12-hour day at the earliest time practicable."

A few days later, after hearing of the company's intentions to end the 12-hour day, President Harding died of a cerebral hemorrhage.

While the President must have been pleased by the impending end of the 12-hour day, the issue's conclusion left Gary in gloom.

"President Harding wanted the eight-hour day because he thought the people wanted it," a subdued Gary told a *New York World* reporter. "Our men will be bitterly disappointed by a shorter day."

Why? "Nine out of ten of them would rather work seven days a week. They make more money in the 12-hour day than they will make in the eight-hour, in spite of the raise in salary. We can only hope they will take it good-naturedly."

Punching a time card took on new meaning for these steelworkers, thanks to the efforts of Judge Gary. He, more than anyone else, was responsible for instituting the eight-hour day which became the norm for the steel industry.

And here it must be asked: Was Gary out of touch with working people? Did he assume laborers shared the same glory in working hard and long that his rural-American, Methodist upbringing instilled in him? Of course his men wanted to work the longer hours. They had to make enough for themselves and their families. With higher pay, they would have gladly accepted a shorter day.

A postscript: During his company's 1924 annual meeting, on April 21, Gary seemed to take a philosophical view of the issue in responding to a question from Charles Mumford. A highly supportive U. S. Steel stockholder with 50 shares, Mumford rarely missed an annual meeting and the chance to quiz Gary. This time, he asked the chairman how much extra the company was paying in higher wages as a result of the switch to eight hours.

Gary's response: "The abolition of the 12-hour day is costing us about $55 million a year. It adds about 10 percent to [our costs]. As to what the net result of that action is, no one man can precisely state, because it involves so many things.... We met a public sentiment, however it may have been created. The Steel Corporation for years has been in favor of abolishing the 12-hour day, not because we believed it was an evil, not because the workmen themselves desired it, but because it seemed apparent there was an increasing public sentiment in favor of that action."

W. J. Filbert   Percival Roberts, Jr.   J. A. Farrell   R. V. Lindabury
Geo. F. Baker   E. H. Gary (Chairman)   J. P. Morgan

FINANCE COMMITTEE, UNITED STATES STEEL CORPORATION, APRIL 14, 1925

United States Steel Corporation
SILVER ANNIVERSARY

THE United States Steel Corporation is twenty-five years old. On February 25, 1901, it was organized under the laws of the State of New Jersey, and began business a few weeks later, on April 1, 1901.

The plan of combining several of the large steel manufacturing companies in different parts of the country into one organization under one general management had its inception at a dinner given in New York on December 12, 1900, by Edward Simmons and Charles Stuart Smith. There were present at this dinner several of the most important steel manufacturers and financial men of the United States, among them the late J. Pierpont Morgan, who was prevailed upon to do what had long been urged upon him by Elbert H. Gary, then President of the Federal Steel Company and one of the great banker's most trusted associates—to undertake the financial arrangements to accomplish the great steel merger.

The enterprise was a gigantic one. It comprised the consolidation of ten separate companies engaged in the manufacture of steel and allied industries, each company prominent in its own particular field. Developments in the iron and steel industry during the closing decade of the nineteenth century had been so rapid and amazing—almost incalculable—that a consolidation of interests had become practically inevitable. Steel manufacturers realized that the old destructive methods of competition must be abandoned and new methods employed which would bring to an end the bitter trade wars which periodically rent the entire industry. Moreover, they realized that the costs of production could be greatly reduced by combining their efforts and making all the processes of steel manufacture, from the mining of the ore to its smelting into iron and the conversion of the iron into steel and steel products, one continuous operation performed under the direction of a single organization, thereby eliminating the waste incident to the processes when performed by a large number of

Shorter shifts may have troubled Gary because of the way they worked out on paper. But it hadn't taken him long to grow proud of the decision to kill the 12-hour turn. After all, Gary was keenly interested in the safety of his employees and the living standards of his workers and their families. He probably was ahead of his time—as a man, anyway—in his conviction that women were at least equal to men in their abilities, and should be granted equal rights, politically and in the workplace.

He celebrated much of what his company had achieved for its workers when U. S. Steel turned 25. The corporation issued a silver anniversary bulletin that reviewed the company's history and looked to the future. The booklet summarized progress in operations and in the value of stock. Much of the publication was devoted to reports on how the company managed to promote the safety of its workers, increase wages and let employees share in U. S. Steel's success through the corporation's stock purchasing plan. Most of the booklet was set aside for photos of the amenities the company had afforded its workers: sparkling kitchens and dining rooms at the plants, and, at the company towns, modern and well-staffed hospitals and schools, and a variety of new and highly livable houses.

It was "look what we did." It was presented in the voice of the corporation. But its optimism and the pride it conveyed in making things better were pure Gary.

The years had been good. The Twenties had been especially good, and continued to be.

In this feverish era the markets were bursting at the seams. To serve them, U. S. Steel invested more than $686 million in new steelmaking facilities, improvements in its non-steel companies, and in acquisitions.

At the top of the agenda was keeping up with Detroit's emerging importance as the world's auto-building center. The corporation built a series of new mills across the country. Sheet and strip mills went up at Gary, and Mercer, Pennsylvania, and Fairfield, Alabama. Bar mills appeared at Fairfield and at the McDonald Mill in Youngstown, Ohio, as well as a double sheet mill at McDonald.

The company beefed up other plants. It put in a 24-inch tin-plate mill at Gary, added to the rail and rod-and-wire mills at Duluth, completed rebuilding of American Bridge's bridge and structural steel plant at Trenton, New Jersey. It added a railway-car plant at Fairfield, 54-inch and 44-inch blooming mills and a structural mill at Homestead, a 40-inch blooming mill at Chicago, seamless pipe and tube mills at Pittsburgh and at Lorain, Ohio. It enlarged the steel pickling and galvanizing department at Vandergrift, Pennsylvania.

The decade also confirmed Andrew Carnegie's vision in starting a couple of small, even experimental, open-hearth furnaces at his Edgar Thomson Works. Carnegie sensed that the open hearths would supplant the Bessemers as the industry's workhorse of choice. He was right. By the Twenties, faster, larger-capacity open hearths were turning out steel as good or better than the Bessemers. New and enlarged open hearths had popped up at Fairfield, Edgar Thomson and Duquesne.

The open hearth supplanted the Bessemer as the industry's workhorse of choice.

Another step forward: The company pursued more seriously something that early steelmakers suspected but couldn't prove because they lacked the technology: that the coal-based chemicals which escaped into the air during the coal-to-coke process would be money in the bank if they could be collected. U. S. Steel had been retiring its quaint, domed, beehive coke ovens in favor of cleaner and more efficient by-product coke batteries as big as buildings. In the Twenties, the company would install more than 1,000 such batteries at Gary, Fairfield, Clairton (Pennsylvania) and at other plants. This coal chemicals business would become one of U. S. Steel's most profitable. The chemicals harvested would wind up in fertilizers and medicines. They would even make possible an amazing new material: plastic.

Elsewhere, U. S. Steel's Universal Portland Cement Company was trying out new dust-collecting equipment at its Buffington, Indiana, plant. The new technology lowered production costs and raised capacity. It also made the work environment healthier. At Buffington, too, the cement subsidiary built a large harbor terminal on Lake Michigan.

Back at the beginning of the steel-producing line were the blast furnaces. These cauldrons bubbled with coal, iron ore and limestone, and made iron. The company built new furnaces at several plants, including the National Works and Duquesne Works, near Pittsburgh.

In 1928, the Corporation also opened a new zinc oxide plant at its Donora Works along the Monongahela River. None of U. S. Steel's officials knew it at the time, but in 1948, Donora's zinc operations would gain a grim fame for a mishap which would focus world attention on the need for industry to do a better job of protecting the environment.

With all the new steelmaking capacity, the corporation needed more coal. It opened vast new mines in Alabama and western Pennsylvania. To deliver the new product, it added 34 locomotives and more than 1,000 cars to its railroads. The Federal Shipbuilding Company fabricated a new 10,000-ton floating dry dock in New Jersey and added 27 new ocean-going cargo vessels, barges and other small craft to its fleet.

During the 1920s, beehive coke ovens gradually gave way to these cleaner, more efficient by-product batteries at Clairton, Gary, Fairfield and other USS locations.

The company also bought some rich reserves of manganese ore in Brazil, and the properties of the Cyclone Fence Company, the outfit that made the chain-link steel fencing that would soon seem to surround every vacant lot.

U. S. Steel's workers benefited from the economic frenzy. They got an across-the-board, 11-percent raise. Workers who went from 12-hour shifts to eight hours got a 25-percent pay increase. Those working 10-hour days, a 10-percent raise.

There was more. During the decade, U. S. Steel advanced more than $15 million in low-interest mortgages to enable employees to buy homes in the steel communities. The company spent millions of dollars, too, for hospitals, clinics, schools, churches, parks and playgrounds for its employees.

U. S. Steel also began to rationalize—a term not yet in use during the Twenties, but one which became a codeword in the 1980s for downsizing, consolidating. During the decade, U. S. Steel sold its Shoenberger plant in Pittsburgh and closed outmoded blast furnaces in Niles, Steubenville, Mingo and Newburg, Ohio; the Painter Works and Clark Works in Pittsburgh; Monessen and Sharon mills near Pittsburgh; the Columbus Works in Ohio and a tube plant in Syracuse.

One facility was rationalized before it got started. This was a new sheet plant the company had been building for its Canadian Steel Corporation at Ojibway, Ontario, across the river from Detroit. By mid-decade, its blast furnaces had been built. So had a cast house and some auxiliary buildings. The beauty of the plant was its location. The company would pay little freight to move product from the plant to the automakers a few miles away in Michigan. But by the end of the decade, what had been built was abandoned. The culprit: tariffs on goods made in Canada and exported to the USA. Suddenly they grew big enough to gobble up any profit the corporation hoped to make.

Gary found another avenue for his creativity: the founding of a centralized research department for the corporation.

He called his presidents to a meeting on May 20, 1926. "The time has come," he told his colleagues, "when the United States Steel Corporation…must be prepared to do anything and everything to advance the art and science of steelmaking and utilization, and our disposition is to leave no excuse for allowing others to get ahead of us, to lead us, in the discovery and development of new things."

After some prodding, Gary got his wish, and in 1927, the General Research Department was established.

In April of that year, Gary was interviewed by Charles W. Word of *Forbes Magazine*, who asked the judge what he was most interested in at the moment.

"I think it is our proposed new technology laboratory. The committee to take charge of it has been agreed upon. Industry, after all, is nothing but the application of human knowledge, and to gather knowledge and organize it is about the most exciting adventure of life. So long as the steel industry keeps on gathering knowledge and coordinating it, it is bound to remain young and vigorous."

Sadly, Gary was not to live to see his vision turned to reality. U. S. Steel's first centralized research laboratory was installed in 1928 in an unused building at the Corporation's Federal Shipbuilding and Dry Dock Company in Kearny, New Jersey.

The years were gaining on Judge Gary. He had overseen his steel empire for more than a quarter-century. He wasn't one to retire. But he was 80, and it was time to look back at all he'd done. It was time for end-of-career reminiscing.

One such session came in the form of an interview by *New York American* columnist Will Irwin. The result appeared as a full-page feature about Judge Gary in its issue of Monday, June 27, 1927. Irwin seems to have uncovered—or *re*discovered—some revelations from the aging steel chairman, who was less than two months from death.

Early in the interview, while he was revisiting the Gary Dinners for Irwin, Gary revealed a detail that seems to have gone uncovered by the press or officials earlier: "Now, we talked very frankly and plainly [at the dinners]," Gary told the columnist. "And I always had stenographers present to take down every word. And every time, I sent full transcripts to the President [of the United States], to the Department of Justice, and to leading members of Congress. That was in line with our policy of conducting our affairs honestly, sincerely, and openly," Gary concluded for Irwin.

It certainly was. But what the steel chairman told Irwin at the end of the interview magnified the power of the Gary openness and cooperation tenfold.

Irwin asked Gary if he were in favor of closer understanding among English-speaking nations. It was a softball, but Gary knocked it over the fence:

"We [steel leaders] had an international meeting in Belgium in 1911, which might have resulted in some very fine things. The big steel men of the world met there and planned to form not so much an organization as a club. It was intended to regulate the business— fairly. To discipline those who didn't play fair to cooperate for the general good. But when I came home with the idea, our government opposed it . . . . They suspected that it was an international price- fixing organization. Of course it wasn't . . . . Without government sanctions we could do nothing.

"If that international organization had gone through, there would have been no war in 1914."

It was a repeat of what Gary had told Rose Feld of *The New York Times* two-and-a-half years earlier. Gary had added that the industrialists might have prevented the World War: "Munitions are made out of steel, and [the steel producers] could have refused to manufacture them.... They could have convinced the political leaders...that harmony could be maintained through friendly intercourse.... Even in October, 1914, if the question had been left to the steel people, there would have been no further continuance of the war."

Irwin must have missed the interview. Perhaps much of the world did. He pressed Gary. How and why could the steel companies prevent the war?

"Because all the steel men were against war—all," Gary replied. "And because, when the clouds gathered, they'd have met at once and decided—practically unanimously—that there should be no war. And that they would furnish no steel for war purposes. How long do you think a war would last without steel?"

Irwin persisted. "You mean that steelmen would have served notice on their own governments that they would not furnish steel for a war?"

"Yes, I do," replied the judge. "Take the German steel manufacturers. If they had been in such a club, honestly and fairly conducted, they could have said to the government, 'No steel and no war.' And they didn't want war. I felt so then, I feel so now."

Whether Gary truly believed industrialists could act together to stop a war (and what *else* could they do?), Gary summed up his story this way: "Just remember this: A big corporation or a big man, or a set of big men, can do the right thing even though they have power and opportunity to do the wrong thing."

Everyone at U. S. Steel's main office knew something was wrong.

Judge Gary wasn't feeling well. His health had been failing for several years. One of his last public acts, according to *The New York*

Times, was on June 16, 1927. Seated in his New York office, Gary started the current that set in operation the newly electrified equipment at the Homestead steel plant. It was an electrical-age version of a ribbon

Judge Gary's mausoleum in Wheaton, Illinois

cutting. A few days later he went home—to the four-story red brick structure with marble-trimmed windows he and Mrs. Gary had built at 1130 Fifth Avenue. It had been two months now and the judge hadn't returned to his office. Only his family and closest associates knew how serious his illness was. And they knew the end was near.

It came at 3:40 in the morning, August 15, 1927. His wife was with him to the end. While the curtains stayed closed in the Gary house, family members called, and a steady stream of messengers brought telegrams, hundreds of them, from friends, including the world's most powerful people.

President Coolidge echoed most of them (though not as poetically as some) in a letter to the *Times*: "He stood foremost among those who find in the great private enterprises of our country an opportunity for public service as well as a medium for financial profit."

The day after Gary's death, the famous train Twentieth Century Limited carried his body on the first leg of its trip to Gary's hometown, Wheaton, Illinois. Services were held in the Memorial Methodist Episcopal Church. The stone structure was a gift from the judge to the people of Wheaton. He was buried in his family's mausoleum, next to his first wife, Julia, who had died in 1902.

In a resolution issued in Gary's honor, U. S. Steel's directors decreed that he "builded so well, and established in the organization methods and policies so firmly founded, that we look into the future with confidence and courage."

Greats of the world stepped forth to trumpet majestic phrases in praise of a man they clearly considered unique in his greatness and

Nation's Business Leaders Pay Tribute to Judge Gary

I WANT to express to you the sympathy and the sense of personal regret which I feel in the death of Judge Gary. He stood foremost among those who find in the great private enterprises of our country an opportunity for public service as well as a medium for financial profit. He upheld the best ideals of commerce and industry and proved that success is attained in largest measure through adherence to the highest standards of American business. His going is a great loss to the nation.—PRESIDENT COOLIDGE *in message to Mrs. E. H. Gary.*

One of the Greatest Figures

JUDGE GARY will go down in industrial history as one of the greatest figures in America. His management of the Steel corporation was unparalleled. His work and devotion to the American Iron and Steel institute, which he originated, were of incalculable benefit to the industry in promoting better feeling. He was a great man and his many friends and associates will miss his advice and counsel.—CHARLES M. SCHWAB, *chairman, Bethlehem Steel Corp., Bethlehem, Pa.*

Most Able Leader and Wisest Counsellor

IN JUDGE GARY'S death the steel industry loses its most able leader and wisest counsellor. The American Iron and Steel institute was of his creation and through it he devoted himself with great earnestness and wisdom to the improvement of conditions throughout the iron and steel industry. He will be greatly missed by his friends and associates, of whom he was always most considerate. —E. G. GRACE, *president, Bethlehem Steel Corp., Bethlehem, Pa.*

A Loss To the Entire World

THE death of Judge Gary is a loss to the entire world. He was the outstanding figure of the last quarter of a century. The United States Steel Corp. has a strong board of directors, capable of properly filling his place. The subsidiary companies are thoroughly organized. Many of the presidents have initiative. Judge Gary's policies permeate the entire organization. The death of Judge Gary is a personal loss. He was my constant devoted friend.—JOSEPH G. BUTLER JR., *Youngstown, O.*

The South Loses a Friend

I AM deeply grieved over the death of Judge Gary. He was one of the country's purest patriots and greatest intellects. There is scarcely a page in the history of the steel industry in which his features are not imaged. He built not only for today in industry, but for tomorrow and for evermore and his policy helped in a splendid way to span the chasm that was once deep and wide between employer and employe, between governmental authority and industry and between people at large and capital. In a large measure because of him it can be fairly stated that there is today a better and more cordial relation and a more friendly understanding between and among all these than there ever has been during any period in the history of the country. His friendly interest in the South and especially in the Birmingham district is attested in

many ways. For inestimable service we render him homage. Voiced in a syllable, the country's verdict is "well done."—HUGH MORROW, *president, Sloss-Sheffield Steel & Iron Co., Birmingham, Ala.*

An Outstanding Man of the Day

JUDGE GARY was without question one of the outstanding men of his day. In force of character and personality he was extraordinary. Passing over his marvelous executive ability which brought about the development of the Steel corporation, his policy of fairness in all business relationships was particularly impressive to those of us who are associated with competing companies as it must have been to all others who become acquainted with his high ideals.—J. F. WELBORN, *president, Colorado Fuel & Iron Co., Denver.*

Admirable As a Man

IN THIRTY years' acquaintance and friendship with Judge Gary I have particularly admired his qualities as a man rather than those as a manufacturer. He seemed to have the secret of placidity, a calm imperturbable philosophy that everything either was right or would be right. I have never seen him flurried, angry or appearing even impatient. This disposition has naturally endeared him to his associates who knew him best. He had the balanced mind of a lawyer merging into a diplomat, watching his speech that he might give no offense and avoid any ambiguity. I regret his loss as one that is personal.—JAMES BOWRON, *chairman, Gulf States Steel Co., Birmingham, Ala.*

Destined to be Pre-eminent

I KNEW of Judge Gary's recent illness but supposed it was nothing serious, and am therefore greatly shocked to learn of his death. He possessed all the qualities of a great leader and would have been pre-eminent in any sphere of endeavor. I have known and admired him for many years. His personality, ability and fairness have endeared him to his friends and business associates and held the respect and confidence of the public. The great company of which he was the genius and directing head since its organization has suffered a most serious loss and the steel industry a great leader and counsellor. I am at a loss for words to express my feelings of personal sorrow.—WILLIS L. KING, *vice president, Jones & Laughlin Steel Corp., Pittsburgh.*

His Life and Work a Guidepost

JUDGE GARY'S sudden taking away must come as a great shock to the steel industry of the world. His position as the outstanding industrial leader of his time has been entirely established. He brought about a new day in industry through the welding into the structure of business high character, fair dealing and recognition of the interest and rights of the worker, the stockholders and the public at large. Over and above all this, Judge Gary proved the value, soundness and practicability of the large business corporation.— GEORGE M. VERITY, *president, American Rolling Mill Co., Middletown, O.*

humility. An old friend, The Reverend James T. Ladd, of Elgin, Illinois, may have summed up the essence of Gary best.

Presiding at Gary's funeral service, Reverend Ladd described the judge as a good churchman, a good singer and someone who "could tell a story, sing a song, act in a pantomime, laugh at a joke, play with the children, give attention to the aged, run a foot race…"

"He exercised the most perfect self-control. I never saw him 'fussed.'
He was as honest as Abraham Lincoln. He was scrupulously careful
for the reputation of anyone of whom he had occasion to speak.
He tried to avoid causing heartache. He was remarkably free from
prejudice. His sympathies were wide and deep. He…made friends,
hosts of them."

It was an epitaph almost anyone would want, but few could hope to earn.

While the Twenties marked the departure of Judge Gary from the scene, it also marked the arrival of a successor who would pilot the corporation safely through the shoals of the Depression. He was Myron C. Taylor, a corporation lawyer with interests in textiles and banking. He joined the board in the mid-Twenties and was ultimately elected chairman in 1932.

JUDGE ELBERT GARY: LOST IN HISTORY

If Judge Elbert Gary has not been unsung, he has been undersung.

Books covering industry's formative years are packed with stories about the dictators of commerce—men who worshiped monopoly, craved power and sought unending riches at the expense of the downtrodden.

But Gary was the reverse image of the devils these writers loved to hate.

He encouraged spending millions upon millions for clean homes, good hospitals and advanced schools for his workers and their families. He ran an employee safety program that was copied around the world. He went out of his way to ask government officials whether his plans were legal, and proper. And when standard business procedure was to freeze out the press and lawmakers, Gary welcomed reporters in so he could air what he and his corporation were up to. In fact, "helping to introduce the present system of candid publicity into corporation affairs" was his proudest achievement, Gary told Forbes magazine's Charles W. Wood.

"The people have a right to know how the people's business is being carried on. And the more they do know about it, the better it will be for business. Big business, like human life, cannot thrive properly in the dark."

In short, Gary was the prophet that the critics of Big Business must have been waiting for. But his coverage in history books is scant or often skewed against him.

Why? It seems Gary was not the kind of "businessman" that leftward-leaning social reformers and populists of the day wanted to talk or write about. He wasn't the devil. He didn't support their case that business was purely evil and must be tightly controlled, if not run outright, by the government. His actions didn't support their agendas.

He had an agenda of his own. He went about converting the hard-bitten business types who once thought his Bible-informed ways of operating were for suckers.

He gave away part of his fortune, but not ostentatiously, like Carnegie. When Carnegie gave a library to a community, he made sure his name was carved boldly over the door. When Gary donated the Methodist Episcopal church in his hometown, Wheaton, Illinois, in memory of his father, he humbly ordered that this inscription be chiseled on the cornerstone: "Donated by a grateful son of Erastus Gary."

He was devoted to opera. Not only did the Garys subscribe to the Metropolitan Opera season, but they were also generous annual contributors to the company.

His character and beliefs must have influenced mighty managers in businesses other than steel. Yet he was your favorite uncle, who asked how you were doing in school and gave you silver dollars.

As a master of management and business savvy, Gary took the long view. He understood the value of investing in research for a long-run payoff. He respected women: "[When] women are given the same opportunity," he told The New York Times, "the same experience about business and about politics, and especially about education and all moral questions, they are keener than men, and... their judgment is... as good as the judgment of the men and perhaps a little better."

He admired hard work and achievement. He admired Babe Ruth. He admired the Japanese and their capabilities—an attitude that would prove on target a few decades later, when the Japanese invaded much of America's steel market.

In a time when politicians went gunning for big business, Gary also admired Teddy Roosevelt for his true aim. Roosevelt "went after big business when he thought it had done wrong," he told the Boston Globe's Olin Downs in 1920. "But he believed in the beneficent effect of big business, properly conducted, and when it was properly conducted, he was always ready to cooperate."

History seems to have forgotten that Gary and Roosevelt were soul mates.

This statue of Judge Elbert H. Gary honors the man for his role in the founding of the city that bears his name. It sits on the lawn of the Gary City Hall and was unveiled on June 18, 1958.

STEEL ON WHEELS

The prosperous early Twenties sent a lot of people out shopping and created the jobs that made it possible for them to pay for the toasters, radio sets and houses they bought. That rang up a lot of sales for steel. And cranking the cash registers hardest was the automobile.

The auto was invented in Germany and fine-tuned by a number of American carmakers in the early twentieth century. It was a rich man's toy until Henry Ford applied his cost-cutting ingenuity.

As James Flink related in The Reader's Companion to American History *(Houghton-Mifflin, 1991), Ford introduced his Model T in 1908. Vanadium steel made it lighter and tougher than other cars, and new methods of casting parts pushed the price down to a fairly affordable $825. In 1913–1914, Henry Ford got his famous assembly line working at his Highland Park, Michigan, plant. The Model T's sticker price tumbled to $360 in 1916 and bottomed out at $290 in 1927. By the 1920s, he was selling more than 2 million cars a year. In 1929, the sale of new cars reached "a phenomenal total of 4.6 million," reported Morris Musselman in his 1950 auto history,* Get a Horse! *(J. P. Lippincott Co.).*

From 1920 to 1929, more than 31 million passenger cars were sold in the United States, notes Musselman. "The automobile became the biggest customer of the coal and iron mines, the steel mills, the plate-glass and the rubber factories and many others. When the motor companies borrowed money to expand in order to build more cars, all the companies that supplied them had to do the same."

The advent of the automobile, typified by the Model T, created a major new market for the steel industry.

The wave of orders sent ripples through other businesses, like road construction and service stations. Steel producers were awash with new business as automakers, their order books growing fatter and fatter, called for more rolled steel for auto bodies. That was just fine with a lot of steel producers. Sheet production didn't require intensive labor. It was profitable even for plants with high operating costs. For a long time, though, steel that was squeezed out into flat sheets or long, thin, rolled-up strip wasn't as useful as rails, heavy plates for ships or even wire. As Oxford University professor emeritus and steel-industry chronicler Kenneth Warren explained in The American Steel Industry: 1850–1970 *(University of Pittsburgh Press, 1988), sheet was useful for railway cars and streetcars. Then came the war economy:*

"By the Twenties," wrote Warren, "there was demand from the office furniture and domestic appliance industries, but far and away the major market, and the most exacting require-ments, were those of the automobile industry. By 1926, American rolling mills shipped 4.9 million tons of steel to the motor industry, of which 2.3 million tons were sheet or strip."

Ford, Chrysler, Hudson and the other auto companies pressed that metal into doors, hoods, trunk lids and fenders for increasingly car-crazy Americans. Warren called the development of "wide" strip mills and "cold reduction" strip mills "the most important technical innovation in the steel industry in the first half of the twentieth century."

WAS JUSTICE BRANDEIS SAYING 'I'M SORRY' ?

Judge Brandeis

History can take strange turns.

We know that U.S. Supreme Court Justice Louis Brandeis did not cast a vote in the U. S. Steel dissolution case. By sitting out the final verdict, he nudged the decision in the corporation's favor, helping ensure the court would not break up U. S. Steel.

But why did Brandeis, a liberal and no friend of big business, decline to vote? He might have had second thoughts about the company's guilt. But there's another possible explanation, one that's far more personal.

In 1911, nine years before the final verdict in the U. S. Steel case, and when Brandeis was practicing law in Boston, he appeared before a congressional committee considering an antitrust matter. During the proceedings, he referred to a news item about a half-million-dollar pearl necklace Judge Gary allegedly had bought his wife for Christmas.

"Is it not," Brandeis intoned, "just the same sort of thing which brought about the French Revolution?"

Whether or not the necklace story was fact, the press was outraged, according to Apleus Thomas Mason, who covered the incident in his 1956 book, Brandeis: A Free Man's Life *(Viking Press).*

Brandeis' complaint was a "cheap bid for sensationalism," howled one paper. Another said Brandeis was guilty of a breach of good taste. Another claimed he was guilty of "a demagogic appeal to class prejudice."

Gary was grief-stricken, according to an account in the December 16, 1911, Boston Globe: "I am surprised that Mr. Brandeis should be the author of such an attack. I did not think he would make such unsupportable statements. I thought he was a bigger man."

Did Brandeis have second thoughts about his necklace hissy? Did he withhold his vote, in part to make amends to the judge?

We can't be sure. But his actions likely squared him with Gary. And the Steel Corporation was allowed to remain in one piece.

Chapter 7

Echoes of the Crash

"Once I built a tower, to the sun.

Brick and rivet and lime.

Once I built a tower,

Now it's done.

Brother, can you spare a dime?"

From "Brother, Can You Spare a Dime," a Depression anthem
sung by crooner Rudy Vallee. Lyrics by E. Y. Harburg.

"The nation has lost a great deal of money, largely at gambling…"

H. L. Mencken

I t was the great market rescue of 1907 all over again.

At least it seemed to be.

On the morning of Thursday, October 24, 1929, in New York City, down in the financial district, a squad of bankers huddled inside the House of Morgan, the great financial firm at Wall and Broad. Their mission: to put together a financial plan to save the nation's stock market, a once-roaring bull that had turned sickly and was on the verge of collapse.

On this day alone, by 11 a.m., the market had lost $9 billion in the value of its shares. People were scared. Crowds of worried investors and other citizens surged up and down Wall Street, trying to detect any turn the market was making.

In another of history's little larks, the rescue crew of banking gurus was meeting 22 years to the day that House of Morgan patriarch J. P. Morgan marshaled bankers and U. S. Steel brass to stop the panic of 1907. The coincidence might have inflated the crowd's hopes. At any rate, when the rescue team emerged, some of its members were smiling. As William K. Klingaman related in his 1989 Harper & Row history, *1929: The Year of the Great Crash*, someone yelled, "It's going to be okay." A few minutes later, at 1:30 on this afternoon of October 24, over at the New York Stock Exchange, a smiling Richard Whitney strode onto the trading floor and over to the U. S. Steel trading post.

Silence replaced the floor's usual hubbub as Whitney, the exchange's handsome and husky president, spoke loudly so everyone could hear. "What was the last bid for U. S. Steel?" he demanded.

"195," he was told.

Whitney's voice echoed again as he placed an order for 10,000 shares at 205 — 10 points higher than the previous high bid, for a purchase totaling well over $2 million.

Everyone on the floor stared in wonder. Then, to their cheers, Whitney marched around to other posts, his heels clicking and his voice loud and steady, placing flamboyant bids on other major stocks. He spent $20 million dollars for 200,000 shares.

It was great theater. Less than buying stock, Whitney was pitching a commodity. It was valuable as gold, and its supply was frighteningly short.

It was confidence. Everyone needed a stiff shot of the stuff — confidence in the staying power of industries, in the country, in the future. Confidence could do a lot to keep the market glued together, the country in one piece.

Wall Street's fix seemed to work. From his estate in England, J. P. Morgan, Jr. — who followed his father as head of the House of Morgan, and Elbert Gary as U. S. Steel chairman — cabled his congratulations.

Things were okay. For a day. For this was the infamous Black Thursday. It was followed by a few days when the market skittered up and down. Then it crashed, dragging the country into the deep, black hole we'd honor for its misery by calling it the Great Depression, capital G, capital D.

H ow did we get into this predicament? Why did times that were so good turn so bad?

For one thing, we got cocky.

We thought the get-rich scene in the American dream would last forever. Speculation in land and commodities became a fever. It snowballed until the economy rested on a pile of paper pyramids. Even farmers kept remortgaging their land so they could plant more and more. Businesses flew into cycle upon cycle of borrowing for future production, and it resulted in overproduction. "In the 10 years between 1919 and

1929," John Garraty explained in *The Great Depression* (Harcourt Brace and Company, 1986), "output per worker in manufacturing rose an astonishing 43 percent."

Producers could sell everything they made or grew, so prices outstripped wages. Workers couldn't afford all the things they, themselves, were stuffing into the cornucopia, but installment plans made it a snap. The debts mounted. When they piled too high, consumers defaulted or stopped buying. Production took a nose dive. So did prices and wages.

The banks? Many were poorly managed, and couldn't handle the chain of speculation. So they shut down—at a rate of 690 a year between 1922 and 1929, Garraty figured.

Then there was Wall Street, pumped full of air. Hundreds of thousands of Americans were buying stock on credit terms that were so generous they were crazy. Volume was furious in March of 1929, but then fell off by 60 percent, noted Klingaman: "Even the news that U. S. Steel established a new domestic record for quarterly earnings in peacetime failed to generate much enthusiasm."

In October, investors felt the pyramid shift dangerously beneath them, and panicked. Over 13 million shares were traded on Black Thursday. More than 16 million were sold October 29. "Wall St. Lays an Egg," moaned *Variety*, the show-biz tabloid. And by November 14, $30 billion in the market value of stocks had evaporated. All over the country, people who'd counted on snowballing investments saw their futures melt.

It went downhill from there. More banks crashed. The next year saw a rash of business failures. Herbert Hoover, who recent historians characterize as reflective and progressive, went into a fit of isolationism. After a thousand economists urged him in a petition to veto the trade-choking Smoot-Hawley Tariff Act, he signed anyway. With his pen, he built the mightiest wall of duties against foreign trade that America had ever seen. Within three years, 33 other countries retaliated, raising their rates on American products.

If the glory days of the Twenties were a huge wave, the wave was followed in the Thirties by a deepening trough.

It wasn't all black. In 1930, for example, opportunities popped up in the form of acquisitions. A lot of properties were put up for sale at bargain prices, and Carnegie's practice of making investments in budget-priced equipment or companies still made sense. It was still a smart way to grow. So, in 1930, U. S. Steel made three major acquisitions:

The Oil Well Supply Company, a petroleum pipelining outfit with a handsome sales record, bolstered U. S. Steel's already strong business in supplying the oil industry with pipe for drilling and delivering oil and gasoline.

The Atlas Portland Cement Company was added to U. S. Steel's Universal Cement Company. This created the largest cement company in the world—Universal Atlas Cement Company—and an even bigger internal customer for the waste slag that poured out of the steel company's mills.

Oil Well Supply became a division of U. S. Steel in 1930. The above ad showcased some of the company products available in 1882.

The Columbia Steel Company, an independent iron and steelmaker operating out of Los Angeles and San Francisco, gave U. S. Steel sound footing in the young and growing Western market. With Gary-like concern for being in the clear with the government, the corporation's general counsel, Nathan Miller, had run the acquisition by Elihu Root, the revered and experienced Washington hand who'd advised Teddy Roosevelt in 1907 that U. S. Steel's purchase of T.C.I. would cause no antitrust problems. Root said he was satisfied the purchase of Columbia Steel would not be unlawful, either. In an act of courtesy, caution, or both, the board postponed action on the purchase until Root could sit in on one of their meetings. He did so, and the board voted to buy.

But everything changed in 1932. It was the Depression's cruelest year.

The stock market slumped to its nadir. During the bull market of the 1920s, the Dow Jones stock averages had climbed to 381.17 on September 3, 1929. Then the Dow Jones began to sag with the October 28th crash. It lost 38.33 points, 13 percent of its value, that day, closing at 260.64. By July 8, 1932, however, it had reached its Depression low of 41.22, having lost 89 percent of its value in just under three years.

U. S. Steel's preferred stock fell from a 1929 high of $144¼ and low of $137 to $113 and $53 in 1932. (Preferred's high in 1933 was $105½.) Common started at a high of $261¼ and a low of $150 in 1929, and slid to $52⅜ and $21¼ in 1932.

U. S. Steel's financial and operating performance echoed the pattern:

Net income fell from a high of $195.4 million in 1929 to a 1932 loss of $91.9 million. Meanwhile, shipments of ingots and rolled and finished steel products dipped from 14.3 million tons in 1929 to a low of 3.8 million tons in 1932.

Employment dropped from 224,980 in 1929 to a low of 158,032 full- and part-time employees in 1932.

Remember those 10,000 shares of U. S. Steel common that Whitney bought so conspicuously that year for $205.00 per share? They were now worth only $21.25 per share. His $2 million investment collapsed to a mere $212,000. Whitney was out $1.8 million, more than an 85-percent loss.

Under these conditions, smart management required running U. S. Steel as lean as possible, meeting orders so customers could stay afloat, delivering to shareholders as much of a return as they could manage. Managers had to be sharp at maintaining promising businesses while selling off out-of-date operations that would put a deadly drag on profits. The company had to be standing when the storm cleared.

As the Depression plunged the country lower and lower into an economic hell, ironworkers from U. S. Steel's American Bridge were erecting buildings higher and higher into the sky. They included the Empire State and Chrysler buildings, which would become national landmarks.

Franklin Delano Roosevelt

Meanwhile, people watched their country, their livelihoods, and their lives unravel, and they screamed for action. The man who seemed most able to give it to them was a man who had been knocked down by a crippling disease, yet kept his head high, his voice full of cheer and confidence, his chin jutted outward, a cigarette holder clamped in his teeth.

Franklin Delano Roosevelt, an old-money patrician, captured the faith of Americans and won the key to the White House in the election of 1932. He'd reside there for an unprecedented length of time, into his fourth term as President. For now, he didn't lose time giving the country the action it wanted. Any kind of action would do, it seemed. No one had a script for reviving the USA. Roosevelt, to a large extent, made it up as he went along, trying social programs and legislation, and, if they didn't work, trying others. It was one of his ways of living the maxim he proclaimed for the people in his March 4, 1933, inaugural address: "We have nothing to fear but fear itself."

Roosevelt's priority was saving the banks. He ordered them closed, and reorganized them. A little more than a week later, the survivors reopened for business. As *American Century* author Harold Evans quotes one of Roosevelt's right-hand men: "Capitalism was saved in eight days."

Capitalism as practiced in U. S. Steel and other companies took a different turn after FDR launched his New Deal. The emergency plan was built on 15 economy-resuscitating bills that, under FDR's prodding, cajoling and inspiration, were passed and signed by the new president in the 100 days after Congress' emergency session.

A lot of the measures were audacious, pushing the powers of the President and government to, even beyond, limits implied in the Constitution. The bills created programs out of ideas that had been circulating for years, some of them by Hoover. Roosevelt put his spin on them. They regulated stock exchanges, bolstered prices by going off the gold standard, and, through mortgage financing, rescued one-fifth of the country's home owners from foreclosure. Bills provided emergency relief for the unemployed, jobs in road repair and park improvement and the like for four million men. The Public Works Administration gave jobs to more people and stimulated the economy by strengthening the threads that held together the country's physical and social fabric: roads, levees, power plants, post offices, schools … and jails.

The make-work programs meant business, and security, for the Steel Corporation. But the program that most interested the managers of U. S. Steel was the National Industrial Recovery Act of 1933. It created the National Recovery Administration, the NRA, which orchestrated codes of "fair competition" for industry. That meant things like regulating production, controlling prices, setting minimum wages and maximum work hours.

Section 7a of the act had huge implications. It guaranteed workers the right to bargain collectively. No more could the captains of industry, for whatever reason, refuse to talk with labor. In its annual report on the year, the company marched right along with FDR. It announced that it was "a member" of NRA's fair-competition code for iron and steel. And it assured shareholders that "[t]he corporation and subsidiaries have given hearty cooperation to plans of the Administration in Washington for bringing about a nationwide economic recovery."

A lot of big changes were coming down from the man elected to the country's top job in 1932.

Big changes had been made that year, too, at the top of U. S. Steel.

The corporation became a member of the National Recovery Administration and subscribed to the code of "fair competition" for industry following the Great Depression.

Who could fill Judge Gary's shoes?

The question was floating about back in 1927, when Gary, after managing splendidly for the entire life of the corporation, was laid to rest in his steel coffin.

In answer, the company decided it would take three men to take the judge's place. Morgan remained chairman, U. S. Steel President James Farrell became CEO. And an outsider appeared: Myron C. Taylor, a New York lawyer and a financial wizard, was named Finance Committee chairman.

But rule by a triumvirate didn't work.

With all his other commitments, such as the business of his father's financial house, Chairman Morgan never could find enough time for the Steel Corporation's affairs. Farrell filled in for him. And while Farrell and Taylor performed splendidly in their jobs, the troika arrangement merely fenced each man in. Isolation from the big picture didn't help them conquer a condition shared by other leaders in industry, banking and government: Depression myopia, failure to focus on how bad the Depression was and what to do about it.

It seemed no one was running the corporation. But the threesome soldiered on, and more than a half-year into the Depression, at U. S. Steel's April 1930 shareholders' meeting, Taylor told shareholders, "The foundation on which we stand today is basically sound…. There is gold in the cargo," he said, borrowing an expression from stockholder Charles Mumford.

The ship may have had gold stashed somewhere in its hold, but it was springing leaks.

During the last half of March 1931, fewer than 80,000 of the corporation's 241,000-person workforce were working full-time. Salaries had been cut in the aggregate by 40 percent. Dividends were eliminated on common stock and reduced by $2 per share on preferred.

It was hard enough to navigate during the Depression, but, at the same time, the corporation was becoming sluggish. The steel business was changing fast, and, as business analysts and other observers pointed out, U. S. Steel's three-men-at-the-top arrangement made it difficult for the corporation to keep up.

The company needed a strongman, and it became clear to other members of the board that they had one in their midst: Myron Taylor. He had cut his teeth in the textiles industry, where he had his own method of turning around the finances of ailing companies. He'd been largely unknown to the public and the business world when he was named to the U. S. Steel triumvirate, but he soon stood out as a master of corporate policy. The Depression was in the future, but the chairman of U. S. Steel's Finance Committee sensed hard times ahead, and took steps to ensure that the company could weather them. In less than two years, he retired $265 million of the corporation's $400-million bond debt, which in turn slashed U. S. Steel's interest charges from $24 million in 1928 to $5 million in 1934.

Taylor's hand in corporate matters had become evident by the spring of 1931. He expanded his activities in finance to include other corporate matters. The country's business community soon realized that Taylor was the principal architect of corporation policy.

He had been the rising star. It was time to formalize his authority. So, in March 1932, U. S. Steel announced Morgan's resignation and Taylor's elevation to the chairman's job. Taylor kept his duties as head of the Finance Committee. Farrell retired and Taylor inherited the CEO title, too.

And by the 1932 annual meeting, the new chairman had changed his gold-in-the-hold tune. "We have been forced by events beginning in the summer of 1929 to retreat from one position to another," he told shareholders, "always hoping to entrench ourselves in a position that would mark the culmination of the Depression."

The worst was yet to come. Operations would hit bottom in 1933, when production would fall to a low of 9 percent of capacity.

So often, when human affairs start to roil frantically, just the right men and women rise to the top and keep the pot from boiling over. They even improve the contents. Myron Taylor was one of them.

Taylor had a brain for numbers and a nose for new ideas, for recognizing when it was time to change the way business and people were managed. But these attributes were oddly packaged. Taylor was an American blue blood. He traced his ancestry to Colonial days. He suffered no physical impairment, but carried a cane. He wore gloves when the weather was fair. And a homburg.

It should be no surprise, then, that Taylor and the aristocratic FDR became good friends. When he had government dealings, Taylor went around cabinet members and White House staffers and phoned the President directly. Or he dropped by the White House to talk things over with the President in person.

Myron Taylor

During his days in textiles, Taylor learned that purely objective eyes did the best job of spotting an organization's shortcomings. Soon after he came aboard U. S. Steel, he instigated an internal audit of the corporation's health. The object of the check-up, from 1928 to 1932, was to find out whether the corporation was losing ground to competitors, and, if so, what could be done to turn things around. The survey, by corporate engineers, called for big changes, especially in the markets the company served and in the facilities that served them.

Soon after rising to chairman, Taylor brought in a big management-consulting firm, Ford, Bacon and Davis, to double-check the findings and recommend actions.

The survey began in October 1933, and "the engineers"—as the consultancy was soon called within U. S. Steel—made their final report in June 1938.

During these five years, no aspect of corporate life escaped the engineers' probe. Every subsidiary, every plant, every office, every product or service was put under the microscope, and the engineers submitted 203 reports containing more than 3,800 recommendations. With pride, they pointed out that only 15 percent of the recommendations were discarded.

For this work, U. S. Steel paid Ford, Bacon and Davis more than $3 million, and in its final report the firm estimated "savings" of $7.7 million "that had been or could be made by carrying out their recommendations." These focused on a diverse range of initiatives related to return on investment, product and markets, customer relations, competition, sales and marketing, foreign business, steel-making and allied facilities, power generation, extracting and processing of raw materials, corporate organization and management.

Many far-reaching results flowed from these studies: new uniform policies for employee relations throughout the corporation, leading to the establishment of an Industrial Relations Department;

changes in the pension plan; adoption of personnel-rating systems; an incentive plan; stepped-up basic and applied research programs; and a strategic planning function.

The consultants' findings were kept confidential for decades, although, in his remarks at annual meetings, Taylor was candid about them. The corporation, the consultants decreed, had become a "big, sprawling, inert giant, whose production operations were inadequately coordinated; suffering from a lack of a long-run planning agency, relying on an antiquated system of cost accounting...."

The corporation, the engineers declared, had turned into a "follower, not a leader, in industrial efficiency." It was a follower in earnings, too.

What had happened? The steel markets had changed right under the corporation.

The demand for all those new consumer goods had caused a revolution in steel product lines. Almost overnight, the industry had to diversify from its old-line, heavy products into light, flat, hot- and cold-rolled steel. The country was moving away from an economy based on such old, steady capital goods as factory equipment, ships, bridge beams and rails. It was moving toward an economy based on quick-turnover products—autos, stoves and other consumer goods.

Another problem was that the transition to new goods was altering the marketing map, and, therefore, the economics of the steel business. As Taylor would explain later: "Iron and steel are basic commodities, and a large part of their cost to the consumer is transportation. The ideal plant location is one where the cost of getting raw materials into the plant and getting the finished products out to the customers is at a minimum." That meant grouping plants around major transportation centers.

The corporation had closed parts or all of more than a dozen plants, old-timers that were scattered about the map, specializing in heavy steel products. They would have been too expensive to convert. Some operations were moved to other plants that were still healthy. But the company had to do more overhauling.

Taylor went into action.

He energized the company's sales and advertising operations and streamlined pricing. In a major step toward efficiency, the company merged its original steelmaking units, Carnegie Steel and Illinois Steel. The Chicago and Youngstown, Ohio, mills were modernized, and others upgraded. Operations that were outmoded or too costly to keep were closed down or sold.

The people side of the business needed attention, too. Taylor gave the management chain a vitamin shot by pushing down decision-making power to the subsidiaries. And he rallied the troops. In early September of 1935, sales managers of all units gathered at one of management's favorite bastions, Pittsburgh's Duquesne Club, to plan a counterattack against younger competitors who were giving them a drubbing. Various presidents and vice presidents parleyed in New York City for the same reason.

Then Taylor brought in new blood. Former Republic Steel executive vice president and former railway engineer Benjamin F. Fairless joined the corporation as president of the new Carnegie-Illinois Corporation.

Another outsider in a prime management post? It was a surprising move for a company whose top operating management almost always came from the ranks. It shook up some insiders who figured they were in line for the job.

And the raw self-assurance of the new man! The *Pittsburgh Press* claimed Fairless agreed to leave Republic to take "perhaps the biggest job in the steel industry," but "only if he would 'run the works' in his own way."

Fortune magazine thought the move was refreshing: "It looks as if the depression had taught Mr. Taylor…that a steel company should be run by steel men as well as lawyers and bankers."

Taylor knew it all along. Fairless was an expert in steel alloys, and the corporation had spent millions building alloy plants in the Chicago district.

Then Taylor performed an encore, bringing aboard Edward R. Stettinius, Jr., a highly respected General Motors vice president. The handsome, silver-haired and silver-tongued, 33-year-old Stettinius joined the U. S. Steel board in 1933, and became vice chairman of the Finance Committee. Taylor also recruited Enders M. Voorhees from Johns-Manville in 1937 where he had been serving as vice president and a member of J-M's board of directors. At U. S. Steel, Voorhees signed on as vice chairman of the Finance Committee, stepping up to the chairmanship of the committee the following year. Voorhees' impact on the corporation, as well as his influence on the careers of later finance managers, is discussed in Chapter 17.

It was clear that Taylor was the right man to follow in Judge Gary's path. He moved quickly, changing things that needed changing, spending money where it should be spent. He was a diplomat and masterful communicator.

At the annual meeting held in the spring of 1933, Taylor delivered to shareholders bad Depression tidings, but with grace.

He reported for the previous year three reductions in salaries "aggregating 40 percent," wage reductions of 25 percent—and a two-dollars-a-share reduction in preferred stock dividend, plus a complete halt on dividends for common stock. His summary smacked of logic and fair play: "There is harmony, there is a mathematical basis, there is almost an exact justice in the way that we have approached the reduction of income to our stockholders and to our employees."

Then, for inspiration, he turned, as he often did, to religious imagery: "It makes me feel, because we are in the presence of Easter, that this sort of cross that we bear is one that all humanity at one time or another in its pilgrimage seems to have borne."

Myron Taylor: Industrial-strength devotion to business and human affairs

LEADERSHIP, TAYLOR-MADE

If ever there was a man who could lead a corporation out of the economic wilderness, it was Myron Taylor.

He was tall and reserved, with a voice one writer described as "gently authoritative and reassuring, like that of a great psychiatrist..." And his counsel was sought from the boardroom to the White House.

He radiated confidence. He also possessed an industrial-strength devotion to business and human affairs. He'd wanted to retire from affairs at the top of U. S. Steel after five years, but stayed for five more so that, as USS chairman and CEO, he could bring the company and country through the Depression. Then he stuck around for 18 more years

as director and member of the Finance Committee, finally closing the book on 30 years of service to the company. He picked his retirement date as January of 1956, a few days before his 82nd birthday.

Taylor might have worn a homburg and carried a cane, but his sensitivities covered the concerns of working men and women. Ultimately, he expressed them in action, working with John L. Lewis to bring in the labor boss's union to represent U. S. Steel workers. He didn't get there just by following his business instincts. His moral compass pointed the way, too.

*B*orn in 1874 of Quaker parents, Taylor spent his boyhood in Lyons, New York. After public school and private instruction, he studied law at Cornell University. He started his law career in 1895, and, as Roger Blough, USS chairman at Taylor's retirement in 1956, put it, "He was almost instantly recognized as the possessor of a fine talent for unraveling the complex in finance [and] for simplifying the scrambled in corporate structure."

Taylor first applied these skills as an investor and chairman of textile companies, replacing old equipment with new, and replacing 12-hour shifts with eight-hour ones. After World War I, he reorganized the financially troubled Goodyear Tire & Rubber Company, likely saving that venerable outfit. He worked similar wonders with banks—then with U. S. Steel.

His attention to workers didn't stop when he put out the welcome mat for the union.

As company documents witness, Taylor advanced wage rates when, as Blough put it, "it might have seemed impossible to do so." During Taylor's administration, the company took enlightened steps, like starting paid-vacation and low-premium group insurance plans for employees. Taylor enriched the pension plan, too. During the Depression, he brought in agricultural experts to help employees grow more-productive home gardens. Besides preserving those employees' self-worth, the gardens produced food that the company estimated to be worth more than $1.2 million. Other companies copied the idea. Taylor made the Depression-era safety net even stronger by authorizing the company to extend more than $7 million in mortgage credit to employees who, otherwise, might have lost their homes.

Said Blough: "So long as United States Steel Corporation undeviatingly adheres to the exemplary standards undergirding every element—financial, physical, human—that Myron Taylor fashioned into every enterprise with which he has been associated, the corporation will continue to be 'an instrument of social progress,' as well as being 'alive...to the necessity of altering its policies to conform to the changing industrial pattern.'"

The word "change" would be used by business managers later in the century as a safely sterile synonym for daring decisions. Taylor was comfortable with constructive "change" back then.

Then Taylor spoke of "the shadow of celestial wings" as he turned to a sad topic, the death the previous winter of Charles Mumford, a shareholder who had so faithfully attended so many meetings. Mumford and Taylor had enjoyed what the chairman called a "rather tender friendship," and Mumford had quoted the "celestial wings" phrase often after Taylor used it at Gary's death. In a warm eulogy to the departed stockholder, Taylor told the assembled: "When I was coming out of the office this morning, one of my associates...said to me, 'Mr. Mumford will be listening today.' I hope he is. And I hope he knows...how assured we are that he is in a much happier situation than we find ourselves in at this time."

By the 1935 annual meeting, there was a glint of good news. Even though this was the depth of the Depression, U. S. Steel's orders had been trending upward for some time. Taylor bucked up the shareholders:

"The great vitality of this nation is only awaiting the assurance that it is safe to begin the next great cycle in the development of an enjoyment of our national resources. The forward movement already begun is plainly gathering impetus, and it should...sweep away all unsound policies which our great prosperity in the past had engendered and many quack notions which have been born of our adversity."

Taylor was Gary-like in his care to head off unsound policies and quack notions from government quarters by keeping clean in the government's eyes. He even sounded like Gary when he told shareholders: "The lines of interest of the corporation considered as a whole and the public considered as a whole must run parallel—for the corporation cannot exist except as it serves the public."

Practicing what Gary preached, Taylor made frequent trips to confer with the powers in Washington. "My mission has been not to seek any special advantages for the corporation nor merely to keep the corporation within the law, but to attune the policies of the corporation to the national policies as part of the corporation's obligation of citizenship."

During Taylor's watch, U. S. Steel elevated metallurgy and pure research to a major division, ranked with production, sales and finance. Gary would have approved. As we'll see in coming chapters, U. S. Steel researchers made important contributions to the company, industry and consumers.

Taylor's style of dealing with publicity differed from Gary's, though. Taylor tightened the tap on blanket news releases, preferring that the company deal directly with the media when the media asked for information.

U S Steel News *makes its debut.*

That he heartily believed in broadcasting what the company was doing and thinking was made evident in 1936, when the corporation introduced the first issue of *U S Steel News*. The magazine delivered background for company activities. It was published for employees, but its editorials and articles found their way into the newspapers, as well. The *News* was loaded with chatty articles about employees. It also mirrored the cultural standards of the day, running fun-but-educational crosswords and anagrams ("Many try color" rescrambled spells "Myron C. Taylor"), and ads featuring boys who imitated their fathers by talking tough over toy telephones. Its last page—"The Last Word"—was reserved for "the little woman," and was loaded with recipes ("hot carrots in mint sauce" in Volume I, No. I). And it was during Taylor's watch that the corporation supported high-tech and high-quality entertainment, serving as corporate sponsor of the "Theatre Guild on the Air," a network-radio series of live dramas.

But as much as Taylor followed Gary's footsteps, he declined to step into all of them.

He took a giant step off the judge's beaten path, and shocked many of his friends in the steel business, when he sat down in January of 1937 to talk turkey with bombastic, bushy-eyebrowed labor boss John L. Lewis.

Lewis was a character. A self-made one, and a commanding one.

For starters, he was a bulldoggish man with eyes that brooded out under eyebrows so thick and long they looked like they could cause flesh wounds. The finishing touch was a gift for oratory that has been compared with Churchill's. Lewis would arm his phrases with sharp words, wrap them in sly humor, then hurl them at his opponents, disarming them.

Lewis' critics claimed he was power hungry. Maybe. What mattered in the end were his political views. And Lewis was no red-tinted revolutionary. In fact, he feared a fatal tip toward communism if America's business leaders did not take substantive steps to bargain with its laborers. Unions, he believed, were the country's salvation.

He was the kind of man Taylor could sit down with. And the two worked together to bring the union to steel—something that once seemed impossible.

P ittsburgh was worried.

It had been proud to be the center of the steel universe. The trade-offs included smoky skies that turned noon into night, but money and jobs kept flowing in as the steel poured out. The country had grown into an industrial giant, and Pittsburgh was its right arm. But new markets were pulling the steel industry westward. It was especially worrisome during the Depression, when U. S. Steel had to go where the action was—for example, by purchasing Columbia Steel on the West Coast.

THE UNION COMES TO U. S. STEEL

Some of the noonday diners in Washington, D.C.'s, elegant Mayflower Hotel couldn't quite believe what they were seeing, but they were seeing history.

It was a lazy Saturday, January 9, 1937. U. S. Steel Chairman Myron Taylor had just guided his wife, Anabel, into the hotel's main dining room. The maitre'd led the couple past a table occupied by Senator Joseph Guffey, a Pennsylvania Democrat, and John L. Lewis, the rotund president of the Congress of Industrial Organization (CIO), whom nature had richly endowed with eyebrows and oratorical talent.

The steel chairman, labor leader and senator nodded at one another. When Mrs. Taylor was seated, Taylor walked over to chat with Lewis and Guffy, whose Pennsylvania constituency included thousands of steelworkers employed in some of the corporation's most important mills.

Later, when they were finished eating, Lewis and Guffy came over to the Taylors' table. Taylor asked the two to sit down, and soon the four were engaged in lively conversation.

Steel and labor at the same table, like gentlemen. A miracle. And when Lewis and Guffey rose to leave, the labor boss told Taylor that he would like to have a further talk. Without hesitating, Taylor invited him to continue their conversation at the hotel the next day. Taylor still didn't like unions. But he'd made up his mind the year before, while vacationing in Europe, that he would come to terms with the union movement.

It would be good for the economy, and it would be good for the company. It was time.

Actually, President Franklin D. Roosevelt had done a lot to change Taylor's mind about unions when he signed the National Industrial Recovery Act (NIRA). It stipulated that American workers had the right under law to organize unions and to bargain with their employers.

Taylor knew U. S. Steel's decades-old bias against unions was doomed. He saw unending conflict in a new practice: Workers were staging "sit-down" strikes. They were powerful. How could a company deal with laborers who were not marching around or throwing bricks, but were passive, immobile?

Taylor also knew U. S. Steel's track record in innovative programs that benefited employees—and, in the process, made them less susceptible to a union's allure. Judge Gary had set up those programs years before. By the time Taylor became chairman, the company had spent some $300 million on doctors and nurses, schools, clubhouses, restaurants, athletic fields, libraries and, at plants, showers and bathrooms that were exemplary for their cleanliness. The corporation had even drained swamps near 22 company towns, reducing malaria cases from 6,000 to 200 a year.

Labor secretary Frances Perkins visited Carnegie Steel Company's Homestead Plant to find out the effects of the NRA code dealing with the steel industry. Courtesy Times World Photos, Pittsburgh Bureau.

With these benefits, who needed a union?

Roosevelt thought the workers did. He saw NIRA as a way to short-circuit the Depression. Besides confirming the workers' right to organize and bargain, the act established price codes that steel and other industries were to follow.

The first provision didn't bring comfort to steel management, but the second did. It let them set prices without setting off antitrust charges. Prices were to be blessed by the government's "code of authority" for steel. But that authority was made up of officers of the American Iron and Steel Institute, the trade group established in 1911.

Still, the steel leaders had to know how the code worked. So Frances Perkins, FDR's labor secretary, invited them to Washington. Besides Taylor, the group included U. S. Steel President William Irvin, top executives from Republic, Bethlehem and Weirton Steel—and their lawyers.

As Perkins summed up the day, the members of the entourage got a shock when they walked into her office. There, waiting to talk with them, was American Federation of Labor President William

Green. The steelmen retreated to a corner to confer with their lawyers. Only the affable Irvin chatted with Green. The lawyers explained what was happening: The steel executives had expected only to meet with her. She replied that Green was there simply to make a statement, probably one supporting the new steel code. They didn't buy it. Green left in a huff, and Perkins scolded her steel-industry guests.

In Homestead, William Serrin recounted Perkins' memory of the sermon she delivered: "I could not resist the temptation to tell them...I felt as though I had entertained 11-year-old boys at their first party."

If the executives had an excuse for their behavior, it might have been that they were upset by a world that was turning upside down.

As Jeremy Brecher pointed out in his book Strike!, the trade-union movement had become practically defunct until the National Recovery Administration came into being: "The [American Federation of Labor] had failed to combat the layoffs and wage cuts that accompanied the Great Depression, and membership, far from increasing with popular discontent, went down with the slump."

Now NIRA was resuscitating the unions.

The United Mine Workers enticed commercial-mine workers into membership. The Amalgamated Association of Iron, Steel and Tin Workers—crushed at Homestead in 1892—gained a second life. By early 1934, membership reached almost 50,000 steelworkers in more than 200 lodges or locals.

*D*espite his uncharacteristic coldness to Green, Myron Taylor could see where labor was heading. His industry would be organized. But he needed time to warm up to the idea.

Time came in the guise of company unions, or "Employee Representation Plans"—ERPs. Steel companies figured these in-house unions would pass NIRA's muster. But the ERPs didn't allow for strikes. Steelworkers could bargain, but they were in no position to make demands. Taylor hired a labor relations professional, Arthur H. Young, to oversee the plans. Young, who had earned his stripes helping to develop strategy which would end labor strife at Rockefeller's Colorado Fuel & Iron, presided as vice president over a new Industrial Relations Department at U. S. Steel.

The ERPs weren't real unions, but they were fine schools for future union reps. And they worked in some places. But not everywhere. Not in the steel companies' mines, the "captive mines."

On June 1, 1933, the corporation's Frick Coke Company opted to keep the United Mine Workers at bay by introducing ERPs. The miners rejected the ERPs, and struck. Two miners were killed. Roosevelt opposed the strike on the grounds it could dampen a then-modest economic upswing. Lewis tried to quell the work stoppage, but the miners refused to go back to work.

The strike dragged on, and steelworkers struck in support. Then the captive-mine companies signed contracts with the UMW for wage increases, an eight-hour day and other benefits, plus government-run elections allowing workers to select representatives. The principles of open shop were affirmed and further campaigns to organize failed.

Success finally came in steel after Lewis forced a split with the American Federation of Labor, which was only interested in representing the craft unions. The laborers could wait.

But Lewis won by the force of his beliefs and his personality.

And his tongue. It was a silver dagger. On one occasion, he thrust it at American Federation of Labor (AFL) President William Green: "It is inconceivable that you intend doing what your statement implies, i.e., to sit with the women, under an awning on the hilltop, while the steelworkers in the valley struggle in the dust and agony of industrial warfare."

What Green intended to do was cut off Lewis' attempt to organize steelworkers. It was an old argument. Lewis had been aboard the AFL, but grew fed up with its insistence in representing only the skilled crafts while leaving laborers to fend for themselves.

In 1935, Lewis and his faction broke away and established the Committee for Industrial Organization (CIO). Its charter: to stand behind longshoremen, teamsters, textile workers, coal miners and laborers in basic industries like autos, rubber and steel.

When it came to steel, Lewis broke from the AFL by putting together the Steel Workers Organizing Committee for Industrial Organizations (SWOC). A CIO maverick, SWOC stood under the AFL umbrella. But it operated with its own board, and in effect operated on its own.

Signing up steelworkers was another matter.

Gary's welfare programs were hard habits for steelworkers to break, especially since employees didn't have to pay for them.

And, as Zieger pointed out, a lot of steelworkers liked the ERPs: "Since the company paid the bills, no dues were required. Company unions were risk-free; indeed employers actively encouraged and in some cases virtually coerced participation."

Some laborers signed up, paid their initial dues, then skipped monthly

John L. Lewis

installments. Some feared that they would lose their jobs if they signed on. Lewis protégé David McDonald admitted in his autobiography, Union Man *(Dutton, 1969)*, that "[t]he biggest problems we had were with the workers." Month after month, McDonald turned up at union rallies at plant gates or in local meeting halls only to find a handful of apathetic workers waiting for the pitch. "What we hoped would be a torrent turned out, instead, to be a trickle."

*L*ewis and Taylor made an odd couple, but they'd learned to trust each other. Their hotel sessions were soon followed by almost a dozen more at Taylor's New York townhouse. The talks were secret; most of Taylor's board and key executives knew nothing about them.

But Taylor had redrafted U. S. Steel's labor policy. Now it read, in part:

"The Company recognizes the right of its employees to bargain collectively through representatives freely chosen by them without dictation, coercion or intimidation in any form or from any source."

In essence, the agreement provided for a 40-hour week, an eight-hour day, time-and-a-half for overtime, seniority for promotions and payoffs, the initiation of grievance procedures and a wage increase of 10 cents an hour.

By mid-February 1937, Philip Murray, president of SWOC, Fairless and their chief lieutenants had signed the agreement.

Steelworkers got their union—not only at U. S. Steel, but, eventually, in all the companies in the industry. But not all of Taylor's peers applauded him for his vision. Many steel executives voiced outrage against the U. S. Steel chairman.

Taylor put the issue into perspective:

"I felt it was my duty as a trustee for our stockholders and as a citizen to make any honorable settlement that would insure a continuance of work, wages, and profits."

Was the company bailing out of the city? The *Pittsburgh Press* dug into the issue in a series of articles in the spring of 1935: "There has been no depression in recent years for the Pittsburgh companies building steel mill equipment," wrote J. Frank Beaman, the paper's financial editor. "They have been busy building mills for other districts—mills which continuously turn out sheets and strip that might have added to Pittsburgh's prosperity."

But the paper was upbeat: "While the record of the Pittsburgh district as the steel center of the nation in recent years has been somewhat discouraging," it admitted in its April 5 edition, "the possibilities for the future are just as great as they ever were—if Pittsburgh's industrial leaders and businessmen will recognize existing conditions and plan constructively for the years to come."

The editors wanted to see an industrial planning commission that would bring new and diversified industries to the region, industries that could grow not just on steel itself, but on the flashy new products that were made of steel. The new air conditioning systems, for example. Or maybe the company could help develop steel housing.

Myron Taylor tried to calm everyone down later in 1935 when he spoke at a luncheon in Pittsburgh. His message: The region's position as a major steel producer is secure.

"In an endeavor to expand the uses of steel and to explore new fields of possible consumption, heavy capital investments are necessary," he said. "The corporation is at the moment spending about $70 million for plant changes, and betterments will be called up to double that amount in the future."

What was not being said was that Pittsburgh's loss of plants and jobs was another city's gain. Still, it turned out, Taylor put more of his company's money where his mouth was.

At Homestead, for example, the company added a 100-inch, sheared plate mill that would roll and finish steel plate in a blazing two minutes. It was designed to produce products including Cor-Ten, a copper-bearing U. S. Steel specialty that was especially strong, and, with its patina, attractive, as well.

Any civic leader who, as the press claimed, was lamenting Pittsburgh's passing as a steel center must have perked up in early 1937, when U. S. Steel announced it planned to spend $60 million on construction and modernization of mills in the Pittsburgh district. A bit later, the company broke ground for its new Irvin Works, near Clairton. The new works, a study in the latest steel technology and named after U. S. Steel's then-president William Irvin, rose on 150 acres, on a hilltop overlooking the Monongahela River.

The hometown revival was great news, but the city fathers cheered even louder over the next "comeback."

In mid-December 1937, U. S. Steel announced that while its corporate and financial management would stay in New York, its operating management, the men responsible for making iron and steel, would move to Pittsburgh.

The huge steelmaker was returning to its roots. It was a great Christmas present, and it called for a party.

The city threw one on December 20. Mayor Cornelius Scully proclaimed "United States Steel Day." Downtown buildings were decorated for the event. Flags flew. Local plants celebrated by blowing their whistles at noon. That night, in the William Penn Hotel, the city staged a hoopla welcoming Benjamin Fairless, the Steel Corporation's newly elected president.

U. S. Steel had come home.

Fairless Day' Salutes Return of World Steel Supremacy to Pittsburgh

SUN-TELEGRAPH   DEC 20 1937

Pittsburgh today celebrated reclaiming its title as world capital of steel.

Mayor Cornelius D. Scully issued a proclamation designating this as "United States Steel Day," in recognition of Big Steel's decision to make Pittsburgh general headquarters for its far-flung organization beginning January 1.

"Fairless Day" was declared by the Pittsburgh Chamber of Commerce in tribute to 47-year-old Benjamin F. Fairless, recently elevated from presidency of the Carnegie-Illinois Steel Corporation, largest subsidiary of United States Steel, to head the parent firm. He is to be honor guest at a testimonial dinner tendered by the Chamber tonight in the William Penn Hotel.

More than 1,000 business men and industrialists will attend the dinner. At the speakers' table will be heads of all large steel firms of th Tri-State area, along with bankers and leaders in various business fields.

WHISTLES TO BLOW

James H. Greene, executive vice president of the Chamber requested that whistles in industrial districts be sounded for five minutes at noon today. Flags were displayed in front of Downtown office buildings.

In a formal statement, Mayor Scully envisioned marked advantages to the city in the coming of a large staff of executives and assistants, and foresaw a boost in real estate values.

He stated:

"The United States Steel Corporation is an old friend of Pittsburgh. It began to 'come back of its own accord' early this year when it announced a plan to spend $60,000,000 o' construction and modernization in the Pittsburgh dic' after many business men l. lamented Pittsburgh's passing a the steel center of the world.

"The return was not made complete, however, until last week when announcement came that United States Steel would centralize its management in Pittsburgh."

KANE'S WELCOME

Chairman John J. Kane, of the County Commissioners, issued a statement welcoming "Big Steel back," and declaring:

"The return of the operating offices will help the district in creating a need for new homes; in providing new customers for our stores and every other type of business establishment and, in general, provide a general impetus of growth at a time when it is particularly needed."

H. B. Kirkpatrick, president of the Chamber of Commerce, hailed the giant corporation's move as "especially reassuring to Pittsburgh business as it expresses confidence in Pittsburgh. Every line of business in Pittsburgh will be benefited."

The Building Owners and Managers Association saw in concen-

BENJAMIN F. FAIRLESS .... THE CITY'S HIS TODAY

Pittsburgh hosted "United States Steel Day" in 1937 in celebration of the city's title as world capital of steel. Sun-Telegraph, December 20, 1937.

Myron Taylor saw his job was done.

He'd planned on retiring five years after he joined the company. The Depression delayed that. Now it was 1938, and he had led the company through the worst economic tempest the country had experienced. He'd tightened up his ship and taken steps he was confident would return gold to the hold. Time to go.

He made his exit with his usual grace. At the last shareholders' meeting at which he would officiate, on April 4, he reminded those assembled of his delayed plans to "resume my place as a private citizen without the responsibility and exacting duties of any kind of office, public or private."

He must have felt a twinge of regret in leaving a career in which he'd led "a corporate army" of more than 260,000 workers (at his retirement) and stockholders "through the years when economic forces of resistless power have been sweeping us hither and yon…. It is a satisfaction to have the corporation emerge better fitted for its work and its destiny than when the Great Depression came upon us."

Taylor picked up his cane, put on his homburg, and gracefully left the corporate stage. His last message to shareholders came in the form of an extraordinary document, a summary of Taylor's stewardship and the company's activities during his 10 years at the helm. It was a showcase for Taylor's talents as a communicator — an engrossing history of U. S. Steel during the Taylor decade, and a remarkably lucid lesson in economics.

But President Roosevelt wouldn't let Taylor retire.

Roosevelt had become a close friend, liked Taylor's smooth and decisive style, and wanted him as a diplomat. Before the end of 1938, FDR chose Taylor as a U.S. emissary to a world conference addressing the problems of political refugees. Then Roosevelt appointed Taylor, who was born into a Quaker family, his personal ambassador to His Holiness, Pope Pius XII. The steel executive held the post until 1950, when President Truman made him "Ambassador on Special Missions."

San Francisco–Oakland Bay Bridge, 8¼ miles long, 4½ miles over water. U. S. Steel's Columbia Geneva Steel Division supplied steel plates and other shapes, and American Bridge fabricated and erected steel and spun steel–wire cables.

Taylor left U. S. Steel's board in 1953, the same year he departed the diplomatic service. He'd enjoyed a varied and distinguished career. But he had detractors. One was Charles White, Republic Steel's president when the Steel Workers Organizing Committee was organizing steel. White was bitter about Taylor's role in ushering in the union. In the November 12, 1951, issue of *Time* magazine, an angry White hinted that Taylor came around to Roosevelt's views on the unionization "in return for the [President's] promise of an appointment to the Court of St. James. Instead he got the job at the Vatican."

The spite falls flat. Taylor's skills and character served two presidents for more than 15 years, and made him an industrial legend.

Soon enough it was 1939. And it was the country's turn to throw a party. Two, in fact. One on each coast.

Just outside New York City, people flocked to the World's Fair, still famous for its two trademarks: a tall, skinny pyramid next to a shining sphere.

The first was the 18-story, three-sided, pointy-topped Trylon. Its neighbor, the Perisphere, was a shiny, 180-foot-wide globe that "rotated" at night over floodlit fountains.

The steelworkers who built the sleek structures called them the needle and the big apple.

U. S. Steel supplied the steel—6,000 pieces for the "apple" alone. The corporation's American Bridge subsidiary erected the two trademarks, which symbolized "The World of Tomorrow," the fair's theme. The company's forecast for how steel would be used "tomorrow" was on view nearby, in U. S. Steel's exhibit building. The structure was an exhibit in itself, a 66-foot-high dome of shiny stainless steel. It housed exhibits demonstrating steel's properties and manufacture. Surrounding these were dioramas depicting how steel would reshape the farm, the city, the home.

BIG JOBS

The Steel Corporation had some good things going for it as it headed into the Depression years: a line on some projects for which it supplied structural steel, and which it fabricated, or fabricated and erected. They were projects that would make any company stand tall.

The Empire State Building, for example. It was built in a little more than a year, an amazingly short time. Most of the work was done in 1930. The skyscraper was erected on the site of New York's original Waldorf-Astoria Hotel, in midtown Manhattan. But its owners had to get U. S. Steel's okay to christen their new prize the Empire State Building. The name was too close to the "Empire Building," which was the official name of U. S. Steel's headquarters at 71 Broadway, even if everyone down there called the building by its address.

The Empire State Building hit the drawing boards during the real estate boom of the Twenties. But when it opened during the Depression, hardly any tenants could afford to sign leases. People called it the "Empty State Building." No matter, the 102-floor Empire State quickly became famous as the world's tallest building, and a trademark of New York and the USA.

Near the Empire State was another soaring project for U. S. Steel, the Chrysler Building. The art deco beauty was the inspiration of Walter P. Chrysler, the auto magnate, which explains the "wheelcovers" that adorn its sides, and the glistening, steel, eagle-head gargoyles—huge "hood ornaments"—

that grace its stainless-steel crown. The building was finished six months before the Empire State, and so held the world's-tallest title of 77 floors for a half-year. Chrysler wanted the "tallest" title badly. So badly that he hid his building's seven-story, steel top inside, then—just before the building was completed—he had it assembled in place in a mere hour and a half. New Yorkers looked up and there it was, this shining crown. It was a dramatic stroke, wrote Peter Gossel and Gabriele Leuthauser in Architecture in the Twentieth Century *(Benedikt Taschen Verlag, 1991). And Chrysler beat the city's next-highest tower by 172 feet.*

A short distance uptown, the corporation supplied most of the steel and fabrication services for Rockefeller Center, the huge, Thirties development orchestrated by John D. Rockefeller, Jr.— the same "Junior" who so aggravated J. P. Morgan, Senior.

A manager at U. S. Steel once said, "Walk along the streets of any major city in the United States and you walk in the shadow of American Bridge."

Over on the West Coast, U. S. Steel helped build another U.S. icon, the mighty San Francisco–Oakland Bay Bridge. At 8¼ miles long, the bridge beat all others in length, depth and number of piers, and in quantity of steel and concrete. U. S. Steel's newly acquired Columbia Steel Corporation supplied steel plates and other steel shapes. American Bridge performed the major fabrication and erection of steel. It also spun the bridge's more-than-two-feet-thick, steel-wire cables.

Out west, too, the company helped build Hoover Dam. The monolith of concrete and steel was a quarter-mile long and almost 80 stories high, and designed to dam the Colorado River and create Lake Mead, irrigating farmland that, in size, was almost a state in itself. There was disagreement for years over whether its name was Hoover Dam or Boulder Dam. One wit wrote the government that the structure should be called Hoogivza Dam.

No one debated its blessing as a job maker.

Above, Rockefeller Center; right, Empire State Building

Across the continent, in San Francisco, the Golden Gate International Exposition took a different twist in its architecture — ornate, temple- and cathedral-like structures reflecting Oriental design. U. S. Steel's exhibits there gave everyone a peek into the future, too. Nearby, the recently completed San Francisco–Oakland Bay Bridge — also a project of American Bridge — gave everyone a real and dramatic taste of modern engineering.

Thanks in large part to steel, the future was going to be great.

But the future would have to be put on hold for a while — at least until the world contended with the trouble that was brewing again in Europe.

Chapter 8

War and Peace, Part 2

The Second World War was the ultimate tragedy.

When it was over, 50 million people were dead.

In the United States, fear congealed as another round of isolationism. The country turned away as Hitler (his friends called him "Putzi") nibbled up Czechoslovakia, and marched along with Mussolini, and embraced the Japanese, who invaded China. When President Roosevelt and U.S. leaders of like mind tried to rev up the American war machine, just a little for safety's sake, the isolationists screamed.

As Winston Churchill bitterly wrote in his *Memoirs of the Second World War* (Houghton Mifflin Company edition, 1959), "the United States had [by 1935] washed their hands of all concern with Europe, apart from wishing well to everybody, and were sure they would never have to be bothered with it again."

Europe was so far away. Even Ernest Hemingway, as macho as anyone, wrote in *Esquire* magazine in 1935 that "…in modern war there is nothing sweet nor fitting in your dying."

Maybe not, but the war engulfed us anyway. And Americans showed they were more than willing to settle the Axis powers' hash—not just on the battlefield, but on the factory floors.

Mobilizing the country for war was such a huge task that, looking back, it seems almost impossible. We did it anyway. Government records show that our armed forces grew from 310,000 men and women in July 1940 to more than 12 million five years later. On the civilian side, war workers grew from a force of less than 49,000 in July 1940 to a wartime high of more than 56 million three years later and an all-time high of more than 60 million in mid-1947.

Industrial output exploded when U.S. industries got the green light to supply Britain and France—and the United States when it got into the fight. The economy started breathing again.

It was a hell of a way to end a depression. But it was precisely this astounding American capacity for production that enabled us to win the war. That's a point made by David M. Kennedy in *Freedom From Fear: the American People in Depression and War, 1929-1945* (Oxford University Press, 1999): By 1945, the United States had turned out 88,410 tanks to Germany's 44,857; 299,293 aircraft to Japan's 69,910. Even America's bases in England, Kennedy said, were "oases of abundance," where the GIs had "more of everything."

More than any war before it, World War II was a war of steel. The fighting men could not advance one inch on land, on sea or into the air without steel. They wore steel and they fought with steel. And they were protected by steel, from the thick steel armor skin that clad the mighty tanks to the steel helmets that U. S. Steel designed and manufactured to seemingly impossible, contradictory specifications. Helmet steel had to stretch just enough to be punched from a flat disk into the familiar GI helmet shape without ripping or splitting. It had to be hard enough to stop a .45-caliber bullet.

The Allies won the war with steel. During the five years that ended with Japan's surrender on August 14, 1945, the American steel industry produced almost $190 billion worth of war goods—a record-shattering 467.3 million tons of steel and steel armaments.

More than a third of it was produced by U. S. Steel.

W orld War II can be written in three chapters.

The first began with the war itself, on September 1, 1939, when the Germans invaded Poland. While the United States sold war supplies to England and France, most Americans wanted to stay out of the fighting. The war was Europe's problem, not ours.

Chapter two, a brief one, opened in March 1941, when the U.S. Congress passed the Lend-Lease Act. America began sending war goods and delivering other aid to the Allies, but still avoided helping them in battle.

In the third chapter, the isolationists lost the debate when, on December 7, 1941, the Japanese bombed Pearl Harbor. Congress recognized a state of war with Japan the next day and, on December 11, Germany and Italy declared war on the United States.

Like it or not, America was in the fray. And the man who led U. S. Steel as chairman during most of that first chapter was Edward R. Stettinius, Jr.

Stettinius broke the mold at U. S. Steel, or at least cracked it, in several ways.

One difference was his youth. He was 33 years old when he joined the corporation, handpicked by Myron Taylor to head the Finance Committee. He was the youngest chairman in the company's history, elevated to that post in 1937 when he was 37 years old. And with his square jaw, cleft chin and dark eyebrows, he looked like he could have been the model for Superman, who showed up in the comics shortly after Stettinius became chairman. Except for one feature: The comic-book "Man of Steel" had jet-black hair; "Stet's" was an elegant silver-gray.

Along with Stettinius' youth came political views that were daringly liberal for a businessman of the day. In some circles, they cast doubt about where his brain was when it came to business. There was talk that his father got him where he was; the elder Stettinius had been a partner in J. P. Morgan & Co. Old money and connections. *The New York Times*, for one, said otherwise. In an article in 1933, after Stettinius joined U. S. Steel, the paper wrote, "It need not be denied that [Stettinius] was lucky in the selection of a father and that the presence of

Edward R. Stettinius, Jr.

the Steel Corporation's directorate of three partners in the Morgan banking firm were points in his favor. But this young Mr. Stettinius, from all accounts, is quite a citizen in his own right."

He was. In June of 1938, he presided over a sweeping cut in steel prices. But he argued to a conservative board of directors that wages should be held. Cutting them, he said, would invite the President's animosity toward the steel company—and that would cost more in the long run than the $10 million the company would save in a wage cut. By reaching out to the workers and the New Dealers, Stettinius earned a pat on the back from celebrity columnist Joseph Alsop: "It is ironical that the chairman of the board of big steel, the mastodon of them all, should play such a part," Alsop proclaimed in his Washington *Evening Star* column. "But," Alsop added, "if there were a few more men like Stettinius, the country might look forward to an era of general good will."

Later in 1938, Stettinius came out publicly in favor of the Social Security Act, claiming in a December speech that the act would give "socially minded employers" a foundation upon which to build group insurance plans and other means of protecting employees and improving their living standards. Corporations existed for more than stockholders' profits. "No longer," Stettinius decreed, "can industry plow a single furrow toward a single, strictly commercial objective."

Plowing through painful speeches for shareholders was a given during these late Depression years, but Stettinius—always graded highly for being articulate and skillful in communicating—did it with grace.

During the corporation's 1939 annual meeting of shareholders—his first as chairman—Stettinius reported grim but not surprising news: After climbing uphill, the corporation's operating and financial numbers had slid downhill again.

"The central fact concerning the steel industry in 1938 is that it was a year of exceptionally small volume of output," Stettinius told shareholders. The total of nine million tons of ingot production for 1938 was half that of the previous year. "The corporation's production in 1938 of finished steel products for sale was less than it was in 1902, the first full year of the corporation's history."

The average number of employees at work had dropped from 261,293 in 1937 to 202,108 in 1938. Average hours worked per week had fallen almost 10 hours. Payroll dropped more than a third, from $442.9 million to $282.2 million. "All salaried employees were put on a five-day week and their salaries were reduced accordingly," Stettinius added.

Shareholder Amzi Lake wanted to go further. Addressing Stettinius, he said, "The salaried people should do without the pension, I think, with the salaries they are drawing. The stockholders go without any income. We have had one dollar dividend on the common stock in 11 years."

Stettinius, in his reply, was tactfully evasive: "The question of pensions," he said, "is very involved and complex because of the difficulties which have come about as the result of the Social Security Act." In fact, he revealed during an answer to another shareholder, Myron Taylor himself was not eligible for a pension.

But the chairman and shareholders looked at a very different picture during the annual meeting held in 1940. The company's war production—steel for the Allies in Europe—had shown up in the numbers. The company's operating performance had jumped from 43 percent of capacity in 1938 to more than 63 percent of capacity in 1939. Steel shipments for 1939 had leaped 25 percent over the previous year.

World War II—A War of Steel
Annual Production in Thousands of Tons

American Steel Industry

September 1, 1939	U.S. Steel 28,885	81,600
December 7, 1941	U.S. Steel 30,550	88,570 Pearl Harbor, U.S. enters the war
1945	U.S. Steel 32,300	95,500

Allied Powers

September 1, 1939	38,200 Great Britain, France, Belgium, Luxembourg, Poland
December 7, 1941	Allies and United States – 119,570
1945	Allies and United States – 138,500

Axis Powers, and Axis-Dominated

September 1, 1939	27,900 Germany, Austria, Czechoslovakia
1943	75,000 Peak of German and Japanese conquests
1945	15,000 Japan, after Germany's defeat

Source: *Steel in the War*, U. S. Steel Corporation publication

Then Stettinius seemed to talk directly to liberals who might have screamed that the figures meant the corporation was reaping bloody profits from the war:

> *"In the annual report for 1939, we said: 'In the latter part of the year the course of business was influenced by the outbreak of war in Europe.' It seems appropriate to state that, quite aside from the humanitarian and moral issues, war orders represent only a fleeting prosperity, and war business is certain to result in a disruptive shifting of our economy. War is certain to cause a destruction of capital that cannot be replaced for years and of lives that can never be replaced. The management of the United States Steel Corporation is convinced that the first requisite for the attainment of a lasting prosperity is peace and the prospect of enduring peace."*

Then he underscored the point.

> *"I want to emphasize that statement. The management realizes continuously the need for policies and attitudes which take into serious consideration the long-term, depressive consequences of war."*

Not that the facts and figures meant U. S. Steel, or the other steel companies, played a minor part in the war. In fact, the chairman moved on to a discussion of U. S. Steel's research work aimed at victory. The company's scientists, he noted, were creating new steels for aircraft and other war equipment, as well as new steels and steel products that would be welcomed by consumers when the war was finally won.

Then Stettinius introduced Dr. R. E. Zimmerman, U. S. Steel's director of research, who proceeded to give a talk on a new U. S. Steel grade of electrolytically plated tin, used principally for making tin cans. He also briefed the audience on "Panelbuilt" housing—quickly assembled structures that were being used in the war and that had great possibility, the company said, for civilian housing.

Zimmerman's lecture was accompanied by lantern slides flashed onto a screen in the now-darkened room. His talk, which lasted at least a half hour as the heat mounted in the room, probably went over the heads of 99 percent of the assembled. Stettinius might have noticed a few shareholders nodding off; when the lecture was finally over, he announced (perhaps with a twinkle in his eye): "Ladies and gentlemen, I suggest the next order of business is the opening of the windows for a few minutes."

Many of Stettinius' pronouncements did anything but put people to sleep.

It might not be surprising, given his politics, that he was credited with encouraging U. S. Steel to sign a contract with John L. Lewis' Congress of Industrial Organizations (CIO). More than that, newspapers like the Douglas, Arizona, *Dispatch*, reported that he favored collective bargaining modeled after the British system.

Such views didn't sit well with some managers in U. S. Steel, or with some shareholders. There were mumblings that Stettinius was playing into the hands of the union. The critics were probably relieved when, a short while later, Stettinius was called to public service.

On May 28, 1940, President Roosevelt named Stettinius to the top position on the advisory commission to the newly convened Council of National Defense. Stettinius could have kept his job as U. S. Steel's chairman, but on May 29, he resigned from that position, and from U. S. Steel's board.

It's interesting to note that his appointment was generally well received. The American Federation of Labor, however, condemned it as a conflict of interest. "His relationship and his responsibility for a basic industry involved make it impossible for industrial identification to be subordinate so far as public service is concerned." And at U. S. Steel, his departure and new career were greeted quietly. The only mention in board minutes is a brief statement about his departure, accompanied by his official letter of resignation. It seems he just stole away.

But now Stettinius was really in his element. He was strongest at U. S. Steel when he played a political role, leaving the heavy financial management to others on the board. In public service, he would climb higher. In 1943, he was appointed Under Secretary of State. The next year, some key Democrats endorsed him for the vice presidency. But, as *The New York Times* would write later, his service "recommended him to President Franklin D. Roosevelt, then on the lookout for big business–government talent that would tend to counteract charges that he was an enemy of the country's businessmen and financiers." And in late 1944, Roosevelt named Stettinius Secretary of State.

Now Stettinius waded deeper into the thick of history. In January 1945, he accompanied President Roosevelt to Russia's Black Sea coast, where Roosevelt, Churchill and Stalin met for the Yalta Conference, the most critical Allied conference of the war. After Roosevelt died in 1945, though, Stettinius was forced to follow political form and resign. He wrote a book about Roosevelt and Yalta. But he didn't have time to do much more. A heart ailment had been whittling away at his health, and, on October 1, 1949, he died.

He was only 49.

Back in 1940, when U. S. Steel needed a chairman to replace Edward Stettinius, the company's directors looked around and gave the job to Irving Olds, a top-flight lawyer who had gained insight into war by working for agencies like the U.S. War Department, where he had been a special assistant. As a publication for investors put it, Olds was "conservative enough to uphold the dignity of the world's biggest steelmaker; he was smart enough to cope with big-time problems; he had enough World War I experience to guide the corporation through a war already started."

Olds was a thoughtful, hair-parted-down-the-middle man who'd gone through Yale and Harvard, then landed a job as secretary to the great Supreme Court Justice Oliver Wendell Holmes. He moved up in a hurry, becoming a partner in a highly respected Wall Street law firm, White & Case, in 1917. And he found himself in the thick of war work even before he officially moved into the chairman's office.

Irving S. Olds

More precisely, on June 4, 1940, he was called on a secret mission to rescue war-worn Great Britain. "I remember the date well," he told a *Detroit Times* reporter after the war, "because I had been named chairman of the company the day before…and the day before that, the British evacuated Dunkirk."

The British defeat had prompted Major General Charles M. Wesson, the chief of Army ordnance, to phone Olds and ask how soon he and U. S. Steel President Ben Fairless could be in his office in Washington. Olds and Fairless rushed to the capital, and into Wesson's office, where the general pointed to a two-inch-thick pile of papers.

"I have a few items here that I want U. S. Steel to purchase," General Wesson said quietly.

The orders were for hundreds of types of ordnance, including millions of rifles, grenades and field artillery. "There's between $36 million and $37 million worth there," the general estimated. Olds was a bit stunned by what was clearly an arms deal aimed at getting around international treaties. After all, U. S. Steel didn't handle products like guns and cannons. Who would purchase this shipment?

"I think Great Britain and France will buy it," said the general.

Olds marched over to the phone and arranged a special board meeting for the next day to consider the unusual purchase. After the board gave its approval, Olds phoned the general to tell him the news.

"That's fine," Wesson replied, "because we started shipping the stuff to you yesterday."

Olds got on the phone and sold the arms to the British and French in 15 minutes. In all, $42 million worth of armaments were loaded and on their way across the ocean. All of it was delivered safely.

"We made only two stipulations," Olds told the reporter. "We insisted on the right to publicize all the details when it was deemed advisable. And we insisted that the stuff be sold without a cent of profit to the steel company."

Then, with a smile, Olds delivered the kicker: "And that is how U. S. Steel practically saved Great Britain. Those were the armaments used to rearm the British after Dunkirk, in which they had lost just about everything they had."

If Dunkirk was Britain's turning point in the war, America's was Japan's devastating, December 7, 1941, air attack on American warships and military installations at Pearl Harbor, in the Hawaiian Islands. (At the same time, Japan attacked Guam, the Philippines, Hong Kong and the Malay Peninsula.) It was a Sunday. The next day, the United States—its fleet crippled—declared war on Japan.

Thousands of lives were changed the moment the first Japanese plane struck.

In steel towns across the land, among the first people to hear the news were the women who had their radios on while they were doing laundry, playing with their children, or, if their husbands were working Sunday shifts, planning what to feed them after they got home from the mills.

Some of them sat in shock or quiet acceptance. Others rushed over to neighbors to talk it all over. They were abuzz with questions: What will happen to us?

They knew the answer but asked anyway. The United States would go to war. So would many of their husbands, sons and boyfriends. So would thousands upon thousands of other young men—women, too—who lived in other cities and villages or off rural roads across the country.

Chapter three of the war had begun, the real fighting for Americans. Company records show that 113,249 of U. S. Steel's employees served in the armed forces during the war. Most of them were men, of course. But while so many of U. S. Steel's young men went off to fight in Europe or the Pacific, there was a serious shortage of manpower at home.

The solution was more womanpower.

An influx of women entered the workforce in the U. S. Steel plants as former steelworkers joined the service.

Women who filled traditional roles as housewives and mothers, or who would have worked at the five-and-dime, suddenly found themselves out on the mill floors or in the yards, tracking "melts" of steel, marking batches of bar or sheet, running cranes, doing what the men did. "A lot of women took a lot of the men's jobs," remembered Rose Kranz, who went to work at the Gary Works when it needed to fill wartime vacancies, and who almost a half-century later shared her war-years memories for this book.

Like many of the women at the mills in Gary and other cities, Mrs. Kranz was part of a steel family. Her husband worked as a "car blocker," battening down steel shipments on rail cars. His name was William, but in true steelworker's fashion, he had a nickname. He was a huge man, a Golden Gloves boxer. So, naturally, everyone called him "Teeny." He went off to serve in the Navy. Mrs. Kranz' uncle and aunt worked in the plant. So did her brother, Milan, who was in the stainless steel department until he joined the Army band. He played clarinet.

The Kranz clan was a real steel family. But everyone who had anyone working at one of the mills back then was part of a big family. War was hell, but the urgency of the cause and the need to support their boys at the front forged a can-do spirit.

"People were different during the war," insisted Mrs. Kranz, who worked at the Gary mill marking huge slabs of steel with data such as customer codes. "People helped one another. They done the job as good as it could be done, and there were no arguments. We got along beautifully." The cause, getting busy with plant-sponsored war bond sales, talking with co-workers about your son, daughter, husband or brother overseas—it all created steel-clad friendships.

Some sparks flew, too. Male-female friendship could grow into something not quite so innocent in a place of heat and dark corners, where men and women worked long hours together, husbands and boyfriends were half a world away, and no one knew what tomorrow would bring. But there were safety programs to deal with this danger, too. The company's National Tube works in Lorain, Ohio, sent around a squad of female counselors to talk with the women and head off hanky-panky. It still happened. Generally, though, workers kept to proper boundaries. Mrs. Minnie Bennett, who was Minnie Cambria when she worked at the Lorain mill during the war, summed it up this way when she spoke with the author: "It was a nice atmosphere. The men respected the women, and they were always willing to help us."

The Lorain mill's workers stood out proudly because they produced the 1,254 miles of 24-inch-diameter pipe that would be welded together to make "Big Inch," an oil pipeline built as a defensive measure against German U-boat attacks off the United States' East Coast.

The subs started to slink up to the coast after Pearl Harbor, picking off U.S. oil tankers that ran Western crude from the Gulf of Mexico to ports on the East Coast. In his Pulitzer Prize–winning history

Lorain Works produced 1,254 miles of 24-inch-diameter pipe for the "Big Inch" pipeline.

of the oil industry, *The Prize* (Simon & Schuster, 1991), Daniel Yergin tallied the destruction: "The number of tankers sunk in the first three months of 1942 was almost four times the number [being] built."

The government watched the sinkings add up and hit on the idea of running a pipeline from Texas to the East Coast, an underground supply route that would be cheaper than railroad tank cars and that could carry oil out of the U-boats' sight and range. The pipeline was to carry half the crude oil that was moved to the East Coast. The Lorain mill started shipping 60-foot lengths of pipe—40 carloads daily—and construction of the line began in August of 1942.

In 1943, the Lorain *Journal* reported that, over in Phoenixville, Pennsylvania, a welder with the unlikely name of Ray Gunn finished Big Inch's final weld, then exclaimed, "Well, baby—you're finished."

The 300,000-plus men and women who worked for U. S. Steel on the home front during the war might have been backstage, but they were just as vital to victory as the men and women in uniform. They made the steel that made it possible to win the war. After the conflict had finally ended, Chairman Olds saluted them proudly: "Their skill, diligence, loyalty, and toil enabled U. S. Steel to produce record-breaking quantities of steel, ships, and a seemingly endless line of other war products made of steel."

U. S. Steel helped the cause greatly, well before the war even began. Its Depression-era investments gave it a head start on war production, and helped the country jump into the war sooner.

During the Depression, the company enlarged and modernized its steel plants to the tune of $600 million. So right after Pearl Harbor, when shipyards and munitions factories started clamoring for steel, the company could send it to them right way.

And it wasn't just steel.

The company's Lake Superior ore mines produced badly needed ore, and the company's carriers rushed it to Great Lakes ports, first leg of the ore's journey to be converted into weapons, ships and war vehicles.

Huge electric cranes, fabricated by U. S. Steel, helped armor plants and shipyards start production earlier than they would have been able to without them. It supplied massive amounts of cement for war construction—including building of the Oak Ridge, Tennessee, plant, where scientists developed the new atomic bomb, which finally brought the conflict to its fearsome finale.

Company records show that, from January 1, 1940, to the Japanese surrender, U. S. Steel spent $470.8 million of the government's money for construction of government-owned, war-materiel plants that were operated by the company. During the same period, the corporation spent $457.3 million of its own money to produce defense goods. And while it was converting and enlarging its plants for war production, its American Bridge and Virginia Bridge fabricating subsidiaries were erecting plants for other industries—plants to make aircraft, tanks, synthetic rubber and other materials.

The company built itself up, too. In October 1941, it began work on a vast new plate mill at its Homestead plant, near Pittsburgh. The plant would cover almost 50 acres, and its 11 mighty open-hearth furnaces would be rated at an annual capacity of 1.5 million tons of steel.

Then the company turned to the West, and to Utah.

Why Utah? As Kenneth Warren explained in *The American Steel Industry, 1850–1970*, "President Roosevelt suggested that, when it came to the nation's supply of steel for the war, the possibility of an invasion of the eastern United States should be taken into account."

The government looked at the map, and the sites of the nation's valuable steel plants were mostly in the East and on the West Coast. Could the Germans launch sea or air attacks in the East and hit some of those plants? Could the Japanese attack from the Pacific and do the same to plants on the West Coast? There was also worry that the Axis powers could attack the Panama Canal, and cut it off as a route for steel shipments.

For safety's sake, the government asked U. S. Steel to submit a plan for a new steel plant, at a safe spot somewhere out West. That spot turned out to be the eastern shore of Utah Lake. It was a safe 700 miles from the Pacific Ocean, some 35 miles south of Salt Lake City, and near Utah's rich reserves of iron ore, as well as coal reserves in Wyoming. The final deal was this: U. S. Steel designed its new Geneva Works to government specifications. The company's Columbia Steel arm got the general construction contract, and the mill was built at no cost to the government. Geneva Steel Company, a new U. S. Steel operating subsidiary, would run the plant for the rest of the war—again, with no charge—turning out plate and structural steel.

The new mill started work at the beginning of January 1944. Its war job didn't last long. After the Japanese surrendered in 1945, war contracts were canceled. The Geneva plant wasn't needed anymore—for war goods, at least. So it was reduced to a standby operation while U. S. Steel and the government negotiated about how to deal with it.

Geneva Works—built for war production and later purchased by U. S. Steel from the federal government.

The outcome: U. S. Steel bought the plant in 1946, for $40 million, and then geared it up to make plate, structural shapes, hot-rolled coils and sheets. It produced coke and coal chemicals, too.

U. S. Steel was into the war business in a big way. Detractors of the company and of industry raged away that the company was making outrageous profits out of an international disaster. Not so. The government put a cap on prices and profits for wartime steel and steel goods. As Irving Olds told shareholders during the company's 1944 annual meeting, the company's profit for 1943 amounted to $63.5 million, having plunged from 1942's $71.3 million and 1941's $116.2 million. In fact, he told shareholders, income for 1943 plus interest on long-term debt represented a return of 3.9 percent on net assets. (It was 4.48 percent in 1942.)

"This relatively small profit for 1943, despite near-capacity operations," he explained, "reflects the inevitable outcome of higher costs pressing against government-imposed price ceilings."

Indeed, Olds told shareholders at the 1946 meeting that the "Navy Price Adjustment Board, acting for all government agencies, found, with one exception, that none of the subsidiaries of the corporation…had realized any excessive profits" under their contracts during the war years. The only exceptions were small refunds in 1942 and 1943 from a shipbuilding subsidiary.

So much for excess profits—and at a time when demand was on the company to produce a reliable supply of especially high-end steel.

What made the wartime steel more special was the rarity of its ingredients. U. S. Steel had to import its critical alloying metals, nickel and chrome. But Axis forces cut off overseas supplies of those vital minerals, and stockpiles shrank in the States. The USA needed enormous quantities for production on the home front, as well as for weapons, ships and planes.

The U.S. government told the steel companies they'd have to use much less of these alloys that make steel hard, because the alloys were no longer available from abroad. But the companies were expected to figure how to produce the same amount of high-grade steel for battle.

And U. S. Steel and the other steel companies did. Together.

U. S. Steel's top metallurgist led an industry committee that devised a way to make high-performance steel for the war, in effect stretching the country's supply of almost priceless magnesium. Science went to war, too. As Olds would say later, "It was providential that U. S. Steel had maintained constant research during the 10 or more years prior to the war."

It was providential because steel was everywhere in the war. Steel pipelines sped up the flow of oil and fuel for steel ships, tanks, trucks, jeeps, troop-landing craft. Doctors, nurses and medics used surgical equipment of high-grade, stainless steel. Planes were held together by light but rugged steel-tube skeletons, their flight guided by steel wire sinews. Soldiers carried steel rifles and wore helmets of pliable-but-armor-like steel made by U. S. Steel. From steel mess kits, they ate "K-rations," instant meals shipped in cans whose tin plate was also made by U. S. Steel.

American Steel and Wire Division produced over 90 percent of the helmets worn by our GIs during the war. The helmets were the toughest ever made—a metallurgical triumph of U. S. Steel.

U. S. Steel built 119 LSTs—Landing Ships/Tanks—and reduced construction time from 260 to 30 days.

THE ULTIMATE WEAPON

Steel in World War II was the Allies' not-so-secret weapon.

From July 1, 1940, to July 1945, U. S. Steel increased its production from 23.9 million tons to 30.8 million tons— enough steel every hour to build 164 four-engine bombers or 703 fighter planes or 63 tanks. But it was formulated and configured in many more ways for many more purposes.

The armaments and other war supplies U. S. Steel produced during the war could fill a catalogue. Most took advantage of high-tech alloy steels for toughness, durability, "bendability"— whatever trait was required.

Some items were U. S. Steel defense specialties:

Helmets: *Unlike the pie-pan hats soldiers sported during World War I, the World War II models were shaped to protect the front, back and sides of the head. They had to be hard enough to protect the skull but "soft" enough to give a little when struck—and to be machine-punched into shape from steel disks. U. S. Steel produced 90 percent of the helmet steel used in the war—enough for 21 million helmets.*

Landing mats: *U. S. Steel invented these prefab runways/landing strips for tough-to-land-on terrain. These 10-foot-long, 16-inch-wide sections were joined by interlocking hooks and slots. A temporary airport for fighters and bombers could be laid out on a beach or marsh in a few hours. U. S. Steel made 214 million square feet of the steel matting during the war, and shared its invention at no cost with other producers. (At one time, 28 companies made them.) General Henry "Hap" Arnold, commanding general of the Army Air Forces, saluted the devices in 1941 as the "outstanding development of the year in aviation."*

Ships: *U. S. Steel converted two sheet steel mills in Pittsburgh and Gary, Indiana, to produce plate. Five weeks after conversion started, plate was delivered to shipbuilders. U. S. Steel itself fabricated 911 ships during the war. Its Federal Shipbuilding and Dry Dock Company constructed 276 vessels, using improved prefabricating techniques the company had developed in World War I.*

Federal Shipbuilding produced 22 percent of the destroyers put into duty during the war, and 10 percent of the destroyer escorts. Federal also made troop ships, landing craft, and, at American Bridge's Ambridge, Pennsylvania, plant, the famous "Landing Ships/Tanks," or LSTs—mighty craft whose bows opened at shorelines to expel jeeps, tanks and troops. They carried railroad cars and supplies and served as sea ambulances to evacuate casualties.

USS-invented prefab steel sections provided a quick, efficient way to create temporary runways and landing strips.

Torpedo nets: *Suspended from booms at a ship's bow and stern, they snared incoming torpedoes.*

Aircraft-arrester cables: *These steel lifelines safely snagged planes as they landed on aircraft carriers.*

Artillery, bombs, shells, rockets: *More than 220,000 tons of steel produced at U. S. Steel plants were fabricated into armor-piercing shells alone. The company "spun" bombs by a superfast method that borrowed from the potter's wheel: Seamless steel tubing, heated at one end to white hot, was whirled in a spinning machine at 1,000 turns a minute. A shaping wheel molded the hot end into a cone—the shell's nose.*

Planes: *High-tech stainless steel was used for building aircraft. A B-29 superfortress required 50 tons; a P-38 fighter, more than 12 tons. Steel stiffened wings and landing gear. Steel tubing held the engine in place and served as the plane's skeleton; wire comprised the interior muscles. Pilots and crew wore steel-reinforced flak vests.*

Tanks: *U. S. Steel research proved alloy-bearing steel armor could be mass-produced in the company's open-hearth furnaces instead of in much smaller electric furnaces. Production of armor plate shot upward. The discovery, plus U. S. Steel-developed welding techniques which replaced rivets, combined to insure an ever-increasing tonnage of armor plate was shipped to manufacturers during an ever-shrinking war deadline.*

Instant bridges: *The speed with which American troops advanced on the heels of the enemy depended in large part on the rate they could rebuild demolished bridges. Prefabricated "Bailey Bridges"* *could be quickly assembled and extended across gaps of up to 240 feet. Steel pins held everything together and made assembly fast. "Treadway Bridges" floated on rivers on pontoons, and had non-skid spans; the heaviest war machines could cross over them.*

Blitz cans: *These boxy, steel containers with the built-in handles and lids were mounted on the backs of jeeps in every WWII movie you've ever seen. The five-gallon cans were filled with gasoline at fuel depots and rushed wherever troops needed gasoline—for tanks, trucks or ambulances.*

Rebuilding bombed-out bridges quickly with prefabricated parts enabled American troops to advance quickly in battle. Shown here is a "Bailey Bridge" under construction in Italy.

Not just any steel could do all this. And not just any steel would do for almost all the uses the metal was put to in the war.

Most of the steel that went to war was very special, a high-grade alloy steel. That made it tough, so it could be rolled into thin steel sheets that became the skin of aircraft, or rolled out in thick slabs to be used as the armor that would bounce shells off ships and tanks—and that could be fashioned into the treads that took tanks over hills, walls and demolished buildings.

That steel was exceptionally versatile. It was tough and supple. It was in the delicate ball bearings that made gun turrets, wheels, aircraft engines and dozens of other mechanisms work smoothly without overheating, seizing up or flying apart. It was in the fine springs that operated gyrocompasses and other instruments that were delicate but had to work while the planes or tanks or trucks they were in were pummeled by exploding shells.

Everything had to perform without a flaw. If you were sprawled out flat on a field in Europe and firing a machine gun at a line of German soldiers who were shooting at you, too, nonstop, you did not want even one of the little steel chains that held together the shells that ripped through the gun to break and cause that gun to jam. Each link had to have just the right touch of springiness.

Life depended on right-on-the-money steel.

Not that the war machine ran smoothly all the time.

There were hitches. For example, in late 1943, the coal miners struck—including those at U. S. Steel's mines. A cutoff in coal threatened the supply of war steel.

Irving Olds connected the dots for reporters during an August press conference in New York: U. S. Steel's second-quarter shipments of finished steel had dropped 260,000 tons below the first quarter. As *The Investor's Reader* reported: "After allowing for waste in manufacturing, 260,000 tons of steel would make 6,000 giant M-4 tanks to batter the

Axis in Sicily or 45 Liberty Ships to carry supplies to U.S. troops in the Mediterranean."

Then there was the odd-couple relationship between the steel industry and Uncle Sam.

The nation that was fighting for democracy as well as its capitalist system was now telling private industry what and how much to make and where to ship it. It was necessary in a war emergency, of course. But anyone who read war-supply documents pumped out by the government would have quickly seen the dangers that could arise when the government overplays its hand.

Consider a 1943 government report with the cumbersome title *Additional Report of the Special Committee Investigating the National Defense Program*. In a section attempting to explain a shortage in the American supply of war steel, the document blamed three factors:

First: "The armed forces seriously underestimated the amount of steel they would need under war conditions.... They are now using as much steel in three months as they previously informed the office of Production Management they would need in a year."

Second: "The desire of the big steel companies to prevent any expansion that might react unfavorably against their control of the steel industry after the war."

Third: The government's War Production Board dragged its feet in converting industry to a war mode. Result: "Untold tons of steel were permitted to be consumed in non-war production until far into 1942."

The report also conceded that "[a]llocation of steel to consumers has been...complicated by the need to plan facilities far in advance for the types of products which will be needed." Leafing through the thick document, one gets the feeling that dropping thousands of copies over Moscow would have scared the communist government away for good from its run-the-economy doctrine.

While cracking the whip over the free market was warranted when there was a war on, there was heavy squabbling, too.

In April 1942, for example, the War Production Board announced charges against Carnegie-Illinois Steel.

"The company," the board said, "gave first preference to customers of its choice, without regard for the Government priority ratings assigned to orders for military and essential civilian needs." In May, Chairman Olds put the issue into perspective for shareholders at U. S. Steel's annual meeting: "With the magnitude of Carnegie-Illinois' operations, it would be remarkable if there have not been some instances since May 31, 1941, where strict compliance with priority orders and regulation has not taken place."

He explained the government's complex priority-rating system and assured stockholders that any straying on the part of their company had been accidental and minor. The issue blew over.

One that did not fade away, however, dealt with allegations that the company had faked tests of the integrity of steel plate it produced for ships. And it brought the company head-to-head with a Missouri senator named Harry Truman.

Truman chaired the War Production Board's Iron and Steel Industry Advisory Committee when officials of United States Steel and its Carnegie-Illinois Steel subsidiary were brought before it to explain more charges against Carnegie-Illinois. The allegations: Employees at the company's Irvin, Pennsylvania, works, near Pittsburgh, were fudging the results of tests on steel plate so they could foist it off on an unwary government.

The investigation had the distinct aroma of politics about it. Truman had no love for big business, but he certainly had his eye on a higher office. And here he was in a position to pillory the biggest of the big in front of the boys of the press. Yet it was clear that U. S. Steel was not lily white in the matter. In fact, there were no black or white tones in the affair, just shades of gray.

The quality of steel plate became an urgent matter for the government after a newly launched tanker named *Schenectady* broke in two at Portland, Oregon, in January of 1943. Carnegie-Illinois had supplied steel for the ship. And investigators for the Truman Committee, responding to mailed-in "tips," found that at least 5 percent of the plant's plate production, something like 3,000 tons of steel a month, failed to meet the Navy's specifications. Yet the plate was being marked as standard, and shipped out.

Carnegie-Illinois employees ran a chemical analysis of each "heat," or batch, of steel to verify whether the steel met specifications—whether it had the right amount of carbon and other elements to give it the strength the customers required, and expected to get. The trouble was, the plant had been converted from rolling steel coil to produce thicker plate—a time-saving but costly and technically challenging change. In the work, some heat codes were lost. Also, some hurried or confused workers had been transposing numbers in the heat codes. These troubles affected about 5 percent of the heats. When that happened—when the chemical analysis of a heat was unknown—company examiners simply made up an analysis for the record book.

But there was more to the plot, as was revealed in testimony before the Truman committee—testimony that began to sound as though someone had shuffled together scripts from the then-popular mystery and comedy radio shows *The Shadow* and *Fibber McGee and Molly.*

One example was testimony given by Murray Stewart, a U. S. Steel quality examiner who was questioned by committee member Hugh Fulton about the inspection system. Historian-writer David McCullough replayed it in his Pulitzer Prize–winning 1992 book, *Truman* (Simon & Schuster Inc.):

> Fulton: *In other words…you would make up a chemical analysis which you thought would fit what the steel should have been.*
>
> Stewart: *That is right.*
>
> Fulton: *And how would you deal with that in that particular record book?*
>
> Stewart: *In order to keep our records so that we would know when it was an incorrect heat number, we would enter it in this book in pencil.*

Fulton: *How were the other entries made?*

Stewart: *They were made in ink.*

Fulton: *And did you, in addition to making them in pencil, put any prefix letter in front of them?*

Stewart: *It was common practice to put an "F."*

Fulton: *What did "F" mean?*

Stewart: *Fake.*

Fulton: *You told our investigator originally that it meant phone.*

Stewart: *That is right.*

Fulton: *But now, under oath, you desire to state it meant fake?*

Stewart: *That is correct. The investigator was a stranger to me and I was sort of pressed for something to say at the moment.*

U. S. Steel's testimony made the company sound devious, or silly. Committee investigators were delayed in being admitted to Carnegie-Illinois headquarters. They had to wait an hour and a half to inspect a record book that, as McCullough described it, had been "taken apart the night before and distributed among several people who were 'doing work' for the company attorney…. How much had been removed or altered they had no way of knowing."

Carnegie-Illinois Steel President J. Lester Perry testified about the "cheating." McCullough paraphrased it: "While management deplored such devious practices as had been disclosed by the committee's investigators—practices that higher management had no part in—even the substandard plates supplied by the mill were 'entirely suitable for their intended use.' "

Furthermore, added Perry, the plate at the point where the *Schenectady* broke was not from the Irvin Works. (It was discovered later that the suspect plate was made at the company's Homestead plant, but the reasons for the fracture remained unclear.)

Truman took the opportunity to lecture the steelmen. When committee member Senator Homer Ferguson bore down on Perry, Truman joined in:

Ferguson: *Why didn't you [meet government specifications]?*

Perry: *We will.*

Truman: *I'll say you will. From now on.*

From U. S. Steel headquarters, President Fairless promised any employees who shipped out plate that didn't meet specifications would "walk the plank." And, as the papers reported, four employees implicated in test faking were suspended.

In May 1944, the company was tried in federal court. One of the star witnesses was Jeanne Nicoden, a former Irvin metallurgical employee who was now a Marine Corps private first-class. Nicoden was described in the *Pittsburgh Post-Gazette* as a "statuesque blonde" who, when asked about her marital status, replied she was "single...sorry." Asked if metal test results were changed, she answered yes, but the changes were "small." Did she feel guilty about "faking" tests? "No."

The episode was embarrassing to U. S. Steel, a company which had earned innumerable production-record awards from the government. It was celebrated as the most solid of corporate citizens. While the controversy raged, Perry and Fairless quickly enforced measures to rehabilitate the corporation's reputation. But the power of the congressional committees can be awesome, and only newspapers like the *Pittsburgh Post-Gazette* put the falsified paperwork issue into perspective.

The end of the case was worthy of Alfred Hitchcock.

A *Post-Gazette* reporter's probing revealed that some facts presented by the government were not "presented in their proper perspective." The reporter also discovered that the War Production Board (WPD) had withheld testimony of Navy and Maritime Commission spokesmen that "would have allayed much of the concern created by the original charges." When the Truman committee issued its official report, the *Post-Gazette* stated on May 24, 1944, it ignored a U.S. admiral's WPD testimony that all plates received by the Maritime Commission had been sound. Also deleted from the press copy of the minutes of the same meeting, according to the paper, was a portion of a statement by another admiral, reflecting his concern over the Truman committee's "sensationalized charges of plate production."

The plates rolled at the Irvin Works had been suitable for their intended use. The Truman probe, said the paper, bungled its job: "The net result of the Senate inquiry has been to hamstring manufacture of steel plates so seriously that Navy and War Production Board officials believe the entire war effort may be in danger...."

Kissing the war goodbye in Times Square. This famous photo captured the nation's mood when V-E (Victory in Europe) Day was announced on May 7, 1945.

Meeting in Hoboken, New Jersey, at the same time, shareholders at U. S. Steel's 44th annual meeting paused "in a slient tribute to those who had fallen...."

Photo by Corbis

Perry had it right when he theorized that the Irvin metallurgists were experienced enough to know that the chemistry deviations were too small to weaken the plates, which were over-engineered for safety. The plates in question were perfectly sound for the use intended—warships. And holding them up would only slow down war production for no sound reason.

When U. S. Steel shareholders gathered in Hoboken, New Jersey, on May 7, 1945, for the company's 44th annual meeting, they were serenaded by the sounds of whistles on factories around the meeting hall.

Chairman Olds explained:

"The whistles you are hearing on all sides announce the end of the war in Europe. A press dispatch of a few minutes ago tells of the signing by the German high command of an instrument of unconditional surrender covering all of the German armed forces. This morning, the German foreign minister, in a radio talk to the German people, announced the unconditional surrender by Germany. Later in the day, we may have an official confirmation of the arrival of V-E [Victory in Europe] Day."

Victory over Japan was sure to follow.

It was probably the best news announced at an annual meeting. And it was followed by perhaps the most touching few moments, when Olds stood with shareholders, heads bowed, in "a silent tribute to those who have so fallen in defense of our country and its sacred principles."

Those who had "so fallen" included a number of U. S. Steel employees, who had served on active duty during the war. Also lost were an uncountable number of stockholders. Associates. Friends. Family.

What was unsaid, but probably filled the minds of most of the people in the big room, was that this must never happen again.

Chapter 9

Peace—At a Price

Finally, the war was over.

The men and women who fought it were coming home to resume their lives. The families of those who didn't return mourned their dead and picked up their lives again. We carried on.

U. S. Steel employees shared the grief and the glory.

In all, 113,249 U. S. Steel employees had served in the war. Most had come home and, with their loved ones and friends, tried to get things back to normal.

"Normal" at U. S. Steel mills, as well as in other factories, offices and stores, meant the men returned to reclaim their old jobs, or to take other jobs. Many of those positions had been held down for them by women, and many of those women didn't want to go back to being full-time homemakers, or on to traditional women's work, like waiting tables. Why should they? They'd shown they could handle "men's work," and many of the men they worked for would have been glad to see them stay.

But it couldn't be. The understanding had been that they were holding jobs for the men who went off to fight. They were expected to give them back. And letting women do the heavy work at a mill? It just wasn't right.

What was "right," of course, would be history soon enough. The USA—the *world*—would not be the same after the big war.

For one thing, England, France, Germany and Italy had lost huge pieces of their infrastructures—highways, buildings, homes and factories. They had to rebuild. But America had been rebuilding its industries during the war, and was in condition to keep building after the fighting stopped. It was the only nation that was strong enough to lead the others. It was the only nation that had "won." It was the new economic power.

A lot of the credit for that belonged to the companies that produced war goods. Naturally, they were accused of shameless profiteering. Never mind that the government had put a lid on profits.

Profiteering? U. S. Steel's war records show that, from 1941 to 1945, the corporation's average, annual, before-taxes profit represented a return on investment of about 4.6 percent. It was hardly excessive, given the huge muscle and money U. S. Steel and its employees and shareholders had put into the war.

That was how Irving Olds saw it.

"I feel strongly that the people who put up the money to make enterprises possible should be allowed a fair return on their investment," he declared in one magazine column. "Otherwise we cannot maintain enterprise."

Or the country, he could have added. A lot of those profits would be put back to work to make things for American consumers. The enterprise Olds spoke of was maintained, and then some, after the war's end, when citizens enjoyed increasing and unprecedented affluence.

Not right away, though.

American victory parade near the Arc de Triomphe in Paris after the end of World War II. In all, 113,249 U. S. Steel employees served in the war.

When the American troops started to return home, and the country started to settle down, it was as though someone had taken a hammer and knocked the safety valve off the national economic machine.

Out burst desires Americans had bottled up for several years, hankerings after the niceties of life. And it wasn't long before they were being satisfied. The war's climax marked the start of an era of unprecedented prosperity for Americans—at least for those in the upper and middle classes.

Prosperity, though, took its sweet time. First came a recession that the country had braced itself for; during the first six months after the peace, the government canceled war contracts. A lot of workers lost their jobs—2.5 million workers, according to Thomas O'Toole, author of *The Economic History of the United States* (Lerner Publications Company, 1990).

But the slump was mercifully short. Steel and other industries had built extra capacity into their plants for the war. They began to convert it to peacetime work even before the war ended. It didn't take long for them to start cranking out shoes, furniture, carpeting, tools, appliances—and, of course, cars. People rushed out to buy.

Not just in the States, either. Europe's factories and shipping lines had been blasted to pieces in the fighting. American companies were exporting mountains of food, clothing, machinery and other goods that were desperately needed overseas. The export business stuffed money into American pockets.

To make things even better, the government rewarded returning war veterans with generous benefits, like free college educations and subsidized home mortgages, courtesy of the GI Bill.

Recovery was helped along, too, by American political leaders. They'd learned their lessons from postwar slumps of the past, and they knew everyone feared another Great Depression. Congress responded by passing the Employment Act of 1946, intended to achieve full employment, and the government took controls off prices and profits. It was a green light to spend.

The economy was humming. As economist and future Secretary of Labor Robert Reich wrote in his 1991 Random House book, *The Work of Nations*, this performance, which would continue through the next decade, would give the American economic system a new gleam:

"If any Americans during the Depression decade of the 1930s or the war decade thereafter harbored lingering doubts about the legitimacy of the large American Corporation or about the viability of American capitalism itself, such doubts were erased by the explosive prosperity of the 1950s. Even the staunchest critics...were convinced."

The steel industry hit a bump when the U.S. Supreme Court took another look at base-point pricing, *á la* the corporation's Pittsburgh-plus method. The court had already ruled in 1924 that the system, which could be traced back to the days of Carnegie, was illegal for setting prices based on shipping rates from Pittsburgh. Now it decreed the Pittsburgh-plus pricing was illegal in the cement industry, as well. The new decision meant that some customers of the corporation's Universal Atlas Cement Company would be paying more for their cement. The surge in consumer demand, and the resulting good times, upstaged the ruling. But it didn't take long for consumers to recognize that the boom came at a price.

That price was inflation. Demand had elevated some prices for goods and services as much as 25 percent. Government measures to buoy employment and wages became institutionalized after the war, locking in inflation. Wage controls were lifted. Factories were winding down from war production, cutting overtime and even downgrading jobs. No longer could workers depend on their jobs. If they worked, they couldn't depend on what they would make, or on what it would buy.

They watched their new buying power dribble out of their pay envelopes. According to the Bureau of Labor Statistics, defense workers were making 11 percent less spendable income in the winter of 1946 than they were in 1941. Between the spring of 1945 and winter of 1946, they lost 31 percent of their weekly wages. Labor writer Jeremy Brecher cited a May 1946 government report which found that "in most cases, wages during the first phase of reconversion were inadequate for the maintenance of living standards permitted by earnings in the year preceding the Pearl Harbor attack."

NEW YORK Tribune LATE CITY EDITION

Section One

10 Cents in New York City and Suburbs
15 Cents Elsewhere

SUNDAY, JANUARY 20, 1946

Steel Shutdown On, 55,000 Already Out; 750,000 to Strike Tonight Across Nation; Hopes of Settlement Fade in Washington

STEEL INDUSTRY IS CLOSED DOWN AS NATION-WIDE STRIKE STARTS; GOVERNMENT MAY SEIZE PLANTS

Strikers to Total 1,657,000 Today

With the strike of 750,000 steel workers and 30,000 farm implement workers set for today, the number of the country's strikers, including those who were already out, will reach 1,657,000.

According to Federal statistics, the year 1919 showed the largest number of workers idle due to strikes, 4,160,000 or 20.8 per cent of the working population. This was the all-time record.

A preliminary survey for 1945 by the Bureau of Labor Statistics indicates that the number of workers involved in strikes for that year was 3,250,000, the highest since 1919.

ACTION IS STUDIED

Truman Aides Are Split on the Advisability of Drastic Steel Step

---

DECISION MAY WAIT WEEK

Pay Dispute Affecting 400,000 Shipyard Workers Comes to Crisis Tomorrow

By LOUIS STARK

750,000 MEN OUT

Arrival of Picket Lines Signals the Start of Big Steel Struggle

---

CLASHES AT PLANTS FEW

Center on Maintenance of Idle Mills—Murray Goes to Pittsburgh as Fires Die

By LAWRENCE RESNER

SEIZURE IN VIEW FOR STEEL MILLS

Continued From Page 1

accrue to industry and permit it to carry on this industrial war" should be discontinued by act of Congress.

Senator Kilgore, Democrat, of West Virginia, charged that the steel industry, by "flouting" President Truman's wage proposal, had "deliberately plunged the nation into industrial civil war" and announced that he would press for repeal of "the tax-rebate provisions which permit United States Steel and General Motors to draw on the Treasury to finance their war on the workers."

Advisers of President Truman

company or an industry would continue to pay the wage adjustment when it was again in possession of its properties.

Adverse Precedents Feared

Since the Smith-Connally Act and the War Powers Acts expire in June, it was felt in these quarters that seizure when the nation is moving into peacetime patterns would set precedents which would be disastrous to free collective bargaining and even to the continuance of a free competitive economy.

There were suggestions, also, that the steel workers would refuse to go back to work even if the Government paid the 18½-cent wage increase unless they believed that the new scale would be continued after seizure was terminated. Seizure, therefore, might not be invoked unless some understanding could be reached that the steel industry would continue the scale.

American workers couldn't keep up. During the war, they had staged a rash of wildcats, strikes their unions hadn't authorized. But the unions had been bargaining with employers, and, to no one's surprise, another surge of strikes—official, this time—came right after the war.

The strikes started in September 1945. Lumber workers, oil workers, auto workers, truck drivers and meatpackers quit working. And with the new year, 1946, came the threat of a nationwide steel strike.

A big steel strike would surely knock the accelerating economy off its tracks, and Harry S. Truman, now the President, was going to stop it if it was the last thing he did.

Ben Fairless

The steelworkers reasoned it was time for a wage hike. They'd earned it, they figured. After all, they'd helped win the war, and the economy was rolling along nicely in large part because they'd given it a big push. So, early in the new year, Philip E. Murray, head of the United Steel Workers (USW) and of the CIO, called for a wage increase of 19.5 cents an hour.

U. S. Steel President Ben Fairless represented the steel companies, who argued they could not afford the steelworkers' demand, and offered 15 cents an hour. Truman stepped in to broker a compromise, proposing that the steel companies grant an increase of 18.5 cents. Murray accepted, but Fairless refused. And in mid-January 1946, some 800,000 steelworkers at more than 1,000 mills across the country went out for what McCullough called "the biggest strike in history."

Philip Murray

It was Truman's worst nightmare: a huge steel strike on top of meatpackers', glassworkers', telephone and streetcar strikes, and all the rest. McCullough, in *Truman*, related the President's thoughts about labor and business at a press conference: "I personally think there is too much power on each side, and I think it is necessary that the government assert the fact that it is the power of the people." Pittsburgh Mayor David Lawrence went on the radio, McCullough added, to plead with workers to go back to their jobs.

Fairless, a convincing communicator himself, took to the airwaves, too. In a January 23, coast-to-coast address over the American Broadcasting Company, he explained to the nation why his company could not go above its offered 15.5-cent-an-hour increase. Part of the transcript:

> *"You will recall that, early in the war, steel prices were frozen by the government at approximately pre-war levels. Labor and other costs in the steel industry, however, have gone up most substantially since 1940. The result of mounting costs pressing against OPA (Office of Price Administration) ceiling prices was that most of our ordinary steel tonnage was being sold at a loss long before the union made its...wage demand.*
>
> *"In order to eliminate those losses, as far back as two years ago, we asked for new and fair ceiling prices, as provided by law. In the face of such facts, we were not able to offer a large wage increase. Yet while these ceiling price applications were still pending—last October— the union made its demand for a $2-a-day general wage increase."*

The union was putting the company in a squeeze, and the government was not easing the pressure. The company had gone back and forth with the union, Fairless added, and with the White House, to no avail. One of the real dangers in all this, Fairless suggested, was inflation. He had a suggestion, he told listeners:

"It is that the President immediately call a conference in Washington
of experienced executives from representative companies which are
now directly involved in the strikes … These men could discuss frankly
with the President, and give him the benefit of their advice on what
kind of a wage increase the economy of this country can endure
without incurring the danger of an inflationary spiral with a
constant race between mounting wages and mounting prices.

"This is a national problem which should be solved not on the
basis of political considerations, but rather on the broad basis of what
is in the best interests of the American people as a whole."

Fairless, of course, made the same arguments to his "opposite" in the strike, Murray, president of the CIO and the USW. Murray looked like a tall leprechaun and spoke with a Scottish burr. He was the son of a coal miner. So was Fairless.

"I explained U. S. Steel's cost pinch time and again to Murray," Fairless wrote in a two-part, 1956 autobiography that ran in the omnipresent magazine, *Life*:

"I said, 'Phil, why argue with me? Why not see OPA? I'll even go
with you.' But he shrugged me off. 'Prices are none of my concern,'
he said. 'That's your problem.'"

Then Fairless added, in parentheses:

(In every negotiation I have heard of, the union has always insisted
that the companies could grant a raise without increasing prices. Yet
the fact remains that, if steel prices had stayed at 1946 levels, every
steel company in the land would have been bankrupt long ago.)

But prices didn't stay put. Various officials tried to talk Fairless into agreeing to the terms, or into accepting limp and iffy compromises. Then President Truman summoned Fairless and Murray to his Washington office and told them they had to settle the matter.

"The general assumption in Washington," Fairless wrote, "seemed to be that I was only kidding about needing price increases, and would eventually give in if enough pressure was applied."

In the end, the parties settled on an 18.5-cent-an-hour raise with a $5-a-ton increase in steel prices. The strike was settled. "At that, the companies got the worst of it," Fairless insisted. "The 1946 strike was the take-off of the postwar inflationary spiral. That…raise was a big one, and it spread quickly into other industries."

And the strikes kept coming.

18.5c Rise Ends U.S. Steel Strike

WASHINGTON, Feb. 15 (INS)—The CIO United Steel Workers Union and the U. S. Steel Corp. reached an agreement tonight for ending the 26-day-old steel strike. The agreement provides for an 18.5 cent hourly wage boost as proposed by President Truman before the strike started. It covers U. S. Steel's 125,000 employes.

A total of 750,000 workers were made idle by the strike. USW President Murray said employes other than U. S. Steels' would remain on strike until contracts were signed with individual companies.

Reconversion Director Snyder announced the settlement to reporters at the hotel where negotiations between the corporation and the union had been in progress for several hours. Truman was notified of the agreement shortly before it was announced by Snyder.

Truman earlier in the day had announced officially the industry would be given a $5 a ton increase in steel prices to compensate it for wage adjustments and other costs.

[In New York, President Fairless of U. S. Steel Corp., said last night that governmental action in raising steel prices had made possible the settlement of the

125,000 Back Monday

Murray said he would instruct the 125,000 employes of U. S. Steel's producing subsidiaries to return to their jobs at 12:01 a.m. Monday morning.

He said negotiations will start as quickly as possible to bring about settlement with the remainder of the 86 basic steel producing companies and more than 1,200 other firms with which the union has contracts.

Labor Secretary Schwellenbach said the new contract will run for one year to Feb. 15, 1947.

The union and the company compromised a disagreement over retroactive payment of the wage increase.

Part Retroactive Pay

Schwellenbach said the disputed retroactivity issue was compromised to provide for a retroactive increase of 9¼ cents for the period from Jan. 1 until next Monday. Mr. Truman had proposed the entire 18½ cents be made retroactive to Jan. 1 but the company objected.

'Bulge in Line'

Truman made it clear Snyder will have veto power over recommendations of Chester Bowles, who last night was shifted from OPA to the post of Economic Stabilizer within Snyder's office.

Truman described the wage-price policy outlined last night for settlement of widespread strikes as a continuation of the old "hold-the-line" program.

He said it is only a temporary "Bulge in the line," adding:

"If all of you cooperate there will be no breakthrough."

He said he expects the "bulge" to be wiped out, which is why he is trying to put price controls on such things as housing and other real estate.

He said Bowles will have authority to make decisions on prices and wages under the new formula, but will be under Snyder in the overall program.

Soon after the President had said there would be a "bulge," Bowles declared the new anti-inflation policy sound.

Harry S. Truman

On April 1, bituminous coal miners went out. By May 1, Irving Olds announced to shareholders at the corporation's annual meeting that "the steel operations of the corporation are now gradually coming to a standstill as a result of the strike." The loss of coal forced the company to cut steel operations from 95 percent of capacity to 45 percent. Then there was a third coal strike in the fall of 1946.

It was the worst surge of strikes in the country's history. And it put steel into Truman's spine. After having been accused of fuddling through his presidency, he got tough when the bevy of strikes threatened the nation's welfare.

He ordered the government to seize refineries to keep fuel oil and gasoline flowing. He broke a national strike of meat packers by taking over packing houses. He did the same with the bituminous coal mines, although the miners stayed out—for a while, anyway. He seized the railroads to head off a nationwide strike of railworkers. They struck anyway, paralyzing the country. But they went back to work when the President threatened to draft them and let the Army run the railroads.

The President may have put an end to the strikes, but U. S. Steel Chairman Irving Olds worried about the damage.

"Because of the steel strike at the beginning of the year, and the effects of the disastrous coal strikes in the spring and late fall, the steel industry lost one-fifth of its expected production for 1946," he wrote in the January 1947 issue of *Commercial West*. "This loss amounted to around 16,000,000 tons of ingots. Naturally, the production programs of all principal users of steel were severely retarded by being deprived of so large a tonnage of this basic raw material."

But, he added, "A new year has dawned. The demand for steel and other products still is great. The opportunity for a sustained period of general national prosperity seems promising."

As Brecher pointed out in his book *Strike!*, most of the union leaders would have preferred to have avoided the strikes. "They led them only because the rank and file were determined to strike anyway, and only by leading the strikes could the unions retain control of them.

"The attitude of top union officials was embodied in the preamble to the 1947 U. S. Steel contract," Brecher added. In that contract, "company officials pronounced that they were not anti-union, and union officials stated they were not anti-company," but were "sincerely concerned with the best interests and well-being of the business."

The apparent coziness between union and management triggered more wildcat strikes—63 during 1946 in U. S. Steel alone. Then, in 1949, there was another steel strike, over whether workers should pay into their welfare and pension funds. It was resolved by a compromise: The workers would not contribute to the fund, but they would pay part of the costs of their health and welfare programs.

The union leaders could not prevent the wildcats or hold off the "official" strikes that followed the war, but, as Brecher maintained, they "managed to keep [the strikes] under control."

The pot boiled over a little, but it didn't blow up.

The rash of strikes didn't dent U. S. Steel management's faith in the future. The company made expansions and improvements, faith worth hundreds of millions of dollars.

In 1946 alone, the company invested $201 million in its facilities. Most of the money paid for upgrades or expansions, but the corporation used $5 million of it to buy a tube mill the government had installed at U. S Steel's Gary Works. And it plunked down $65 million for government-installed facilities at Homestead, Duquesne and Edgar Thomson.

The dollars translated into jobs. At U. S. Steel's annual meeting in 1947, Olds announced the company had hired or rehired 141,000 World War II veterans. Sixty thousand of them were former employees. The whole batch of hires included 1,500 ex-servicemen who had been handicapped during the war, 862 of them former employees.

There was more work to do.

IRVING OLDS: GENTLEMAN OF STEEL

"A chairman performs the same functions as a piece of parsley on a dish of fish."

That was how Irving Sands Olds responded to a woman who, at an annual stockholders meeting, asked him what a corporate chairman did.

When the laughter died down, he turned serious and answered the lady at length as to what duties he performed under the by-laws of the corporation. But the original quip was a measure of his humility and warmth, his down-to-earth refusal to play big shot. He could be tough when toughness was called for, as when he rounded up the guns and bombs that "saved England" during World War II, and when he accidentally smashed his favorite wristwatch with a gavel while trying to rein in an unruly shareholder.

Typically, though, he operated on a smile. Fred LePell, U. S. Steel's public relations director during Olds' tenure as chairman, wrote in a brief tribute that Olds was the nicest man he'd ever met. LePell penned the biography after Olds' death and during his own retirement.

Behind Olds' usually mild façade ticked a generous portion of brains that helped him get from what he described, in LePell's words, as a "rather uneventful life of the usual youngster in a city of around five thousand" to a wartime command of a huge corporation.

The city was Erie, Pennsylvania. But Olds would not stick around there. He was bound for Yale, then Harvard Law School, where he received his law degree in 1910. It was a launching pad to an impressive position: secretary to United States Supreme Court Justice Oliver Wendell Holmes. Then he caught the eye of the folks at the New York law firm, White & Case. He became a full partner there.

The man who would lead U. S. Steel through World War II spent time as counsel for J. P. Morgan & Co., dealing with British and French purchases of World War I supplies in the United States. He then served as counsel for the British War Mission in the United States, later as a special assistant to the U.S. War Department.

It was when he went to work on corporate legal matters, however, that he came to the attention of U. S. Steel Chairman Myron C. Taylor. With Taylor's blessings, he was elected to U. S. Steel's board and Finance Committee. In 1938, after being appointed the corporation's special counsel, he labored over an industry study requested by the government. The New York Times *judged it to be "the most exhaustive and illuminating analysis of its kind ever made." After he was named chairman on June 4, 1940, he "camped himself behind impressive doors," said* Investor Reader, *and "from there he has quietly and efficiently run the affairs of Big Steel through one of the toughest periods of its 42-year corporate experience."*

But Olds was not one to warm chairs. He made it a point to make the rounds of U. S. Steel facilities, to learn firsthand of progress and problems and to demonstrate that interest to U. S. Steel's employees. See and be seen. And LePell pointedly wrote that Olds' interest in keeping U. S. Steel shareholders as informed as possible led the corporation to supplement its annual

Irving S. Olds

reports by launching, in 1947, its quarterly financial reports.

The circle of common interest that Olds drew around his company and its constituents was of a generous circumference. He urged corporations to support independently endowed colleges. He was instrumental in establishing the U. S. Steel Foundation and served as a trustee for seven years after his retirement in 1952. He also served for a while as chairman of the Council of Financial Aid to Education. The circle extended even further: In its January 25, 1945, issue, the magazine Finance *summed up Olds' philosophy of public responsibility: "In his opinion, a corporation's standing with its neighbors is dependent upon its contributions to the well-being and social progress to the community. Stemming from that premise, the public relations emphasis in United States Steel has been on basic policy...."*

The sentiments were clear enough for the Times *to characterize Olds in its November 7, 1948, issue, not only as "the clear-thinking, get-it-done type," but as "one of the liberals added to the directorate of Big Steel in 1936."*

He was a man who could get angry about a righteous cause and devote almost as much creative energy to a humorous prank—as was evidenced by the time and work he put into training his cocker spaniel, Tony. According to LePell, the dog would bolt under a table and lie with his paws over his eyes, whimpering, if a guest in the Olds home mentioned the name "Roosevelt." And, later, "Truman." Even Olds' jokes bore a message.

Overall, Olds maintained a soft voice and impeccable manners, his studious side expressing itself through his favorite hobbies—writing about early American naval history and collecting historical naval prints, lithographs and paintings.

His book, The United States Navy, 1776–1815, *was published in 1942 by the Grolier Club in New York and contained some of his 500 prints of America's naval engagements. Later, he asked LePell to help him assemble a complete catalogue of the collection. This volume was printed in 1951 in a limited edition of 500 registered copies. Many of the prints had been hand-tinted by Olds' wife, Evelyn, a talented watercolorist.*

This collection hung in U. S. Steel's 71 Broadway headquarters for many years. When the office was moved to Pittsburgh in the 1970s, the Olds Collection, as it was known, moved too. Largely ignored in Pittsburgh, the collection was placed in storage, in an environmentally controlled room where the prints received gallery care. But no one ever viewed them. In 1999, however, the collection was returned to New York and now decorates the corporation's offices at 350 Park Avenue.

Olds retired in 1952 to live the quiet life, spending as much time as he could at home with Evelyn. The couple had no children.

Olds was a gentleman, at a time when quiet courage was priceless. Under his wartime leadership, the corporation out-produced the steel industries of Germany, Italy and Japan, achieving a productivity rate of 106 percent of capacity.

U. S. Steel's construction and expansion in the late 1940s included a new battery of by-product coke ovens at the Lorain (Ohio) Works of National Tube Co.

The company put in a new seamless pipe mill at its Lorain Works, in Ohio. (As the name implies, this variation of tubing and large pipe was free of an end-to-end, welded seam—and stronger for it.) It modernized its Fairfield Works, in Alabama, installed machinery for hot-rolled coils at Geneva, Utah, and put in a "cold-reduced sheet" mill at its works in Torrance, California. In 1948, U. S. Steel committed $20 million a month—or about half a billion dollars over two years—for even more improvements, including higher-capacity, by-product coke ovens, blast furnaces that would boost iron capacity by a million tons in 1948, and new facilities to make more steel ingot, wire, tin plate and tubular products.

Chairman Olds covered the expansion sprees in a perspectives-on-steel essay he wrote for a November 1947 issue of *Financial Times*:

"Despite the materially increased cost of steel production—resulting from sharp advances in labor rates, higher prices for purchased goods and services, and greater transportation costs, as well as much higher costs of installing new facilities—steel prices in the United States have advanced since the end of the war far less than almost any other commodity."

We were getting a good deal from steel, and it would continue, because the industry would be very busy for the rest of the decade and into the next. Investments were needed to satisfy Americans' new hunger for goods of almost every kind.

On top of that, Olds added in his *Financial Times* column, "the American steel industry is also faced with the probability of being asked to furnish large tonnages of steel for the rehabilitation and reconstruction of Western Europe."

American steel had accounted for a third of the world's output before World War II. Now the USA produced almost half the world's steel. The country had been promoted to giant, partly because Europe's steel capacity had been crushed, and partly because, as Olds put it, "the steel ingot capacity of the United States was increased 19 percent between 1938 and 1945 to provide necessary implements of war."

The Secretariat, one of three UN buildings, as it neared completion in 1950. American Bridge Division fabricated and erected the structural steel for all three buildings.

War? We didn't want to worry about it anymore.

Just maybe, given the senseless waste of two sizable clashes between multiple nations within four decades, we'd try methods other than shooting at each other to short-circuit aggression and settle our political differences.

Giving substance to the dream was a remarkable new building that U. S. Steel's American Bridge Company was fabricating and erecting with more than 34,000 tons of steel rolled in the corporation's Carnegie-Illinois mills. In 1949, work started in New York City on the United Nations building. The structure, a glass-clad tower flanked by two meeting halls, would be the new home of the young association that was dedicated to peace, and whose membership totaled almost 60 nations.

It was just the thing for the coming new decade.

It was made of glass, concrete and steel, but mostly it was made of hope.

Chapter 10

The Fifties:
Hits and Myths

We tend to remember the Fifties as a series of photographs, moments frozen in black and white and served up again and again in magazine retrospectives and the picture books that replayed twentieth-century America.

In U. S. Steel's archives is a photo that captures the mood of the decade as surely as any of the snaps of Elvis or the Edsel.

The picture records the official startup of U. S. Steel's thoroughly modern Fairless Works, at Morrisville, Pennsylvania, 30 miles north of Philadelphia, on December 11, 1952. In the photo, Ben Fairless smiles proudly as his seven-year-old granddaughter, Nancy, lights a ceremonial fuse that will ignite the mighty blast furnace named in her honor.

It's all there, in reassuring tones of black, white and gray. Grandpa in his coat and tie, granddaughter in her Sunday bonnet, the fuse spraying light like a Fourth of July sparkler. Family. Celebration. Anticipation for the future.

But the photo reveals as much by what it does not show. For in the shadows, invisible to everyone at that stage of history, were forces that would transform the steel industry, and with it, the nation's economy. More strikes. More government investigations, more inflation, but more productivity and prosperity, too.

Life itself in the Fifties seemed, in retrospect, to have been a blissfully secure time when we lived at a slower pace, enjoyed unprecedented prosperity and looked for an even better tomorrow.

The truth is more complicated. As journalist-author David Halberstam wrote in his acclaimed 1993 study, *The Fifties* (Villard Books), "Social ferment…was beginning just beneath this placid surface." Technological and economic ferment, too. The decade seeded ideas, attitudes and options that, in the following years, would transform us in amazing ways. It also kept feeding us shots of nuclear-war paranoia.

The steel industry went along for the ride, plunging into the Fifties. But it, too, was on an unexpected trajectory when it emerged. The biggest turn, as we'll see, was 1959.

So the Fifties was Ozzie and Harriet, hula hoops, porkpie hats and buying a cool new car and taking the family to the drive-in to get burgers and shakes that were served on a tray attached to the car window.

But the decade also was about the polio vaccine and sit-ins for racial equality, as well as *Playboy*, the pill, communist witch hunts, the Bomb, flying saucers, rock and roll and other things that got us all shook up. The new affluence? It was pretty much limited to the middle class.

Moreover, we soon found ourselves immersed in another war: Korea. By that time, we were so tired of fighting that we downplayed this spin-off of World War II by rating it a "conflict," or an "action," or an "incident," as though these were nicer labels. It still looked and sounded like a war to the guys sent overseas to duck bullets.

"Call it a war, call it an international incident, call it what we will," lamented *U S Steel News*, "we're at it again." And by April of 1951, the company was dedicating more than 40 percent of its steel production to special-grade steels—Man-Ten steel plates for tanks, Tri-Ten steel for portable bridges, Cor-Ten for trucks—plus alloy steel for bazooka rockets and other war materials on a list that sounded like it was copied from the World War II order book.

New in the catalogue was a .45-caliber sub-machine gun with a barrel that was curved 90 degrees. It was for shooting around corners. Ingenuity persisted. Also new: In munitions for Korea, the company was replacing rare alloying elements with much-cheaper boron. It was made from borax, mined from abundant deposits in America's Southwest.

But Korea was the sideshow for the main event, the Cold War, which began when the Soviet Union drew a line in the dirt. Any day now, we'd be lobbing nuclear weapons at each other. Everyone just knew it. And so the corporation was supplying bars, rails, wire rope and other material for secret goings-on at the Atomic Energy Commission's facilities at Los Alamos, New Mexico and Oak Ridge, Tennessee—and for government work in South Carolina on an unimaginably powerful new "hydrogen" bomb.

Our hopes and fears set our wish list. We wanted new homes and cars and those amoeba-shaped chairs we could sit on while we watched TV. We wanted peace and time with our families, too. But to get it, we decided we had to go into a permanent, defensive crouch, always producing, always ready to spring new weapons on Russia. Still, the defense research, mixed with peace-time R&D, set the scene for unbelievable technological advances.

It was a weird and worrisome formula, yet stimulating. And steel was factored into it in large numbers.

Fairless Works' ore storage yard and blast furnaces

When it came to steel, the Fairless Works was an industry showplace.

In the spirit of the nation's anxious gearing-up of its Cold War defenses, the company claimed the Fairless Works as part of its official "Expansion for Defense Program." Pennsylvania Governor John S. Fine declared the plant was an aid to peace. He hinted at the possibility that the Cold War would turn hot when he told the papers that the peace "will be accomplished either through a successful but unwanted conflict, or by making the United States and its allies so strong none will dare defy our desire for peace."

U S Steel News proudly proclaimed the Fairless startup as "another thrilling chapter in the story of steel," and pointed out that the plant had gotten to work "just two weeks after the history-making event at Homestead," that event being U. S. Steel's production of its billionth ton of steel.

A sleek and shiny giant nestled along the Delaware River, the works was a technical wonder. It was fitted out with nine open hearths. Each furnace was electronically controlled and lined with enough brick to build 125 six-room houses. A long series of huge rollers and powerful shears flattened the steel and trimmed it, forming it into long, thin rolls. Fairless himself likened it to rolling out dough.

But his real pride was the Works' continuous hot-strip mill. It was more than a half-mile long. Red-hot slabs of steel glided slowly into the first of a series of mighty rollers. As the rollers pressed the slabs thinner and thinner and longer and longer, the steel had to move along faster and faster. At the end, a glowing strip of metal, stretched hundreds of times its original length and squeezed to a fraction of its original thickness, came shooting out at a blur to be cooled and coiled, ready for customers.

USS officials and plant personnel celebrate the company's production of its billionth ton of steel at Homestead Works.

The mill's ahead-of-the-curve technology included environmental equipment that was a preview of the "greener" things to come in industry in a couple of decades. Fairless liked to tell about how clean the plant was, how thousands of ducks made its grounds their refuge during fall and

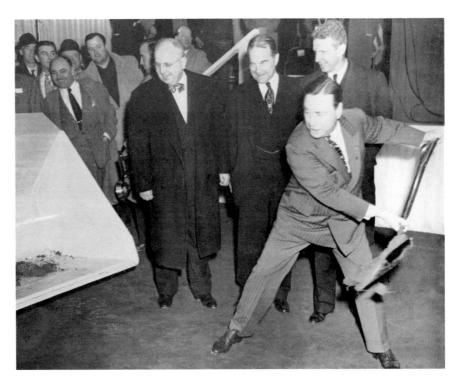

Benjamin Fairless turned the first spade of earth for the new Fairless Works. Looking on (left to right) are Pennsylvania Governor John S. Fine, USS Board Chairman Irvin S. Olds and New Jersey Governor Alfred E. Driscoll.

spring migrations, how the plant drew 250 million gallons of water every day from the Delaware River, then returned it to the river as clean as it was before.

Since the plant was built out in the country, on farmland, the workers needed homes. So U. S. Steel built Fairless Hills, a community that had grown by the middle of the decade to 2,000 homes—plus a bowling alley, golf course and swimming pool. Fairless Hills was a pleasant eight-mile drive from the mill.

All of this was something to behold, and Ben Fairless—named U. S. Steel chairman just six months before his namesake mill started making steel—was proud of it. The Fairless Works was his baby. He followed the mill's design detail-by-detail, and he turned the first spade of earth for construction on March 1, 1951, one month before the corporation's fiftieth anniversary.

He had even located a source for the ore that fed her, that made it possible to bring her to life to begin with.

That story went back to 1945, when Fairless was still president. As he told the story in his *Life* memoir published in 1956, he was

Cerro Bolivar—Orinoco Mining Company's rich mountain of iron ore in Venezuela

at his desk in Pittsburgh one afternoon when he got a phone call from John G. Munson, the U. S. Steel vice president in charge of raw materials.

"Ben," Munson said, "I have a man in my office I think you should meet. His name's Mack Lake, he's a mining engineer and he has a very interesting story to tell."

"Come right on up," said the curious Fairless.

Within minutes, Munson was introducing Fairless to Lake, a large, tanned, middle-aged but energetic man.

"My story's very simple," Lake said. "I think there's iron ore in Venezuela, south of the Orinoco River. Nobody's ever gone in to find out, or at least the Venezuelan government had no record of it. So I'm interested in finding somebody who'll put up the money to prove whether I'm right or wrong."

"How much?" Fairless asked.

"It'll cost some money," Lake cautioned. "Say $50,000 right off the bat. That'll pay for the aerial photography."

"Go ahead," said Fairless. "We'll pay for it."

"We" certainly would. World War II had put a drain on ore, and Lake Superior reserves were dwindling at a discomforting rate. U. S. Steel and other steel companies had been prospecting for new reserves, mainly in Canada and South America. Fairless offered the money without blinking.

BEN FAIRLESS: A NICE GUY WHO FINISHED FIRST

Jimmy Cagney, in his straight-shooting, George M. Cohan mode, could have played Ben Fairless. Or picture an earnest, slightly awkward Jimmy Stewart reenacting a soliloquy that the real Benjamin F. Fairless performed for a San Francisco Chronicle *reporter who was about to interview him in his California hotel suite:*

He stalks through the suite, peering in one ash tray after another for a cigar butt.

"Ah-ha!" he declares in triumph. "Here it is." He sticks the stub of a cigar into his lips, lights it and inhales luxuriously.

"With these new salaries," he announces, "you just can't ignore short cigars."

This was November of 1942, a war year, and the government had clamped a lid on salaries. Fairless, paid $156,010 the previous year, according to the Chronicle *was being held this year to $25,000. Fairless knew that even the slashed salary would be a fortune to most people. His short-cigar routine was a joke on himself, his way of poking a hole in his own ego.*

It was pure, down-to-earth Fairless—Fairless the likable guy who starred in his own poor-boy-makes-good-through-brains-and-fortitude drama.

*B*enjamin Franklin Fairless was born in the little mining town of Pigeon Run, Ohio, May 3, 1890, to Welsh immigrants, Mr. and Mrs. David Williams. When Ben was two, his mother was seriously injured in a runaway-wagon accident, and Ben had to be sent to live with his Aunt Sara and Uncle Jake Fairless, three miles away in Justus. The couple adopted the boy, and Ben Williams became Ben Fairless.

Young Ben hawked newspapers and shone in school. He also taught school, in a one-room schoolhouse, to earn money for college. During college terms separated by stints in semi-professional baseball, he earned a law degree at Ohio Northern University, in Ada, Ohio.

The turning point of Fairless' life came when he hopped aboard an interurban train bound for Massilon, Ohio, where "General" Jacob Coxey was gathering his second jobless "army" for a march on Washington. Fairless was curious about Coxey, but when the train passed the muddy construction site of a new steel plant, he hopped off. With a job in mind, he headed straight for the superintendent's shack.

A week later, he was a civil engineer for the Central Steel Company. By April 1930, Central Steel had been folded into the new Republic Steel Corporation, and Fairless was executive vice president. His talents for organization and for coming up with winning ideas at the right times won the attention of U. S. Steel Chairman Myron C. Taylor; and, in 1935, Taylor's blessings in the form of the presidency of U. S. Steel's Carnegie-Illinois Steel Corporation. He advanced to chairman and chief executive officer in 1952,

Benjamin Fairless received the Medal for Merit, the highest civilian decoration by the American government, from Secretary of War Robert Patterson. The award recognized Fairless' service as a volunteer advisor to the Army Service Forces during WWII.

remaining president until Clifford F. Hood was elected in 1953.

U. S. Steel experienced one of its greatest periods of expansion between 1938 and 1955, under Fairless' guidance. His success rested on stratospheric intellect plus down-to-earth affability. He could agree to disagree, sometimes harshly, with labor leaders, even as he retained their respect and friendship. But he could turn his words into cold, hard chisels when he had to.

He felt he had to when, as a spokesman for the steel industry, he was called to testify at hearings in Washington. After critics blasted U. S. Steel first for expanding too slowly during war, then for being "too big" during peace, he shot back: "No one has yet invented an accordion-pleated steel plant that will contract conveniently under the glowering eye of the Department of Justice, and then expand obligingly in times of national peril."

A year after he retired, Fairless was called yet again to Washington. This time, the summons came from the President. Eisenhower wanted Fairless to chair a committee to study the country's foreign aid programs, to identify and correct overlapping and waste, and generally to recommend ways to make the programs perform better and at the right cost.

From the end of December 1956 to the middle of February 1957, Fairless and his colleagues prowled the globe, visiting 17 countries. The panel was a blue-blooded cross section of business, labor, government, academe and journalism including: John L. Lewis, labor leader; Walter Beedle Smith, diplomat and former undersecretary of state; and Whitelaw Reid, chairman, New York Herald Tribune.

On their international swing, panel members interviewed presidents, premiers, ambassadors and foreign-aid officials. And they reviewed dozens of aid programs. When the trip was over and the fact-finding completed, the principals filed their report. It included nine major recommendations, some still relevant today: Although the U.S. economy can bear the cost of essential aid, the United States cannot risk the weakening of its own economic strength; business investment abroad is far superior to governmental investment; American grants in military aid should be accompanied by a willingness on the part of each country to bear its share of the cost of common defense; and the United States should reconcile itself to the fact that collective security costs are not temporary.

Fairless was in high demand by the news media when he returned. The report had resonated well in government and with the American public. During the following year, 1957, he authored two long magazine articles describing the trip and its findings—one in the April 29th issue of Life magazine, the other in the July 23rd issue of Look magazine.

Lake came back a few weeks later with news:

"The pictures show there's ore there, all right. The question is, how much and how good is it? We ought to go in there now with a diamond drill and take some samples."

"What will you need?" asked Fairless.

"Maybe half a million."

"Go ahead."

He did, and tracked down rich, high-grade deposits that could be shipped north to the U. S. East Coast. It filled holes in the corporation's ore supply line.

That Venezuelan mine paid off big, but it became a worry to own and operate. There was always the threat that it would be nationalized by the Venezuelan government. Later, it was. Still, as Fairless pointed out, it was the Venezuelan ore that made the Fairless Works possible.

There are two more telling facts about Fairless Works. First, it was, at the time, the biggest steelworks ever built from the ground up. Second, it was the first steelworks in the post–World War II era to be built from scratch.

First Shipment Of Orinoco Mining Company Iron Ore From Venezuela To Fairless Works
(USS)
January 20.1954

Iron ore prospects at Cerro Bolivar eventually paid big dividends, becoming a major source of supply to Fairless Works.

As metals expert Christopher G. L. Hall declared in his 1997 analysis, *Steel Phoenix: The Fall and Rise of the U.S. Steel Industry* (St. Martin's Press), "In only one case did a major integrated company build an entirely new, 'greenfield' steel mill at this time…. The bulk of steelmaking investment was geared toward upgrading or 'rounding out' facilities at existing mills…chiefly because incremental expansion was far cheaper than the greenfield route."

It was a frustrating trade-off. Running flat out to produce war steel brought in the money, but it also wore out mills. And producers postponed improvements so they could get out the war goods.

The Fifties weren't perfect.

The era was young yet when Ben Fairless found out the decade had its flaws.

Offsetting the optimism and promise of good times were fears of Communism and continuing suspicion, even paranoia, of various factions and institutions. Whom could you trust, really, in this hidden, non-shooting war? Dark looks were cast toward Big Government, and Big Business, despite the job they'd done together on the previous war. There was even talk about nationalizing steel and other industries, or at least breaking up the big companies into smaller pieces, shattering their supposed power at controlling prices and touching off inflation.

Inflation, the "I" word, was very much on the mind of rough-edged Brooklyn Representative Emanuel Celler when, in January of 1950, he summoned U. S. Steel's executives to Washington for an inquiry before his Joint Committee on the Economic Report. Specifically, Celler demanded to know why, in December of 1949, U. S. Steel had dared to wave a red flag at the bull of inflation by raising prices on some of its products.

As U. S. Steel's public relations official Fred LePell later summarized the affair, then-Chairman Irving Olds opened testimony by stating his hope that "the statements presented to the committee will clarify [U. S. Steel's] position that increased costs of operation justify increased prices to cover such higher costs, and that stockholders as well as employees are entitled to consideration when determinations are made as to how United States Steel is to be operated."

Then came a line of U. S. Steel expert witnesses: Ben Fairless, Finance Committee Chairman Enders M. Voorhees, Vice President for Raw Materials John Munson, Vice President of Sales David F. Austin, and others. They presented, and explained, facts and figures demonstrating the math and the facts behind the price increases.

One member of the panel, thinking he'd trap Fairless with a trick question, demanded that the president explain the industry's seemingly complex and covert basing point system.

Without blinking, Fairless picked up three paper cups that were near a water decanter, and maneuvered them on the table in a demonstration of how the system worked. "It was the fastest explanation on record of the [pricing system]," recalled LePell. "Even the carping Celler, who thought he knew a little something about the steel business, was utterly flabbergasted by this unique demonstration showing how simple the system actually was. He promptly recessed the hearing to the following morning."

A few months later, from April 26 to 28, 1950, the same cast of executives faced yet another group of inquisitors on Senator Estes Kefauver's (D-Tenn.) Anti-Monopoly Sub-Committee. They were concerned that the corporation had been exercising destructive "monopoly powers." Fairless reviewed the necessity of profits in keeping businesses—and the nation's economy—healthy. He traced the proliferation of small businesses, told the committee how U. S. Steel relies on small businesses for its operations, and testified that U. S. Steel's competitors had grown almost four times as much as U. S. Steel since the corporation's founding in 1901.

"Since 1935," he added, "the corporation's ingot capacity had increased about 1.4 million tons. But our competitors during this period have grown 14 times as fast as we have."

Other U. S. Steel executives and experts followed. Sales Vice President David Austin described the race for quality and the dynamics of pricing, and told how steel had to compete with aluminum, copper and even glass. And he proclaimed the steel market as healthfully dynamic.

Company economist Bradford Smith cut to the quick by acknowledging that "legislation has been suggested to this subcommittee under which any company with $25 million or more of assets would have to register with a government commission and justify its continuation as a single business enterprise." Then he marched out graphs and tables to demonstrate why, in any industry, bigness should not be confused with badness.

The numbers and squiggly lines communicated the idea that, given the overall wealth and security of the country, bigness could be equated with goodness.

It's probable that at least a few of the committee's members were on an honest fact-finding mission, eager to expand their knowledge of economics and the workings of "big" business. But the familiar scent of politics was once again wafting about.

The committee proceedings and the talk of breakups reached shareholders, and provoked paranoia-tinged talk at U. S. Steel's annual meetings.

At the 1950 meeting, a shareholder stood and referred Fairless to "clippings from newspapers throughout the country in which there are persistent attacks on the United States Steel Corporation," and cited "grave fears" that the company would be nationalized.

Another shareholder, Catherine Curtis, who identified herself as representing the Women Investors in America, and who was one of the new generation of "gadflies" who needled corporate leaders to hold them to their organizations' agendas, felt obliged to deliver a clarification of her motives. It was a good example of the jumble of worries that were floating around, and it was wrapped in a warning:

> *"I feel that the stockholders should realize that we are in a totalitarian war today, the forces of labor-socialism with its agitation, the Stalin-communism forces, working against the private enterprise system and the owners, commonly known as capitalists.... Our [association's] members... feel that we are in the army of private enterprise, and we want to help fight the war. We don't want to agitate or embarrass or harass. We want to help so that our ship of capitalism will not flounder on the rocks."*

In June 1951, the Korean War had erupted, and the corporation again started a series of expansions and improvements.

The projects started in the Pittsburgh and Chicago districts. Then the company focused on its facilities in the South and West, regions where the steel market was growing. It added open hearths and stepped up blast-furnace capacity at its Tennessee Coal, Iron & Railroad Company in Alabama, and boosted ingot capacity at its Utah works.

By 1952, the company had increased its capacity by 4.3 million tons over what it had been at the end of World War II. And in 1952, besides turning up the juice at its physical operations, the company modernized its ship of capitalism on paper, streamlining its structure as a business entity.

At the start of the year, the corporation combined four subsidiaries— United States Steel Corporation of Delaware, Carnegie-Illinois Steel Corporation, H. C. Frick Coke Company and United States Coal and Coke Company. This was a move to keep up with the times, and the other guys. It meant that the corporation was shedding its structure as a sprawling holding company in favor of life as a streamlined, single operating company that was compact, quicker, more responsive to markets and customers.

United States Steel Company is Formed
January 1, 1952

United States Steel
Corporation of Delaware

Carnegie-Illinois
Steel Corporation

H. C. Frick
Coke Company

United States Coal
and Coke Company

USS

United States
Steel Company

The sleeked-down result was the United States Steel Company which was, itself, merged into the U. S. Steel Corporation at the end of the year, completing the reorganization.

(It's an intriguing legal tidbit that some smart company lawyers made a heroic effort to garner tax advantages via an argument worthy of science fiction writers. Merger papers were to be filed in New Jersey by midnight, December 31, 1952. In filing tax returns in New Jersey, the corporation declared that the mergers occurred at "a moment which is neither a part of one year nor a part of the ensuing year." New Jersey's Supreme Court was not having any of it. Its members concluded there was no interval of time that was not part of some day or year.)

But a "new" company deserved a new headquarters. It was located in Pittsburgh, at 525 William Penn Place, a gleaming, 41-story, steel-and-stone tower that made it clear Pittsburgh was the capital of steel. No surprise, the building was Fifties-sleek, its steel fabricated and erected by American Bridge.

The new company also got a new chairman. On May 6, Irving Olds reached the corporation's mandatory retirement age. The torch was passed to Fairless, who continued to hold the president's chair, as well, at least until the beginning of the next year. Then it was occupied by Clifford F. Hood, who'd started with the company some 35 years earlier as an operating clerk at an American Steel & Wire plant, and had advanced by 1951 to U. S. Steel Company's executive vice president for operations.

Nineteen fifty-two was turning out to be quite a year. The bad news was it saw another steel strike, one serious enough to compel an angry President Truman to call Chairman Fairless on the White House carpet one more time.

The stage for the 1952 strike was being set before the previous labor agreement's expiration on the last day of 1951.

U. S. Steel Labor Relations Department records show that the United Steel Workers union (USW) presented the corporation with 22 demands. They included increases in shift differentials, reporting allowances and vacation benefits.

Two demands topped the list. The first was for a wage boost of 35 cents an hour. Unlike workers in the electrical and auto industries, the steelworkers had been granted no pay raise since 1950. They figured they'd done their part in raising tonnage, and they saw that profits had gone up.

The second demand was the traditional sore point, a call for a closed shop. All workers were to sign up with the union.

The company refused to negotiate over what it considered an unreasonable package (unreasonable, especially, because of the call for the closed shop). So the union served notice that it would strike when its current contract expired at the end of 1951.

President Truman didn't need this. A steel strike, he insisted, would disrupt the flow of weapons to Korea. It also would threaten the supply of munitions and supplies going to NATO forces that were building up in Europe, and that the President considered critical to the Cold War balance of power, and to peace.

Truman turned the dispute over to the Wage Stabilization Board (WSB), and the union agreed to hold off the strike until April 8. The members of the WSB listened to weeks of hearings, then recommended a 26-cents-an-hour wage hike for the steelworkers. The union said fine. The steel companies said they couldn't live with the proposal unless it came with an okay to boost the price of steel $12 a ton. The negotiations deadlocked.

Truman thought the pay increase was reasonable. He looked at the fast-approaching strike-holdoff deadline and decreed, "We are holding the line [in Korea] with steel and not with the lives of our troops." Steel must be made.

Truman was genuinely angry at the steel companies for what he saw as selfish greed. He resorted to the measure he used to stop the railroad strike of 1946: seizure. He signed an order for the government to take

U. S. Steel's new 41-story steel-and-stone headquarters in Pittsburgh.

over steel mills across the country on April 9. "The President has the power to keep the country from going to hell," he assured his staff. And in an April 8 radio address, he told the nation, "The plain fact of the matter is that the steel companies are recklessly forcing a shutdown. They are trying to get special, preferred treatment."

On the morning of April 9, 1952, at steel mills across the country, workers went to their jobs as usual. The mills were now being run by the government. But not for long.

Congress declined to grant Truman power to take over the mills. Major papers and news magazines attacked Truman; he'd been "high-handed" and had "grossly usurped the power of Congress." It was a balance-of-power issue. "Nothing in the Constitution," intoned *The Washington Post*, "can be reasonably interpreted as giving to the Commander in Chief all the power that may be necessary for building up our defenses or even for carrying on a war."

It was a humiliating defeat for the President, and the strike went on for what was then a record, 54 days.

Truman had had enough. He called Murray and Fairless to the White House. As Fairless described the scene in his *Life* memoir, Truman looked across his desk at him:

"Ben," he said, "you can settle this strike."

"Alone?" Fairless responded.

Truman looked at Murray.

"Phil, you can settle this strike."

No answer.

Then Fairless and Murray were ushered into an outer office and left alone.

In that room, the pair rehashed a compromise that Fairless had proposed earlier, that steel would require that new employees sign a union application, but that they would have a 30-day grace period in which to withdraw it. Murray accepted the compromise within five minutes, recalled the steel chief. When Fairless said, "Fine, let's go tell the President," Murray countered, "Oh, no. Think of all those newspapermen out there. We've got to make this look more difficult."

"So," Fairless wrote, "we sat and talked baseball and swapped jokes…. Murray, a good Catholic, told me a story about a priest at a prizefight…. The priest, an old fight fan, took along a Protestant minister who had never seen any boxing. In the first fight, one of the boys crossed himself before leaving his corner. 'Father, will that help him?' the Protestant asked. 'It will if he can fight,' said the priest.

"After an hour, Murray said, 'All right, let's go,' and we broke off our talk session and announced that the strike was over."

Fairless would insist that, for Murray, the whole strike was really over a closed shop. That made the compromise finally palatable to the labor leader.

But there was a larger lesson here.

The Murray–Fairless White House gab session demonstrated how well the two men got along, despite their differences. They treated each other with respect, agreeing to disagree when they had to; agreeing on issues where they could. When Murray died not long after the 1952 strike, Fairless worked to build the same kind of relationship with Murray's successor, affable, pipe-puffing David McDonald.

"Despite the strikes and near strikes, management and labor kept making progress toward understanding one another," Fairless said in his memoirs. "By the time Phil Murray died and David McDonald moved up to the president of the United Steelworkers, we had come so far that McDonald and I were able to try something completely unique in management–labor relations."

And so, on November 17, 1953, the two started off on a tour of U. S. Steel plants.

This was no junket, but a serious effort to get to the heart of what the steelworkers and managers at each site had on their minds.

Before the fact-finding mission, Fairless, now chairman, went before the union's wage and policy committee in Washington to help McDonald sell them on what the two had in mind.

"We are not going just to brush by," he told the committee members. "We are going to sit down and talk with the union's representatives and management's representatives in the various locations. In that way, I hope to find out what is in your mind, what you are thinking. And I hope that you, in turn, may learn something of my problems."

The two traveled separately, and met at the plants for the visits. They started in Cleveland, and from there went to other mills in other districts. They talked with workers in the mills and across the lunch table, in what McDonald described at the outset as a mission "to find the causes of industrial peace rather than the causes of industrial strife."

Fairless was careful to clarify for the workers his and his company's agenda: "[that] we wholeheartedly accepted the union, and that we would in no way attempt to weaken or destroy it."

"I also made it clear that I thought the union had grave responsibilities, that in order to represent its members properly, it must recognize the problems and duties of management and the fact that the stockholders also had important rights.

"McDonald, for his part, always said the union recognized the right of management to manage the business. He agreed the public had a right to be recognized, and that it was imperative that management and labor work together as a team in the best interest of all concerned."

U. S. Steel President Benjamin Fairless (left) and David McDonald, president of the United Steelworkers, embarked on a tour of U. S. Steel plants in 1953 to help foster better management–labor relations.

The two were criticized for being too cozy with each other, but only history would judge how much the tour advanced company-union relations. "But I would do the same thing again if the occasion arose," Fairless wrote later, "and I believe McDonald would, too."

Fairless' tenure as chairman was short and uneventful compared with his years as president, when he had scuffled with a U.S. President and Congress, and kept pushing U. S. Steel's capacity upward. There'd been quite a few highs back then, though. Lows, too, like the amusing moments during the company's annual meeting in May 1954.

Fairless probably saw it coming when Wilma Soss rose to speak.

Soss was president of the Federation of Women Shareholders, and by now had addressed those assembled at several of the corporation's annual meetings. She'd delivered some constructive comments and suggestions for the good of shareholders, but she'd gained a reputation as a notorious activist. Just before the 1954 annual meeting, she wrote to Fairless on behalf of the members of her organization, encouraging him to take some "deflationary" actions.

"As stockholders of U. S. Steel, we note with concern that you appear to have put on a considerable amount of weight. With so much publicity being given to the importance of maintaining a slim and youthful figure to avoid heart and other ills, [we'd] like to see our board chairman keep in good physical trim."

The prescription was not really about Fairless' health, of course. The *Pittsburgh Press* relayed the clarification Soss made before the other shareholders: "The boys begin to live pretty well when they become executives.... We don't like them to sit on too many boards, and we want them to conserve their health. It's better for business—and our dividends."

The *Press* did not record Fairless' reaction, but the minutes of the meeting preserved his playful rejoinder. Not until he received Mrs. Soss's letter, he said, "did I realize that I carried any great weight with the kindly (lady), nor had I suspected even remotely that (she) was concerned with keeping my blood pressure down.... I am glad to report, in fact, that I lost several pounds, that I have had to pull in my belt a couple of notches and that I am in excellent fighting trim."

During the 1954 meeting, too, several women shareholders lamented the absence of a female on U. S. Steel's board. Mrs. Soss even proposed such a candidate, the former chairman of the American Silk Spinning Company. The nomination failed. But it prompted a swift chauvinistic comment from one shareholder, Dr. Frederick Griffith: "Until U. S. Steel starts making nylon stockings, steelmaking is no job for the petticoats."

Fairless was able to swerve during the meeting from harsh opinion to hard facts: Fairless Works had started production; first shipments of concentrated taconite ore had begun flowing from Minnesota; the production and shipment of iron ore had commenced at Cerro Bolivar, in Venezuela.

He also proudly announced to shareholders: "[In] 1953, sales equaled almost $4 billion…. [Our] biggest year during World War II was just over $2 billion."

The following year's annual meeting was a Fairless lovefest.

The chairman announced his retirement, and the shareholders gave him a standing ovation. During his career as president and chairman, he'd helped lead the company through war production, overseen the purchase of the Geneva plant, converted the company to peacetime production and dealt with the union in a way that was positive and fresh. Arguably, he had accomplished more than most—perhaps all—of the men who preceded him.

Following Fairless as chairman was a man who would take the corporation and its employees into an era tougher than any which had gone before it.

Roger M. Blough

Roger Miles Blough, son of a just-over-subsistence truck farmer, had worked his way up from plowing fields and laboring at U. S. Steel's Johnstown plant to a glowing career with a New York law firm, White & Case. There, he helped advise U. S. Steel on legal matters. His preparation and research caught the eye of U. S. Steel executives, and, in 1942, he was appointed the corporation's general solicitor in Pittsburgh and given the responsibility for preparing and executing the plan that would transform U. S. Steel from a sprawling holding company into an integrated operating company. It became increasingly obvious that behind Blough's modest demeanor were considerable talents, and a mind so sharp about company affairs that rumor soon had it that its owner would be tapped as chairman.

Rumor turned out to be fact. Blough was named chairman in May of 1955.

Blough didn't talk a lot, preferring to listen to all facts and opinions before proclaiming a decision. *Fortune* magazine summed him up this way: "Wary and prudent, he seems determined to avoid uttering a single word that might someday be held against him." But behind the spectacles and the cautious façade were a refusal to take nonsense from anyone and a sense of humor that was dry as a desert. *Fortune* related the way, back in 1950, counselor Blough had used both traits to deflect heat at the Celler Committee hearings. One of the committee members was baiting the corporation's witness with the controversial but decades-old Ford, Bacon & Davis engineering study about U. S. Steel. It was like a teacher making a student stand in the corner for something his grandfather had done. "And what," Blough interjected quietly, "do you think an engineer's report on Congress would look like?"

Not long after he moved into the chairman's office, Blough found himself before still another congressional committee dedicated to getting to the heart of inflation, the Senate subcommittee led by Senator Kefauver of Tennessee.

Kefauver had made a name for himself for taking a couple of runs (in 1952 and 1956) at the Presidency, and for wearing a coonskin hat when campaigning. In 1950 and 1951, he had toured the country at the head of a traveling, televised, state-by-state series of hearings on organized crime. Witnesses included crime boss Frank Costello and gangster Bugsy Siegel's girlfriend, Virginia Hill, who, McCullough reminded us, wore a $5,000 silver-blue mink stole and pronounced a curse on the committee: "I hope a goddam atom bomb falls on every goddam one of you."

If there was a threat of guilt by association, U. S. Steel had nothing to hide. Concerned about public ignorance of the real causes and effects of inflation, the corporation printed a book containing statements from U. S. Steel officials including Blough, and made the book available to employees and some of the nation's thought leaders.

At the top of one of the first pages was a photo of Blough, gazing solemnly just above the reader's head, his hands clasped in an apparent prayer that the servants of the public good might finally grasp the mysteries of inflation and leave him to his work.

Blough must have had fun writing the testimony. It was a wry address which seemed to come from a bemused teacher whose fifth graders could not pass social studies by impressing him with knowledge, so they tried to baffle him with balderdash.

"I have read with deep interest, and with understandable perplexity, the conflicting testimony of the distinguished economists who have appeared before you at these hearings," Blough began.

"I have studied their differing definition of the term 'administered prices.' I have sought to comprehend that stillborn economic concept called the 'zone of relative price indifference.' I have struggled with the impossible paradox known as 'monopolistic competition,' and pursuing my research even farther into the semantic stratosphere of economic literature, I have encountered 'atomistic heteropoly' and 'differentiated polyopoly.' Clearly, this is no place for simple iron puddlers, so with your permission, I'll just try to keep it simple by avoiding the pitfalls of economic theory.... "

Then, in testimony that brought back memories of the Celler hearings seven years earlier, Blough and other U. S. Steel witnesses set out to dispel the myths of inflation, and the corporation's supposed role in perpetuating it.

Blough, himself, cited a contemporary *New York Times* analysis that demonstrated that it was the price of services, not industrial products, that had been increasing: "Edwin L. Dale, Jr., the *Times* economic correspondent," Blough announced, "showed...that the price of *things* which people bought [since 1952] had remained relatively stable, but the price of services—or non-things, such as transportation, medical care, laundry, haircuts, rents, and so on—had risen substantially."

Then he quoted the *Times*:

"Though it may seem surprising, the price of steel could practically double and the cost of living would hardly show it. Between 1951 and 1955, the price of steel rose 14 percent; but the price of household appliances...actually declined by 13 percent."

Misunderstandings about economics and policy were part of the job, sometimes a source of amusement, usually the origin of frustration. Other events brought heartbreak. These were the disasters, and Blough was weighed down by more than his share. During his term as chairman, U. S. Steel and its people suffered three great tragedies. Two struck in the Sixties (we'll learn about them in a later chapter).

The first of three—the November 18, 1958, sinking of the limestone freighter *Carl D. Bradley*—floated a black cloud over the corporation for years. Thirty-three seamen were lost. The toll included the ship's 52-year-old skipper, Captain Roland Bryan, who, according to a *Detroit News* account, radioed a "May Day! May Day!" message as the ship foundered a mere 100 miles from her home port of Calcite Harbor, Michigan.

The Steamer Carl D. Bradley, *second largest vessel in Michigan Limestone Division's Bradley Transportation Line, sank on storm-tossed waters of Lake Michigan on November 18, 1958. Only two of the ship's 35-man crew survived.*

Only two of the ship's 35-man crew survived to tell their tragic story:

The 639-foot-long *Bradley*, one of the mighty vessels of U. S. Steel's Great Lakes fleet, had discharged a load of open-hearth limestone at the corporation's Gary Works and was cruising northeast on Lake Michigan, bound for Lansing Shoal in northern Michigan, when it ran into a violent storm and buckled amidships. She sank within minutes. As cold water struck her hot boilers, they exploded, signaling the end of what was then the largest ship to be lost in the Great Lakes.

Most of the crewmen were able to board a lifeboat before the *Bradley* went down. But the violent waves capsized the small craft, tossing the men into the frigid waters of Lake Michigan. Four other crewmen took refuge aboard a life raft. But towering waves kept capsizing the raft, and only two men—the wreck's only survivors—managed to stay with the raft through the night. "I got pretty scared when I found out there was ice forming in my hair and there was ice encrusted in my jacket," one of the survivors, First Mate Elmer Fleming, told a reporter from the *Presque Isle County Advance*, a paper based in Rogers City, Michigan.

Why had the *Bradley* sunk? There are no clear answers.

In a letter written to his wife 10 days before the wreck, Captain Bryan suggested that the 31-year-old ship was suffering wear and tear—that it was "getting pretty ripe for too much weather." But, as newspaper accounts revealed, the vessel had a history of consistently proper maintenance. It had been inspected only a half-year before its sinking, and pronounced seaworthy. In fact, as the Soo (Michigan) *Evening News* reported on June 12, 1959, "Ironically, the *Bradley* was lost seven months after the Bradley Line received the National Safety Council's highest award for establishing a new world safety record for the marine transportation industry."

The Coast Guard conducted studies, including sonar scans of the hull under 30 feet of water. But the sonar scans revealed no signs of catastrophic structural damage that could have caused the wreck. The only suggestion the Coast Guard could offer was that the ship had developed recent, undetectable, structural weaknesses.

Soon after the disaster, the people of Michigan and other states set up a fund for the children of the victims. Although U. S. Steel was not charged with negligence or wrongdoing, it was legally liable, under maritime laws, for a settlement of $575,000. The corporation's final settlement—which went into the children's fund—was $1.3 million.

Money couldn't heal all the heartache, but Roger Blough knew words could help. Soon after news of the sinking broke, he flew to Rogers City, Michigan. The town was home to most of the *Bradley*'s crewmen, and it was to their families and friends that the chairman spoke.

During a personal address, he told the townspeople that Christian Beukema, president of the corporation's Michigan Limestone Division, would soon visit their grieving families.

Then he added: "To many of us [at U. S. Steel], the men of the *Bradley* have long been personal friends as well as business associates. Words cannot express the sympathy we feel for the families and loved ones of those men who perished."

Fortunately, few of Blough's actions as chairman had to do with events that were so disheartening. One of his first was even rousing: the orchestration of a whopping $2.9 billion modernization of the corporation's plants.

The huge upgrade, to be implemented from 1955 to 1962, was applauded by *Fortune* in a January 1956 review of U. S. Steel: "Thanks to a swiftly rising efficiency, the Corporation…is setting a postwar record in profitability….

> *"To keep pace with the economy's growth, the Corporation this year will probably spend several hundred million on replacements and new plant, including a large addition to its great new Fairless Works. And its new chairman, Roger Blough, who had remarked that one of the most important changes the Corporation has undergone is change itself, looks forward to many more changes."*

The magazine cited renewed resolution to compete: "The Corporation has grasped the fact that the greatest service any company can render society is steadily improving its efficiency. It had integrated operations wherever it could, eliminating duplications and overlaps in manufacturing, sales, research, and purchases. But it has made its most dramatic advances out in the plants, where…it has increased its efficiency about 25 percent in five years."

A lot of that increase came by exercising brainpower. "Most of the Corporation's improvement in plant efficiency is to eliminate the bottlenecks that prevent each piece of equipment from being used more intensively," *Fortune* noted. "Corporation engineers are constantly hunting these bottlenecks." At Gary, for example, the company added a reheating furnace and some controls to a 1936 vintage hot-strip mill. "By 1956, the mill was rolling more than three million tons—employing no more man-hours than it took to roll 600,000 tons in 1936."

The company and its engineers had a word for this ratcheting-up of efficiency: beneficiation. *Now*, of course, was always the time to do things more efficiently. But the corporation was concentrating even more on improving what it made, creating new and better steels by working right down at the level of molecules.

Science was on everyone's mind. The company had already bought one of those giant computers, a UNIVAC, an awesome assemblage of cabinets with spinning tape wheels and refrigerator-door–sized control panels loaded with lights and buttons and switches. The corporation was one of the first metal companies to get a UNIVAC after Remington Rand started selling them to industry. The "electronic brain" sprawled over 3,000 square feet of National Tube's general offices in Pittsburgh, and figured out the payroll at breathtaking speed. Employees called it "Friday," after the detective on the popular *Dragnet* TV show.

Science was on U. S. Steel's mind in another way, as well. In May of 1956, hundreds of community leaders joined reporters and customers flocking to a hilltop in Western Pennsylvania to behold the corporation's latest investment in tomorrow: an elegant, college-campus–like research center.

Partial view of U. S. Steel's new Applied Research Laboratory which covered 142 acres near Pittsburgh's Monroeville suburb

Constructed as several joined buildings, extending over grounds that totaled 142 acres near Pittsburgh's Monroeville suburb, this would be the place where, eventually, 1,700 chemists, metallurgists and other technologists would bend over microscopes, spectroscopes and X-ray machines. This is where they would engage in the heady business of probing the internal mysteries of steel, applying their discoveries to improve the grades the company made, and to create steel that, until now, the industry could only dream about.

Judge Elbert Gary had dreamed of such a place when he headed the corporation in the early Twenties. It took years, some ironing out of differences, and some disappointments before the company could build a lab this sophisticated. Still, its science wizard had formulated stronger, higher-performance, marvelous new kinds of steel. Dream steel. Who knew what wonders they would perform in this new lab?

Creating wonders was important because they could take some of the heat out of the tense, U.S.–Soviet Union relations. And U. S. Steel was on guard. It was even working with the National Advisory

Committee for Aeronautics—NACA—to develop rocket planes that blazed through the sky at more than 2,000 miles an hour.

There were problems to be worked out. Problems such as how to make a plane fly that fast or faster without cracking its skin, or cracking up or burning up because of air friction. U. S. Steel worked with NACA on a wind tunnel made of the company's tomorrowish "T-1" steel, and that could cook planes at more than 4,000 degrees Fahrenheit without melting.

The cold war, and NACA's heat war, grew more urgent the next year when the Soviets spun a beeping, metal beachball called *Sputnik* around the globe. To its harried agenda the nation added beating the Soviets in space, and NACA soon evolved into NASA—the National Aeronautics and Space Administration.

For flying, and other purposes, steel was the right stuff, and U. S. Steel *was* learning more about how to beat the drum over the metal and its futuristic uses.

The company's image makers and marketing people were getting more sophisticated at the art of persuading the public to see the extent to which steel was—or should be—part of their lives.

Viewers knew steel was special when they watched the opening of the classy and popular television show the company sponsored, when the steelworkers sent a torrent of sparks flying across the TV screen as the announcer intoned: "It's The United States Steel Hour."

U. S. Steel *was* steel. It meant industry. It was a national icon.

The new "Steel Hour" was the popular radio show brought to television. Its premiere play dealt with psychological problems of American servicemen returning from Korean prisoner-of-war camps, and it was hailed by critics and viewers as a TV triumph.

The play was gritty and timely. Gary Merrill portrayed an Army psychiatrist, Richard Kiley his soldier–patient. Rosters for following broadcasts included Eddie Albert, Rex Harrison and Lillie Palmer.

Performed "live," before the days of videotape, the shows were electrifying.

Television clearly was powerful as a communication tool, and the company used it in ways that were clever and tasteful. Later, some called this the Golden Age of Television, the era when Rod Serling and the other Young Turks of Hollywood wrote grown-up scripts, and when plays were acted by top stars.

In 1960, U. S. Steel would recruit John Sutherland Productions, Inc., to produce an animated, educational film for schools and TV, in which elegant cartoon characters took viewers through the history of steel. Famed composer Dimitri Tiomkin wrote the musical score for the film, *Rhapsody of Steel*.

During these days, U. S. Steel was doing things that made the heart race.

U. S. Steel and American Bridge wound up the Fifties by finishing the Mackinac Bridge, the world's longest suspension bridge, a five-mile span that tied Michigan's upper peninsula to the rest of it.

The corporation supplied much of the 57,000 tons of steel that went into the nation's newest aircraft carrier, the *USS Independence*. The ship carried more than 100 jets. It was almost a quarter-mile long, and was topped with a four-acre flight deck.

The hood of a new car looked like an aircraft carrier flight deck when viewed from the driver's seat. Cars were getting more popular, and bulkier. We loved them.

Tempting to shoppers, too, were all the other good things made of steel, from clocks to cookware, from furniture that was made of steel that was vinyl-coated to furniture that was made of steel that was not. Mountains of products. The company made a mountain, too, by fabricating and erecting the 450 tons of steel beams that supported the Matterhorn, a new attraction at Disneyland.

Popular actors and actresses appeared in "The United States Steel Hour," which was televised "live" from New York.

What would life be without steel? That was the point when U. S. Steel and the rest of the industry put on "Steelmark Days," a festival in which towns across the country that made and sold anything that was steel joined in a festival to the metal.

It was a blitz to sell steel, and a time to celebrate steel, to feel good about making it. It was parades, floats saluting steel and local steel plants, and lots of coverage in the papers. Posters in the windows of appliance stores displayed the steel industry's new symbol, the Steelmark, a cluster of three starlike shapes emblazoned on tags and labels stuck on products made of steel—and on the helmets of the Pittsburgh Steelers.

For decades afterward, trivia buffs would stump their friends by asking them what the steel industry called those pointy, starlike shapes. The answer: hypocycloids.

Steel was anything but trivial, and it was riding high. But on the horizon, events were stirring that would nudge steel off its throne.

The first, in 1959, was a 110-day strike that would play a big part in turning what was a trickle of steel imports into a stream. The stream would grow into a river, the river into a flood that threatened to drown American steel.

Nothing would be the same.

HIGH TIME FOR RESEARCH

We were bombarded with TV reports about harnessing the atom. We were in orbit over the "space race" and its visions of rockets to Mars. We explored magazine imaginings of future cities, forests of towers amid tangles of elevated, computer-run highways. Our cars would drive us where we wanted to go.

At first glance, the Fifties seems the perfect decade for U. S. Steel to have opened a sleek, central, campus-like research and technology lab near Pittsburgh—to gather its best brains in one spot, let the sparks fly and illuminate new ideas.

That was what U. S. Steel's Monroeville lab, opened in 1956, was about. But why did U. S. Steel wait until 1956 to open its dream lab, stimulating and promising as it was? Why not 1920? Or right off the founders' bat, in 1901?

The reason has to do with a permanently established tug-of-war being fought in industries of all kinds over these questions: Where should we put our research dollars? Should we use them to chase big ideas that could turn out to be phantoms? Put them into ideas that were obvious moneymakers?

Many U. S. Steel scientists and technicians and like-minded managers argued for "pure" research, probes into the mostly uncharted waters of science and technology. This required expensive equipment, and a central lab, where researchers could build on each others' knowledge and ideas. And it was highly speculative, a hefty gamble fishing in these waters with hopes of snagging new processes or creating new materials— maybe entirely new technologies. Such catches were rare. But they often were worth fortunes.

Then there were those who were more conservative, and those of more practical bent who argued the company should do more prodding into technologies and materials that were already proven. Discoveries in well-traveled waters weren't usually big "eurekas." They usually didn't pay off as generously. But they happened more often.

The debate about research and development—R&D—in U. S. Steel goes back to the days before the company was U. S. Steel, when Andrew Carnegie's inventive Captain Jones tinkered with Bessemers and the very earliest open-hearth furnaces. Experimentation went on at most, if not all, the mills right from the start.

It was Judge Elbert Gary who took the first steps to stimulate inventiveness further by centralizing research.

This building in the Oakland district of Pittsburgh was the first full building to be utilized as the corporation's research laboratory.

*F*rom the early 1920s until his death in 1927, Gary lobbied his board and the presidents of U. S. Steel's constituent companies to establish a central lab that would coordinate and expand the research being done at plants and other sites throughout the country.

Most of these projects were basic, focused on improving the specific steel product made at each plant or company. In R&D at these sites, the emphasis was on the "D"—development. At American Sheet and Tin Plate Company, for example, technologists worked away in a converted row house, and pioneered in adding copper to steel to fight atmospheric corrosion. The work led to corrosion-resistant Cor-Ten steel. National Tube's Pittsburgh lab tackled the problem of corrosion in pipe.

But all too often, the results of this development remained local secrets. The reason: egos. Plant superintendents didn't like to share research findings. Many didn't even know or understand what their own engineers were up to. Those engineers played it close to the vest, too; the boss might pinch pennies if he found out what they were doing.

The secretive, helter-skelter approach guaranteed that projects would be duplicated, and results hidden.

Gary had watched all this, and, in 1926, he took action.

A few weeks after the 1926 stockholders meeting—where a shareholder had groused that the corporation had no facility to compare with Bell Telephone's much-in-the-news, highly inventive central lab—Gary called together his presidents.

"The time has come," he told them, "when the United States Steel Corporation . . . must be prepared to do anything and everything to advance the art and science of steelmaking and

Dr. John Johnston, first director of U. S. Steel's centralized Research Department at Kearny, New Jersey

utilization, and our disposition is to leave no excuse for allowing others to get ahead of us, to lead us, in the discovery and development of new things...."

Then Gary formed a committee, whose first, unsurprising recommendation came within a month: "The United States Steel Corporation should establish a General Research Department."

Gary had won. Now came a round of visits to industrial laboratories by Gary and his ally, George Crawford, president of Tennessee Coal, Iron & Railroad Company. Crawford was a board member, and a central-lab advocate. The two were searching for models for a U. S. Steel lab. They were also looking for research directors, and, during one of his forays, Crawford found their man.

He was Dr. John Johnston, chairman of Yale's chemistry department and a consultant to Bell Laboratory's president, Dr. Frank B. Jewett. (Jewett, in turn, would become a consultant to U. S. Steel.) Dr. Johnston was enthusiastic about his new role in the corporation. But he was a visitor from academe, and he would soon be bitterly disappointed in this new world.

One of the first jobs Johnston assigned himself was a fact-finding tour of U. S. Steel's subsidiaries, and visits with those subsidiaries' research people. In a brief memoir he wrote in 1948, after retiring, he noted that he'd come away from those meetings convinced that some nagging problems were getting "rather casual and superficial attention." But facts were hard to get. Employees were reluctant to even talk about problems, "particularly in the presence of superiors..., that some men who thought they had some special knowledge of some piece of the art obviously wished to keep it to themselves."

The visits hardened Johnston's and Gary's conviction that their new laboratory should be far from U. S. Steel's plants, politics and petty jealousies. Johnston checked sites near New York City and U. S. Steel's headquarters. But when he returned to headquarters to report his findings to Gary, he was shocked to learn that Gary, his champion, had died.

Now Dr. Johnston reported to U. S. Steel President James Farrell, who was cool to centralized research. Johnston knew Farrell had been overheard to observe, "This research department is just a gesture."

It was a painful remark, and another setback. But Dr. Johnston returned to his hunt. Finally, he decided on acreage in Harrison, New York. It was well-served by utilities and transportation, and near an attractive residential neighborhood.

It would be a stimulating retreat for science, and a nice place for scientists to live and raise their families.

On a snowy day in March of 1928, President Farrell and the rest of the Finance Committee toured the site. And they vetoed it. Why build here? U. S. Steel already owned a perfectly fine piece of land in Kearny, New Jersey, at the company's Federal Shipbuilding & Dry Dock Company. That site even had an unused building that could be converted into a lab.

Dr. Johnston, stunned, checked the Kearny location. What he found crushed him, but he tried to make the best of it: "I like neither the location nor the building," he wrote in his memoir, "yet (I) had to admit that the west end of the building could be altered so that it would serve as a . . . temporary laboratory."

Far from temporary, it would serve Dr. Johnston and the staff he assembled for more than two decades, until the eventual move to Monroeville. Despite his letdowns, Johnston was determined to make the best of the hand he was dealt. He signed up a star team, a roster that included Robert Sossman of the U.S. Geophysical Laboratory, and Edgar Bain, who'd done research for an alloy steel company before joining Union Carbide. By the end of 1929, the research staff numbered 18.

The lab was in business. And its first challenge was to attack cracks in steel rail, a low-tech problem, but a headache which dated to Carnegie days. Steel produced the fissures, which caused the rail to fail. Customers said the rail was inferior. Steelmen claimed the railroads were at fault, that they'd run trains that were too heavy, or that they didn't maintain the track. Johnston had observed that rails rolled in winter were more likely to crack than rails rolled in summer. He deduced that summer rails were stronger because they cooled more slowly. Soon the mills were slowing cooling rates—and producing top-of-the-line rail.

By the mid-Thirties, Bain was well along in his studies of "solid-state metallurgy," which dealt with steel after casting in molds. In his memoir, Pioneering in Steel Research, a Personal Record *(American Society for Metals, 1975), Bain wrote about hypotheses that were once considered "unorthodox" and "wild," but that resulted in major advances in metallurgy.*

Put together the right brains, and they make the impossible happen. It would happen again and again in the minds and laboratories of the corporation's research department.

Dr. Edgar C. Bain served as U. S. Steel's vice president—research and technology from 1942 until his retirement in late 1946. The Edgar C. Bain Laboratory for Fundamental Research at U. S. Steel's Research Center in Monroeville, Pennsylvania, is named in his honor.

TOOLS AND TOYS

For the rocket-powered, supersonic Fifties, steel was the thing.

What else—aluminum? It was creeping up on steel, but it didn't have the heft, the serious feel of steel.

Plastic? Please.

Steel was it. The stove, refrigerator, clothes washer and dryer and the hand-cranked can opener mounted on the kitchen wall were steel. So was the vacuum cleaner, which was built like a tank, but still looked good; steel was strong, yet it could be formed into the curvy, streamlined shapes that symbolized the era.

Strength plus style, that was steel. It made a lot of products look good, especially products of shiny stainless steel, or chrome-plated steel. How many people carried shiny Zippo lighters?

American consumers served food in steel bowls, wore steel jewelry, sat on sofas and chairs that had spindly, minimalist, steel legs. Steel was in the cool clock that replaced numerals with little spheres, and that looked like an ad-man's drawing of an atom. After all, this was the start of the atomic age. U. S. Steel's Gary Works even made the steel for the 80-foot-diameter, 10-story dome that capped the nation's first nuclear power plant, at Lemont, Illinois.

In atomic or conventional power plants, as in factories and machines, steel worked hard for us. But kids still played with steel. It was in toy trains, cap guns and the metal forts and doll houses parents patiently assembled for their youngsters on Christmas morning.

The family had fun, too, watching the TV, whose picture got bigger and better, thanks in part to U. S. Steel; the company built a steel cone that reinforced TV picture tubes, and that allowed manufacturers to make those tubes—and the image—larger and larger. Paired with image was sound; steel was incorporated in new, truer-sounding hi-fi equipment.

We couldn't get away from steel, but why would we want to? It was no-nonsense, sleek. It said industry, science, progress, speed.

The place it said those things loudest was in our cars.

Fifties Fords, Dodges and Caddies were rolling showcases of steel. Relatively demure in style at the start of the decade, the automobile kept growing in bulk, and chrome baubles. At their biggest and brightest, they looked like yachts. Or circus wagons. At the same time, they grew in power, running on mighty, usually-eight-cylinder engines that belted gasoline like there was no tomorrow. But we loved them—enough to pay the car companies extra to retool every year for a fall event that ranked with the World Series: the Unveiling of the New Models.

By the end of the Fifties, cars were starting to tone down. The 1959 models were longer and lower than the previous years, though. And they still sported dinner-plate-sized taillights, massive

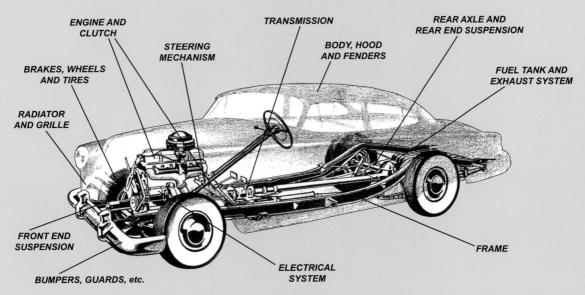

ENGINE AND CLUTCH

STEERING MECHANISM

TRANSMISSION

REAR AXLE AND REAR END SUSPENSION

BODY, HOOD AND FENDERS

BRAKES, WHEELS AND TIRES

FUEL TANK AND EXHAUST SYSTEM

RADIATOR AND GRILLE

FRONT END SUSPENSION

BUMPERS, GUARDS, etc.

ELECTRICAL SYSTEM

FRAME

This cutaway shows the uses of steel in a typical 1952 four-door sedan by a large auto manufacturer. Castings of iron and steel are not included.

chrome-steel bumpers, and grinning, chrome-steel grilles. The fins were there, too. On the '59 Chevy, instead of upward and backward, they swept outward, suggesting a giant, steel gull.

What wasn't visible, though, was the more than 100 different grades of steel that were used in the '59s.

"In terms of what today's steel can give to the modern motor car in strength combined with beauty," crowed U S Steel News, "it can be truly said that steel is autodom's most precious metal."

U. S. Steel's carbon sheets, alloy steel and stainless were common in cars by 1959. New was aluminum-coated sheet steel, a grade that combined the otherwise competing metals in a way that added to a muffler's ability to fight heat and corrosion. Not new, but used in greater quantities, were shiny stainless steel, and United States Steel Par-Ten, an

unusually strong, "carbon-vanadium" alloy ideal for bumpers.

Whatever steel they were made of, though, cars were big, heavy and fast. But catching up with these models was a relative newcomer, the funny-looking, stripped-down, shrunken-down Volkswagen. Accessories? It didn't have much more than four wheels and an engine, and it putted along on four cylinders.

The "Beetle's" appeal was the car's simplicity. It hardly broke, and it was easy to fix. It was happy to be basic. And it was attracting a counterculture— army vets who'd been hooked by the little cars in Germany, and economy-minded college kids who thought the "bug" was cute.

Detroit, though, was looking at the VW in the rearview mirror, and laughing. But not for long.

Chapter 11

The Turning Point

American steel entered worrisome territory in 1959.

For one thing, 1959 turned out to be the first year that the United States imported more steel than it exported. Imports first exceeded exports in December of 1958. But 1959 takes the dubious honor as the pivotal year for imports, and the beginning of the era in which domestic steel users would buy increasingly more steel from abroad than from producers at home.

Also turning 1959 sour for U. S. Steel and its fellow producers was a costly, bitterly fought, national steel strike that lasted for a record 116 days. It would have gone on even longer, except that President Eisenhower—following a tradition established by his predecessors—got fed up and forced a settlement.

The two milestones, the surging imports and the strike, were related symptoms of a worsening economic illness. But the first, the tip toward foreign imports, rang the loudest alarm: Once a symbol of American might, domestic steel was being beaten in its own home.

It was still king of the hill, but it was slipping. The signs that it was in trouble had been there for some time for whoever cared to read them.

Behind all the Fifties hope and hype was a discouraging truth: If the nation was enjoying a boom, steel was not.

Certainly, as the Fifties rolled out, sales and profits seemed encouraging enough. In 1950, U. S. Steel reported record sales of $2.9 billion, and a net profit of $215.5 million. Sales wavered up and down, hitting another record, $4.4 billion, in 1957. Net profits peaked at $419.4 million that year.

But other numbers revealed a worrisome trend, one the industry spotted too late: No matter how the overall economy fared, demand for American steel remained flat between 1950 and 1960. In a chart in his book *Steel Phoenix*, metals consultant Christopher Hall told the story in one snapshot: After starting at 70.2 million net tons in 1950, consumption of American steel took a few hops up and down, but ended up in 1960 at 71 million tons.

U. S. Steel's production of finished products followed the trend. The company produced 22.6 million tons in 1950, and, with the exception of a few blips, remained level through the Fifties. Furthermore, it would stay level into the Sixties.

One reason for the stagnation was those imports. They kept nibbling away at U.S. producers' share of their markets. As Donald F.

Steel imports contributed to the drop in demand for American steel during the Fifties. This shipment of structural steel arrived in Chicago from Antwerp, Belgium, via the St. Lawrence Seaway.

Barnett and Louis Schorsch set the scene in their book *Steel: Upheaval in a Basic Industry* (Ballinger Publishing Company, 1983), the United States produced more than 45 percent of the world's raw steel in 1950. But, as Barnett and Schorsch acknowledged, this "awesome status was an anomaly." Steel's standing would decline as U.S. producers lost business to competitors in Japan, Great Britain, Germany, even Russia.

The real question was why, compared to its competitors in other countries, was America's once-mighty steel industry regressing?

A number of forces and factors were at work. Among them:

A global wage gap: Foreign producers paid lower wages than Americans. It was an impressive difference—especially during the 15 years after World War II. By 1957, according to a chart printed in *U S Steel News*, American steelworkers were earning $2.92 an hour while hourly wages were $1 in Australia, just under 75 cents in West Germany and about 45 cents in Japan. U.S. steelworkers were more productive, but by only enough to make up for half the wage differential. American steel's ability to compete on price kept eroding.

Competition from other materials: "The U.S. economy's steel intensity—the consumption of steel per million dollars of Gross National Product, adjusted for inflation—fell by 25 percent during the decade of the 1950s," according to Hall. The reasons: Concrete, aluminum and plastics were replacing steel in many applications. Lighter gauges of steel—which meant less steel—were being used in products such as automobiles. Most important, according to Hall, was a "shift within the economy toward products that were less steel-intensive, as heavy, capital goods declined in importance compared to the rise of personal consumption goods."

Temporary demand for heavy steel, such as war goods for the Korean conflict, didn't do much to offset the trends. Meanwhile, observed Hall, Japan and most of Western Europe were "still growing in the steel intensity of their economies, as they promoted the growth of industrial sectors such as heavy machinery."

The rebirth of foreign steel plants: Wartime destruction of their plants left producers lagging behind. But, with the benefit of financial aid from the United States, they had completed most of their rebuilding by 1950. The plants that rose from the ashes of the war were among the world's most modern. As industrial economists-analysts Barnett and Schorsch insisted, those new plants still lagged America technologically. Still, the gap kept shrinking.

Playing it safe with new technology: The U.S. steel industry had enjoyed a healthy lead in technology—an advantage that, according to Barnett and Schorsch, more than made up for economic disadvantage imposed by the gap between U.S. steel wages and what foreign producers paid their workers. But the technological and wage advantages withered as American producers grew conservative when it came time for them to invest in new technologies.

American producers had made healthy investments at the ends of their lines by putting money into new hot-strip mills, which pressed steel out into finished, flat rolls. The producers' objective: to meet a growing demand for flat-rolled steel. But it was a different story at the front of the line, where the basic iron and steel were made. There, U.S. producers stuck with what they knew, spending millions during the Fifties on new open-hearth furnaces. But the open hearths were soon to become dinosaurs. Steelmakers in other countries, notably Japan, were passing them up in favor of newly emerging Basic Oxygen Furnaces, or BOFs, which cut heat times, and therefore costs, dramatically. BOFs became the technology of choice in the Sixties. By then, foreign producers had the edge. (U. S. Steel installed its first BOF in 1963, arguing that the technology had not been proven until then.)

Overexpansion: On the other hand, American producers were anything but conservative when they planned for needed expansions of plant capacity. They kept overshooting the mark when they forecast economic growth and how much they should expand.

A big reason for the apparent overoptimism was pressure from the U.S. government. As Barnett and Schorsch wrote, by the late 1940s,

The rebirth of foreign steel plants, featuring the latest in modern equipment, helped foreign producers compete successfully in the international market.

government economists, "some of which had little direct connection to the steel industry," drew up projections of steel demand, using a full-employment economy as their model. According to their estimates, steel-production capacity was inadequate; steel supplies would be a bottleneck for an economy that grew under their assumptions. President Truman even hinted that the government should sidestep a steel crunch by building and operating its own steel plants.

U. S. Steel and other producers objected to the government's assumptions and pressure. "Subsequent events," wrote Barnett and Schorsch, "showed that the industry's perception of capacity needs was more accurate than the government's.... Nevertheless, it would be fair to say that the government won the dispute, although the victory was a dubious benefit to the national economy. Steel capacity expanded rapidly soon after the issue was joined."

To the surprise of those government economists, and even the steel planners, growth in steel *demand* proved to be sluggish—so sluggish, in fact, that the market essentially went flat.

Monday morning quarterbacks had a field day lambasting the steel companies for betting on the wrong technology, overshooting market growth, overexpanding and making other calls that turned out to be wrong. Second-guessing was easy *after* the results were glaringly obvious. But back when the steel companies had to commit to investments, marketing strategies and vastly expensive changes in technology, the signs they had to read were blurry. At least that was their argument.

When all was said and done, as Hall summed it up, U.S. producers approached the end of the Fifties burdened by some weaknesses but bolstered by some strengths.

On the minus side, they had overbuilt and invested in obsolete technology. They were in a vice, squeezed between uneconomical, lower-than-projected operating rates and higher operating costs. More, they needed cash. Hall wrote: "The industry's capacity expansion in the [Fifties], at a cost of $10 billion, could not be financed from earnings except in the boom years, 1955 to 1957, when the industry exceeded $1 billion a year of gross profits."

The industry's long-term debt had tripled during the decade to $2.5 billion. That meant more borrowing. Its share of world production had taken a bad tumble since World War II. (By 1956, wrote Hall, it would account for 27.7 percent of global output.)

In the plus column, added Hall, was America's labor productivity, which was greater than Japan's or Europe's. U.S. producers' raw material costs were lower. Also, the U.S. steel industry had "by far the largest internal market in the world for its products, and that market commanded the highest prices for steel in the world, so that there was little need or incentive to export."

As for U. S. Steel, Hall noted that the company "had 30 percent of the domestic market, and announced price changes with which the other producers quickly fell in line."

Then came 1959, which many people in the American steel industry remember as the year the industry turned a very bad corner.

By 1959, the *modus operandi* of steel industry-union bargaining had changed. So had the mood.

Gone was the two-decade-old pattern in which U. S. Steel did the talking with the union, reaching a deal that, by and large, was followed by the other steel operators. The year 1956 had seen the start of formal, industry-wide, collective bargaining between the major integrated steel companies and the United Steelworkers of America. Now representatives of most of the big steel producers, a dozen companies, sat around the table. The result, after a brief strike, was a settlement that raised hourly employment costs by 30 percent over three years, including a cost-of-living adjustment—a "COLA."

On the day the contract was signed, as Christopher Hall recorded in *Steel Phoenix*, U. S. Steel announced a general price increase of $8.50 a ton. "As wages were adjusted upward during the contract," Hall wrote, "so, too, were prices, by $21 a ton in total."

(All of this further fueled a suspicion favored by certain editorialists and politicians that "big steel" and the unions—without directly making any behind-closed-doors deals—actually were in cahoots. Bargaining, it was said, was really play-acting, in which both sides dutifully huffed and puffed at each other, in the end driving up the price of steel and going home happy.)

In any case, the 1956 settlement was inflationary. So was U. S. Steel's price hike. But the economy was in good health, and U. S. Steel and the other producers could live with the deal.

Roger Blough didn't like it, though. The settlement was a huge victory for the union, and Blough felt he had been railroaded. When the contract came up for renewal in 1959, *Time* magazine ran a grumpy statement from U. S. Steel's chairman: "We would like to do better than we did in the 1956 negotiations."

The chances were excellent that Blough would get his wish. Economics and the mood of the times were stacked against a big raise, or even a tiny one, for steelworkers. As *Time* paraphrased Blough, U.S. steelworkers had, since World War II, won "four healthy wage settlements totaling $1.31 an hour." American steelworkers' pay was far above the wage scales of the steel industry around the world, and, at $3.10 an hour, was well above the U.S. industrial scale.

McDonald didn't argue with that, but he pointed out that productivity in the mills had risen an average of 4.7 percent a year over the last two years, and claimed the industry could afford a pay hike. Industry profits for the first quarter of 1959, as *Time* said, "had reached a near-record $374 million, an 11.7-percent return on stockholders' investment on an annual basis, slightly better than the returns of all U.S. industry."

The steel companies countered that, yes, during the first half of the year, they'd made nice profits—but the profits were largely due to stockpiling, overbuying by customers who feared a strike that would deplete their stocks. Anyway, those profits didn't count as a windfall; the steel operators would have to plow them back into their mills to make them even more productive, the better to compete in the future with the newer mills overseas.

Actually, despite the glowing numbers, the steel companies were in poorer shape than they'd been a few years earlier. Before the traditional, pre-strike rush of stockpiling orders, noted Hall, they had been operating at an inefficient, money-burning two-thirds of capacity. U. S. Steel was running at 60 percent capacity for the second consecutive year.

More alarming was the fact that the American economy itself was now in poorer shape. And the clincher was this: The twin specters of inflation and steel imports were scratching at the door, and, during bargaining, would be breathing down the negotiators' necks. They seemed bigger and meaner than before. Any handsome gains by the union would only feed them further, touching off additional, even-more-threatening cycles of inflation, steel imports and layoffs.

Inflation had become a national fixation, and with good reason, considering the way it was already sapping the country's wealth and will. It was at or near the top of every lawmakers' worry list. Senator Estes Kefauver, chairman of the Senate antitrust and monopoly subcommittee, brought together experts and witnesses for yet another investigation into how the steel industry's habits might be aggravating inflation.

Senator Estes Kefauver
"The price...of steel is...
the business of all the people."

Not long before the steel wage contract was to expire, Kefauver also floated a bold suggestion: that the United Steelworkers of America peg any wage increase to productivity increases—with the average of productivity improvements throughout the industry to be determined by an impartial board selected by the companies and the union.

USW President David McDonald was not pleased when he heard about that idea. His answer, as quoted by papers including the *Pittsburgh Press*: "I wish Senator Kefauver would learn to keep his nose out of my business."

Kefauver shot back via the papers (the Gary *Post-Tribune* headlined its coverage, "Kefauver Nose His Business"). "The price of steel," declared the senator, "is not just Mr. McDonald's business. It's not just the business of Mr. Roger Blough, chairman of U. S. Steel. It's the business of all the people."

Then he took his argument to the doors of the Steelworkers: "As Mr. McDonald must realize, inflation is just as hard on the members of his union as it is on the people everywhere."

But steel and the USW declined to follow up on Kefauver's idea to tie wage hikes to higher productivity. Trying to pin down increases in productivity probably would have been no easier than traditional bargaining for wages. As one paper evaluated Kefauver's plan, "The formula the Tennessee legislator set forth … is not so simple as it probably appears to the uninformed." The reason: "So far as the steel industry is concerned, there is no incontrovertible definition for 'productivity.'"

Another government official was keenly interested in the outcome of the bargaining.

President Eisenhower, like his predecessors, was worried enough about the outcome of the strike to intervene. Before and during the bargaining, he warned steel management and the union not to sign a contract that was inflationary—defined as any contract large enough to force an increase in steel prices.

$\mathbf{I}$f Presidential participation had become routine in steel contract negotiations, there were factors that set the company-union talks of 1959 apart from those of the past. The 1959 negotiations dragged on longer, and the steel companies stood much tougher.

As *Time* wrote a little more than halfway through the sessions, in its July 9 issue:

> *"For the first time in 23 years, the nation's third most powerful union (after the teamsters and the autoworkers) had run—to its shocked surprise—into a stone wall. After years of giving in to union demands for wage raises, the steel industry this year met labor with a hard new line, refusing right up to this week to give the union a penny that would raise overall wage costs."*

At the bargaining table during the 1959 contract negotiations, U. S. Steel representatives were seated on the right of the table, union negotiators on the left. *World Wide Photos*

The steel companies were emboldened by a compelling argument: Inflation's disastrous domino effect had to be stopped.

Wage hikes, the companies said, would necessitate price increases. Price increases would open the door wider to imports of steel—steel purchased by American manufacturers who had to try to keep down the costs of cars and electric can openers so *they* could avoid inflation and stay alive. But it wouldn't end there. Workers in aluminum, railroads, shipbuilding, meatpacking and other industries would expect *their* new contracts to measure up to steel's. Then, the pay hikes in steel would ripple through the economy.

Articulating this "hard line" during bargaining was R. Conrad Cooper, U. S. Steel's executive vice president, a chief negotiator for the industry. But the inflation strategy's main author, said *Time*, was Roger Blough, "perhaps the foremost advocate of a new look in U.S. labor-management relations...

He feels that the U.S. is no longer a 'laboristic society,' that U.S. business, after sweltering for years in a climate that considered labor invincible, can and must check the unions' power, simply because it can no longer accept the high costs of labor demands. Looking over the whole economy, Blough knows that, when it comes to inflation, foreign competition, and other new factors in the economy, labor and management are in the same boat; what hurts one also hurts the other."

Union chief McDonald dismissed the inflation issue as a hoax, a "fictitious monster," and charged the steel companies with trying to "bewitch and bewilder the American public."

But the inflation-run-wild argument was backed by unsubstantiated and largely unchallenged statistics.

"When steel prices were raised 4 percent in 1957 after a 6 percent raise in steel wages," *Time* reminded its readers, "a major steel consumer had to pay $420 more for the steel that went into a power shovel. But the manufacturing company also had to give a wage hike prompted by the steel industry's wage rise. The wage cost of producing the shovel jumped $3,444, or more than eight times the price increase."

The Journal of Commerce agreed, reminding readers that "any boost in prices could mean an increased flow of imports."

Economic lessons like these, especially in the mainstream press, were reinforced in the minds of consumers, who remembered the trouble they had adhering to household budgets, and all the items they'd bought and needed that were made of steel. Many of those consumers concluded that, for now, anyway, a raise for steelworkers was not a good idea. As the bargaining sessions ran into July, the Gallup Poll organization released results of a survey in which 51 percent of the people polled said that steelworkers should get no pay raise.

The big surprise was that 40 percent of the families of union members felt that way, too.

Confident in their position, U. S. Steel and 11 other major steel companies made an unusual first move on April 6—before the official opening of bargaining. After slicing and dicing costs, projected demand for steel, numbers based on the ephemeral concept of production and the potential damage an inflationary contract would do, they proposed a one-year extension of the existing contract.

Three days later, USW rejected the proposal, suggesting measures including a freeze on steel prices during the coming contract, plus wage increases based on output per man-hour and profit.

On April 15, the companies rejected the union's suggested freeze as illegal, and its wage hike as inflationary. There followed on-and-off rounds of negotiations during which the union and steel companies sat around a table in the Roosevelt Hotel in New York, making and rejecting offers, and arguing economics and the industry's and country's ability to absorb any substantive wage hikes.

It was becoming painfully apparent to the steel companies that the union negotiators had no intention of even discussing a contract that did not include increased wages and benefits. As U. S. Steel's Conrad Cooper told a Minneapolis *Star* business columnist, union leaders had hailed the "highly inflationary contract of 1956" as the greatest ever, and promised "to come back to their own members with an even greater contract in their pocket."

The union had put itself out on a limb. So, on June 10, the steel operators upped the ante. In a move aimed at recovering some of the rights they had bargained away in *past* negotiations, they suggested contract changes they said would enable them to improve operating efficiency, and make real economic progress, to the ultimate benefit of the company, shareholders, consumers and workers.

The companies wanted to change contracts so they more clearly recognized management's function in establishing incentives and standards, and management's right to change work schedules when business conditions demanded flexibility. Specifically, they wanted to eliminate duplications in benefits and reinforce contract prohibitions against wildcat strikes, slowdowns and picketing.

More important, they wanted to modify ambiguous and restrictive contract language that had tied management's hands when it wanted to adopt more-efficient processes and procedures. Cooper would later put these "contract issues" into perspective during a U. S. Steel-sponsored radio interview:

"...[T]here are instances where men put in only three or four hours of work a day but get paid for eight. Now, this is not only wasteful of the energy and skill of the employees involved, it also endangers the future security of all employees and the company alike, especially in view of the keen competition we face from foreign steel producers and other domestic materials that can be substituted for steel."

The real culprit, Cooper admitted, was a monster he had helped create: a fuzzy clause that had been written into the 1947 labor contract. The union interpreted it as supporting payment for hours not worked. The clause also served as a hook on which workers could hang arguments against changing work practices when the companies switched to new equipment—machinery which needed fewer workers or which required different tasks to run at top productivity.

"I confess with considerable chagrin," Cooper shrugged, "that I was one of the six negotiators who put that language into the contract. And David McDonald, on the union side, was another. [The insertion] was written and approved at four o'clock in the morning by six brain-weary men who were racing to beat a strike deadline. In the years that have followed, it has been interpreted in arbitration to mean many things that it was never intended to mean."

R. Conrad Cooper (left) and David McDonald, principal players during the 1959 steel contract negotiations.

USW's McDonald thought otherwise, arguing that a revision of the clause would "turn the clock back" for the unions, and deprive workers of rights they'd worked hard to win.

And the talks dragged on.

On June 28 came the initial strike deadline. But the USW and the steel companies deferred a strike—for now, at least—by extending their current contract, a measure suggested by President Eisenhower. Negotiations were recessed until July 1.

Despite the extension, workers staged a rash of wildcat strikes in lake shipping and at steel plants across the nation. With ore carriers sitting still in the water, U. S. Steel's Oliver Iron Mining Division suspended production. McDonald ordered workers back to work, but contract negotiations were postponed because of the strikes.

Things were not going smoothly. McDonald had been worried for some time about the outcome of the bargaining. In mid-May he had seen President Eisenhower in New York, a visit aimed at winning government pressure to wrap up the talks. Now, in early July, McDonald slipped off to Washington for a private talk with Vice President Nixon.

"McDonald pleaded for government help to break the deadlock," said *Time*. "He remembered the record 62½-cent, three-year wage package won by the steelworkers in 1956 after Labor Secretary James Mitchell and Treasury Secretary George Humphrey pressured management, [and he] knew that this time both Nixon and Mitchell were anxious to see a no-strike settlement. But the Administration stuck firmly to its hands-off policy."

The companies and union went around and around, and, as a strike appeared imminent, the President appealed to both sides to continue operations during the talks.

On July 13, seeing no break in the contract deadlock, the companies began to prepare for a shutdown.

The next day, McDonald, as *U S Steel News* later put it, "disclosed for the first time that the union was asking for a 15-cents-an-hour package increase for each year of a one-, two- or three-year contract, with continuation of the cost-of-living escalator."

Cooper's response: "Much as we regret the hardships that will result from a strike, we cannot in good conscience be party to another round of the inflationary spiral. Strikes are bad—but we believe the long-range consequences of acceding to the Union's demand would be worse."

Negotiations stopped, deadlocked. The next day, July 15, the sixth union-called strike since the end of World War II began.

T he steel plants shut down, and the nation—in fact, the world—watched and waited.

And thought. Debates and soul-searching about bargaining, prices, profits and imports continued.

The New York *Journal American's* financial editor, Leslie Gould, citing the companies' second look at the ambiguous contract language and their bargained-away authority, decreed, "The big issue in the steel strike is the right of management to manage. Wages are only secondary."

Washington syndicated columnist David Lawrence raised a more alarming issue, asking, "Do the American people want a regulated economy—with the government fixing wages and prices?"

The question prodded American fears of socialism and communism. But, Lawrence told readers, David McDonald seemed to be saying yes:

"[McDonald] declares that the government 'cannot help but get involved' in the steel strike, and adds, 'We have always welcomed the involvement of government.'"

Yes "we" had, as was apparent when McDonald visited the President and Vice President to appeal for intervention. Government intervention—politics above economics—was precisely what Roger Blough did not want. He made a promise: "Whatever the length of the strike, and whatever the eventual outcome of the negotiations—as long as they are voluntary—we in United States Steel do not intend to raise the general level of our steel prices in the foreseeable future."

President Dwight Eisenhower ordered the Justice Department to issue a back-to-work injunction that stopped the strike in its 116th day.

Blough repeated his promise, adding that he intended to stick to his pledge "in the absence of an involuntary settlement mandated by some public body or authority." Like the President.

Life backed Blough: "… [U]ntil the union starts espousing a price cut instead of a cost increase, the public might better play along with Blough, who at least offers a way to keep prices level."

Many opinion shapers agreed. Famed columnist Walter Lippman did not. He was appalled by Blough's gentlemanly way of telling the President to "keep your nose out of my business." Rather than being vexed because he thought Blough rude, Lippman was sounding off because he favored intervention. "The national interest demands that the major industrial conflicts be settled under conditions which are good for the economy as a whole," he contended in his October 13th New York *Herald Tribune* column. "Some agency has to have the authority to speak for the national interest when a conflict arises."

Labor Secretary James P. Mitchell (center) looks on as R. Conrad Cooper (left), chief negotiator for the steel industry, and David McDonald, president of the United Steelworkers, signed contracts to signal the end of the strike. UPI photo

To a lot of people, that sounded close to advice that could have come from a famous guest. Nikita Krushchev, the feisty Soviet premier, was touring America at the invitation of President Eisenhower. Ike wanted "Mr. K" to see the steel strikers, a demonstration of free bargaining between unions and management in action. Krushchev was more likely to interpret the strike as proof that capitalism was in chaos. And he wasn't likely to disagree with another complaint from Lippman, that the country "had not learned how to substitute law and order for unconditional industrial warfare."

If this was warfare, President/General Eisenhower was determined to put an end to it. In early November, he told the U.S. Justice Department to obtain an order for the steelworkers to return to their jobs. The back-to-work injunction, issued under economic-emergency provisions of the Taft-Hartley Act, stopped the strike on its 116th day, and directed the strikers to return to work for 80 days while government officials brokered a settlement.

The steelworkers went back to their plants, and the plants restarted their furnaces and began making steel. Meanwhile, Cooper and the other steel negotiators resumed their talks while they watched the calendar; the injunction would expire January 26, 1959.

During this bargaining round, the steel negotiators were joined by Eisenhower's appointees, Vice President (and Presidential candidate)

"We All Lost!" was the way the U S Steel News *illustrated the 116-day steel strike in 1959.*

Nixon and Secretary of Labor James P. Mitchell, who coaxed the parties to a settlement based on compromise and politics. The steel companies had good reason. If the standoff continued, the strike was likely to resume, and the dispute would end up in Congress. And as J. A. Livingston, financial editor for the Philadelphia *Evening Bulletin*, put it, Nixon convinced the steel executives that "the industry would be clobbered if the dispute got to Congress."

At Nixon's suggestion, the steel negotiators and the union ended up splitting the difference on their best offers for a wage-benefit package. The result, agreed upon in January of 1960: several wage increases over the next two and a half years, plus pension increases and other benefits. The package was worth about 40 cents an hour, boosting steelmaking costs $16 per ton, according to the editors of *Steel, The Metalworking Weekly*, in an analysis of the contract published in 1960.

Presidential intervention took Blough and the steel companies off the no-price-increase hook. But the issue of work rules, the steel companies' biggest bone of contention, was another matter. The government and union teams won a decision that disagreements on work rules were to be settled by negotiation in local plant committees. That put changes to the rules in limbo.

"The companies have lost this fight," *Journal American* Financial Editor Leslie Gould concluded. But Livingston thought that McDonald "should be able to cooperate in eliminating unnecessary work practices."

In the end, the only winners were the foreign steel producers.

Almost 520,000 steelworkers had struck, idling almost 90 percent of the American steel industry's capacity. "By the end of the strike," wrote Hall, "[the steelworkers] had also caused 25,000 workers in other, steel-dependent industries to be laid off as stockpiles were exhausted."

Early on, as was customary when a steel strike loomed, appliance companies, contractors and other steel customers had laid in huge stockpiles of steel to weather them over. The nation had expected a strike. Back at the end of May, as the pages of *The Washington Post* and *Times Herald* had reported, Republic Steel Chairman Charles M. White had told reporters that anyone who had not started to hoard steel "would be an utter damn fool."

Most observers, however, had predicted a strike of three months at the most, not almost four months. "Steel buyers," noted Hall, "began to look overseas for steel as their stockpiles were consumed, and imports surged from 1.707 million tons in 1958 to 4.396 million tons in 1959."

Meanwhile, as Hall added, exports of "scarce and expensive U.S.-made steel dropped to a low of 1.677 million tons."

For the first time in the twentieth century, the United States imported more steel than it exported. The wedge of imports was firmly planted in the hides of the U. S. steel companies. It would cut deeper, taking more and more business that once had belonged to American steel, not to mention jobs that belonged to American steelworkers.

The pattern was set. The rebuilt foreign steel plants were up and running. There were no stories of long strikes in England, or Japan, or, for that matter, Russia, now the second-largest overseas producer. American manufacturers could feel safe with the supply of imported steel, and they wouldn't have to slow down or shut down because of a shortage.

Worse, those manufacturers, added Hall, liked what they got: "To many users' surprise, foreign steel was acceptable in quality...."

On top of that, imported steel was cheaper, even if it had to be shipped across the oceans.

During U. S. Steel's 1960 annual meeting, on May 2, in Hoboken, New Jersey, Blough gave shareholders two dramatic and discouraging examples of what they and the company they owned were up against.

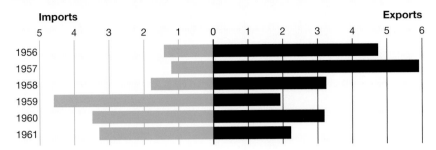

U.S. Imports and Exports of Steel Products
Millions of Tons

Imports		Exports

Source: American Iron & Steel Institute

"Within view of an American steel fabricating plant in Los Angeles," he said, "a building is being erected whose 770-ton steel skeleton is entirely of structural steel fabricated in Great Britain instead of in the Western United States. The steel for this building was shipped across the Atlantic, through the Panama canal, and delivered virtually next door to an American plant in the same business."

Example two: "Japanese steelmakers can buy scrap on our West Coast, transport it across the wide Pacific to their mills in Japan, and then ship finished steel products back to California shores, and despite all their shipping costs, undersell domestic producers."

Did Blough have any solutions?

Several: First, to keep developing new and better products, and second, to keep improving services and sales. Most important, he added, was to find a way to "overcome the underlying cause of employment cost inflation."

Number three was especially critical, he told shareholders, because "wages of American steelworkers are from three to seven times those of steelworkers abroad."

Chapter 12

JFK Faces the SOBs

"Thanks, Mr. President,
For all the things you've done,
The battles that you've won,
The way you deal with U. S. Steel
And our problems by the ton,
We thank you so much."

> —Sung by Marilyn Monroe to the tune of "Thanks for
> the Memory" to President John F. Kennedy at a May 19, 1962,
> party at Madison Square Garden to honor his 45th birthday.

John Fitzgerald Kennedy was furious.

It was spring of 1962, and the young president was at war with an old enemy: inflation. Kennedy wanted to slay this particularly fearsome dragon. It was battering the walls of Camelot, and one of the men who could most help him defeat it—Roger Blough—was not helping. In fact, he was proving to be a turncoat, abandoning all trust and honor, preparing to loose a new barrage of higher prices against Kennedy's kingdom.

At least that was how President Kennedy read Blough's behavior during the pair's 1962 feud over steel prices.

The fight would go down in history, even though it lasted only a few days in April. But that was long enough for the President to take some mighty swipes at U. S. Steel with the government's terrible swift sword. As part of his offensive, he blackballed the company from government contracts and sent FBI agents to subpoena U. S. Steel executives' personal records.

In the minds of Kennedy and his men, the executives were guilty of tyranny. They'd just announced they were going to raise steel prices—against Kennedy's clearly expressed wishes.

As for Roger Blough, he could only shake his head in quiet frustration. To him, the commotion was all about economics, and shouldn't be confused with politics or power plays. He was amazed by the overreaction:

"Never before in the nation's history," he wrote in a post-feud account in the January 29, 1963, *Look* magazine, "had so many forces of the federal government been marshaled against a single American industry."

The marshaling really began on August 22, 1961, when anti-inflation bulldog Senator Albert Gore, Sr., D-Tenn., took the floor in the U.S. Senate, calling on President Kennedy to stop the steel companies from raising prices.

It was almost time for the next series of wage and benefit adjustments, announced under the 1960 steel-labor settlement, to kick in. That, Gore reasoned, presented the clear danger that the steel companies would slam those increases right back at consumers in the form of higher prices. Result: more inflation.

Gore exhorted the President to use "his great powers, both legal and moral," to block any attempt the steel companies would make to raise prices. If the companies defied the President by raising prices, Gore proclaimed, the Federal Trade Commission and the Justice Department's antitrust division could take punitive action against them.

"If all else fails," Gore railed, "steel prices can be brought under utility-type regulations."

It was tall talk. Blough said as much in his *Look* reminiscences, which he shared with journalist Eleanor Harris to put on record his views of his scrap with JFK:

"To my knowledge, this was the first time any President had been publicly called upon to exercise control—without authority of law—over the prices of an entire industry, and to initiate or participate in a whole series of administrative and legislative actions of a punitive nature, if that control were not accepted."

Two weeks after Gore's Senate-floor rant, President Kennedy wrote identical letters to the chief executives of the country's top dozen steel companies, asking them to refrain from raising prices. They wouldn't have to. Kennedy assured them they could "look forward to good profits without an increase in prices."

Blough and other industrial leaders were disturbed by Kennedy's hold-the-line pressure. "The President's attempt to predetermine the prices of the steel industry," Blough wrote, "was…an unprecedented move in the history of our country in peacetime."

Furthermore, Blough begged to differ with Kennedy's view of profits. The President's evidence for "good profits" consisted of the same economic forecasts that Gore had cited to back up his arguments against any price hikes. Those forecasts had been drawn up by the Council of Economic Advisers, and Blough was sure they were too rosy. (In time, they proved to be far from accurate.)

From where Blough sat, steel profits looked parched and withered. And they wouldn't rebound soon. As of 1961, U. S. Steel and its competitors had not raised prices in almost four years. When they thought they could, they had to back off; recession had undercut demand, and therefore prices. Meanwhile, wages and benefits had kept marching uphill, fixed by labor agreements.

The blunt truth was that money was going out faster than it was coming in, and Kennedy was telling the steel companies to keep it that way. It was hardly a formula for "good" profits, or, for that matter, for the steelworkers' job security. Given the beating steel was taking in the market, no responsible authority in the industry could promise to keep holding prices down. It would only make the bleeding worse.

That was the message Blough wrote back to the President, only in words that were more statesmanlike:

"We in United States Steel cannot forecast the future trend of prices in any segment of the steel industry, and have no definite conclusions regarding our own course during the foreseeable future."

He pressed down a bit harder on his pen when he told Kennedy that his letter to steel executives had raised "questions of...serious import, including [questions about] the future of freedom in marketing...."

Then Blough received an invitation from Kennedy to visit him at the White House. He took it as a good sign, an offer to become better acquainted with the President, perhaps to help him better understand the problems of the steel producers, and why they had to raise prices.

In fact, Blough went off to the White House several times to chat with Kennedy about the whole steel-pricing situation.

On September 21, 1961, he sat across from the President, explaining that "no one man could speak for the industry about prices, that there was no question about the freedom of any company to change prices—to act, that is, as a competitor in a competitive market." And he left the meeting convinced that "the President was under no misapprehension on this matter, although my associates [at U. S. Steel] and I believed that competitive conditions precluded a price rise on October 1, when wages would automatically advance."

Roger M. Blough, chairman of U. S. Steel Corporation, visited President John F. Kennedy at the White House, September 1961, to discuss steel industry problems. World Wide Photo.

Three months later, on January 23, 1962, Blough was back at the White House, again by invitation. This time, Arthur Goldberg, former USW counsel and now Kennedy's Secretary of Labor, was there. So was USW President David McDonald. In five months, the current steel labor contract would expire, and the White House wanted the group to discuss an early start to talks for the following contract.

By now the President's agenda was clear. In his 1994 Touchstone biography, *President Kennedy: Profile of Power*, columnist Richard Reeves summarized the meetings this way: "With inflation on his mind, Kennedy had begun talking regularly to Blough and McDonald late in 1961. [He was] trying to persuade them that their restraint was the key to checking inflation, then running at 2.5 percent a year (almost double the 1.4 percent average during Eisenhower's second term)."

"'Wage Restraint'...'price stability'...'statesmanship' were phrases [Kennedy] repeated again and again to the two men," Reeves claimed.

The message surely was in the air during the second session with the President, and it gave Blough reason to remind Kennedy, Goldberg and McDonald about a few economic facts of life:

A) U. S. Steel had not raised prices for almost four years.

B) Meanwhile, U. S. Steel's costs "had shot skyward, partly because each year, we had raised wages and benefits."

C) Something like 80 percent of the cost of steel was labor. Half of *that*, or 40 percent, consisted of direct costs U. S. Steel paid its workers. The other 40 percent was employment costs, too—the costs that U. S. Steel's vendors and suppliers incurred, and passed along in the prices *they* charged for goods and services.

Besides quantifying the cost-price pinch he was in, Blough shared some legal realities with the three men: He could never enter negotiations that even touched on the issue of steel prices. "Such a discussion," he later explained, "during multicompany labor negotiations could be claimed by the Department of Justice as a violation of the antitrust laws—[as] 'collusion' or 'indirect conspiracy.'"

Blough was being extra careful, registering his views well in advance of any negotiations or raised prices. He wanted no surprises.

But he would get a few.

The first came the day after the steel negotiations (which did start early) were essentially concluded. It was then that President Kennedy telephoned his congratulations to each of the negotiators and to Blough, ending the conversation with optimistic words: "It [the contract] is obviously noninflationary, and should provide a solid base for continued price stability."

Blough was troubled by this remark. "I had repeatedly told him that cost increases were basically the cause of the nation's recent inflation, and that a price rise was long overdue U. S. Steel." It was Blough's favorite chant. (Ben Fairless, master of what would later be called the soundbite, had said it this way: "Steel price increases cause inflation like wet sidewalks cause rain.")

Blough, of course, meant that companies couldn't survive by swallowing cost increases they incurred. They had to raise prices to recoup the lost cash so they could rebuild, invest in research, and, they hoped, produce more and more for each dollar they spent. In the end, *that's* what kept prices down, raised the wall against foreign steel and helped to preserve American jobs.

Blough repeated the mantra to anyone who would listen.

But who was listening? Most Americans didn't have bad dreams about foreign steel, about hoards of steel beams wading out of the sea to stomp American steel plants and laser-beam steel jobs into vapor. Their worst nightmare was the constantly swelling prices in their grocery stores and the bloated payments recorded in their checkbooks. That was inflation. Saying costs caused inflation sounded like some meaningless riddle, like the one about the chicken and the egg.

Meanwhile, the President's apparent optimism over the steel contract suggested it was time to set *him* straight, too, on economic realities.

Blough huddled with the company's Operations Policy Committee, U. S. Steel's top ten executives. "After considering every aspect of our cost-price situation, we unanimously decided to recommend a price increase of about 3.5 percent on products, or about $6 a ton," Blough said. The board approved the increase on April 10, and Blough got on the phone and set up an appointment with Kennedy.

He arrived at the White House at 5:30 that afternoon, and well before 6 p.m. he was in the Oval Office, seated on a couch, facing the President, who sat in his famous rocking chair.

Kennedy was not sure why Blough wanted to visit. He was wary. He'd heard rumors that U. S. Steel might raise prices. And as U. S. Steel would go, so would the other producers.

His fears were confirmed when Blough said, "Perhaps the easiest way I can explain the purpose of my visit is to give you this," and handed the President a copy of a news release that U. S. Steel had just distributed to the press:

> *"For the first time in nearly four years, United States Steel today announced an increase in the general level of its steel prices. The 'catch-up' adjustment, effective at 12:01 a.m. tomorrow, will raise the price of the company's steel products by an average of about 3.5 percent—or three-tenths of a cent per pound...."*

Kennedy read the release and looked up. He was furious, according to Reeves. "You have made a terrible mistake," he told Blough. "You double-crossed me."

Blough, Reeves added, was shocked by Kennedy's anger, and "protested that he had never said he would not raise prices."

Kennedy called in Goldberg, who, as he walked into the room, was arguing against price hikes. "Wait a minute, Arthur," Kennedy said. "Read the statement. It's already done." Now Goldberg was furious.

And Kennedy kept turning up the heat, according to Hugh Sidey, the journalist who covered the Kennedy–Blough battle in his book, *John F. Kennedy, President* (Atheneum, 1963).

The President, Sidey learned, "sharply criticized Blough for sitting in the meetings whose sole purpose had been to prevent a price rise and never hinting that a price increase was intended; indeed, on the contrary, accepting all along the offices of the President to help get a favorable labor contract and, having achieved that, announced the price increase."

At a TV news conference, President Kennedy lashed out at the steel industry for increasing prices, and accused it of an "unjustifiable and irresponsible defiance of the public interest."

The meeting went on for 50 minutes, Kennedy and Goldberg repeatedly asking Blough to reconsider, and Blough repeatedly explaining that the industry had to raise prices. The agony continued even after Blough returned to the Carlton Hotel. For almost two hours, according to Sidey, Kennedy paced his office, flopping now and then into his rocker, venting his anger, hypothesizing to Goldberg black deals between Blough and Nixon, throwing out ways to get back at Blough.

It was probably during these agonizing hours that Kennedy famously condemned the captains of private enterprise:

"My father warned me that all businessmen were sons of bitches, but I never believed him until now."

The comment must have touched off a rash of head-shaking and grinning as congressmen, journalists, police chiefs and political stagehands measured it against old Joe Kennedy's reputation for womanizing, vote-buying and hobnobbing with gangsters.

It's doubtful Blough would have thought it funny, and he had even less reason to smile about the heavy-handed actions the President and his men would take next.

Kennedy was determined to get back at U. S. Steel. He couldn't do much but vent his anger the night of Blough's visit, although he did manage to bring his brother, Attorney General Robert Kennedy, into the fray. That very night, the Justice Department announced it would "take an immediate and close look at the current situation…." And Bobby Kennedy himself announced that a Federal Grand Jury in New York would investigate the price increase.

The next day, the 11th, the President staged a brutal, televised press conference, one, Sidey said, designed to "lay [Kennedy's] outrage before the people."

By then, five more steel companies—Bethlehem, Republic, Jones & Laughlin, Youngstown and Wheeling—had announced price increases that matched U. S. Steel's.

Looking grave and aggrieved, the President struck back hard from his first sentence, and he pushed as many emotional buttons as he could:

> *"The simultaneous and identical actions of United States Steel and other leading steel corporations, increasing steel prices by some six dollars a ton, constitute a wholly unjustifiable and irresponsible defiance of the public interests.*
>
> *"In this serious hour in our nation's history, when we are confronted with grave crises in Berlin and Southeast Asia, when we are devoting our energies to economic recovery and stability, when we are asking reservists to leave their homes and families for months on end and servicemen to risk their lives—and four were killed in the last two days in Vietnam—and asking union members to hold down their wages; at a time when restraint and sacrifice are being asked of every citizen, the American people will find it hard, as I do, to accept a situation in which a tiny handful of steel executives, whose pursuit of private power and profit exceeds their sense of public responsibility, can show such utter contempt for the interests of one hundred eighty-five million Americans."*

"Reporters," recalled Reeves, "were literally gasping. Kennedy heard them, and poured it on."

He went through a litany of dire consequences he said would spring from the price increases—boosts in the costs of homes, autos, appliances "and most other items for every American family." The prices

Chairman Blough takes a question from a reporter during a radio and TV news conference in which he presented the company's stand on steel price increases. World Wide Photo.

would "seriously handicap our efforts to prevent an inflationary spiral from eating up the pensions of our older citizens...."

Then he made his wildest claim, attributing it to Defense Secretary Robert McNamara:

"[The increase] would add, Secretary McNamara informed me this morning, an estimated one billion dollars to the cost of our defenses, at a time when every dollar is needed for national security and other purposes."

The steel settlement itself? Kennedy blessed it as noninflationary, and he patted the union on the back: "The steelworkers' union can be proud that it abided by its responsibilities in this agreement."

It was a masterful performance. Back in New York, in U. S. Steel's boardroom, Blough and other U. S. Steel executives watched the show in stony silence. Media requests for interviews flooded the switchboard. Blough knew he had to respond to the President's misleading claims and charges.

The next day, the 12th, Blough took to the airwaves in his own televised press conference. He was filled with frustration over the President's remarks, but, characteristically, he rejected stridence over calm dignity. In his horn rims, in his usual patient and measured manner—ever the lawyer—Blough justified the price increase.

He opened with a long statement, explaining the companies' need for profits to keep upgrading so they could stay competitive with the new steel plants in Japan and Western Europe. He summarized the need to remedy U. S. Steel's cost-price relationship, and described his responsibility to shareholders.

Then *he* sized up the effect of the price hike.

"The rise of three-tenths of a cent per pound in the price of steel adds almost nothing to the cost of steel which goes into familiar, everyday products that we use."

Turning to a chart, a professor lecturing his class, he ticked off the real additional costs the hike would impose on products. Intermediate-sized cars would go up by only $8.33; ranges, 70 cents; refrigerators, 65 cents; toasters, 3 cents.

Then Blough turned to McNamara's overkill claim that the steel price hike would add $1 billion for defense. Blough's figure, based on a newspaper survey he trusted, was an increase of $18 to $20 million. It wasn't pocket change, but it was a far cry from a billion dollars. Blough dryly reminded his class: "That's $980 million less than the secretary's estimate."

When Blough called for questions, the press nailed him, sidestepping economics and going straight for the political angles.

First to pop up was CBS's Walter Cronkite, an admirer of Kennedy. He set the tone by reminding the chairman of a joint, Blough–McDonald press conference, and demanded: "I wonder if you can tell us why there was no denial at that time, or in this week that has passed…whether an increase was intended?"

Other reporters, Reeves related, dug in deeper. Why was Blough defying the President and the national interest? Helping the foreign competition? Raising the defense budget?

When one reporter asked Blough why the steel companies did not raise prices in 1960, under a Republican administration, Blough, Reeves wrote, gave his only humorous answer of the day: "Well, I think you gentlemen can readily see that I do not know anything about politics."

If the reporters' questions had that certain ring of being planted by the White House, they were. Some of them, at least; according to Reeves, the President had the day before taken command of what could only be called a campaign to "get" U. S. Steel. As part of the plan, staffers had phoned reporters with questions to ask Blough at his press conference.

That wasn't all. Cabinet members were assigned statements to make to the press. Friendly congressmen and senators were asked to hold antitrust hearings. *The New York Times* reported that high-ranking

Kennedy staffers called steel executives to hold their old prices or rescind any raises they'd made to meet U. S. Steel's price.

The anti-U. S. Steel campaign kept unfolding. On April 11, Senator Kefauver announced his Senate Subcommittee on Antitrust and Monopoly would investigate the corporation's pricing actions. In the House, Rep. Emanuel Cellar, D-N.Y., called for an inquiry by the House Subcommittee on Antitrust. He was chairman. Not to be outdone, Federal Trade Commission Chairman Paul Rand Dixon launched an investigation of his own.

On the 13th, the day after the Blough press conference, Secretary of Defense Robert McNamara checked in with an announcement that the government would buy steel only from companies which refrained from raising prices.

"The President's attempt to predetermine the prices of the steel industry was, to my knowledge, an unprecedented move in the history of our country in peacetime."

Excerpted from Blough's comments in the January 19, 1963, issue of Look *magazine, following his celebrated clash with President Kennedy in late 1962.*

Robert Kennedy was toughest of all. "We're going for broke," he proclaimed right after Blough's White House visit. One of the steel companies had matched U. S. Steel's hiked price. That looked like price fixing to Bobby, so he convened a grand jury to look into the matter. He told his men to subpoena the other steel executives' phone records, expense accounts, personal records. The agents followed orders to the point of phoning executives in the middle of the night. There was evidence that they tapped steel executives' phones and pulled their income tax returns for scrutiny.

Blough himself said later that, while his press conference was in progress, "two FBI men called at my office and asked to talk to several of our executives." The FBI, he added, "served subpoenas on three of our executives for appearances before a [federal] grand jury just 48 hours later."

Whatever influence these tactics really had, doubts were growing that the new steel prices would stick.

As of dawn on April 16, more than a half-dozen steel companies had raised their prices. But the rest were holding at $6 lower. And the

Administration figured it was worthwhile sitting down again with U. S. Steel.

So Roger Blough, U. S. Steel President Les Worthington, and Robert Tyson, chairman of the company's Finance Committee, joined Secretary Goldberg and Clark Clifford, the distinguished Washington lawyer and Kennedy confidant, at New York's Hotel Carlyle for lunch. Even before they ordered, each member of the USS delegation was sure it was time to throw in the cards. At noon, Inland announced it would not raise its prices. Shortly after that, Kaiser Steel announced it would hold to its old price schedule. When a phone call informed them that Bethlehem had rescinded its increase, the three knew it was over.

As Blough said philosophically, "No one has yet discovered a way to sell steel in a buyer's market at $6 a ton more than his competition."

The siege was over. Kennedy took some swipes in the press for bullying. But one question still hung in the air.

Why did Kennedy step on steel so hard?

Theories included a need for Kennedy to ingratiate himself to the union, to pay for a past debt. "His earlier stand against a 35-hour week had displeased the labor unions," Blough pointed out. "I believe that he [Kennedy] and Secretary Goldberg felt an increase in steel prices, following the early wage negotiations, would be viewed as evidence that the Administration's policies were adverse to labor's interests."

There was another possibility, however. April had been unkind to Kennedy. A year before, he'd been mired in the Bay of Pigs operation, and he was humbled when the planned overthrow of Cuban dictator Fidel Castro turned into a debacle. Now, a year later, he was not going to be humiliated by Roger Blough.

These events could account for Kennedy's urgent insistence that prices be held. Still, that doesn't answer another question. Why—after he had congratulated McDonald and Blough for a "noninflationary" contract—did Kennedy blow up when Blough delivered his bombshell of a news release? Had he been listening to Blough?

Blough, after all, had repeatedly told [the President] that a price rise was long overdue U. S. Steel.

Blough had sketched U. S. Steel's cost-price position, dropped the fact that the company had not raised prices in four years. He hoped that Kennedy would come to what Blough thought was an obvious conclusion: A price increase was probable.

But, as Reeves emphasized, "Kennedy was a politician, not an economist." More than once, he'd asked his chief economic advisor, "'Now, tell me again, how do I distinguish between monetary and fiscal policy?'"

Kennedy the politician never got Blough's hints. He assumed Blough was following his marching orders.

The two men had been talking on different channels.

T he time came for Blough and Kennedy to smooth things over.

Kennedy was not a sore winner. Soon after the price fiasco settled, he invited Blough to the White House. The two sat again in the Oval Office.

"I saw him... in an atmosphere of mutual cordiality," Blough said in *Look*. "The subject of the price controversy never came up.... Instead, both of us spoke with real concern about the importance of business confidence." (The subject proved timely. A few weeks later, the stock market took a disastrous drop, a loss of $20 billion. It was worse than the huge two-day loss of the 1929 crash.)

After their talk, Kennedy told the press that "this Administration harbors no ill will against any individual, any industry, corporation or segment of the American economy."

Only 12 days later, the President sought to reassure Blough on a personal level.

Blough was at Yale, his alma mater, to receive the Law School Association's highest honor, the Citation of Merit. In a no-hard-feelings mood, according to a New York *Herald Tribune* account of that day, April 29, the President sent his personal "good wishes" to Blough. And to the delight of 400 Yale alumni at the luncheon, Kennedy—a Harvard man—said he would contribute to the Yale Law School capital drive.

It even seemed as though some of Blough's economic lessons and worries had sunk in. During an address to the U.S. Chamber of Commerce, Kennedy told those assembled: "Our domestic programs call for substantial increases in employment, but it is business, not government, who must actually perform these jobs.... [B]eneath all the laws and guidelines and tax policies and stimulants [government] can provide, these matters all come down, quite properly in the last analysis, to private decisions by private individuals."

Never once during the whole disagreement did Blough repeat quotes or drop innuendoes that would have made the President look bad. He just relayed the pertinent facts as he saw them. He stayed on that diplomatic course when, a couple of weeks later, he summarized the price uproar for shareholders during the company's 1962 annual meeting.

He could not characterize the final steel pact as non-inflationary, but he told shareholders it "represented real progress, and gave us reason to expect that it would not aggravate our cost-price problem as greatly as the previous contracts had."

Blough took a lesson, too, from the pricing-inflation flap: First, the nation had to understand how, over the past 12 years, corporate profits had deteriorated, and with them, the nation's industrial strength.

The second "great area of misunderstanding," he added, was the belief that there was "something special—something economically inhibitory—about the price of steel."

After all, over the past four years, many other industrial products and services had gone up, raising prices in industries other than steel. Prices had gone up for basic necessities, too, such as bread and milk.

But, added Blough, there was one sector in which prices had run wild. It was a sector that added not one cent to the economy. Yet no one seemed to point at *it*.

"The Federal Budget itself—or the cost of government, if you will—has increased a total of 24 percent in the past four years with 9.3 percent of that increase in the past year. Yet it would appear that a rise of 3.5 percent... in the price of steel somehow constitutes an intolerable threat to the security and economic welfare of this nation with all the strength and vigor that it possesses."

Blough never surrendered his belief that the 1962 price increase, had it held, would have helped the economy in the long run.

Steel prices, of course, couldn't stick where they were forever. A year after all the agonizing over steel prices, they went up. This time, though, U. S. Steel was the sixth company to announce it was raising prices—but not across the board. The company applied boosts of $4 to $7 a ton on a wide range of sheet and strip products—auto and appliance steels. There was no interference from the White House. Its response was restrained, almost supportive.

A few months later, Kennedy was dead.

Blough was free to say more about the events of April 1962—to have the last word on his fight with the President. Instead, he refused interviews on the matter.

"No," Blough would say to such requests. "It would be unfair since Kennedy can't respond."

Chapter 13

When the Sky
Had No Limits

While some of the media portrayed the Kennedy-Blough fracas as a political power struggle—the big corporation against a hero of the common people—others captured the underlying economic lessons.

Tough-guy newsman Walter Winchell followed the feud. Then he sat down at his typewriter, pushed his fedora back on his head and punched out a column that cut right to the moral of the story.

He reminded his readers what U. S. Steel really did with its money. Some of it went to repair, replace and upgrade its machinery. Almost half was turned over to the employees, who helped sustain other workers by buying houses, food and lawnmowers and by sending their kids to college. A nice-sized chunk of the company's cash was turned over to the government in the form of taxes.

If there was anything left, U. S. Steel returned it to shareholders as dividends on the money they'd invested in the company—although, as Winchell noted, "It's the rules of the game that the stockholders' money goes in first and comes out last."

"It certainly appears," concluded Winchell, "that the government is in the best business of all…. No investment, no work and a sure return."

Winchell wound up his column with his verdict on U. S. Steel: "A company which provides for the employment of 200,000 men, sends

600,000 kids to school, and pays $300 million in taxes, rates as a darn good citizen, one deserving a pat on the shoulder and not a kick in the pants."

The steelworkers would have summed up Winchell's lesson on wealth distribution this way: "What goes around comes around." The trick was to distribute the right amounts of money at the right times to the various people who kept the whole machine running.

In a few years, another U.S. president would take it upon himself to shepherd the steel industry through some critical business: the settlement of another steel-labor pact. For the most part, and without the help from above, the USA in the Sixties was a great example of how that wealth-recycling machine worked.

America was on the move. It was taking President Kennedy up on his challenge to land a man on the moon by the end of the decade. It didn't seem possible. But the young President's message was: We can do it.

And we did, as part of an unprecedented burst of "can-do-ism."

We had places to go, and not just to the moon. We were building a new, national system of interstate highways so we could get into our cars and shoot over to Des Moines or down to Miami. We had things to do, like step up our fight against communism on the Southeast Asian front. U. S. Steel was part of it all.

Unfortunately, it was an agenda that created division. People faced off over the Vietnam campaign (another nonwar that required real guns), and argued whether the highway and moon money would be put to better use rebuilding urban neighborhoods. But the work fattened up industry's order books, jump-started new technologies and preserved some jobs while it created new ones. As a result, U. S. Steel employees got busier—especially those who worked in the company's structural steel and concrete businesses.

The most ambitious project by far was the interstate highway system, the national network of roads envisioned by President Eisenhower.

Earning the distinction as the nation's largest public works project, the system was well under way by the mid-Sixties. Construction crews crisscrossed the map with a web of superhighways. They scooped out troughs for rights-of-way that circled cities. A good piece of the work entailed building bridges. Bridges over rivers and valleys. Bridges that wound over and under each other at pretzel-like interchanges. Buried *in* all the concrete, invisible, was mile after mile after mile of netlike, steel reinforcing bars. The job called for mountains of cement and steel.

Pablo Picasso's striking 50-foot-tall sculpture in Chicago was fabricated from U. S. Steel's Cor-Ten steel by American Bridge Division.

Many of the cities motorists drove to, or through, grew in prosperity and grace, thanks to the space-age buildings, stately bridges and other structures and projects U. S. Steel was part of. Some looked like works of art.

One *was* a work of art.

In the summer of 1967, Pablo Picasso collaborated with U. S. Steel to create a 50-foot-tall, steel sculpture for the plaza of Chicago's Civic Center, downtown. This was not art that imitated life. It was a 3-D version of one of Picasso's abstract figures, its eyes, mouth and nose floating off its face. It was his shoulders-up interpretation of a woman.

A woman? You (or, rather, Picasso) could have fooled a lot of observers. Still the "Chicago Picasso" was commanding, in part because American Bridge fabricated the daring piece at its Gary, Indiana, plant, from U. S. Steel's Cor-Ten, the steel that weathered to an attractive russet brown. The sculpture "echoed," as artists put it, the Cor-Ten on the Civic Center building itself.

Artworks, defense goods, great-looking buildings, awesome bridges, space stations, the national network of highways…it all tempted U. S. Steel employees to brag to their neighbors, if just a little. But the project that surely got more employees talking was the company's new and stunningly different corporate headquarters, being built in the heart of U. S. Steel's hometown, Pittsburgh.

The company broke ground in March 1967 for what it said would be the second-largest high-rise office building in the world, surpassed in office space only by New York's Pan-Am Building. It would be the tallest office building outside New York and Chicago. And it

The first steel column— a 16-ton section that towered 37 feet—is lowered to its anchor plate for U. S. Steel's new headquarters building in Pittsburgh.

U. S. Steel's corporate headquarters as it looks today. Featuring a facade of USS Cor-Ten steel, the 64-story triangular tower rises 841 feet over Pittsburgh's famous Golden Triangle.

would be three-sided—an 841-foot, triangular tower rising over Pittsburgh's Golden Triangle.

The design was *practical, U S Steel News* was careful to explain. "[It] offers maximum office space and minimizes the over-all cost." Into that maximum space—almost an acre per floor—would move headquarters personnel who had been scattered throughout 10 separate buildings, including their "old" headquarters, the 1951-vintage Mellon-U. S. Steel Building. The company would occupy more than half the new structure, leasing out to other tenants some 800,000 square feet of prime space.

Any Pittsburghers who expected the "obvious" building—a big box of shiny steel—had to have been pleasantly surprised when the company unveiled the new tower's design. It looked like no other office tower. Its lower lobbies were encased in glass, and recessed, making an already spacious and inviting public plaza appear even roomier. Its external framework of vertical and horizontal beams and its notched corners served up a visual feast—the more so because the facade of the building was fabricated from USS Cor-Ten steel, whose satisfying, earthy hue would mellow with age.

Copper-bearing, element-defying Cor-Ten steel had been available since the Thirties. It was great for railroad hoppers and boxcars. Life on the road and in the switchyards was tough on the cars. They got knocked around. Their paint chipped. Then they rusted.

Cor-Ten was the solution, even though the steel was a paradox.

Alternating rain and sun caused it to form a dark-brown patina—a coat that was a cousin to rust, but that was stable and tenacious. It blocked further corrosion. It never had to be painted. It looked good, and stayed good-looking. Besides, Cor-Ten was especially strong, rated at 50,000 pounds per square inch. The qualities explained the name: *Cor*rosion resistant, *Ten*sile strength.

Steel had long been a given for the frames of buildings, but architects had shied away from the metal as a design element. Steel lacked texture. Architects preferred wood and stone. It wasn't until the Sixties that they discovered Cor-Ten. One of the first was Eero Saarinen.

He was won over by the steel's rich patina, and the fact that it was tactile, pleasing to the touch.

Saarinen had just the commission for the unusual steel: the John Deere Company's new headquarters in Moline, Illinois. Built in a park-like setting, amid lawns, trees and paths, it was a masterpiece. It won awards. Its earthy texture captured the essence of John Deere's real business: working the earth.

In time, the company found that Cor-Ten had its downside. Unless architects, fabricators and contractors followed U. S. Steel's instructions to the letter, the metal could cause trouble for its clients. The "weathering" would not be uniform. Wind would blow surface rust off the exterior and onto other buildings, cars and pedestrians.

As a result, suits were filed against U. S. Steel over Cor-Ten, and the company eventually stopped selling it for architectural applications. But where the steel was properly installed, the final result was—and continues to be—spectacular.

Rounding out the stable of USS steels were Ex-Ten, Man-Ten and Tri-Ten. They were all in the 50,000-pounds-per-inch strength range. Even stronger were high-stress, T-1 steel, used in tunneling machines and other heavy mining equipment, and HY-80, HY-100 and HY-140, armor steels used in ships and special craft such as, for the navy, a compact, deep-diving mini-submarine. Stronger steel meant less steel could be used in various products and applications. Less was more. Construction beams kept their strength even though they were slimmed down and lighter, giving way to more usable space in buildings, trimming the mass, weight and costs of buildings and bridges. Then there were anti-corrosion steels for bridges, and other structures that had to tough out sea salt.

These supersteels were the creations of the metallurgists and other researchers at the company's laboratories in Monroeville, Pennsylvania. (The research staff had moved in the mid-Fifties from the company's former lab in New Jersey to a new research campus in suburban Pittsburgh, a short drive from U. S. Steel's headquarters.)

Those researchers developed other steels, not all of them skyscraper mighty, but tailored for other, very specific needs.

A sampling: high-pressure, seamless, superstrong, weldable steel tubing; single-strand, lower-cost barbed wire; tempered steel for nuclear power plants; rocket-flame-resistant, steel-wire-mesh parachutes designed to lower space capsules to earth safely; wall panels whose interior was a light-but-rugged steel honeycomb; and actual steel honeycomb, prefabbed for beekeepers and their bees.

The center built an experimental house for developing applications of steel in home construction.

Elsewhere on the home front, steel was fighting the can wars, competing against aluminum as the material of choice for the familiar "tin can," which was really tin-coated steel. U. S. Steel's volley of ideas included two-piece aluminum cans, "thin" tin (for cans and other packages); steel-foil laminate for the inside linings of orange juice containers; pull-off, "snap-top" lids for beverage cans.

In a join-'em, don't-fight-'em switch, the company adopted a process for making aluminum-coated steel cans. A beam of electrons vaporized aluminum, then painted it as a veneer on steel strips that were rolled into cans.

Then there was Curvemaster Rail, especially tough, and installed at roadbed curves, where rail got its worst beating. And residential steel siding. And enameled and painted steel sheet for appliances.

Company research and marketing experts often put their heads together to sell new uses for steel. They tackled big problems, such as the growing need for economical urban mass transit. The result was "SCOT," the Steel Car of Tomorrow. It looked like a subway car for the year 2020, but it could be much more. USS ran the car by urban planners and transportation experts, reminding them that SCOT cars could be busses, too, or monorails, or elevated trains.

Impressive as the researchers' experimental furnaces, mini–rolling mills and muscular, metal-testing presses were, their most awesome piece of equipment was a million-volt electron microscope. It stood 17 feet tall and weighed 15 tons. Using magnetic fields for lenses, it allowed scientists to "see" steel at the molecular level, and its images were thrown onto a phosphorous screen. What the researchers "saw"

The million-volt electron microscope at U. S. Steel's Research Center allowed scientists to "see" steel at the molecular level.

helped them engineer steels that were stronger, tougher, more resistant to corrosion.

When the microscope was installed at Monroeville in 1966, it was the largest in the Western Hemisphere. It looked like the viewing end of a submarine periscope. Scientists used it to probe the lunar rocks that Apollo astronauts brought back to earth. The studies lasted two years and helped NASA crack riddles about the moon's composition and the forces that made it. The rocks also told scientists that gamma rays, once thought to be a serious threat to astronauts, were not so dangerous.

Science was a serious piece of U. S. Steel's business. The April 1966 *U S Steel News* reported that 1,800 employees were working on 1,300 projects in laboratories, on pilot test lines or in small-scale steelmaking facilities. "In the past two years," the publication noted, "more than 100 new or improved products have been marketed by U. S. Steel."

The company plowed money back into its business through R&D and marketing work during the decade. It also invested great sums in coke-oven gas processors, anhydrous ammonia plants, and new plate and cold-reduction mills. And into improvements in its pipe mills, largely for the benefit of the oil industry.

But it was in the early Sixties that the company made what had to be its biggest commitment to technology, investing in two revolutionary technologies that went back to stage one of steelmaking.

As earlier chapters pointed out, American steel producers lagged behind their foreign counterparts in installing basic oxygen furnaces (BOFs) and continuous casting equipment. They opted to monitor these new technologies—to wait until overseas plants worked out the bigger bugs—before they sank breathtaking sums into the costly new technologies.

There was good reason why American steelmakers were late in adopting new technology. Soon after World War II, the U.S. government began urging steel companies to add capacity, something steel executives were reluctant to do. But then the Korean crisis exploded. Producers, including U. S. Steel, began building new open hearths.

In Europe, meanwhile, the basic oxygen furnace was being perfected. It could make steel many times faster than the open hearth. But the American industry could not immediately install the new technology. Not with all those new open hearths. Having bowed to government pressure to increase capacity, the American steel industry now found itself losing the competitive race to the thoroughly modern steel industries in Europe and Japan, largely rebuilt after the war.

But the new BOFs and continuous casters were the future. A BOF furnace amounts to a souped-up Bessemer converter. It is jug-shaped. Through its top, crews load molten, blast-furnace iron and a precise amount of steel scrap—old fenders and bedsprings. Then, through a tube, they blast pure oxygen into the mix, triggering a violent reaction that cooks the impurities out of the steel.

A BOF can make a heat of steel in less than an hour, versus 6 to 10 hours in an old open hearth. And all the heat the BOF needs is right there in the molten steel itself. The BOF eliminates the old step of cooking the steel with costly natural gas or oil.

Producers multiply their savings in time and fuel costs when they couple their BOFs to continuous casters, major innovation number two.

The old casting method went like this:

Crews cooked up a melt of molten steel, then poured it into molds. The molds formed "ingots," monoliths of raw steel. Overhead cranes transferred these to "soaking pits," where they steeped in more heat—a step that assured the ingots cooled uniformly, preserving their chemical integrity.

Then the ingots were squeezed and sawed into working pieces, such as blooms (long, squared rails which became girders, beams or train track), slabs and billets (thinner bars—round, square or triangular, made into pipe and wire).

Continuous casting collapsed all those steps into one: molten steel to blooms or billets. It is steel's twist on the production line, and an awesome process to watch.

At the head of the line, huge ladles carry molten steel right from the furnace, and pour it into a stationary mold. The steel begins a slow descent—through water sprays that cool it between rollers that press it into its required shape for billets or rails. Still pliant, the ribbon takes a long turn onto a horizontal conveyor, cooling and solidifying as it glides toward machines that will cut it into billets or blooms.

There are no soaking pits, no need to remelt the steel for rolling. There are lower fuel bills, plus much less handling, and less scrap.

Typically, continuous casters operate in tandem, producing glowing steel in flat bands or round strings. It is a spectacular show, and

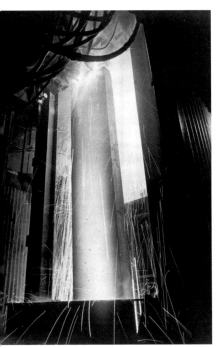

Continuous casting represented a major innovation in steelmaking.

one that became more common as BOFs and continuous casters gained importance as "tools" (as the company likes to call equipment and processes). By 1971, the company was operating continuous casters at its plants in Illinois, Indiana, Pennsylvania and Texas. Fairfield, Alabama, followed in the mid-Eighties.

Critics especially castigated the company and its U.S. competitors for their supposed delinquency in installing BOFs. Roger Blough refuted the charge in the October 1967 issue of *Iron and Steel Engineer.*

Early BOFs, installed in Austria and other countries, were primal, said Blough. They made a limited range of steels. They lacked adequate air pollution controls, and would have generated so much pollution that, in the States, they would have been shut down.

"To have scrapped hundreds of millions of dollars worth of good and serviceable open-hearth furnaces in order to replace them with a process that was then in its relatively primitive stages would have been wasteful," concluded Blough.

But the company hadn't been sitting on its hands. As it watched BOFs mature, it was busy improving its open hearths, almost doubling their production capacity between 1950 and 1963.

The truth, Blough insisted, was that U. S. Steel commanded a formidable battery of steelmaking machines in the Sixties—especially when one factored in the company's electric furnaces with powerful electrodes that melted scrap steel down to molten steel, and vacuum processing units, which briskly gasified and expelled contaminants lurking in the molten steel. Both technologies were golden when it came to making the high-performance alloy steels that the times demanded.

Continuous casting had one shortcoming, a serious one. It made inferior steel slabs—the wider, flat shapes that were rolled into plates or sheets. But the company was taking care of that problem. It was perfecting, at Gary, a breakthrough "continuous–continuous" caster. A U. S. Steel technical team designed it. In the early Seventies, Gary crews took it to commercial production, turning out top-quality, lower-cost slabs that were 50 feet long and more than six feet wide.

Reprint of the news article from the December 7, 1962, issue of The Wall Street Journal *concerning the Robena Mine disaster. Photo reflects the grim faces of a crew of miners as they prepare to exit Robena's Frosty Run elevator after a night shift of rescue work.* Courtesy of Lonnie and Rita Miller.

Blast at U.S. Steel Coal Mine Traps 38 Men Deep Underground

Rescue Teams Strive to Reach Victims in Pennsylvania Mine; Fear Fire at Explosion Scene

CARMICHAELS, Pa.—(AP)—An explosion trapped 38 men deep underground in a soft coal mine, and rescue crews worked feverishly to make contact.

More than seven hours after the blast rocked the mine, rescuers were an estimated 1½ miles from the trapped men some 650 feet under the surface.

The explosion ripped through a shaft of the Robena No. 3 mine. The mine is in southwestern Pennsylvania about 80 miles southwest of Pittsburgh.

The Robena mine, owned by U.S. Steel Corp., is among the world's largest soft coal mines and is highly mechanized. It is under a 59,000-acre tract in Greene County.

Several years ago, the mine was divided into three geographic sections known as Robena No. 1, No. 2 and No. 3.

Pittsburgh seam coal from the Robena facility is barged to U.S. Steel's Clairton Works, near Pittsburgh, where it is processed into coke for blast furnaces. Robena has produced as m̄u̅c̄h̄ as 20,000 tons of coal a day, enough

There was bad news, too—in the form of two more accidents that would haunt Roger Blough's term as chairman.

The first came on December 6, 1962, at the company's Robena coal mine complex, about 60 miles south of Pittsburgh. Early that afternoon, an explosion rocked a section of the complex's No. 3 mine, near the town of Carmichaels, in Greene County. The blast instantly killed 37 miners. As the *Uniontown* [Pennsylvania] *Herald* wrote in a summary a year later, the explosion was so violent that miners working in the tunnels almost 8,000 feet away were knocked off their feet.

Yet, up on the surface, people weren't sure what had happened until they saw a cloud of dust boil out of the mine shaft. Indeed, on

December 6, the fate of the mine crew was not clear. Where were the miners? How many men were trapped? How many were dead? No one would know the answers until rescuers reached the section of the mine where the victims had been working. That would take most of four days.

It was a long time to hear of the fate of friends and loved ones, but during those long days, the victims' families waited and prayed together on the surface, in the building that housed the entrance to the mine shaft. They knew, as did the U. S. Steel and union officials standing watch with them, what people elsewhere did not: For the rescuers, digging their way to the trapped men would be frustrating and slow work.

Why? Because a coal mine is another world. As Lonnie Miller explained in *Robena: A Chronological History of Robena Mine in Greene County, Pennsylvania* (self-published, 1997), the Robena complex, one of the world's biggest mines, sprawled a mile below, a virtual subterranean city of intersecting streets and alleys. "Describing the size of the mine is hard," wrote Miller. "It's like trying to give the size of the New York subway system ...."

The rescue mission was massive, as well. At its peak, it was conducted by 13 teams of six men each—miners from West Virginia, Kentucky, Indiana and Alabama, as well as from Robena and other Pennsylvania mines. As a December storm piled snow on the ground outside, teams assembled in the shaft house and checked their gear. As they started down the mine shaft, they passed under a sign that was intended to bring joy, but now only added to the sadness. "Merry Christmas," it read.

"For four days and ten hours, weary miners battled their way through jumbled, gas-filled passages deep under the ground," the *Uniontown Herald* remembered in a piece on the tragedy 20 years later. "Their progress was agonizingly slow and dangerous, as they inched their way into the dark blast-wracked, gas-filled corridors of the mine." Wary of volatile pockets of methane gas, they "had to reconstruct ventilation as they went, because of the danger of new explosions, as they pushed the 'fresh air base' forward."

At 4 a.m. Saturday, December 8, the rescuers sighted the first victim. By Monday night, December 10, hope—already dim—flickered out as the team found the last of the dead miners. The *Uniontown Herald* summarized the toll: 31 miners, a foreman, two assistant foremen, two mining engineers, and one 18-year-old, a local high school honors graduate who had been studying mining engineering at Penn State while he worked in U. S. Steel's mines as an engineering trainee.

But what caused the explosion? After conducting hearings and investigations, the U.S. Bureau of Mines laid the blame on a temporary change in procedures that made ventilation sluggish, causing an accumulation of methane and coal dust that was touched off by a spark from an unknown source.

As the *Pittsburgh Press* summarized the bureau's findings on February 26, 1963, "A new mining routine aimed at opening a new set of entries in the affected section made the ventilation more difficult to direct and control." Quoting the bureau's report, the *Press* added: "Apparently the fact that this deviation…would adversely affect ventilation…was overlooked."

Every tragedy has its ironies. The December 11, 1962, *Pittsburgh Press* singled out one of Robena's: "Robena, the largest mechanized coal operation in the world and known as one of the safest, had lost its once-proud reputation by the worst mining disaster in six years."

But tragedy was not finished with U. S. Steel.

On May 7, 1965—almost two and a half years after the Robena misfortune and seven years after the sinking of the *Bradley*—another ship of U. S. Steel's Great Lakes Fleet was lost.

This time it was the freighter *Cedarville*. It was rammed by the *Topdalsfjord*, a Norwegian freighter, as the two vessels attempted to pass each other in the fog-shrouded Straits of Mackinac.

Reinforced to break ice, the *Topdalsfjord*'s bow ripped a 20-foot gash in the *Cedarville*'s hull. After stopping his vessel and dropping anchor, the *Cedarville*'s captain surveyed the damage to his ship…and made a fateful decision. Hoping to beach his ship near Mackinaw City, Michigan, he ordered the engine restarted and the anchor raised, and soon the *Cedarville* was limping toward shore. But before the ship reached safety, it rolled over slowly, and sank. Of a crew of 35, 10 drowned.

The Coast Guard investigated the tragedy and put much of the blame on the *Cedarville's* captain. His ship was traveling at nearly full speed, despite a fog that limited visibility to about 300 feet. His license was suspended for a year. But he never sailed again.

This facility at Irvin Works, Dravosburg, Pennsylvania, produced long-terne steel, cold-rolled sheets that were in demand for automobile gas tanks, air and oil filters and TV chassis.

It got better. In the mid-Sixties, the company marched into new markets, introducing new products: embossed steel for decorative touches in buildings and for appliances; color-coated steel; and Nexus, a chemical-based adhesive that, bonded between steel structural panels, dampened sound and reduced vibration.

The corporation installed a continuous, long-terne sheet line at its Irvin Works in Pennsylvania. The line produced long-terne sheet steel, cold-rolled sheets that were coated with a lead-and-tin alloy in demand for automobile gas tanks and air and oil filters and TV chassis.

Gary added an 80-inch, five-stand, cold-reduction mill. It turned out exceptionally thin sheets for autos, appliances and containers.

And at the company's National Works, in McKeesport, Pennsylvania, crews installed what *U S Steel News* proclaimed as the "most advanced electric resistance weld pipe mill in the industry." This breed of pipe was used for long-distance transmission of gases and materials such as bauxite. It was thinner, longer and smoother than the pipe it replaced. That translated into less handling and fewer welds in the field, and into smoother-running pipelines.

In 1966, the corporation embarked on yet another round of rebuilding at select mills. It was three years and $1.8 billion worth of work. It included lines for galvanized steel sheet, new electric furnaces, new BOFs, upgraded rod mills—and a lot more. The targeted works: Gary, Fairfield, Fairless and a half-dozen others.

It seemed the company would never be able to stop pumping money into its plants for new and better "tools" and products. To survive, it had to keep renewing itself.

On January 1, 1964, U. S. Steel remade itself yet again, on paper, and in terms of the way its operating and corporate staffs interacted. It began to gather, under one umbrella, its domestic steel-producing, mining and lake shipping operations. Michigan Limestone, Oliver Iron Mining, Pittsburgh Steamship, American Steel & Wire, Columbia-Geneva Steel, National Tube and Tennessee Coal & Iron were consolidated with the company's central Operations Divisions.

Packing the companies into the same operating boat would eliminate excess bureaucracy. The units could be swifter and surer.

Then the corporation "moved."

Since its creation, U. S. Steel had been incorporated in New Jersey. But during the next 60-plus years, other states adopted advanced incorporation laws. Delaware had emerged as the most progressive, pro-business state. It let directors meet via telephone conferences. It updated requirements for corporate finance and securities. If that weren't enough, reincorporating in Delaware would save the corporation taxes.

On January 1, 1966, U. S. Steel became a Delaware corporation.

Somewhere, though, some steel-industry wit must have jested that, instead of trying to reduce its taxes, producers should think about

National Works' new electric resistance weld (ERW) mill was considered the most advanced of its kind at the time and was capable of producing the longest length of pipe in the world.

paying more. That would allow raises for the Presidents and their staff members who volunteered so much help to the steel industry in managing its affairs. It had happened again during the summer of 1965, when the steel companies and the union stalled in their efforts to reach a new contract settlement. President Lyndon Baynes Johnson offered his services in breaking the impasse.

Johnson was famous for the "Johnson treatment," his method of cajoling senators or representatives into supporting a deal or a bill he favored.

He would press his body within millimeters of his human target. Staring into his trapped victim's eyes, he would explain a law's good points, hint at favors, drop names—smiling all the while.

As president, Johnson elevated the technique to the group level, mass-Johnsonizing the parties deliberating the steel settlement of 1965.

His chief targets were R. Conrad Cooper, U. S. Steel's balding and fatherly executive vice president for personnel services and the steel industry's chief negotiator, and I. W. Abel, the newly elected, bespectacled, grandfatherly president of the United Steelworkers.

A new steel wage and benefits package had been a work in progress for some time. Negotiations had begun in Pittsburgh, on December 14 the previous year. The negotiators had already postponed an earlier settlement deadline, and now they were either going to sign an agreement—or hunker down for a strike—at midnight, August 31, 1965.

With that agreement to postpone, the workers won an 11.5-cents-an-hour interim wage increase. It was mounting for them in escrow accounts until the final contract was reached. But the talks hit a wall when the steel companies failed to agree on a level of improvments for pensions, insurance and other benefits for a three-year contract.

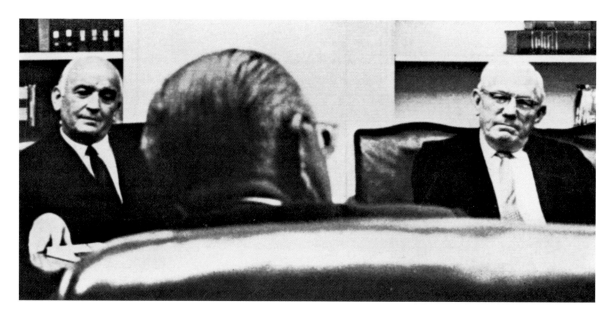

The trouble stemmed from union and industry differences about the number of steelworkers who would benefit from a sweeter package. The companies projected more beneficiaries than the union did—and therefore priced out the benefits higher than the union did.

When everyone did the math, the two sides sat staring at each other across a benefits gap that could be figured at from 12 to 16 cents an hour, depending on whose calculations one accepted. And that's where

The Johnson Treatment— R. Conrad Cooper (left), U. S. Steel executive vice president personnel services, and I. W. Abel, president of the United Steelworkers of America, meet with President Johnson during the 1965 steel crisis.

they stayed, while U. S. Steel and other operators began shutting down their furnaces.

Johnson wanted a wage-benefits hike that was fair to steelworkers but that wouldn't spoil the producers' profitability or pump the bellows under inflation. He was worried, too, that the deliberation impasse would trigger a long strike, and therefore a steel shortage that would cause an economic relapse and hurt his campaign in Vietnam. Yet he didn't want to take the drastic step of commandeering the industry under the Taft-Hartley Act.

So he stepped in. He pressed the negotiators to postpone the strike deadline. They did—for eight more days. And he summoned them to Washington to continue bargaining under his watchful eye. They came that day.

That night—the evening of August 30, just shy of a Labor Day weekend—Johnson went on national television. He introduced Abel and Cooper (and Labor Secretary Willard Wirtz and Secretary of Commerce John Connor) to the TV audience. He announced the eight-day strike extension and praised the negotiators for agreeing to the reprieve. After his speech, Johnson strode out of the White House TV studio. Wirtz, Connor, Abel and Cooper filed out silently behind.

The Johnson treatment continued. The President put the negotiators to work for the next few days in the historic Executive Office Building, next door to the White House. In effect, he locked them in, seeing to it that they worked until after midnight, keeping them at the bargaining table by sending over sandwiches and fish soup.

When the producers granted a key concession by agreeing to increase workers' pensions by $5 a month for each year of employment, Johnson decided to take advantage of the momentum. He went next door to chat up the group.

"Mr. Johnson's visit to the negotiators mostly was designed to prod the union to give a little more," said *The Wall Street Journal*…

"For the first time in his many recent utterances on the steel dispute,
Mr. Johnson trotted out a series of figures designed to show that the average
steelworker already has it pretty good financially; average hourly earnings
for steel industry employees are 33 percent above those for all other factory
workers, he told the negotiators, and steel employment in the first half of
1965 was 59,000 greater than in the second half of last year."

Johnson, said the *Journal*, reminded the producers that "steel-industry profits are high" and observed that "profits this year could reach a record if there's no strike."

Then he sounded a "between-us-men" chord. He admitted that he, like them, wanted to spend the Labor Day weekend at home, and jested that "his wife was calling him almost every hour wanting to know whether he would be coming down to the ranch or whether she should come to Washington."

The President left, convinced that an agreement was close, that the negotiators needed one final nudge. So he sent Wirtz and Connor over with what *The New York Times* called "suggestions for resolving six or eight points of difference on wages and pensions."

The deadlock broke in 90 minutes.

In the final settlement, workers gained raises of between 49 and 51 cents an hour over 35 months, the union claiming the lower figure and industry claiming the higher.

There was no strike. In fact, there had been no strikes since the 166-day strike of 1959. There would be close calls, but no strikes, until 1986. The company was in the midst of a virtually strike-free quarter-century.

The plant expansions, the construction boom and the dearth of strikes were all good news. But they couldn't erase other trends threatening the steel industry. Anyone who stopped to listen could still hear alarm bells.

A particularly loud one rang early in 1966, when U. S. Steel announced it had to close one of its veteran mills because time had passed it by.

The Donora Works began operations in 1905, on the Monongahela River, not far from Pittsburgh, and grew up with the town of Donora. It was built by William H. Donner on land owned, in part, by Pittsburgh financier Andrew W. Mellon, and christened in honor of its founder, the "Don" in Donora, and Mellon's wife, Nora. Four years after its startup, the works was purchased by U. S. Steel's American Steel & Wire Company.

The mill's chief businesses were producing steel and steel wire and rod. But it staked a claim to infamy in the fall of 1948, when a freak temperature inversion trapped, right over the milltown, a blanket of smoke and fumes from the mill. When the wicked smog lifted five days later, 6,000 of Donora's people were sick, and 20 dead.

As the next chapter will reveal, good was gleaned from the tragedy: The disaster so shocked the nation that a cry went up for a war against air pollution. It was the beginning of the environmental age.

In the late Fifties, for environmental and market reasons, the company shuttered the mill's zinc works (zinc was used for coating steel sheet and wire) and began dismantling furnaces. Left operating were the mills that produced steel rod and wire, and products like baling wire (which would become extinct when farmers went back to the basics, baling their hay with hemp rope.)

The final blow came when domestic competitors on the Eastern seaboard—smack in the heart of Donora's main market—installed facilities to make competing products, and delivered them almost "right now."

"All three [competitors] give overnight service to customers," shrugged a spokesman for U. S. Steel. "Donora can't do this."

The company had seen the trouble coming. It had lined up jobs at other mills for 700 Donora employees, and was looking for more jobs. A year later, it shut down the rest of the works. It sold the 700 acres to a nonprofit organization whose mission was to spearhead the area's redevelopment.

The truth was, Donora was a dinosaur. How many other U. S. Steel mills were headed for extinction?

One that was especially iffy was the Geneva Works in Provo, Utah. It had been built during World War II, far inland, where it could produce war goods safe from enemy subs or planes. Its location back then was its strength. Now, in the Sixties, location was its weakness.

The Geneva Works, observed *U S Steel News* in 1966, was 700 "overland" miles from the market for 80 percent of its products—700 miles farther away than its domestic competitors. The shipping costs were a killer. More troubling was the fact that Japanese steelmakers were shipping their products across the Pacific—and *still* undercutting the American producers, right in their backyards.

Out-of-the-way Geneva had to get tougher as a competitor. It had to shave costs tissue-thin. It had to shoot for perfection in quality and service.

It would be hard, but Geneva employees—a majority of them Mormons, members of the Church of Jesus Christ of Latter Day Saints—pulled together. Their fighting spirit glowed during a huge rally, one attended by 9,000 people—employees and their spouses, U. S. Steel executives, union officials, public officials and church leaders. They kicked off the plant's "Errors Zero" program, a formalized striving for perfection in quality, delivery and service.

Donora Works as it looked before being shut down and dismantled in 1967 due to environmental concerns and declining markets for its products.

In a fight for survival, Geneva Works in Provo, Utah, launched its Errors Zero program in an all-out effort to help the plant remain competitive.

Could they run a ship that was tighter than anybody else's?

Yes, Conrad Cooper told them: "Most of the conditions by which you must compete are as different as our own thumbprint from those faced by [other steelmakers.] The total of these differences…sets the ground rules by which you must make and sell steel at adequate returns."

Then Eldon Tanner, first president of the church, rallied the crowd for the job ahead. "The spirit of a man is best cleansed by the sweat of his own face," he proclaimed.

The spirit reflected those of other U. S. Steel employee rallies, sessions staged to convince employees that everyone needed to pump the absolute last measure of quality into the products they made. There was a Zero Defects drive at Homestead, and an Errors Zero campaign at Christy Park Works in McKeesport, Pennsylvania. They were like pep sessions at plants in other industries all across America, although *U S Steel News* opined that the company's quality drive was the first.

But what was going on?

Since when did steel employees have to be reminded to do the best job possible? To make the best products they could? To deliver A-plus service?

Since the late Fifties. It was then that employees in all kinds of industries contracted a strange, self-destructive disease. It sapped their desire to excel, drained them of any will to compete, afflicted them with the hallucination that they were "set," and could get away with doing less than their best.

The bug struck just about everywhere, from the auto industry (where customers watched window cranks fall off their two-year-old cars and warned friends not to buy cars made on Mondays) to basic steelmaking where pipe and rail didn't come up to snuff. The attitude was, "If it's gray, ship it. " For pipe: "If it has a hole in it, ship it."

Where this apathy attack came from is hard to say, but it survived well into the Seventies. It was crazy, especially at a time when quality and service were the highest cards steel producers had to play against producers in Japan and Europe.

There was more craziness. With one hand, an American producer sank millions into equipment, to raise productivity and lower operating costs. With the other hand, he paid more in wages and benefits. It happened again in the 1965 settlement. "Wage and benefit increases cost another 50 cents an hour; and steelworkers were guaranteed the right to retirement on a full pension after thirty years' work, regardless of their age at the time of retirement," noted Christopher Hall in *Steel Phoenix*.

Anticipating a strike, customers stockpiled steel, triggering a surge of steel imports.

"Perhaps the biggest cost to the industry," Hall added, "was the rise in imported tonnage from 6.4 million in 1964 to 10.4 million in 1965, including for the first time significant tonnage of flat-rolled products brought into the domestic industry's heartland, the Great Lakes ports. Imports reached 10.3 percent of apparent consumption...."

Three years later, added Hall, it was more of the same:

"The next strike deadline, in 1968, saw yet another last-minute, generous contract and yet another surge of imports to a new peak, of 17.96 million tons, or 16.7 percent of the market. The integrated mills were slowly withdrawing from, or being pushed out of, markets in which their production and freight costs now greatly exceeded those of overseas producers."

There was stockpiling in 1968, too.

J. Michael Curto, a U. S. Steel marketing vice president, sighed on the pages of the July-August *U S Steel News* that, "Yes, part of the big increase [in imports] this year comes from customers buying ahead for protection against a possible strike.... Unfortunately, we've found in the past that, at the end of labor negotiations, imports don't drop back to their old level."

It was becoming such a pattern that you could almost hear imports being ratcheted upward: Strike negotiations, stockpiling, higher imports, *CLICK!* Strike negotiations, stockpiling, higher imports, *CLICK!*

As he prepared his address for U. S. Steel's May 1968 shareholders meeting, Roger Blough could be excused if he was sighing in relief. After almost 14 years as chairman, 14 years of hearing the dreaded *CLICK!* right over his head, he would soon get out from under it. He had announced his retirement. It wouldn't come until early 1969, and after it did, he would stay on for some time as a director. But no longer would he sit in the hot seat. And the 1968 annual meeting would be his grand finale.

The meeting was held in Pittsburgh, where the corporation's new headquarters was rising in all its Cor-Ten glory. Was the building a symbol of a new company? Blough would have said so. At the annual meeting, he painted a verbal picture of the company that must have sounded to many shareholders like a minor makeover.

It wasn't a steel company. It was a materials and services company.

"U. S. Steel is a producer of a variety of materials and services in addition to steel," Blough said. "While the production and marketing of steel continues to be the principal function of the company, profit opportunities in related activities are being pursued vigorously in markets that are growing significantly."

The company was broadly hedging the shareholders' bets through its rounded investments in chemicals, plastics, cement—even through a joint venture in titanium, "a superstrong, lightweight metal in higher demand for aircraft, space and defense, oceanography, and the chemicals industry...," Blough pointed out.

Add to these crushed limestone and U. S. Steel Homes' line of "pre-engineered" apartments, school rooms and dormitories.

Blough's perspective on the company's diversity was a welcome goodbye present for shareholders who had come to admire, trust and respect him. After the meeting, shareholders crowded around to thank him and wish him well.

He was the subject of a farewell gesture during the meeting, too—a little ceremony that turned out to be touching, but for a while had Blough holding his breath.

Roger M. Blough discusses the corporation's progress at a press conference before his last annual meeting as chairman of the board in 1968. His retirement on January 31, 1969, brought to a close a distinguished career that spanned 27 years of association with U. S. Steel.

Evelyn Davis, a much-seen-and-heard professional gadfly, had taken the floor. She specialized in sparring with CEOs. Blough was her favorite. She had lit into him for "allowing" aluminum to creep into automobiles, beverage cans, appliances, construction materials— markets that steel once had locked up.

Today, she argued with him about the same subject: aluminum. But today was different. Today, Davis wore a dress made of the rival metal.

The verbal battle ended, and, to the consternation of management and delight of the shareholders, Davis climbed to the stage and approached the podium, and Blough—her aluminum dress flashing in the auditorium lights.

By the time she stood next to the chairman, the vinegar was gone from her attitude and voice. She smiled. She praised Blough for 13 years of leadership and for putting up with her antics.

Then she announced she was giving the chairman "a present." While Blough watched, frozen, the not-unattractive Ms. Davis slipped off her aluminum dress, and handed him the rattling garment.

Underneath, she wore a respectable and well-tailored black sheath. And as shareholders applauded, and bemused boardmembers smiled, Blough accepted Davis' gift, and her final tribute—a peck on the cheek.

FROM
THE EARTH
TO THE MOON

For much of the Sixties, America was building. A national highway system, bridges, schools, office towers, Arctic defense lines, spaceports. It was a spike in business for U. S. Steel and its divisions.

Through projects like these, the corporation helped America define what it was, what inspired hope and fear in its people.

The bonus was that much of the work was daring and striking.

Steel was downright majestic when it took form as St. Louis' sweeping Gateway Arch, completed in 1965 to coincide with the city's bicentennial.

The graceful, stainless-steel curve soars 630 feet into the air (75 feet taller than the Washington Monument) and spans 630 feet. Half its steel was produced at a half-dozen U. S. Steel plants. Universal Atlas Cement supplied 100,000 barrels of concrete, 90 percent of the total used in the arch and its underground museum.

The arch was built to commemorate the spirit of the pioneers who opened the West beyond the Mississippi. U. S. Steel created a visual echo of the more-recent past when it put up the 12-story Unisphere at the 1964–1965 New York World's Fair, in Flushing. The giant globe was the 1939 New York World's Fair sphere brought up to date, a spherical grid of longitude and latitude lines over which floated the continents. Circling this interpretation of the globe were several rings, the suggested paths of orbiting satellites.

In this artist's rendering, the spirits of the pioneers who opened the West pass through St. Louis Gateway Arch.

U. S. Steel supplied steel and fabrication for the buildings on the fair's grounds. And many of the visitors to the fair got there by driving over the new Verrazano-Narrows bridge, erected by U. S. Steel's American Bridge Division. The $325 million suspension bridge, spanning the entrance to New York harbor and linking Staten Island and Manhattan, opened in late 1964. Employees at more than a half-dozen U. S. Steel mills worked two years to produce the cables and components for the bridge, a double decker with 12 lanes. Its main span took the world's record, at 4,260 feet long. It was 60 feet longer than the Golden Gate Bridge, and no less graceful in design.

(A week before Thanksgiving in 1963, ironworkers were inching along the topmost structurals of the bridge, joining girders hundreds of feet above the

Unisphere—a 12-story symbol of the 1964–1965 New York World's Fair

water. A young ironworker suddenly stopped what he was doing, stood up and whipped off his hard hat into which he had taped a small radio. Staring into the hat with a look of disbelief, he shouted to his crew, "Someone just shot President Kennedy!")

*T*here was even a kind of cold beauty to structures U. S. Steel helped create for the government, even if those structures had to do with events more ominous than fairs or river crossings. These were projects for the cold-war market, structures built to alert America should she be invaded by enemy planes or missiles.

"Cold" was the word for the Ballistic Missiles Early Warning System. "BMEWS" stretched from Alaska, across Canada, through Greenland, to Iceland, and its job was to protect the USA from a surprise attack by enemy missiles. It was designed to spot a missile 3,000 miles away in space, and alert U.S. bomber and missile crews to the threat. The system's eyes were huge radar antennas, concave grids of steel webbing. They looked like backstops for a baseball game played by giants, even if U S Steel News eyeballed the vertical face of each antenna as being the size of a football field.

U. S. Steel's National Tube Division signed on to make the tubing for four of the antennas at a station in Greenland, a little more than 900 miles from the North Pole. This was a land of Arctic gales and temperatures that fell to 65 degrees

below zero. This was metal-cracking cold. But a USS specialty alloy—National Seamless Carbon and Nickel Alloy Tubing—could take it. More than a mile of tubing made of the alloy was woven into each antenna. The work on the first array was finished in mid-1960, and more antennas were planned at other BMEWS stations.

The flip side of government defense projects was the government's space program. It was about discovery, about creating things.

The corporation was a busy partner with NASA, and active at the space agency's Florida launch site, the home of the monster Apollo-Saturn spacecraft that took the astronauts into space, and to the moon.

Ultra-strong, ultra-heat-resistant steels from the corporation were used throughout the spaceport. It was used to build the port's two huge "crawler-transporter" flatbeds, each of which appeared to be carried by four Army tanks. These monsters transported the spacecraft to the launch sites, creeping along with the big rockets on their backs. Brawny U. S. Steel beams and tubing went into equipment for fueling the monster rockets with liquid oxygen, into facilities for testing the rockets, and into the rockets themselves. The company also supplied beams and other components— 45,000 pieces in all—for the giant moonship's "hangar," the Vehicle Assembly Building. The structure comfortably held four Apollo-Saturn Vs. It was 525 feet *high and more than 700 feet long and 500 feet wide. It was the world's most capacious building.*

While steel was proving itself an even more versatile building material, concrete was coming into its own as the material of choice for a building's decorative outer shell—the "curtain wall." Architects were learning they could mold strong, economical concrete into buildings of unique shapes, textures and colors.

Proving the point was the Pan-Am Building, the 59-story office tower that sprouted during the early Sixties next to New York City's venerable Grand Central Terminal, right over tracks serving the terminal. U. S. Steel's American Bridge Division fabricated and erected its steel. American Steel & Wire furnished reinforcing steel for the 13-by-6-foot, precast, white, concrete panels that covered 600,000 square feet of the building's exterior. The panels were made of cement supplied by the company's Universal Atlas Cement Division.

Against Manhattan's gray canyons, the new Pan-Am Building was a dazzler. It was one of the world's largest commercial office buildings, although its economy of space and eye-pleasing, horizontal rows of concrete panels kept it from bossing its neighbors.

U. S. Steel's construction arms were busy in other cities, too.

In Boston, American Bridge fabricated and erected 38,000 tons of steel for Prudential Center—a 52-story office tower with a bank, shops, a hotel and a convention hall clustered around its feet. National Tube supplied 1,200 tons of pipe, American Steel & Wire pitched in with wire mesh, reinforcing bars, electrical wire and 24 miles of elevator rope. Universal Atlas Cement supplied more than two million bags of cement for the entire project.

Topped off by its 750-foot tower, the complex added a touch of modern grace to Boston's blighted Back Bay section.

The John Hancock building in Chicago climbed skyward as it neared its full 100-story height.

Late in the Sixties, American Bridge ironworkers "topped out" Chicago's latest entry in the race for the sky: the 100-story John Hancock Center. This is the dark, tapered monolith with an external skeleton consisting of a series of load-bearing, crisscrossed beams up each side. U. S. Steel's Gary and South (Chicago) Works rolled the 42,000 tons of steel required for the tower. Hidden inside, suspended from the final beam, is a space-age cornerstone: a conical, space-capsule-shaped container holding mementos.

Across town, American Bridge got busy with what for 20 years would be the world's tallest building, the 1,468-foot Sears Tower. Opened in 1974, the tower was built on a frame consisting of a squared bundle of nine huge, vertical, steel tubes. The system offered incredible strength for the amount of material used (think of a cluster of cardboard mailing tubes) and packed in an exceptionally generous quantity of floor space. It was the brainstorm of the building's structural engineer, Bangladesh-born Fazlur Khan. The affable "Faz" is a Chicago hero. Visitors like to find his likeness on his bas-relief memorial in a Sears Tower lobby and rub his nose for good luck.

On the other end of the size scale, United States Steel Homes Division offered a variety of factory-built homes (12 basic models with 83 different floor plans in 1962) that promised extra strength because their frames were made not of wood, but of steel studs. (It was a good idea that became even better later in the century, when people worried more about depleting forests, and lumber prices soared.)

American Bridge fabricated and erected two steel bridges and fabricated 37 tunnel sections for the almost-18-mile-long Chesapeake Bay Bridge Tunnel, off the East Coast. Each tunnel section was the length of a football field.

U. S. Steel supplied almost half the yard-wide pipe used to build the colossal Colonial Pipeline, the world's longest petroleum pipeline. Running 1,600 miles between Houston and New Jersey, under highways, across mountains and over rivers, the line was designed to move 27 million gallons of gasoline and other petroleum products a day.

In support of science, the company supplied more than 20,000 tons of high-strength steel, fabricated at American Bridge plants, for the structures supporting the world's largest and most

U. S. Steel supplied more than 40 percent of the large-diameter trunk line pipe for the Colonial Pipeline, which stretched 1,600 miles between Houston, Texas and Linden, New Jersey.

powerful movable radio telescope. The device amounted to a huge "ear," a dish whose surface approached seven on the football-field scale. Sited in West Virginia, the big ear caught radio waves from space that, translated, allowed scientists to "see" farther into the universe than they ever had with other radio or optical telescopes.

Deep in the earth, inside a mountain near Colorado Springs, American Bridge crews hollowed nearly three miles of tunnels and erected 11 steel buildings. They were the nerve center for NORAD, the North American Air Defense Command. Its mission: detect and defend against air or space attacks against the continent.

The moon station, the space ear and the NORAD control center were a few of dozens of defense and space projects

(more than 100 in progress in 1964 alone, according to U S Steel News), in which the corporation took part. Vietnam accounted for no small share of them, and it had the company on its toes, again, producing arms and other defense goods to life-over-death specifications.

But the Cold War had upped the ante. As the U S Steel News put it, new weaponry demanded a quality of workmanship never before dreamed of. "An Atlas ICBM (Intercontinental Ballistic Missile) alone has more than 40,000 separate parts…. Once airborne, it has no one aboard to correct a malfunctioning part."

Built inside a mountain, the NORAD Project was the new combat operations and nerve center for the North American Air Defense Command.

Chapter 14

Doing the Impossible

As he reflected on his years at U. S. Steel's helm, Roger Blough must have cracked one of his wry smiles over the ways the business had changed.

He had redefined his company. Now it was more than a steel company. It was a *materials* company. Considering its moon-probe and earth satellite projects, it was a space-age company. Surely its new versatility was more obvious to shareholders and other investors. Surely U. S. Steel managers, as they formulated their strategies for this new company, would make mental leaps over walls that once restrained them.

Still, re-identification was no fix-all. As broad a label as "materials company" was, other materials—notably plastics and aluminum—were muscling their way onto the corporation's turf.

Meanwhile, operating costs continued to balloon. For one thing, the corporation was going to have to work harder to gather cash for costly equipment designed to keep smoke, toxic chemicals and other harmful pollutants out of the air, rivers, streams and lakes. Reason: The environmental movement was going through a growth spurt strong enough to encourage the corporation to add environmental protection to its official list of social responsibilities.

Blough first put the company on record as recognizing its environmental duties when, in the corporation's 1966 annual report, he wrote environmentalism into a discussion of an ad campaign the company was running to make people aware of its endeavors as a corporate citizen:

> *"Built around the general theme that U. S. Steel is a good neighbor and a good place to work, these advertisements dealt with safety, training programs, suggestion awards, United Appeal Drives, long-service employees, new facilities, unusual jobs and the ever-present problem of air and water pollution control."*

It was a brief statement, and it acknowledged growing concern about mounting pollution from factories. But it could not hint at the soon-to-arrive era of confrontation and confusion—a period ushered in by the 1970 passage of the federal Clean Air Act, and during which U. S. Steel and government officials would butt heads over environmental targets before switching to a mode of cooperation.

Blough's annual report remark also failed to reflect something else: the time, energy and money the corporation's executives, operating hands and research personnel had already poured into technologies and methods to limit—*eliminate*, if possible—the wastes their plants were dumping into the air or waterways.

In fact, the environmental movement had been building for more than a half-century.

President Theodore Roosevelt had elevated the public consciousness about the need to protect nature when he pronounced as untouchable vast stretches of American wilderness. But that land was far, far away from most Americans—especially those who lived in the cities, and who still put up with blackened skies and fouled rivers. Zoologist Rachel Carson brought environmental sensitivity home by writing *Silent Spring* (Houghton Mifflin Company, 1962), a celebration of nature and a warning that indiscriminate use of pesticides was destroying animals and

The Monongahela River Valley of Donora (left) and Webster, Pennsylvania as painted by Charles C. Shinn. "The Week of the Smog" gave rise to local, regional and national laws to reduce and control factory smoke, culminating in the Clean Air Act of 1970.

The week of the smog

During the last week of October 1948 a heavy smog settled down over the area surrounding Donora, Pa. Weather men described it as a temperature inversion and anticyclonic conditions characterized by little or no air movement, prevailing over a wide area encompassing western Pennsylvania, eastern Ohio, and parts of Maryland and Virginia. This prolonged stable atmospheric condition was accompanied by fog and permitted the accumulation of atmospheric contaminants resulting in dense smog, particularly in highly industrialized areas. Smogs of short duration are not unusual and except for discomfort due to irritation and nuisance of the dirt and poor visibility, no unusual significance is attached to such occurrences.

This particular smog encompassing the Donora area on the morning of Wednesday, October 27, it was even then of sufficient density to evoke comments by the residents. It was reported that streamers of carbon appeared to hang motionless in the air and that visibility was so poor that even natives of the area became lost.

The smog continued through Thursday, but still no more attention was attracted than that of conversational comment.

On Friday, however, a marked increase in illness began to take place in

plants. The book caused a great stir. To cautions concerning wilderness lands and air and water quality, it added a call to protect animal and plant life. By writing it, it has been said, Carson launched the modern environmental movement.

However the campaign began, it sharpened public fears that industrial contaminants were threatening the world. Pressure mounted for federal legislation for controls of industrial emissions. Overnight, it seemed, environmental concerns rose to a top priority for most of society.

But the alarm had rung 20 years earlier for U. S. Steel—the entire American steel industry, for that matter. The time was the fall of 1948. The place: the town of Donora, Pennsylvania, where U. S. Steel's American Steel & Wire Company operated a mill and zinc works.

As of the late Forties, steel mills and factories had spewed smoke and gas into the air over the Monongahela Valley for 75 years. Smog often blocked the sun, turning day into night. Soot dusted the countryside, foul odors permeated the air. But, like people in industrial towns around the world, the folks of the "Mon Valley" saw the billowing smokestacks as a sign of prosperity. Their economy was booming, thanks to factories and mills. The smoke was annoying, but they were willing to put up with it. It was just an inconvenience.

Until Wednesday, October 26, 1948.

That night, as the people of Donora (a town of nearly 14,000, 35 miles south of Pittsburgh) slept, an unusually stubborn temperature inversion clamped a layer of dense air on Donora like the lid of a metal pot. The inversion trapped the smoke and gas from local industrial plants. When townspeople awoke Thursday morning, they could barely see through the fumes. And the foul blanket grew thicker while the townspeople—most of them unaware that they were in any danger—tried to go about their business.

On Friday, October 28, the town held its traditional Halloween parade. By Saturday, fans had to grope their way to the local stadium to watch a high school football game. They could barely see the players. Still, most of the townspeople didn't understand what was happening. They didn't worry. But when fire alarms shattered the eerie stillness that night, they knew something was terribly wrong.

The whitish smog, laced with sulfur dioxide, was burning the eyes of the townspeople and attacking their lungs.

"Thousands of people suffered severe abdominal cramps, splitting headaches, nausea and vomiting," the *Pittsburgh Tribune-Review* said in a solemn summary of the tragedy 50 years later. "Strong men and women with no previous health problems were struck down."

Then elderly people, most of them asthma sufferers, began dying. The town's doctors were deluged with calls. The fire squad was dispatched to administer oxygen to victims. But the devil fog fought them all the way. "It almost got to the point where it was claustrophobic, it was so dense and thick," fire department veteran Bill Schempp remembered 50 years later. "It took us at least one hour to go to someone's home only five blocks away. We had to feel our way along the fence."

On Sunday, the skies began to clear. The disaster was over, but it left 20 people dead. Some 6,000 residents—more than a third of the town's population—were ill, 1,440 of them seriously.

At the Donora operations, officials had "followed the book" in curtailing production as the skies grew dense with the polluting smog. But, in the face of the emergency, the procedures in "the book" proved to be grossly inadequate, and the zinc works was not shut down completely until most of the harm was done.

A lengthy investigation by the U.S. Public Health Service (paid in part by the steelworkers' union) uncovered evidence that the deaths and sickness were caused by gas and zinc dust emitted by American Steel & Wire's zinc works' smelter. After the probe came lawsuits. In the end, the *Tribune-Review* reported, the company paid individual, out-of-court settlements that ranged from $1,000 to $30,000.

U. S. Steel never formally admitted any company responsibility. Indeed, as the *Birmingham (Alabama) News* editorialized on April 21, 1951, "the degree to which the company was at fault is a matter of much doubt."

Rather, the doubt rested largely on the question of whether the company could reasonably have been expected to foresee a tragedy, which, as the *News* pointed out, the Public Health Service blamed in part on unusual atmospheric conditions, a quirk of nature.

But Donora was a wake-up call.

The city fathers of Pittsburgh, U. S. Steel's hometown, had awakened during World War II to the troubling truth that their town's midnight-like noons repelled families, businesses and jobs. Fearing Pittsburgh was dying, city leaders including U. S. Steel's Ben Fairless worked hard to sell a plan to clear the city's famously smoky skies.

In 1948—the year of the Donora smog—they won enough support to pass an ordinance ordering factories to switch from notoriously smoky, soft coal to cleaner-burning hard coal.

For its part, U. S. Steel built at its mill in McKeesport a new boiler plant which replaced 57 old and smoking chimneys with four stacks equipped to trap fly-ash before it got into the air. Within a few years, the company also installed equipment that cut back the emissions from the coke ovens at Clairton and reduced the dust that was escaping from furnaces in other plants.

With industry pitching in, the Pittsburgh plan did partially clear the air. And it cleared the way for clean, green Point State Park, and hastened downtown revitalization. Other cities were adopting similar programs to make their air more breathable. But the nation was still expanding its view of environmental responsibility.

If any good can be said to have come from the Donora tragedy, it was that it focused widespread attention on environmental dangers.

The October 29, 1998, *Pittsburgh Post-Gazette* reminded readers that a series of University of Pennsylvania investigations conducted soon after the tragedy "marked the first time that there was an organized effort to document health impacts of air pollution in the United States." "The investigations," added *Post-Gazette* reporter David Templeton, "prompted Public Health Service recommendations for a warning system tied to weather forecasts and air sampling."

In 1955, Pennsylvania enacted its own Clean Air Act, the first law to control air pollution in the Commonwealth. It was formulated and passed in direct response to Donora. "When the U.S. Clean Air Act was passed in 1970," the *Post-Gazette* pointed out, "the impact of smog on Donora was a key issue in Congressional debates."

Donora certainly shook U. S. Steel and other producers, and made them take a harder look at their processes and equipment, especially in light of the quirks of nature. The tragedy was a key issue in U. S. Steel's initial formation of a committee whose job it was to police the corporation's plants for environmental trouble spots and get them fixed.

The corporation's Committee on Air and Water Quality Management sprang to life in 1952, as the environmental movement was beginning to heat up. It was four years after the Donora alarm rang, and a decade before citizens' worries about environmental hazards led scores of municipal, state and federal agencies to take on the job of environmental watchdog.

U. S. Steel's environmental committee reported to the corporation's top administrative unit, the Operations Policy Committee. Its members represented research, law, personnel and production. There still was a lot of skepticism in the air—at least in a lot of corporate meeting rooms—about spending good money on air and water. Yet, between the time the U. S. Steel environmental committee was formed and Roger Blough referred to environmental protection in the 1966 annual report, U. S. Steel had spent $200 million for devices to cut air and water pollution.

The price tag should not have shocked anyone. To begin with, steelmaking is a dirty process. Keeping the process clean calls for pollution control "devices" that have to be tailor-made for each mill, and for installations that are far from small. As the company stated in its August 1966 quarterly shareholders report, some of those devices towered 10 stories high. Others covered tracts the size of a city block. Most needed constant and costly maintenance to keep running.

Extensive, complex electrostatic precipitators cleaned the air by trapping dust from open-hearth furnaces.

Lagoons, such as this one at Geneva Works, held process water that could be reused in steelmaking or treated with chemicals before being discharged safely into lakes, rivers or streams.

They included pits and lagoons to hold process water that would be reused in steelmaking, or disposed of safely. Other devices skimmed off residual oil that had been used in making steel. Chemicals neutralized acids in the process water before it was discharged into lakes, rivers and streams.

Polluted air got a lot of attention, too.

Air from the steelmaking furnaces came out loaded with dust or other particles. Before the environmental era dawned, this smoke simply drifted out of the stacks, into the air. Now, though, mechanical contraptions spun the contaminated air, creating little cyclones that flung out the heavier particles. It was just one method of erasing smoke from the sky, and one of several environmental technologies that U. S. Steel developed or adapted for its mills.

This huge clarifier, used to settle out blast-furnace dust, was an example of U. S. Steel's efforts to minimize air and water pollution. The resulting clean water was returned to the plant for other uses.

Smaller, more stubborn particles remained in the exhaust vapors. They were bombarded by injected water, scrubbed out in environmental science's version of the washing machine. Or those pollutants were zapped out of process air as it passed through electrostatic fields, or sucked into the dust-collection bags of what amounted to huge vacuum cleaners. Harmful or obnoxious gases were incinerated.

Other waste-treatment technologies were—or soon would be—in the works. The environmental pros at Gary were working on an unusual way to get rid of a process waste that had an unusual name. Before the decade was out, they were injecting spent "pickle liquor" down a special well, into a bed of porous rock almost a mile underground.

But all these systems were add-ons. And they were not the best way to get rid of pollution.

A more efficient, more economical way of dealing with pollution was to build control technologies into new steelmaking equipment. That was the beauty of the new BOPs, the Basic Oxygen Furnaces. Besides making steel some eight times faster than the old open hearths they replaced, the BOP shops stopped pollution in its tracks, and did it more economically than open hearths could. This was because BOPs were equipped with scrubbers and other anti-pollution equipment as they were being constructed. The pollution preventers were built right in.

This massive BOP cleaning facility contained spray chambers, scrubbers and cooling towers as well as water clarifiers.

Naturally, U. S. Steel had a campaign to install as many BOPs as possible. By early 1971, it had a half-dozen BOP shops up and running at, among other plants, its Duquesne works near Pittsburgh, Chicago's South Works, the Gary Works and at its mill in Lorain, Ohio.

None of this was cheap, neither the BOPs nor the anti-pollution add-ons. And Blough had a complaint: The time was past due for the steel industry to get the tax breaks it deserved for environmental spending—breaks that would help assure it could continue to build pollution-abatement facilities.

"Expenditures for these facilities do not add to the value of the product produced," Blough insisted, "but they do add measurably to construction and operating costs....

"U. S. Steel feels...that such expenditures should be considered an operating expense as incurred and hopes that Congress will permit acceleration of the write-off for income tax purposes."

Still, there were other ways to stretch the environmental dollar. Take the built-right-in method a step further and you have the concept of building an entirely new steel works that is super-efficient and super-economical because it was built from the ground up. No retrofits; everything original and engineered from scratch.

That's exactly what U. S. Steel did in Texas.

In the late Sixties, the corporation began work on a "greenfield" plant 35 miles from Houston. U. S. Steel's new Texas Works was rising on undeveloped land, smack in the heart of oil country, and the folks in oil country were busy. They needed pipe and other steel components used in oil exploration and drilling, and oilfield products would be the new works' stock-in-trade.

Texas Works takes shape as a "greenfield" plant 35 miles east of Houston. It opened for business in 1971 with a product line consisting of pipe and other steel components used by the oil industry.

The Texas Works opened for business in 1971. It did not look like a steel plant. There were no platoons of towering smokestacks because, essentially, there was no smoke. No bell-shaped furnaces to be seen from the surrounding fields, no mazes of pipe or open-sided, shed-like buildings. The place was a neat collection of clean, box-like structures. It could have been an assembly center or research lab for electronics.

But it was a steel works. In fact, it was a showcase of the newest steelmaking technology, from electric furnaces and continuous casters to the latest environmental gear. One national magazine called it "the first steel mill ever to make an effort to be clean clear through."

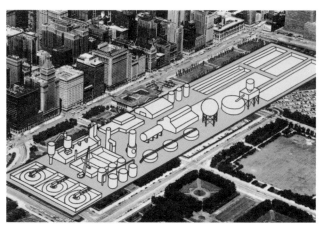

A diagram superimposed on Grant Park in downtown Chicago dramatized the size of Gary Works' mammoth new water treatment facility. In this diagram the facility, which covered 35 acres, stretched from Randolph Street to Congress Parkway.

Many of the plant's installations—particularly the public-swimming-pool-sized settling basins and the other water-treating facilities—took up a lot of space. The company made the point visually in the January/February 1969 *U S Steel News* by superimposing a diagram of the Gary Works' new water treatment installations—just the water treatment plants—over a photo of downtown Chicago's Grant Park. The environmental facilities "covered" 35 acres, an area of the park about seven blocks by three blocks.

Size was no small problem when it came to retrofitting older steel plants with the gear required to pull the steelmaking wastes out of water and air.

Many of U. S. Steel's older works were hemmed in by rivers or lakes, or by factories, roads and even houses. Development had encircled them.

The company might be able to shoehorn in a cooling tower for process water over here, a vacuum cleaner for air over there. But where could it put a water-cleansing lagoon? Or one of the pits used to collect and recycle process oil or the scale that was sloughed off steel during a process called pickling? Or, for that matter, the facilities that cleansed "used" air—small factories in their own right?

And when it came to technology to make steel and technologies to maintain clean air and water, the steel companies were chasing their tails. To stay competitive, they had to invest in newer steelmaking equipment. It was more productive. But it demanded further spending to raise the capacity of the environmental equipment that served it.

And as we'll see, U. S. Steel and the other steel companies grew increasingly irritated because they were being pushed over the cliff of diminishing returns. The first two-thirds of a pollutant could be contained, treated or eliminated at far less cost than the final 5 or 10 percent, and the technology to wipe out the final percentage points of pollution didn't exist.

Still, environmentalists kept raising the bar.

U. S. Steel President Edgar B. Speer complained about this "ever-changing character of specific control problems" when, in 1970, he spoke at the National Executives Conference on Water Pollution Abatement.

The session was in Washington, D.C., and it was conducted by the U.S. Department of the Interior. (Interior Secretary Walter J. Hickel had recently commended U. S. Steel for the pollution abatement job it was doing at its facilities on the Great Lakes.)

"With the changing requirements of states and federal agencies," Speer told his audience, "steelmen often find themselves in the position where they feel they have completed a job begun under one set of official standards, only to discover they are faced with additional requirements....

> *"When we consider the effects of criteria changes, with the time-consuming research, engineering and construction they frequently entail, the futility of measuring water conservation programs in terms of absolutes becomes apparent.*
>
> *"As vitally as we are concerned with water pollution abatement... we oppose treatment for treatment's sake.... That is, unless some user receives value as the result of the treatment given the waste, then the money spent for pollution control is removed forever from productive use."*

Speer had a point. And he was articulating it more politely than he would have back in his office. There, he would have used sharper language.

Then-chairman Edward Gott would have, too.

Gott and Speer were mad. At a time when they were trying hard to keep their balance sheet in shape, they were being told to punch a hole in earnings by pouring money into unproductive environmental installations.

Laws varied by state and community. The *Birmingham News* looked at the corporation's environmental record and, in its May 5, 1970, edition, summed up its findings: "Abatement efforts have been extremely uneven and vary according to the strength of the law in the states where U. S. Steel plants are located.... Control efforts are most advanced in Pennsylvania, where the laws are strongest, but at the U. S. Steel works in Fairfield, Alabama, there are no air pollution controls whatever, with the result that the factory spews out an estimated 45 million pounds of dust annually."

True enough, the steel industry had to deal with a hydra-headed environmental bureaucracy. Like the bosses in other "smokestack" industries, they had to sort out and meet a multitude of environmental regulations that had been issued by states and local communities. Some federal laws were on guard, too, but they weren't strong enough to satisfy a lot of federal legislators.

These agencies bumped into each other as they tried to administer protection for rivers, lakes, forests and the air—subjects that knew no political boundaries. If it wasn't pure chaos, it was not the way to get the job done, either.

Policy makers argued that the federal government should be granted stronger authority over this confusion. One official in particular, President Lyndon Johnson, pushed hard for federal-umbrella powers to set industry-wide limits on the release of pollutants into the atmosphere.

In 1970, after he'd left office, Johnson got his wish. Through the efforts of his successor, Richard M. Nixon, Congress passed the national Clean Air Act and created the powerful national Environmental Protection Agency—the EPA—to enforce it. A national Clean Water Act would follow two years later.

The war against pollution was being waged by big generals with big guns. And now began a period marked by confrontations that often bordered on the surreal.

A good example was the lunchtime raid that a busy environmental activist known as "the Fox" launched on one of U. S. Steel's offices.

The Fox's antics were designed to expose and embarrass companies that environmentalists characterized as willful polluters. He had been busy. By the time he got around to U. S. Steel and its alleged environmental sins, he had gained a sympathetic audience and the attention of the press.

Chicago was the Fox's main theater of operation, and, in late 1970, he pulled a lunch-hour raid at U. S. Steel's Chicago office.

He slipped into the building, and through a doorway marked as the office of Edward Logelin, a U. S. Steel vice president. Logelin was out to lunch. After announcing to a receptionist that he had a gift for Logelin, the Fox began untwisting the cap from a large bottle of foul-smelling liquid, a disgusting cocktail he claimed he'd collected from a drain that emptied into a stream from U. S. Steel's Gary Works in Indiana. He sloshed the disgusting potion on Logelin's nice white carpet, and, by accident, on the foot of a secretary who was approaching him to see what he was doing. She screamed, and the Fox fled—out the door and down an emergency stairwell.

Ed Logelin: "Why didn't [the Fox] come when I was here?"

This piece of guerrilla theater was written up by nationally known Chicago newspaper columnist Mike Royko. He had become the Fox's main contact in the press, and he now printed Vice President Logelin's protest: "Why didn't he come when I was here?" the usually affable, now-fuming Logelin asked Royko. "I'm a big boy!"

Royko's readers could tell the columnist was chuckling as he typed up his report. Between Royko's lines, many of them read that the small and helpless—themselves—had scored one against a mighty corporation.

Right on, Fox!

But who was the Fox? There were those who suspected he was a prominent priest turned protester. But he could have been any of a number of frustrated citizens. Much of the world, it seemed, was angry with U. S. Steel and other industries because of their supposed penchant for polluting.

Whoever the Fox was, his assault on U. S. Steel was right on cue.

Not only did 1970 bring Congressional passage of the first Clean Air Act (a revised act would follow), but it was the year of the first Earth Day, when 20 million people around the globe gathered to celebrate nature and to raise a red flag against society's degradation of the environment.

When it came to environmental matters, the government spoke and acted through the EPA. Its mission: enforce environmental regulations previously policed by agencies which had no teeth.

The EPA *did* have teeth, and it was soon flashing them at the steelmakers.

Wrote Christopher Hall in *Steel Phoenix*: "[EPA] immediately began to focus on the steel industry, which it estimated to be responsible for one-third of all industrial waste-water pollution in the United States, and 10 percent of the total air pollution emissions."

EPA wanted to fix that. Between 1971 and 1973, said Hall, it sued almost every American steel producer to compel them to reduce emissions in water and air. As a result, U. S. Steel and the other domestic producers faced huge expenditures to clean up their operations during a time when they needed to invest in new facilities to produce steel more efficiently—facilities that would help them compete with offshore mills.

In the eyes of the EPA regulators, cost was no object, and fines became the agency's biggest weapon. Working under the provisions of the air and water acts, the agency adopted a standard procedure of pressing industries to meet its mandated reductions in air and water emissions by specific deadlines. It didn't matter that the required technology didn't exist. Find a way or pay, Uncle Sam demanded. This tactic was called "technology-forcing." The steel managers would have called it extortion.

When environmental protection should have been a business–government partnership, it was reduced to a shoving match. And both sides seemed to like to play rough.

Veterans from U. S. Steel's environmental brigade agree that the EPA set targets that *were* unrealistic, then refused to budge. But, they add, during most of the Seventies, U. S. Steel's management was in no hurry to meet the standards and schedules. And with good reason. The company needed time to assess the massive environmental requirements it was expected to meet. Then U. S. Steel's environmental and engineering staffs had to determine how technically to comply. Or, as a very likely alternative, to consider the option of shutting down some operations when the cost of compliance could not be justified.

Remarkably, corporate records show that the U. S. Steel Law Department considered marching off to court to fight all of EPA's pollution-control mandates. But it didn't take long for the lawyers to conclude that the real issue was not *whether* the corporation should abide by EPA's directives. The anti-pollution regulations were too popular to fight, and who could argue with their objectives?

No, the real issue was whether the corporation would have enough time to do the job right—to allocate enough money and technical problem-solving to perfect and install effective anti-emissions technology—without going broke.

The corporation decided to buy that time. The objective became negotiating EPA consent decrees, including permission to stretch out the deadlines for meeting EPA's emissions standards.

One victim of this resistance mindset was Earl Mallick. He was the corporation's first vice president of environmental affairs. As such, he was a human tennis ball, whacked back and forth between insistent EPA officials and resistant corporate officers.

"I'd go out to the agencies and get beat up all day," Mallick shrugged during an interview for this history. "Then I'd come back to the headquarters and get beat up there."

Mallick wasn't an environmental scientist, but an electrical engineer who had studied law at Harvard. That was okay, because he started on the corporate law staff in 1949 and progressed through labor arbitration, lobbying, and community and industrial relations jobs in Pittsburgh and Birmingham. The experience probably prepared him as well as any schooling could for the negotiating, cajoling and quarreling he would get into with environmental regulators.

Earl Mallick, the corporation's first vice president of environmental affairs

"The government set standards which were, in many cases, unobtainable," Mallick asserted. "Then it would insist we meet them. We'd argue nose-to-nose about what we were going to agree to, and they'd threaten us with anything possible if we didn't agree to meet them.

"Gott and Speer were really angry about what the government was trying to force them to do," added Mallick. "Their attitude was that they were doing a good job."

Mallick himself became associated with "the enemy."

One morning, while in his office in Pittsburgh, Mallick received a phone call of complaint from a U. S. Steel vice president. Allegheny County officials were insisting that the corporation's Clairton Works was emitting a thick blanket of smoke. The works could take steps to diminish the smoke, but that would cost money. Besides, the vice president claimed, the Clairton plant was running clean. Mallick could see for himself by looking in the mill's direction, up the Monongahela River.

"Those county guys are nuts," the caller told Mallick. "Look out your window. Look at the sunny day!"

Mallick did more than that. He took a ride over to check the readings on an air monitor the Clairton Works had positioned at a school near the plant. He didn't have to read the device: "The smoke was so thick around the school that I couldn't see out the windshield."

Mallick returned to his office and told the VP to cut the smoke.

"He was trying to sandbag me," Mallick insisted.

What sense did this make? "By fighting [with the agencies] the way we did, we brought on more trouble," Mallick later insisted. "We'd have done better if we'd adopted a more cooperative attitude."

By remaining blind to that wisdom, Gott drove himself and the company into an embarrassing jam.

The trouble had to do with the Clean Water Act. Soon after its passage in 1972, its enforcers decreed that, by 1975, U. S. Steel would have to obtain environmental discharge permits at every plant, one for every drain that emptied water into a river or stream. That meant certifying that the water going down every single drain was "clean." If it wasn't, track the source and fix the trouble.

Mallick's successor, Dr. Philip Masciantonio, found himself in the middle of this rush job. Masciantonio held a Ph.D. in chemistry from Carnegie Mellon University in Pittsburgh. He joined U. S. Steel's Monroeville research center in 1955, and soon became involved in environmental research.

Of the outfall chase-down, Masciantonio later admitted: "We thought it would be impossible for us to comply. We had 87 operations, and 314 outfalls."

Not only would trying to carry out the EPA's order be a frantic exercise, it might paint the corporation into a legal corner. At least that was the advice of one of the corporation's attorneys. The reason: The company representatives would have to sign what amounted to a promise to fix all the outfalls when, in all likelihood, it couldn't. To the lawyers, that sounded like a fat lawsuit, or jail.

Almost every other steel company signed similar agreements, Masciantonio recalled, "even though they couldn't make the numbers, either. Ed Gott, though, took a stand. He refused to sign. He thought the government would back off. But he was wrong.

"He had to go to Washington," said Masciantonio, "to tell Attorney General John Mitchell that we were going to keep running without the permits. Mitchell warned him—you'll end up in a serious problem. Congress says you have to sign.

"We came back home with our tail between our legs."

At about the same time, the corporation suffered the "Thanksgiving Day Massacre." On this particular Thanksgiving, Pennsylvania officials had marshals deliver subpoenas to U. S. Steel's top executives—subpoenas ordering them to appear before a grand jury to answer charges that they were violating the Clean Air Act.

Dr. Philip Masciantonio inherited an environmental headache from the EPA and helped to soothe it.

"The government didn't pursue the case," said Masciantonio. "But it was depressing for people who worked [in environmental jobs], and who knew they could be brought up on criminal charges."

There were more embarrassing and stressful incidents: The time Speer, after rising to chairman, reneged on promises to install environmental equipment at certain plants; the other executives who dictated to, and dressed down, environmental authorities; the two Homestead plant guards who were arrested for obstructing justice because they refused to let two credentialed, state environmental officials through the plant gate; the Gary Works general superintendent who refused to accept the responsibility to let an EPA inspector enter the plant, and who phoned Speer to get the okay. It was a time during which conflicts with environmental agents were not rare, noted Masciantonio. "There were a lot of shouting matches…people walking out of rooms… slamming of desks. We promised to put on every bell and whistle at new plants, but not at old plants. And the government didn't like that."

Throwing gasoline on the flames was the company's distrust of government. "It went back to Blough's confrontation with Kennedy,"

Masciantonio contended. "It created bad blood [between the corporation and the government] that lasted a long time."

The hard feelings spilled over into the media. It was politically correct for TV and print journalists to ignore technology and timing and turn the environmental conflicts into a morality play, with government taking the role of the white knight, industry the villain.

Chicago Tribune writer Bob Cromie's editorial page column of January 22, 1971, was typical. It covered pollutants that U. S. Steel's South Works had been releasing into Lake Michigan. Regulators had granted the plant five years to halt the discharges. "Five Years to Stop Polluting [the] Lake?" Cromie cried in his headline. In the column, Cromie wondered why halting the pollution should take so long—and "how long it would take United States Steel to straighten out some flaw in its manufacturing process if [the flaw] were polluting the product."

Was the trouble a mere "flaw"? Why should it take a whole five years to fix the problem? Cromie only asked the questions. He had no answers. He did no research into anti-pollution technology and its costs. To Cromie, apparently, the solution to the problem of emissions was a matter of throwing a switch. Just stop polluting.

Such oversimplification in the press and by the regulators drove U. S. Steel management up the wall.

Ed Gott often took a defensive, "we're-not-the-only-ones" tone. In a March 1971 *U S Steel News* roundup of the company's environmental pressure and progress, he complained that "governmental bodies must correct their own pollution."

Speer even seemed intent on spreading the hard feelings to the communities around the company's plants. In a series of editorial advertisements placed in local papers when he was chairman, he addressed the environmental operations spending conflict, the fact that the company had to put money into expensive environmental installations and operating measures, money that could raise its steel productivity and competitive strength.

But the conclusions were arrogant, even threatening.

One ad was headlined: "U. S. Steel has spent millions of dollars on major expansions at Neville Island. I hope they won't be the last." In the text, Speer summarized the environmental improvements the corporation had made at the Pittsburgh-area chemical plant, but the message was "enough is enough." Speer's conclusion: "…We can't continue to commit people and money if we're asked to go beyond what is technically practical in pollution controls—or held to unreasonable timetables."

"Did we make a mistake by locating our new headquarters building in Pittsburgh?" asked another ad. Speer totted up the salaries the company paid in the Pittsburgh area, reviewed the investment it made in plants to preserve jobs and mentioned the suppliers it supported in the Pittsburgh area. Could the company maintain these kinds of investments? "I'd like to think so," said Speer. Then he asked: "Will the governmental and environmental climate favor selection of the Pittsburgh area? We hope it does!"

There was nothing specific here, but the threat was clear: U. S. Steel could move its operations to other cities with more favorable governmental and environmental "climates."

And where could the corporation—any corporation—go to escape such steep environmental obligations? Just *how* steep was revealed in a study commissioned by the American Iron and Steel Institute and conducted by the Arthur D. Little, Inc., engineering and consulting firm.

In their findings, released in 1975, the Little researchers concluded that meeting the mandates would require the steel industry to spend $12 billion to $14 billion by 1983. That broke down to about $1.4 billion a year—a full quarter of the steel industry's expected total capital requirements. On top of that, the report projected, steelmakers would have to raise their operations costs by 10 percent. That translated into a $25- to $30-a-ton hike in the price of steel.

That wasn't all. Running plants with environmental gear would use more energy—the equivalent of 23 million barrels of fuel oil each year. And half that energy increase would be needed to control "visible fugitive emissions." These were small, random leaks whose removal previous reports had termed "cosmetic."

The report's authors asked this question: Was getting rid of them worth spending $3 billion in extra energy costs?

"Yes!" cried the regulators, politicians and much of the public. "Zero pollution" was their wish. But, as U. S. Steel Vice Chairman R. Heath Larry insisted, zero pollution was totally unrealistic.

Larry was speaking in his role as chairman of the U.S. President's Committee on Health Education, but the environmental groups said his view didn't count. In comments picked up by the *Pittsburgh Press* on January 11, 1972, Michelle Madoff of GASP (Group Against Smog and Pollution) protested, "There are many who feel that the appointment by President [Richard M.] Nixon of R. Heath Larry, a member of good standing of the board of directors of U. S. Steel…is a blatant example of the fox guarding the chicken coop."

The burden of battling pollution was greatly eased, though, when the EPA relaxed its schedule and negotiated more reasonable requirements. The agency granted the steel industry "consent agreements," under which producers agreed to spend specific sums of money to lower emissions to specific levels by specific—extended—deadlines. In effect, the decrees legitimized the industry's strategy of delay in meeting environmental orders and recognized EPA's unrealistic demands. They made financing of environmental improvements easier. Things got done.

The steel market helped. It was good to the producers during the decade's early years, and the resulting profits made it easier for them to spend for environmental processes. "In the three peak years 1975 to 1977," Hall pointed out, "the steel companies spent $1.2 billion on pollution control capital investment, or 13.5 percent of their total capital expenditures."

In fact, U. S. Steel made impressive environmental progress during the Seventies—even with the burdensome costs and political aggravation.

In 1971, the U.S. Justice Department filed a suit against the corporation's Fairfield Works for polluting the Warrior River. Justice withdrew the suit in 1972, after the corporation agreed to build the necessary facilities to treat process water it released into the river. Construction began in 1974, and the "facilities" turned out to be 19 water- and air-pollution control projects that the company said would ring up at almost $60 million.

One of the Fairfield projects was a new, even-cleaner version of the basic oxygen process which U. S. Steel had refined from a German development. In creating the "Q-BOP" technology, the company's engineers effectively turned the former BOP furnace upside down. Oxygen for steelmaking had been shot into the top of the BOP. In the Q-BOP, it was blown in at the bottom, and the result was more steel-making efficiency.

Work on the Fairfield Q-BOP started in mid-1973, a few months after the corporation unveiled the new technology at its Gary Works. Gary management agreed, under a consent decree, to cut soot emissions, which the new technology made it easier to do. Then Gary management said they would install $166 million in new water pollution controls. But the announcement came after state and local environmental authorities sued the corporation for excessive discharge at Gary.

Meanwhile, in Pennsylvania's Allegheny County, the company's Edgar Thomson Works was planning $5 million worth of gear, plus operational changes, aimed at cleaning up air emissions. This was after the corporation tested the constitutionality of Allegheny County's air pollution control law.

U. S. Steel was upgrading environmental systems and adding new ones at other plants, too. But, when it came to pollution, the corporation's biggest problem by far was the coke plant at its Clairton Works, 15 miles up the Monongahela River from Pittsburgh.

Turning coal into coke for steelmaking is the dirtiest end of the steel business. The corporation and the residents of Clairton and Liberty Borough nearby were reminded of that in November 1975, when they

(Above) Gary Works' new Q-BOP facility launched a new era of high-volume steelmaking. The Q-BOP technology was a new, cleaner version of the basic oxygen process.

(Right) This complex gas cleaning system serviced the three-furnace Q-BOP shop at Gary Works.

found themselves to be the victims of an air pollution emergency that was disturbingly reminiscent of the Donora disaster.

An EPA study released a half-year later indicated the crisis may have contributed to the deaths of 14 people.

The corporation was again in the hot seat. As the *Pittsburgh Post-Gazette* said in a May 11, 1976, summary of the crisis, "Two issues in the dispute were whether U. S. Steel acted quickly enough and whether it was only the pressure of possible federal court action that forced the steelmaker to act at all."

"Acting quickly enough" meant, at the first sign of trouble, reducing coke emissions by stretching the coking cycle from the usual 18 hours to 48 hours.

The event reminded everyone of the urgent need to clean up cokemaking. It produced potentially harmful particulate matter, hydrogen sulfide, sulfur dioxide and benzene. Into the Seventies, a large portion of these pollutants escaped into the air when crews opened the coking ovens to charge them with more coal. This was the biggest environmental problem in cokemaking, and probably in steelmaking. Pollutants also leaked out from around the closed battery doors.

In the Seventies, U. S. Steel engineers—and Clairton employees—put their heads together and came up with a new way to seal the doors. U. S. Steel also installed equipment that prevented much of the pollution during charging. More improvements would come later. Today, Clairton is among the cleanest cokemaking facilities in the world, the example EPA asks others to match.

Looking back at the environmental frenzy of the Gott-Speer era, it is possible to sympathize with both men's truculence concerning environmental spending.

At the outset, they were simply protecting the resources of their company from what they considered were EPA's ill-advised clean-up standards and compliance timetables. To Gott and Speer, it seemed apparent that the standards and timetables were unreasonable and unattainable because the technology to create the controls didn't exist. So, they stubbornly defended their company from a government they felt was reacting irrationally, prodded by an American public which had suddenly discovered a close-to-home cause to espouse—clean air and clean water.

One of the most baffling features of this whole drama is that men like Gott and Speer—leaders who were affable, even-tempered, well-liked by the men in the plants and highly respected in the business community—continued a policy of confrontation when the time for compromise was clearly at hand.

Whatever the psychological and personal reasons behind the bad blood, it stopped flowing after David Roderick ascended to the U. S. Steel chairmanship.

Battling chairmen: Edward Gott (left) and Edgar Speer led the charge in U. S. Steel's confrontation with the EPA during the late 1960s and early 1970s.

We'll learn more about Roderick, a former World War II Marine with a talent for cool analysis and for decision making that weighed political and social realities.

For now, it's enough to know that, soon after he first sat down at the chairman's desk, he began mending fences in the environmental area. As Masciantonio put it, "Roderick immediately started to end the trench warfare—and that's what we called it. He decided that life could not go on the way it had with the Sierra Club, the wildlife groups. They had us tagged as public enemy number one."

Roderick didn't let ego block his view of reality. He could see that, demanding as environmental regulations were, waging war on the people who enforced them was futile and dangerous.

As Roderick told the author, "They always tell you never to fight with a guy that has a gun, and never to fight with people who buy ink by the ton."

Chapter 15

Boom and Gloom

At the start of the Seventies, U. S. Steel's top managers squinted into the future and declared that, all in all, the new decade looked good.

But they had reservations. For one thing, a growing breed of smaller steel producers—"minimills"—was nipping at their heels. For another, the company would have to choke back emissions even further. That meant more costs, at a time when income seemed to be "trending" down: After reaching what was then an all-time record of $253.7 million in 1968, income retreated to $217.2 million in 1969.

On the other hand, during the same period, consumption had been growing steadily—at an apparent rate of more than 4.3 percent a year, according to Christopher Hall, author of *Steel Phoenix*. U. S. Steel sales had picked up steam, reaching almost $5 billion in 1969.

Further, with its new Q-BOPs and a new-from-the-ground-up mill in Texas, the corporation was making nice progress in modernizing.

Certainly, when Edwin H. Gott, who had succeeded Roger Blough as U. S. Steel's chairman, addressed the company's 1970 annual shareholders' meeting, he delivered a sunny forecast for steel.

"Before the decade is out," he declared, "the world will become a billion-ton-a-year customer of raw steel.... With our resources and capabilities in metals and minerals technology, and with our skilled manpower, U. S. Steel will participate profitably in this world of opportunities."

Gott was careful not to predict *how* profitably. But his optimism was not unfounded, given the numbers and trends U. S. Steel and just about everyone else were divining.

Also encouraging was U. S. Steel's diversity. Quite logically, considering events like the import squeeze, the company had been carefully depositing its eggs in other baskets. As Roger Blough characterized the corporation at his farewell annual meeting, U. S. Steel was more than a steel company. It was a materials company. It made steel and chemicals and cement. It erected buildings and bridges, and ran other operations that danced to different business tunes. When the steel business was down, the other businesses could be up. Given this potential built-in insurance, it's easy to see why Chairman Gott was bullish on the future when he addressed shareholders in 1970.

U. S. Steel Chairman Edwin Gott addressed shareholders in 1970 with bullish optimism.

Gott was the picture of optimism, anyway. Silver-haired and photogenic, he liked to transmit assurance at his press conferences by smiling at the cameras as, theatrically, he counted on his fingers the points he was making. Still, from where he and the shareholders sat, the future—the *near* future, at least—looked like a good bet.

But all bets were off a few years later, when a consortium of oil-producing countries put a stopper in the United States' oil supply, orchestrating an economy-crippling "energy crisis."

Many Americans didn't know it, but their nation's supplies of oil and therefore gasoline were short from the start of the Seventies. American tempers got short, too, when, in 1973, the Organization of Petroleum Exporting Countries—OPEC—started closing their oil spigot.

Almost all of OPEC's members were Middle Eastern Arab nations, and they wanted to teach the United States a lesson for supporting Israel in the October 1973 Yom Kippur War—the fourth and fiercest of a series of wars Israel had fought against Egypt, Syria and other Arab nations.

The OPEC nations had plenty of sand and oil. America needed the oil. So, flexing its muscles as an oil monopoly, OPEC cut back supplies to the United States, creating shortages of crude, and, therefore, heating oil and gasoline. The OPEC producers also got together and raised their price for Middle Eastern crude from $3 to more than $11 a barrel. By 1979, according to the American Petroleum Institute (API), a barrel of crude rose to nearly $13. In response, the average retail price of gasoline in the USA shot up from 38.5 cents a gallon in May 1973 to 55.1 cents in June 1974. It would reach 85 cents a gallon in 1979, API indicated, before easing downward. Meanwhile, U.S. imports of oil from Arab countries virtually dried up, plummeting from 1.2 million barrels a day to 19,000.

This was a shortage created by politics. And the federal government fought back with more politics. It commandeered the distribution of gasoline, dusting off an old, emergency allocation system based on old consumption data. As Daniel Yergin explained in *The Prize: The Epic Quest for Oil, Money and Power* (Simon & Schuster, 1991), the emergency plan "assured, perversely, that gasoline could not be shifted from an area already well-supplied to one where it was needed."

While the government delivered gasoline where it was plentiful, drivers jammed gas stations where it was scarce. They formed lines up to two miles long to insure they got their share of what gas there was, or to "top off" their tanks with a few insurance gallons.

Aerial view of a section of the Trans-Alaska Pipeline route as it winds its way between Prudhoe Bay and the port of Valdez. More than 36,000 "shoe assemblies" were fabricated by American Bridge Division to support the elevated sections of the 800-mile pipeline.

Anger mounted. Motorists crashed lines and assaulted the pump jockeys. Others quietly stewed while they idled in line, burning gas and listening to their car radios—perhaps to news about the planned Trans-Alaska Pipeline. This 800-mile-long, $100 million steel tube was going to deliver oil from Prudhoe Bay, a crude-oil jackpot on Alaska's Arctic, northern coast, to a port on the state's southern coast. Huge tankers would then shuttle the oil south for distribution in the "lower 48" states.

In 1977, the pipeline was finished. It shot across Alaskan plains, slithered through gorges and ducked underground for long stretches. That year, it pumped over a million barrels of crude daily for an oil-thirsty nation.

The largest construction project in the nation's history, the Alaska pipeline had required unimaginable quantities of steel. Steel for workers' dormitories. Steel for the pumping stations that kept the oil flowing. Steel for the stilts engineered to keep the pipeline safely stable over stretches of Alaska's often-mushy "permafrost" surface. U. S. Steel won contracts for the steel "shoes" the pipeline "wore" so it could stand on those stilts.

This was the mother of all pipelines, and, since its inception, American steelmakers had been rubbing their hands together at the thought of manufacturing even small pieces of it.

The real prize would be a contract for the 48-inch-diameter, high-grade pipe that would comprise the pipeline itself, the 800-mile-long artery for oil. But as it turned out, no American steel producer was equipped to bid for it.

That main pipeline, designed to deliver American oil to energy-hungry American homes, automobiles and factories, was built by... the Japanese!

A consortium of Japanese steel companies, to be exact. Some of the same steel companies that, subsidized by their government, had been raiding the American producers' home turf, pecking holes in the American firms' profits and shooing away American jobs.

For America, it was a sad irony.

For American steel, it was a slap in the face.

OPEC's embargo and price hikes made everyone pay dearly, and not just at the gasoline pump. They jacked up the price for all crude oil, and, as a result, for all kinds of goods and services down the line.

"In 1974 alone, retail prices increased by 11 percent and wholesale prices by 18 percent," recalled James T. Patterson in *Grand Expectations*, a United States history published in 1996 by Oxford University Press. "The impact of the embargo and of other structural flaws in the economy touched off unsettled times that lasted until 1983 .... And by the end of the decade the United States was dealing with double-digit inflation as well as double-digit unemployment."

"Recession" became a familiar word.

For U. S. Steel, the immediate turmoil of the so-called energy crisis was partly offset by some reassuring facts and events.

Busy oil crews needed more drill rigs, drill bits and pipe. Especially hot drilling zones were under the oceans, along the continental shelves, and they were risky and expensive to drill. Now, though, they commanded higher prices, and they were worth going after. The call went out for more offshore drill rigs—huge steel islands that floated drilling crews out and over the ocean-bed oil targets.

Since our oil and gas supplies looked iffy, demand climbed for coal as a sure substitute for industry's boilers. Orders for coal from U. S. Steel mines shot up. So did orders for the mighty mining machines whose spinning steel cutters drilled into the coal beds or shaved coal away in long, repeated sweeps.

This was good news for steel, but it was overridden by the bad.

Who knew how much fuel oil or natural gas would even be available at any given time in the future? Natural gas was a big worry. Its supplies were especially prone to shortages.

And who knew where energy prices would go? High fuel bills pulled the carpet out from under non-energy businesses. Demand for the steel they used took a spill, too. Adding insult to injury, the corporation had to manage the higher energy costs at its fuel-devouring but now semi-idling plants.

Right after the 1973 oil embargo, the corporation started to cover itself. It devised a strategy to squeeze every BTU it could out of the fuel oil and natural gas it had to buy, and it scoured its plants for ways to switch from oil and gas to cheaper, surer fuels.

There was good reason, especially, to scrimp in the steel mills. They ate up 90 percent of the energy consumed by the entire corporation. This was the case even though a lot of their fuel consisted of by-product gas drawn from the company's coke ovens. These ovens converted coal into coke. And since the corporation ran its own coal mines, a big fix for skyrocketing fuel bills was finding ways to substitute coal for other fuels—especially shortage-prone natural gas.

Another good thing the mills had going was the new generation of steel hardware. The multiplying Q-BOPs, electric furnaces and continuous casters didn't guzzle energy like the machinery they replaced. In comparison, they sipped it politely.

Still, there were a lot more BTUs to be saved, and the corporation's engineers and researchers set their brains to the task.

They devised systems to fire coke oven batteries with waste gas from the blast furnaces. They retrofitted equipment to round up escaping heat. They computer-calibrated the flow of energy to the operations, and fine-tuned furnaces so they used fuel more efficiently. They installed souped-up emission-scrubbers that allowed some mills to burn coal directly, cleanly.

Energy saved here and there added up, and, in 1978, the technical wizards hit a conservation target they'd set for 1980: Using 1972 as a base year, they shaved energy consumption almost 10 percent. Still, they kept modifying processes and controls. Looking further ahead, they partnered with the Department of Energy to develop systems that would harness solar energy and substitute natural gas with methane from the coal mines.

In the 1980s, U. S. Steel implemented a program inspired by the oil shortage. In its steelmaking plants, the company installed equipment allowing crews to operate on either gas or electricity, choosing the fuel that happened to be the cheapest at the time.

Cracking the whip over errant BTUs became a pastime for all industries, and it consumed lots of money and time.

Especially irksome was the fact that energy shortages were aggravated, if not created, by government policies. Enough was enough. In 1977, a new U. S. Steel board chairman, Edgar B. Speer, lit into federal energy-policy drafters for their crunch-causing directives.

Edgar Speer succeeded Gott as board chairman.

He got vocal. As the nation was emerging from one of the iciest winters ever, Speer blasted the "cold hand of government" for natural gas shortages that worsened the cold's bite, shut schools, stores and businesses, and put millions of people out of work.

Speer blamed government caps on gas prices: "The Federal Power Commission has held the wellhead price of this clean-burning fuel at artificially low levels since the mid-1950s. As a result, there have been no economic incentives for energy companies to locate new reserves."

Ultimately, the government unchained natural gas prices so they could float upward to their real value, so energy outfits had reason to drill. Meanwhile, the controls reminded Speer of the regulatory policies that put a chill on steelmaking.

To illustrate the point, he cited a federal Council on Wage and Price Stability study that listed regulations influencing steelmaking.

The council didn't report *all* the "regs." But it did manage to catalogue 5,600.

They had been issued by 27 agencies.

Running-wild energy costs were all the steel chiefs needed.

They were already fighting the battle of the dumped steel. They were getting hoarse arguing that employment costs were slowly strangling them. Choking them, too, was the frenzied, pre-steel-bargaining three-step: the frantic hedge-buying and stockpiling of steel (unfortunately including foreign steel)…the plummeting orders as customers worked down their inventories…and the increasingly loud whoosh of incoming steel imports.

They pleaded their case from behind podiums and into lawmakers' ears. But who was listening?

Steelworkers' union president I. W. Abel was. He decided to add his voice to those of the producers—at least on the issue of strikes.

Abel, who was elected United Steel Workers president in mid-1965, had for some time been thinking about a "no-strike" agreement. He had watched the sorry stockpiling-to-imports cycle replay itself every time the steelworkers' contract came up for renewal. And he worried that it was crippling the steel industry. His workers, his people, might be striking themselves out of jobs.

Abel's fears flared up after the contract round of 1971. He had emerged from last-minute bargaining with a huge victory for his steelworkers: a contract with wage increases that worked out to 10 percent immediately and 31 percent over three years. The deal also reinstated the COLA, the locked-in cost-of-living hikes that had been shelved during earlier talks.

But as John P. Hoerr related in his 1988 book, *And the Wolf Finally Came* (University of Pittsburgh Press), "The steelworkers' joy about the 1971 wage increases evaporated in the months ahead.

"Steel customers had stockpiled about 17 million tons of steel," Hoerr wrote. "After the settlements, layoffs, begun in June, accelerated. About one hundred thousand steelworkers were furloughed in the next few months, and ninety thousand were out of work for six months."

The destructive cycle cost the industry $80 million in 1971, and fueled Abel's growing belief that industry-wide strikes might be outmoded. Hoerr summarized the question Abel was wrestling:

> *"If the price of threatening to strike was that one hundred thousand members would be laid off while the remaining two hundred thousand received the immediate 10 percent pay hike, would the jobless members think the price was worth the principle?"*

Abel didn't think so. In late 1972, he started talking with the steel industry's new chief bargainer, U. S. Steel's R. Heath Larry. The result

I. W. Abel (left), president of the United Steelworkers of America, and R. Heath Larry, vice chairman of U. S. Steel and the industry's chief bargainer, jointly announced the unprecedented agreement known as the Experimental Negotiating Agreement, or ENA, in March 1973.

was an unprecedented deal known as the Experimental Negotiating Agreement, or ENA.

To the steel managers, ENA spelled miracle. The deal was a guarantee that the union would not strike. No strikes, no reason for customers to hoard emergency steel. At long last, the producers could plan production without fear of strikes that raised their costs while opening the door wider to imports.

The producers had to pay a price, too. For their part of the bargain, the steelworkers won guaranteed annual pay increases of 3 percent plus the inflation rate for the COLA, the cost-of-living adjustment. The industry had bought labor peace at a high and accelerating cost in wage rates. "Once this machine started operating, its generative ability was awesome," Hoerr concluded.

He was right. Under ENA, the companies made seemingly small concessions in the 1974, 1977 and 1980 contract negotiations. But the costs kept multiplying, outpacing earnings.

This was not what Abel had in mind. The steel producers? It would take them almost a decade to admit they had a monster on their hands, one that had to be tamed.

In 1976, the economy was still chilled by the cold breath of recession. Markets were weak, and, after investing in new facilities and new capacity, the company was cash-tight. So were the other major American steel operators. Their solution was to post a 6-percent price increase on almost half their shipments in December.

Again they got flak from the government—this time, from the inflation-battling Council on Wage and Price Stability.

The price increases stuck. Even so, Time magazine reported in its January 3, 1977, issue about two-faced policy makers: "The flap illustrates a hardy truism: steel-price increases arouse more political excitement than increases in the price of almost anything else....

> *...[As] steel men note caustically, aluminum makers in November announced price increases as much as 11 percent on some products without drawing any special political comment.*
>
> *"Even more striking, Du Pont raised the price of Dacron staple fiber up to 10 percent; yet Du Pont Chairman Irving Shapiro was welcomed to a long conference between [President-elect Jimmy] Carter, his economic aides and some businessmen at which the participants discussed, among other things, what to do about steel prices."*

The steel industry, it seems, had to follow the rules of some kind of fantasy land. It was depended on to make jobs and help keep the economy afloat. But it was not expected to make the money it needed to work these wonders.

As if it wasn't enough to have to keep their eyes on lopsided regulations, irksome foreign competitors and rocketing employment and environmental costs, U. S. Steel was beginning to sweat about a pack of pesky bantams that were scampering underfoot.

These were the "minimills," operations that—especially when they emerged in the Fifties—tended to be highly specialized, and markedly smaller, than the integrated producers.

It's easy to imagine the CEOs and marketing managers of major producers looking askance at these upstarts and shaking their heads in amused skepticism. What were these squirts trying to prove?

But the smiles faded as the minimills sliced deeper into a tight but lucrative niche with the precision of a master surgeon. They had claimed a piece of a market they thought they could command not through size, but stealth. By the Seventies, they were proving that they were right.

Minimills, such as the one shown, gave the "big" steel producers a run for their money by concentrating on lower-cost, lower-end and lower-tech goods.

Minimill. As in *miniature, mini-market* and *miniskirt.* The label announced these guys were streamlined for the times. They worked hard so they could get down to the bare bones. They liked the image. It was lean-and-mean chic.

In his book, *Steel Phoenix*, Christopher Hall listed the characteristics that set the breed apart. Its defining trait was thrift. Not just businesslike economizing, but conspicuous frugality that started at the top. As Hall pointed out, Nucor Corporation, one of the best-known minimills, "takes pride in its Spartan headquarters, located in a suburban shopping mall, with a [corporate] staff of less than 20 people including the chairman."

In operations, the minimills passed up made-to-order equipment for cheaper, off-the-shelf technology.

In marketing, they liked to act like "Steel 'R' Us," selling only through supermarket-like service centers, tagging their products with prices that were non-negotiable. They offered discounts for quantity, but it was all in the catalogue. There were blue-light specials, but no hidden deals.

Products? The minis concentrated on lower-cost, lower-end, lower-tech goods, mainly the stock steel bars that their customers turned into products. They made everything by remelting scrap steel in electric furnaces.

And they grew. They spun off new mills. They graduated to higher-tech products—flat-rolled steel, for instance—and they were good at it. Meanwhile, the majors had been adopting minimill ways, trimming down plants, adding electric furnaces, running more scrap. They were learning something from the minimills.

By the Seventies, it was getting increasingly harder to tell where the minimills ended and the integrated producers began. There was no crystalline definition for the minimill species. Their essence, though, seems to have been captured by Richard Preston in *American Steel* (Prentice Hall Press, 1991), which traced Nucor's startup of its Crawfordsville, Indiana, minimill.

For Preston, the mill's defining characteristics were efficiency, compactness, computerization.

"It was a desktop steel mill," he wrote.

Why couldn't the major producers be desktops, too?

In time, they *would* tend toward highly computerized, stripped-down minimill-like operations. But they had to remember this fact: Sleek, computerized plants didn't mean much if the people running them weren't, themselves, operating at a high megahertz level.

It was an old theme: Maximize worker productivity. It didn't mean simply replacing fast machines with faster ones or making employees work harder, faster, themselves. It meant working smarter. The steel companies had been preaching that sermon for years. Now they were joined by an unlikely ally, Steelworkers' union chief I. W. Abel. After divining the latest economic signs, he decided to join the producers in spreading the gospel of productivity.

In October 1973, he took the word to all Americans by way of an editorial, paid for by U. S. Steel and run under his photo—the image of a concerned and wise grandfather—in a half-dozen major magazines, including *Fortune*, *Time* and *Sports Illustrated*.

At the invitation of United States Steel, I. W. Abel made a pitch for increased production in U S Steel News. *The editorial also appeared in several national publications as part of the corporation's "We're Involved" advertising campaign.*

"If we adopt a don't-give-a-damn attitude," Abel warned, "we risk becoming a second-class economic power." He called on "every American to enlist in a crucial battle to improve our lagging productivity...."

"By last year, 18 percent of all the steel sold in this country was being produced elsewhere.... Jobs have gone down the drain and families have suffered lower living standards as a result.... How can we improve?"

His answer: Naturally, by improving technology. But also by stepping up each worker's efficiency and chance to contribute.

"Does this mean work speedups, job eliminations? Hardly. It does mean cutting down on excessive absenteeism, tardiness, turnover and overtime. It does mean more effective work incentives—and really listening to the man at the work bench."

Abel's message was rather remarkable, coming, as it did, from a union leader, and sharing space with the logo of the biggest steel operator. The message also had a timely ring. In 1973 and again in 1974, the nation experienced steel shortages. Steelworker productivity was part of the trouble, but a bigger problem was the industry's total capacity.

U. S. Steel's far-reaching program of modernization and expansion was captured in this facility montage which appeared in the December 1975 issue of U S Steel News.

At U. S. Steel, capacity and other troubles were now the official worries of a new chairman, Edgar B. Speer. He sounded the alarm in a 1974 speech before a joint meeting of the St. Louis chapters of The Steel Service Center Institute and the Purchasing Management Association.

"In my own industry, some 25 million tons of new steel output will have to be added over the next six years, to keep supply in balance with domestic demand. And that's assuming a certain percentage of the market will continue to be supplied by steel imports."

The Arthur D. Little consulting company validated Speer's concern when it concluded a study of steel capacity. The firm's findings: The American steel industry would have to spend about $5.5 billion a year to expand its output to meet steel demand, replace equipment as it wore out, and meet government regulations on pollution control.

But, Speer pointed out, the report had been ignored by the Council on Wage and Price Stability, the federal government's inflation watchdog. The council had issued its own estimates of America's steel requirements, and of the capital the industry needed to meet them. Its figures had come in remarkably lower than Arthur D. Little's.

While U. S. Steel's numbers experts debated productivity with their counterparts in the wage-and-price council, the corporation kept investing in technology that raised the efficiency at its mills.

In its December 1975 issue, *U S Steel News* checked off the company's recent work:

Two new electric furnaces and two continuous slab casters were being built at the corporation's new Texas Works. They would double the plant's capacity for steel plate for energy projects, shipbuilding and construction in the South and Southwest.

At Fairfield, Alabama, the corporation had added replacement capacity—two, 200-ton Q-BOP furnaces, successors to 12 open-hearth furnaces, and was building a third—plus a new blast furnace to replace three old ones.

Gary had just added another blast furnace and was installing new coke ovens. Chicago's South Works was about to start up a new 100-ton electric furnace.

Other projects had just been finished or were in the works. A new caster, electric furnaces and other equipment would increase Fairless Works' output of high-quality rod and wire. The Pittsburg, California, plant had hiked its plate capacity. Geneva, Utah, had, too—and was raising output of billets and plate.

The corporation was opening new coal mines. It also was expanding its taconite-pellet production capacity in Minnesota, mining new ore reserves there. Those reserves proved to be an especially fortuitous find in 1977, when Venezuela nationalized the company's Orinoco mine. U. S. Steel would have to walk away from the very mine that had been Ben Fairless' pride and joy.

Pride and joy were in abundance as management surveyed what U. S. Steel had become in the Seventies.

It was, as U. S. Steel was quick to proclaim, more than "just" a steel company. It was a *family* of firms that took the corporation into a variety of businesses. They balanced each other. It was a nice, round package. It even included service firms, and companies whose wares were technology, or ideas.

The head of the family was still steel manufacturing. The rest—the nonsteel businesses—was a diverse group of brothers, sisters and cousins. Some raised questions about whether they even belonged in the family album.

The lineage ranged from business that mined and shipped ore, to plastics and resins producers, to real estate services. Also considered a service was U. S. Steel Supply Division. It sold bar, sheet and other products at 28 steel service centers—in effect, a coast-to-coast chain of steel supermarkets.

The natural resources businesses ran operations from coal mines that supplied the company's mills with coking coal, to ore mines which fed their critical raw material to the steel operations. Ore was shipped by U. S. Steel's own rail, ship and barge company, whose subsidiaries shipped ore and other bulk commodities internationally.

The nonsteel divisions included companies which obviously meshed with the steel business: bridge-and-building-fabricator American Bridge, and the Oilwell Division, which supplied the oil drillers and the pipeliners. Closely related materials operations included the familiar Universal Atlas Cement and the not-so-familiar Bahama Cement Company.

A powerful performer, and a business group unto itself, was USS Chemicals.

USS Chemicals' products were derived from the company's coke-making operations and sold for conversion into other products, such as industrial chemicals, resins and plastics. Agri-Chemicals produced fertilizers and other farm products. Molded Plastic Products made plastic fence posts and marine docks.

One of steel manufacturing's in-laws was USS Engineers and Consultants, a wholly owned U. S. Steel subsidiary. Its wares: patented processes and "proprietary" products. For hefty fees, it offered technical advice to steelmakers in foreign countries, including Poland, Romania and Brazil. Such aid did not significantly raise America's incoming flood of foreign steel. It did, however, allow foreign steelmakers to offer more and better steel to their markets at home.

There was Alside, Inc., which made and retailed home insulation, roofing and siding. USS Realty Development, which owned properties, dealt in mortgages, and built shopping centers, industrial parks and condos and resorts. In the early Seventies, it designed and built two signature hotels at then-under-construction Disney World: the space-agey "Contemporary Resort Hotel" and the worlds-away Polynesian Village. Hughes Boat, located in Canada, made fiberglass sail boats.

In a class by themselves were the overseas operations, the best known of which were Quebec Cartier and Orinoco, both involved in mining and processing iron ore. Starting in the 1960s and extending well into the next decade, U. S. Steel established a series of far-flung joint ventures with partners in Europe, South America, India and South Africa, primarily in exploration and development, mining and manufacturing. Included were these operations with exotic names: Amazonia Mineracao (exploration for iron ore, Brazil); P.T. Pacific Nikkel (exploration for nickel and cobalt, Indonesia); Compagnie Miniere de l'Ogoone (mining of manganese ore, Gaban); Associated Manganese Mines of South Africa (mining of manganese and iron ores); Prieska Copper Mines (South Africa); Marico Fluorspar (mining of fluorspar, South Africa); Union Miniere (mining the sea bottom to harvest nodules containing copper, nickel and cobalt); Acieries de Paris et d'Outreau (production of ferromanganese and steel castings, France); Feralloys Ltd. (production of ferromanganese and ferrochrome, South Africa); Altos Hornos de Vizcaya and Altos Hornos del Mediterraneo (integrated steel production, Spain); Societa Finanziaria Finsider (producer of structural steel and a steel fabricator, Italy); Terninoss (producer of stainless steels, Italy); Triangeler Daemmstoffwerk (producer of automobile components, Germany); Mapri (manufacturer of automobile components, Brazil); Zuari Agro Chemicals (producer of fertilizer, India). There were also Navigen and Navios, ocean transportation companies.

These ventures demonstrated the diversity of U. S. Steel and its presence across the globe. But by the late Eighties and early Nineties, these ventures would be gone, Orinoco Mining to expropriation by the

Venezuela government and the others sold with additional assets the corporation would determine did not fit with its core business.

The company, however, wasn't getting enough out of steel. It wasn't getting enough even though its steel shipments had climbed 25 percent from 1972 to a then-record in 1973 of 26 million tons. That wasn't enough, even though the company's steel sales had crossed the $7 billion mark.

As *U S Steel News* paraphrased the corporation's 1973 annual report: "By the end of 1973, steel prices should have been some 6 percent higher than they were just to recover cost increases incurred...."

One reason was the government's program of price controls. New President Richard M. Nixon had been experimenting with these formal restraints on prices as a way to hog-tie inflation. Whatever their intended purpose, the controls put a chill on incentives to produce, and on profits. They also assured domestic steel output would fall short. They did this by disallowing the price increases the American producers claimed they needed.

Income for 1973—more than $325 million—was more than double that of the previous year. It still wasn't enough. As Chairman Edgar Speer would tell shareholders at the annual meeting the following year, the 1973 return (4.6 percent on sales) was about half the company's typical rate for periods of comparable sales—not enough to attract the amount of capital the corporation needed to replace steel facilities, and to expand its steel operations.

Business Week looked back the following March and called the less-than-9-percent return on equity "a poor showing compared to most manufacturers, and below that of most rival steelmakers." It quoted Speer: "With the lines of business we are in, we should be earning 15 percent on equity."

Not enough. Speer had to act. The March 1974 *Business Week* said this: "The 57-year-old Speer will need to be tough to carry off the task he has set for himself: revitalizing a company that has been a challenge to managers since the day it was founded, 73 years ago."

Again, too much slack had crept onto the organization chart. Again, it was time to tighten the lines of responsibility. Speer, who had occupied the chairman's seat for only a year, was known as a "steelman's steelman." He knew what to do: Reorganize.

As the same issue of *Business Week* put it, Speer "reversed a decades-long process of concentrating power at the top by creating five super divisions, whose managers have been given more operating authority and more responsibility for profits than divisional heads ever had before."

In steel operations, Speer replaced two operating divisions and five sales divisions (none of which had responsibility for profit) with four production-and-sales divisions, based in Pittsburgh, Chicago, Birmingham and San Francisco.

The fifth division handled raw materials and shipped them on the Great Lakes.

In just two months, *Business Week* said, the restructuring looked like it was "breathing new life into an enterprise that for years seemed on the verge of atrophy."

The year 1974 brought good news, too. Despite a recession, it was a healthy year for steel. For U. S. Steel, it was a year of records.

Earnings reached a then-all-time high of $635 million on what were record sales of $9.3 billion. More than 75 percent of those revenues came from steel manufacturing. Still, that meant that almost a quarter of the revenues was generated by chemicals and the other nonsteel operations.

If the non-steelmaking businesses looked sweet to shareholders in 1974, they were an outright blessing in 1977, when corporate-wide sales and revenues were a strong $9.6 billion, but total income was only $138 million—a breathtaking $272 million drop from the preceding year. The culprit was steel manufacturing, where rising employment costs, inflation and the creep of imports had contributed to a $45 million loss. The other operations remained profitable. As the company's annual report pointedly stated, those other operations were "substantial, growing segments of the Corporation, and their future is promising."

That message was emphasized in 1978. Earnings from steelmaking improved, but they were still depressed, accounting for only 14 percent of the company's operating income for the year.

The numbers meant trouble. But as Edgar Speer watched the red light flash over steel manufacturing, he learned he must face a worse crisis yet, one that was personal.

He had cancer. That meant he would have to step aside as chairman to undergo medical treatment. He died October 13, 1979.

The man who replaced Speer in early 1979 was David M. Roderick. And he was of a different breed.

Speer and Gott had come up through the steel business. They were steelmen to the marrow, up from the mills.

Roderick, on the other hand, was a former World War II Marine sergeant. After his hitch, he studied at Robert Morris College, and later at the University of Pittsburgh where he earned a degree in economics and finance. He went to work for Gulf Oil and two U. S. Steel-owned railroads before joining one of U. S. Steel's accounting offices in 1953. He started climbing the ladder, reaching the vice president of International Operations rung in 1967. He was named chairman of the Finance Committee and a member of the board in 1973. In 1975, he was named the corporation's president. Four years later, he became chairman.

David M. Roderick was elected chairman of the board and CEO, succeeding Edgar B. Speer, in early 1979.

Roderick was a self-made man, one who insisted that the discipline of Marine Corps life enabled him to march out of the old Pittsburgh neighborhood he was born in and up a steeply rising career track.

Sections of that track, though, caused him frustration, even anger.

The problem was this: Newspaper writers and politicians would scan his biography, note its absence of experience in mills, and point to its accent on accounting and finance. Then they would say Roderick was an accountant, a numbers man, even a bean counter.

The portrayal was way off center. But it would be useful to adversaries later in the Seventies and in the Eighties, when smothering costs would force Roderick to put non performing, unsalvageable, behind-the-times mills on the chopping block. Sacrificed with these facilities would be a lot of steelworkers' jobs. Only a bean counter would do that, cried those who insisted the plants could be saved.

The accusations were unfair. Quite the opposite of causing tunnel vision, Roderick's education and experience sharpened his view of the big picture. He explained it so often, it became his mantra. He explained it again for this book: "I was never a financial man. I was never in general accounting. I've never been in a treasury department, an audit department, a tax department—never a comptroller of anything. All my accounting exposure, all my background, was analytical.

"I analyzed businesses. That's what I did."

Well before he was made chairman, in fact, Roderick was casting his analytical eye around the corporation, studying its springs and gears, determining which parts meshed, which were worn out. He was like a master jeweler. Was the watch working properly? If not, was it worth fixing?

His vision for weak versus strong operations was sharpened during a turn in Europe. This was during his time in the corporation's International Department, before he became a vice president or headed up the Finance Committee. Management had their eye on him and liked what it saw. Roderick, still in his late thirties, was sent to Paris to help oversee the launch of a mine the company was running with the French. The mine was in the Congo, but Roderick's main base was Paris. He was the only U. S. Steel employee stationed there.

After the mine was up and running, Roderick got another assignment: Scope out every steel plant in Europe. The job had him hopping around to mills in Belgium, Luxembourg, Germany, France, Italy, Spain, the Netherlands and England.

When the jeweler compared what he saw with U. S. Steel's older, outdated, and cost-burdened plants, he formulated some advice.

"I told our people these other people had modern facilities and low-cost labor—in some cases a third of *our* labor costs. We couldn't compete! Our market was like a piece of red meat to a mad dog, and they were going to keep coming after us. I pleaded that we had to shut things down.

"I gave that lecture to the Long-Range Planning Committee, the executive VPs, the chairman, and anybody else who would listen."

But his sermon was met with silence. The young analyst was still damp behind the ears. There was no need to worry.

It was all part of a management culture that belonged to older days, but refused to die.

"We had a concept that was called normal volume," Roderick explained. "It said you normally ran at 75 percent volume, and kept 25 percent of capacity on standby for times when the economy surged and you wanted to do better. Think about that. What it really said was that 25 percent of your capacity would not be used 80 percent of the time."

But the plants were still paying for that fat. It was like throwing cash into the blast furnaces.

Things changed after Roderick strode into the chairman's office. The situation he inherited was not pretty.

The plants were sinking in a swamp of costs, but Roderick was in a position to take his own advice. Close the plants that were going to go down anyway. Why should they take the others with them?

The talk was that Gott and Speer, steelmen to their souls, would have further tinkered with the organization chart, or looked for other ways to get their chain of mills on track and intact. How could they shut operations they had come to cherish? They had both begun at one of the plants that was now weakest, Youngstown—Gott as a young engineer, Speer as a "metallurgical observer." They still had friends there, hourly steelworkers. Closing Youngstown or any other works wasn't in their blood.

But sentimentality did not burden Roderick, the analyst. Marginal mills—the older, outmoded, under-competing plants—had recorded losses for four consecutive years. They had to go.

Roderick drew up a hit list of steelmaking and fabricating plants. Fatefully, they totaled 13. They'd once been strong links in the chain, but they, too, had to go. U. S. Steel's board members agreed.

So the company shut down Youngstown, as well as its works in New Haven, Connecticut, and Torrance, California. It kept open a rod mill at its Joliet-Waukegan, Illinois, works, but closed everything else there. It shut down the wire and 140-inch plate mills at the Fairfield (Alabama) Works; the wheel and axle operations at McKees Rocks, Pennsylvania; Gary's 80-inch, hot-strip mill; South Works' iron foundry; and Pittsburg, California's, rod mill.

A Year of Hard Decisions

Steel operations marked by plant closings; nonsteel businesses show significant progress.

Marginal operations shut down

Following a comprehensive review of all operations, management recommended and the board of directors approved the permanent shutdown of a number of facilities. Operations at these facilities have been marginal and, in total, recorded losses in each of the last four years.

Major facilities being permanently shut down include Youngstown (Ohio) Works; New Haven (Conn.) Works; Torrance (Calif.) Works; Joliet-Waukegan (Ill.) Works, except for a rod mill at the Joliet plant; the wire mill and 140-inch plate mill at Fairfield (Ala.) Works; wheel and axle manufacturing operations at McKees Rocks, Pa.; the 80-inch hot-strip mill at Gary (Ind.) Works; the iron foundry at South (Chicago, Ill.) Works; and the rod mill at Pittsburg (Calif.) Works.

Steelmaking capability will be reduced about three percent due to the shutdowns. For the most part, this is a reduction of peak operating capability only, since a number of the products produced at the affected locations will continue to be furnished to customers from other USS mills.

Units being shut down in nonsteel industry segments include American Bridge Division's steel fabricating plants at Los Angeles, Calif., and Gary, Ind.; Universal Atlas Cement Division's Universal (Pa.) cement plant and the gray cement facilities at Buffington, Ind., and Northampton, Pa. (see page 9 regarding sale of UAC); and United States Steel Supply Division's container manufacturing plants at Chicago, Ill., and Camden, N.J.

The year 1979 was marked by a number of critical decisions such as were reported in this brief pullout from the corporation's annual report to employees.

In 1980, the corporation shut down the 48-inch plate mill at one of its oldest works, Homestead. That action sent a chill through the town, whose people wondered about whether the rest of the mill had a future. In other mill towns, workers and families worried about their fate.

Some of the silent mills would be sold to other steelmakers, and to other companies who would adapt them for their own manufacturing operations. U. S. Steel employees who lost their jobs received unemployment compensation, supplemental unemployment benefits, deferred pensions. Some took jobs in other U. S. Steel mills.

But it was painful, and this was only the first round of closings. There were stirrings in the steel communities. Forces that intended to fight plant closings began to gather—church leaders, town officials, worried citizens.

There already had been protests. In 1979, a coalition of steelworkers filed suit to halt construction of a new mill U. S. Steel had said it was going to build on Lake Erie, in Conneaut, Ohio.

A mill at Conneaut had been a gleam in the eye of the company's managers for a century. The location was great. A plant there would be served by the railroads, and it would straddle crucial shipping lanes.

Andrew Carnegie had announced plans to build a tube mill there in 1900, but it seems he wasn't serious. That was when he was trying to coax J. P. Morgan into buying his interests. Talk of a mill at Conneaut was imaginary icing on the cake.

Still, Carnegie had bought land around the town, and the company still owned it in the Seventies. Edgar Speer reopened the plans to build a plant there, a mill which might even be named in his honor. That plant was his dream. The people of Conneaut liked the idea of a new steel works, with new jobs. But steelworkers from Pittsburgh plants sued to stop it. They feared, probably rightly, that a gleaming new Speer Works would spell doom for their older mills.

The mill died anyway, of economics. Roderick's analysis told him a greenfield mill there defied profitability. "We can't afford it," he told the steelworkers.

Conneaut never saw a Speer Works. But a few years after the steelworkers' suit, land, consisting of more than 3,000 acres of woodlands, wetlands, and bluffs overlooking Lake Erie, was turned into a wildlife preserve. It was named in Roderick's honor.

This four-stand billet caster at South (Chicago) Works was among the new and upgraded existing facilities that helped to streamline production and increase efficiency during the early 1980s.

While Roderick was going about the sad task of writing off his hopelessly antiquated mills, he was looking hard at nonsteel operations; the days were gone when the company could keep marginal contributors under the same roof.

One of the first "*non*-core" businesses to go was Universal Atlas. It had once been the nation's largest cement manufacturer, but, for several years, the corporation had not deemed it a worthy recipient of cash transfusions. Atlas no longer made sense as part of the corporation. In 1980, Roderick and associates sold it to a West German cement manufacturer for $138 million. More nonsteel business would leave the family later.

Over in steel, while it was shuttering money-losing mills, the corporation was upgrading the keepers—for example, by adding more new-generation steel casters.

Huge infusions of technology were only part of the answer. There were all sorts of small technical improvements waiting to be made, old headaches and new "minor" problems which, when solved, could be worth a couple casters themselves.

But the opportunities could slip through the cracks. Why? Because the people responsible for spotting the needed fixes were, by and large, members of the corporation's engineering and research staff, the technical experts who were based at the home office in Pittsburgh. They were far away from the problems, professionally and physically.

The corporation took care of this by transferring the responsibility to the technical pros at the front. Twenty mill employees were given the rank of process engineer. They led local teams that scoured their mills for quality and technical glitches. And they found them. Texas Works' troubleshooting squad, for example, boosted their pipe mill's output, and reduced cracks on slabs coming out of their continuous caster.

During 1979, the locally empowered flying squads tackled 50 projects. They reworked equipment, added computer controls and in other ways streamlined production and enhanced quality. The company priced their improvement as being worth $30 million.

Roderick was especially interested in the fixes at the South, Gary, Fairfield and Texas Works. As he told shareholders at their 1981 annual meeting, the corporation had identified those four works as "problem plants." They were getting extra help—for example, through capacity-hiking expansions. And they were turning around.

Again, it all added up. For 1979, the year it shed a number of steel facilities that were incurably inefficient , the corporation wound up with a loss of $293 million, of which $102 million came from steel manufacturing. Much of the steel loss resulted from costs associated with closing the mills, including employee benefits. But in 1980, the steelmaking segment returned to the spotlight of profitability, racking up an operating income of $58 million. Depressed markets had reduced its raw steel production for 1980 to 23.3 million tons—a 34-year low—but the steelmaking group had bounced back to the tune of $160 million.

And, at the 1981 annual meeting, Roderick told the shareholders, "We are turning these problem plants into moneymakers."

The corporation was leaner and meaner, but not by enough. Roderick was keeping his eyes peeled for properties to sell off. "Sleeping assets," he called them.

According to *Fortune* magazine of April 6, 1981, Roderick had started looking for salable "snoozers" back in 1975, not long after he became U. S. Steel's president. He'd been at a party when a stranger approached him and offered to buy 49,000 acres of timberland U. S. Steel owned in southern Alabama. The stranger's price: $28 million. Roderick checked out the property. "He…found it was worth a lot more than he'd been offered," observed *Fortune*. "International Paper bought it for $65 million."

A light had gone on over the chairman's head.

"Roderick," said *Fortune*, "figures that, with the largest raw-materials base of any steel company in the world—5.7 billion tons of iron ore, 3.3 billion tons of coal, 4.3 billion tons of limestone, half a million acres of timber—U. S. Steel has plenty of other somnolent assets it can profitably awaken without affecting its long-term steelmaking capability."

A while later, U. S. Steel sold more timberland. It leased coal properties to Conoco. Then it sold a package of coal mines and reserves for $700 million to the Standard Oil Company of Ohio—"Sohio." The oil company had been looking for places to invest the flood of cash that had been pouring in since oil prices had started soaring. Coal looked good to the energy company. And the deal was touched with nostalgia. Standard of Ohio was what was left of the original Standard Oil, the company founded by none other than John D. Rockefeller, J. Pierpont Morgan's crafty nemesis.

Roderick insisted his corporation couldn't afford to be sentimental. His motto, said *Fortune*, was "No more sacred cows."

"I think in the past we sometimes suffered too long trying to figure out how to break even at, say, Youngstown, rather than trying to figure out how to double the profit of our Oilwell division," he told the magazine. "We're saying now, 'Let's manage assets we can make money on rather than sit there nursing a sick cow.'"

If the sentiment was harsh, it was realistic. One fact, printed in *Fortune* in April 1981, sent the message: "The company-owned barge lines and railroads that haul ore and coal from U. S. Steel's mines to its mills and semifinished steel from the mills to the fabricating plants have been carrying an even weightier cargo lately…. For three years running, they've turned in the largest operating income of any of the groups, while producing only 5 percent of the revenues."

(By 1988, USX would sell all its railroads, bargelines and the USS Great Lakes Fleet, Inc. to a new company called Transtar, Inc., jointly owned by the corporation and other partners, including The Blackstone Group. USX retained a 44 percent interest.)

Meanwhile, the corporation was tending its healthy cattle and it was also talking about expanding the herd. It had cash—especially after the Sohio deal. It could shop for a profitable business, perhaps one that would be "up" when steel was "down."

What might it buy? Roderick wouldn't say, although he dropped a hint to *Fortune*. "Any acquisition should fit into the company's major nonsteel lines of business."

The suspense would soon be broken.

CULTURE CLASH

Edwin H. Gott and Edgar B. Speer made it to the top of "The Corporation" during times that would have tried most chairmen's souls.

Both were steelmen to the core. Gott started his climb to the top from the mill floor, where he got his hands grimy as an industrial engineer. Speer, too, started in a technical job, "metallurgical observer." They were products of a let-me-roll-up-my-sleeves-and-get-to-it era, and they ran smack into an age in which, in their view, loopy lobbyists and overzealous lawmakers sought to tie their hands and feet.

Their major frustration was the environmental movement. It hit the industry like a storm, spinning off regulation after regulation that called for choking back air and water emissions, often to the point where compliance was impossible. Gott and Speer, like other managers of their generation, saw this as an outrage.

And they said so. In December of 1972, for example, Gott took to the podium at a meeting of the Illinois Manufacturers Association and let loose his frustration. "The machinery of government," he complained, "has cranked out a profusion of anti-pollution laws, some of which are without scientific basis and all of which are saddling industry with costs that are already straining financial resources and affecting our competitive position in world trade."

Speer was even more outspoken. He authored a series of newspaper editorial-advertisements in which he argued that his corporation was spending huge sums to cure incurable problems. "Can U. S. Steel really stay in your community?" he asked in one headline. It was posed as a question, but it sounded like a threat.

Both men sought to stifle environmental clean-up demands they considered excessive and—issued by local, state and federal governments— often contradictory. They acted firmly to conserve the corporation's resources, refusing to crack the corporate checkbook for exorbitantly expensive, but unproven, pollution-control equipment. They never softened their get-tough—some said truculent—tones. But their attitudes were not exceptional for the times, especially since both men were show-me-the-numbers, up-from-the-mill-floor steelmen.

*G*ott wore overalls and smudged his hands when, in 1937, he joined the corporation's Ohio Works, in Youngstown. He was an industrial engineer, a

Edwin Gott (left) and his successor Edgar Speer (right) fought long and hard to protect corporate interests against overzealous environmental lobbyists and lawmakers.

"production man," when it was rare for production men to beat lawyers and financial experts to the top of the corporation. But the Lehigh University grad did just that. After sprinting up the ladder at the Clairton and Gary works, he returned to Youngstown as general superintendent of U. S. Steel's sprawling Youngstown District. From there it was a few hops to higher management positions. In 1967, he was named corporate president and chief administrative officer. A year and a half later he succeeded retiring Roger M. Blough as U. S. Steel's CEO.

Business Week sized him up: "Gott is said to be a tough but fair administrator who likes to run a taut ship [and who] knows the production end of this company more thoroughly than any president it's ever had." Under Blough, Gott had played a big part in modernizing U. S. Steel.

Yet under Blough, the corporation's share of domestic steel sales had slipped from 30 percent to 25 percent. (Critics claimed Blough had been too slow in upgrading his plants.) As Time noted in December, 1968, one of Gott's goals was to hike that share back up to 30 percent. But, with an economy that dragged until almost his last day in the chairman's chair, Gott barely had a chance.

As the Pittsburgh Post-Gazette pointed out in a February, 1973, story on the chairman's retirement, the "'Gott years' coincided with national recession and a great cream-skimming of the market by imported steel…. So the management

Gott is presented with a portrait by Explorer Scout David Bajek. Retired at the time, the former U. S. Steel chairman actively supported the scouting movement for over 25 years.

seeds planted by Gott never were able to sprout into visible profit growth before the man himself suddenly turned 65… in the midst of 'excellent' steel orders!"

Gott died in 1986. And as for character, his favorite private activities say it all. He was a vice president and board member of the National Boy Scouts of America, and he put many hours into youth activities. As one writer put it, he deeply believed in helping to develop the young.

*I*nterestingly, Edgar Speer also did Boy Scout work in his later years. It didn't stop the media from describing him as "two-fisted," and "tough-minded" on the job. And Speer had a tough job to do: pick up where Ed Gott had left off in pumping new life into his corporation.*

Speer was born in 1916, in Pittsburgh, but his family moved a decade later to Philadelphia. He soon proved not only tough, but cerebral. He enrolled in pre-med classes at the University of Pennsylvania. He had wanted to study

During his chairmanship, Speer reshaped the corporation's traditional centralized decision making by creating four super divisions.

psychiatry, but he never reached that goal. And in 1938, at 21 years of age, he returned to Pittsburgh in search of a job.

It was not a good time to look for work. The nation was recovering from depression, and there were plenty of bright young men competing for good positions. But luck was with Speer. He walked into U. S. Steel's office. While he was being interviewed, the phone rang. The caller was the chief metallurgist at the corporation's Ohio Works. He needed a "metallurgical observer." Young Speer caught the first train to Youngstown and got the job.

Working full time at the plant, attending college classes in metallurgy and related subjects, and studying into the night, Speer got into the habit of sleeping only four hours every night—a practice that would stick with him through his career. He soon gained an industry-wide reputation as an expert in steelmaking processes. His knowledge and drive propelled him through a sequence of supervisory and managerial

jobs at several plants, and, in 1958, he came to corporate headquarters as general manager of operations for steel. By 1969, he had advanced to corporate president, and became chairman March 1, 1973.

Technical expertise did not dull Speer's vision for the mechanics of management—or for signs that the organization was bogged down by bureaucracy. In 1974, he launched a massive restructuring. This was only a year into his chairmanship, but, as Business Week put it, he had made a "formidable start" toward making his steel operations "leaner and meaner."

"In his most dramatic step Speer has reversed a decades-long process of concentrating power at the top by creating [four] super divisions, whose managers have been given more operating authority and more responsibility for profits than divisional heads ever had before."

At the annual meeting the following year—1975—Speer (who would die four years later) was able to announce that the reorganization was producing good results.

The reshaping was a break from the corporation's traditional centralized decision making. It was a daring move, especially for an operations man.

It was "tough" in the best sense of the word.

Chapter 16

White Knight
to the Rescue

David Roderick decided soon after he became chairman that it was time to go shopping for another company.

Drawing up a shopping list, of course, had to be done methodically. Roderick decided he needed a strategic planning department. Not a *business* planning department; U. S. Steel had those in the past, and they merely focused on finding better ways to conduct the businesses the corporation had. Their members asked questions like, "What new products should our steel business make?" Or, "Would this new sector of the plastics industry be a good place to sell chemicals?" Or, "Should we sell this business?"

Roderick asked a different question: "Are there any businesses that are totally new to us that would make sense for us to buy?"

He asked the question because he was convinced that the corporation had to pare down its steel business, trim away the under-performing and obsolete mills and make the remaining operations more efficient. It was an unpleasant job, but, as we've seen, Roderick soon began taking care of it.

There was more to fix. Roderick knew the corporation had to do something to offset steel's down cycles, to smooth out the market's hills and valleys. The way to do that was to acquire companies in industries that complemented steel by swinging in the opposite direction—especially upward when steel was in a down phase.

An ideal acquisition would be unlike steel in other ways, too. It would not be energy- or labor-intensive, or a constant victim of low-cost, foreign competition. It would be smart, also, to pick a company that could benefit from the knowledge and talent possessed by the people in U. S. Steel's traditional operations.

Come to think of it, *two* more companies, in two nonsteel businesses that reacted to somewhat different market ups and downs, would give the corporation more stability.

"The idea was to have three lines of business that were somewhat interrelated," Roderick said during interviews for this history. "That would give us diversification that was balanced. I always referred to it as a three-legged stool."

To start building his stool, Roderick established within the corporation a new corporate strategic planning group. For its leader, Roderick tapped Charles A. Corry, a U. S. Steel executive who had joined the corporation's Tax Department right out of law school in 1959, then cruised through jobs in tax, accounting and finance.

Then in his late forties, slim and somewhat gangly, Chuck Corry still looked like the varsity tennis player he'd been when he attended the University of Cincinnati. He had a good, analytical brain, and he'd seen a lot of the company. Roderick made him a vice president.

Corry's thinking matched Roderick's when it came to the need to hunt for a complementary business.

"We foresaw that the steel industry was facing tough times," Corry said in an interview. "There were the high labor costs…the never-ending imports. The Sixties and Seventies hadn't been good to steel, but now we were looking at ourselves as the largest company in an industry that was in decline, and we didn't see any quick end to the problems."

Corry went right to work, examining the corporation's businesses, determining which should be pruned away. Turning to the acquisition side of the strategic planning equation, he began browsing among other industries, checking out various companies. He pumped

As head of the corporation's strategic planning group, Charles A. Corry spearheaded the acquisition of Marathon Oil Company.

analysts. He made sure that the preparatory legal work required to acquire other companies was ready so U. S. Steel could move swiftly when an opportunity arose.

Working with others in his group, and with Roderick, he began drawing up a shopping list. It grew to about 10 corporations that looked like good acquisition prospects. It included major manufacturers in numerous industries, and, of course, in oil. In fact, Roderick and Corry chatted with some of the CEOs of companies that wound up on Corry's list of possible acquisitions.

Then came a chain of events that almost pushed the right partner—Marathon Oil Company—into U. S. Steel's arms.

I n late spring and early summer of 1981, successive tender offers for Conoco, the American petroleum producer and marketer, were oversubscribed and hostile. Clearly, the non-major, middle-tier oil companies were up for grabs.

As anticipation mounted over still other acquisition attempts, stock values for mid-sized oil companies climbed. On July 8, *The New York Times* listed possible acquisition targets that included Cities Service, Phillips Petroleum, Pennzoil and Diamond Shamrock.

Also mentioned was Marathon, a mid-size oil company that Chuck Corry had checked out very closely. Impressed, he had placed what he had learned about this Midwestern outfit in his "possible acquisitions" file.

Marathon looked like a nice fit. Based in the city of Findlay, on Ohio's flatlands, roughly halfway between Detroit and Cincinnati, it was an established, independent oil producer and gasoline marketer. It owned and operated four refineries with a total capacity of over a half-million barrels of gasoline a day. People throughout the Midwest knew well the bright red M on Marathon's service station signs. But Marathon also operated under other familiar and successful brands—Bonded,

Speedway, Gastown and Consolidated. It explored for and owned oil reserves. It operated a fleet of oil tankers.

Better yet, with business highs and lows that ran counter to steel's, Marathon fit nicely into U. S. Steel's complementary business plans. In 1981, Marathon ranked as the country's 17th largest oil and gas company. But it was expanding aggressively, and pursuing petroleum reserves outside the USA. And it was going places. Back in 1976, it had acquired sizeable, undeveloped, offshore reserves in the United Kingdom's oil-rich North Sea. It held a 49.5-percent interest in the Yates Field, a Texas oilfield that, in size, was second only to the Prudhoe Bay Field in Alaska among domestic fields.

Artsist James Dietz captured a Yates Field gusher in this oil painting.

Under the direction of Harold Hoopman, Marathon's rough-hewn president and CEO, Marathon was doing pretty well—especially for an independent. "Hoop" was the kind of "big boss" who mowed his lawn and pruned his trees on weekends, and he was understandably proud of the successes scored by his mid-size company with its Midwestern heritage. The last thing he wanted was an unwelcome takeover.

But he got one.

Mobil Corporation, one of the country's oil giants, had been licking its wounds after two failed acquisition attempts (one of them being Conoco) and was now looking hungrily at Marathon.

In his book *Big Deal* (Warner Books, 1998), investment banker Bruce Wasserstein explained why.

"Heavily dependent on Saudi oil, Mobil desperately wanted to expand its U.S. reserves. In fact, the company had spent $4.3 billion on domestic exploration and production between 1976 and 1980. Yet U.S. reserves were down 6 percent over the period. Mobil chairman Rawleigh Warner and president William Tavoulareas sought to reverse the decline."

Hoopman found this out at about 10:45 in the morning on Friday, October 30, when he received a terse phone call from Rawleigh Warner.

Mobil, Warner informed Hoopman, was making a tender offer to buy up to 40 million shares of Marathon stock—68 percent of the company's shares—at $85 a share, a price Hoopman knew was too low.

The call, made the day before Halloween, did not suggest a friendly deal. This kind of trick or treat didn't appeal in the slightest to Hoopman. Still, he had seen it coming. He had anticipated an attempt at a hostile takeover by a larger member of the petroleum fraternity, and he had gathered his management team around him to formulate a defense.

On Sunday, November 1—two days after Mobil struck—Hoopman and his board members met to discuss what to do about Mobil's offer. They concluded it was "grossly inadequate." Weighing heavily on their minds was the prospect of huge Mobil ingesting Marathon—oilfields, gas stations and all. It would be like being gulped down by a whale. Their company would simply disappear.

They began to fight back. One of the first defensive measures Hoopman and his crew took was to check their list of prospective "white knights," companies that Marathon had identified as attractive matches.

On that same Sunday, Marathon filed suit in the United States District Court in Cleveland to block Mobil's bid. The grounds: that Mobil's acquisition of Marathon would violate antitrust laws by diminishing competition in the Midwest.

The court acted that very day, issuing a temporary restraining order that, as amended November 11, prevented Mobil from purchasing any shares until Marathon's suit was resolved.

It was a busy Sunday. And during the even busier days that followed, Marathon's management began exploring the possibilities of being acquired by another company. During this time of acquisition fever, they knew, they were ripe for a takeover. Better it be a friendly one, by a company that would not erase the Marathon name and heritage from the face of the earth.

They were soon to hear from a suitable hero.

When Chuck Corry heard the news about Mobil's run at Marathon, he remembered his filed notes on the oil company. He immediately dialed up Dave Roderick.

Corry later reconstructed the conversation:

"I reminded Dave that we had sold quite a few assets and we had two billion dollars available for acquisitions. I told him that I had just heard that one of the companies we'd had our eye on was the subject of a hostile offer by Mobil. We discussed it a bit, and he asked, 'Do you know anyone over at Marathon?' I said I'd talked to a guy there to sell them some coal reserves. Why don't I call him and see what they think?" Go ahead, answered Roderick.

In fact, Roderick had met with Harold Hoopman himself. As U. S. Steel lore has it, Roderick had stopped in the previous year at Marathon's headquarters in Findlay to have a little chat with the chief. Roderick was helping another CEO who was strengthening his relations with the people in New York City by doing some fundraising for the Metropolitan Opera. Would Hoopman care to give a little to the cause? Maybe a million dollars?

According to the story, the crusty Marathon boss looked straight at Roderick and gave his answer concerning the opera: "Well, New York is a long way off. We can hardly hear that thing out here. But I'll tell you what. We'll give a million dollars to the Met in New York if you give a million dollars to the Findlay High School Band."

Findlay was not New York, but it was a nice town. In a Marathon centennial book published after the Mobil takeover attempt, Marathon editors referred to Findlay as "a city of churches and neatly manicured lawns." It was a city of 38,000 people, more than 2,000 of them on Marathon's payroll. Later, when the townspeople heard that big-city-based Mobil was gnashing its teeth at their oil company, they showed their fighting spirit, staging demonstrations. They handed out "I Love Marathon" buttons while the high school band played a number composed for the occasion, "I Believe in Marathon."

Now, though, Hoopman heard only the clicking of shark's teeth. And he was more than willing to talk a deal with Roderick.

Reprinted with permission from The Blade, *Toledo, Ohio*

Corry phoned Marathon and talked with John Strong, his corporate-planning counterpart at the oil company. Strong verified that Marathon would fight Mobil. Further, Corry learned that Marathon was compiling a list of companies that might want to buy it. Corry popped the question: Would Marathon welcome U. S. Steel as a white knight? Strong said he would check. The next day, Roderick and Corry were aboard a company jet, winging their way to Findlay. There were other flights to follow, carrying an assortment of U. S. Steel officers and executives.

Much later, evidencing his sharp eye for humor amid sobriety, Chuck Corry revealed that the flying executives thought they were traveling low-profile when, in fact, they might as well have landed at Findlay aboard Air Force One.

"Marathon had been talking to other companies, and corporate planes had been flying in and out of Findlay, and this news was getting picked up. Findlay had a small airport, so it was easy to check the tail numbers of aircraft to see who was flying in and out."

The FAA numbers on the tail of U. S. Steel's jets soon became familiar to reporters stationed at the airport, and they spread the word. Soon the investment community knew the corporation had designs on Marathon.

Participants in the dealings included Bruce Thomas, U. S. Steel's chief financial officer, and William Lewellen, the company's treasurer. A chief player on the Marathon team was CFO Elmer Graham. Each side had a cadre of lawyers and investment advisors. As U. S. Steel's Bruce Thomas explained later, "Keep in mind, nobody in our stable had any history of a major acquisition—especially in a hostile situation. So investment bankers were very, very important to us."

At one point, Mobil raised its bid for Marathon. To no avail.

In Roderick's opinion, Marathon seemed almost destined to go in with U. S. Steel. "Marathon's guys had a monkey on their backs," he said. "They weren't in the best bargaining position, and they liked us because we couldn't integrate them into steel. With us, they would remain an identifiable entity. That had great appeal to Marathon, its communities and its employees."

That was apparent by one of the final U. S. Steel-Marathon negotiations, which took place at U. S. Steel's Pittsburgh headquarters. *Big Deal* author Bruce Wasserstein, the investment banker with First Boston, one of the investment banking firms Marathon hired to help work through the negotiations with U. S. Steel, was in Pittsburgh that day. (Later, he made a name for himself as chairman and CEO of the investment banking firm Wasserstein Perella & Co.)

According to Wasserstein's account, it was clear that the members of U. S. Steel's acquisition team had ridden a steep learning curve since their self-advertised landing in Findlay.

"As our plane [without markings] touched down, it was quickly whisked directly into a separate hangar. The scene was out of a James Bond movie. Ground crew members, dressed in neon orange suits, stood all around the hangar along with security guards. We were ushered to…a helicopter waiting to take the Marathon team to the U. S. Steel building. The helicopter landed on the top of the Pittsburgh skyscraper, we climbed down one flight of stairs, and were in the U. S. Steel executive offices."

Then came the day for the final signing. The date: November 18. The place: New York City. Each company held a board meeting to gain final authorization of the acquisition before putting any ink on paper.

Harold "Hoop" Hoopman (left), president of Marathon Oil Company, and David M. Roderick, U. S. Steel's board chairman and CEO, joined forces at a press conference to announce the proposed U. S. Steel–Marathon merger.

Marathon's board and negotiating team met at Marathon's boardroom, at 630 Fifth Avenue. But, for U. S. Steel, a complication arose.

U. S. Steel, of course, no longer had a boardroom to call its own in New York. It had been renting one from General Motors. But, as part of a program to raise cash, U. S. Steel had also been subletting the boardroom to other corporations. And Union Carbide had booked the room for November 18. On this, one of the most important days in their corporation's history, U. S. Steel's board had no place to meet—until Dave Roderick called up GM chief Roger Smith and got the okay to use GM's boardroom at 767 Fifth Avenue.

The site was convenient, being only a block away from Marathon's offices. At one point, Hoopman walked over to GM's headquarters with his chief financial officer plus Wasserstein and one of his associates. The quartet answered questions. And Hoopman gave U. S. Steel's board a presentation reviewing Marathon and its operations—a slide show filled with pictures of drill rigs and gas stations that U. S. Steel's Bruce Thomas thought would "go on forever."

The Marathon party rejoined its board down the block. A while later, Hoopman received a call from Roderick. Hoopman took it over a speakerphone so his board could hear. Roderick informed them that his board had unanimously authorized him to propose a tender offer. Its terms:

- U. S. Steel would acquire 51 percent of Marathon, at a price of $125 a share, paid in cash.
- After Marathon shareholders approved the merger, U. S. Steel would acquire the remaining 49 percent of the Marathon shares with notes. (At the time the offer was officially announced, the notes were valued at $86 a share. Given this value, the shareholders would get a "blended average

price" of about $106 a share, and a total purchase price of about $6.4 billion.)

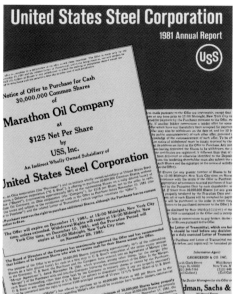

- As insurance, U. S. Steel would be given two options, one to purchase 10 million newly issued common shares of Marathon at $90 a share, and one to buy Marathon's interest in the Yates Field in Texas for $2.8 billion. The Yates option would kick in only if another company wound up buying Marathon.

Roderick went through some details and reminded the Marathon board members about a condition he'd mentioned earlier in the dealings: that his company's offer would be open only until that evening.

Hoopman's board discussed the offer, and in the end concluded it was, as the meeting notes recorded, "in Marathon's best interest" to accept it.

After they wound up their business, Marathon's directors joined U. S. Steel's board to celebrate.

B
ut it wasn't over until it was over. Now came a flurry of lawsuits, aimed at halting the U. S. Steel-Marathon agreement.

Two days after the U. S. Steel-Marathon agreement, Mobil sued the two companies in the United States District Court for the Southern District of Ohio, sitting in Columbus, challenging the validity of the Yates Field option and the stock option. Mobil was granted a temporary restraining order that precluded U. S. Steel from purchasing shares of Marathon until a date to be established by the court.

Eventually, U. S. Steel surrendered both options and was permitted to continue the acquisition. The day after it obtained the temporary restraining order, Mobil raised its tender offer to $108 a share.

But Mobil's case was faltering. On November 30, Federal District Court Judge John Manos rendered an opinion that Marathon had shown reasonable probability that it could win an antitrust suit against Mobil, and he issued a preliminary injunction. Judge Manos also declared Marathon would suffer irreparable harm if the injunction weren't issued. Mobil appealed the ruling to the Sixth Circuit Court of Appeals. But the court backed Judge Manos. Then, on December 30, 1981, and again on January 6, 1982, Supreme Court Chief Justice Warren Burger rejected requests by Mobil to delay the U. S. Steel-Marathon deal.

One very important lawsuit, spawned by U. S. Steel's acquisition of Marathon, could have damaged U. S. Steel. It was a class action filed in early January 1982 in Federal District Court in Cincinnati, Ohio, purportedly on behalf of all Marathon shareholders. The plaintiffs claimed that U. S. Steel and Marathon had violated federal security laws and state law in connection with the tender offer and merger—that certain appraisals of Marathon's assets should have been disclosed in the tender offer; that the tender offer was coercive; that Marathon's board had structured the transaction to preserve its control over the company.

There was a lengthy trial in the summer of 1983. David Roderick, Charles Corry and U. S. Steel board member Neil Armstrong were among those who testified. So compelling were their arguments, evidently, that the jury quickly returned a verdict in favor of U. S. Steel, a verdict upheld on appeal two years later in the Court of Appeals for the Sixth Circuit.

Meanwhile, dissension was rising among other Marathon shareholders. Three months after the corporation announced its tender offer, *The New York Times* reported formation of a "Marathon Shareholders Committee" to block the merger. The merger was subject to approval by two-thirds of Marathon's shareholders, and reports in the press strongly suggested that the Marathon shareholders' vote on the deal might be a cliff-hanger.

The reports were wrong.

In an emotional special meeting held in Findlay on March 11, 1982, Marathon shareholders overwhelmingly approved the merger.

Effective that day, Marathon became a wholly owned subsidiary of U. S. Steel.

At U. S. Steel's annual meeting on May 3 in New Orleans, David Roderick proclaimed to shareholders that theirs was a "new" company, a "resource powerhouse."

"In the new U. S. Steel," he said, "steel accounts for 38 percent of our asset base. Oil and gas [accounts for] an equal 38 percent, with the remaining 24 percent divided among our other businesses, such as real estate, chemicals, utilities and transportation."

The news was even better than that, according to Bruce Thomas. "We never actually transferred money from Marathon to steel," Thomas told the author 17 years after the acquisition. "But one of the biggest benefits of that acquisition was that Marathon's assets and earnings created what I call a credit umbrella. It extended over the steel assets. We were able to borrow money for upgrading the steel facilities that we otherwise would not have been able to upgrade.

"Marathon had good earnings, and that umbrella helped a lot during the worst period for steel, which came right after we bought Marathon. It enabled us to reenergize our steel business."

Harold Hoopman (at podium) looks on at a Marathon shareholders' meeting as votes were tallied concerning the USS-Marathon merger.

MARATHON: OIL ON ROUGH WATER

Towering drilling rigs that poked holes deep into prairies and the ocean's bed? The corner filling station where Dad gassed up the family Buick and picked up free drinking glasses for the kitchen cupboard? What did these have to do with United States Steel?

Not a lot, and that was the point. Big Steel needed a well-run, successful company that acted as a life raft, smoothing out the corporation's ride on the roller-coaster sea we called the economy. The wisdom went like this: When the steel market swelled, petroleum might descend into troughs. When steel crested and sank, oil could bob up again. Overall, that meant smoother sailing.

So, in early 1982, when U. S. Steel announced with pride (and relief) that it had acquired Marathon Oil, the corporation was really acquiring a solid and dependable set of shock absorbers. These were Marathon's oil and gas exploration team; drilling and production unit; crude oil and gasoline pipeline operations: oil tankers; special tankers for shipping condensed natural gas; refineries; a busy network of service stations, many of which doubled as convenience food stores; and 16,000 employees in 21 states, Canada and far-flung corners of the world. There were bonuses, such as a petrochemical refinery in West Germany, and interest in a refinery in Spain.

The package came wrapped up in sales that, in 1981, totaled $9.8 billion, and a net income of $343 million. But the contents sure were different. Making it a

bit of a surprise package were the people who made it work, and their heritage.

Petroleum lore is packed with characters. There were the rough-and-tumble wildcatters who chased after oil in the lush lands east of the Mississippi and in the dry and dusty West, and who, after a day's work, washed the oil and sweat from their faces and rode into town to patronize the bars and bawdy houses. There were the cool-headed geologists, who deduced the locations of the favorite hiding places for oil and gas. There were the bewhiskered dandies who grubstaked the deals, playing big bucks on hunches that they were standing on top of rich pools of crude.

Despite what popular history infers, even the early drillers weren't wild-eyed gamblers. They did their homework. They drilled on the basis of solid clues. One representative of the breed was Henry M. Ernst, the fabulously mustachioed first president of The Ohio Oil Company—the company that would become Marathon.

Ernst was with a group of wildcatters who joined forces in 1887. They had been watching nervously as John D. Rockefeller's mighty Standard Oil combine came snowballing across the landscape, snatching up small drilling outfits in its path. They reasoned that, together, they could hold out against John D. and "The Standard." They were wrong. Together, they only made a bigger target for the oil tycoon, who succeeded in buying "The Ohio" in 1889.

Henry M. Ernst, first president of The Ohio Oil Company, which later became Marathon

Rich reserves of oil were discovered by Ohio Oil prospectors under the harsh and barren landscapes of Wyoming.

saw its production soar, doubling between 1926 and 1930.

Oil people use colorful names to catalogue their fields, places overflowing with history.

Grass Creek Field. Elk Basin. Big Muddy Field. Each figured into The Ohio's oil hunting in Wyoming. In 1912, Ohio Oil sent people out there to go prospecting. It was rocky, dry, treeless, thankless country, where the noonday sun seared everything in sight. Finding oil was a tough proposition. Ohio Oil's seasoned field manager, John "Uncle Jack" McFadyen, learned that fact when he drilled a wildcat on the Tilsdale Ranch, a hundred miles north of Casper. It turned out to be a $250,000 dry hole.

Other finds were like picking gold dollars off the sidewalk. In some spots in Wyoming, oil leaked out of the ground. A lot more was down there for the taking, and leases to drill were cheap. In any case, McFadyen and his crew got lucky, making big discoveries at Grass Creek and Elk Basin. Keeping big finds was another thing. Often enough, it required a good rifle and a sharp eye to discourage claim jumpers, who could move in and take over your rig. If you succeeded in running them off, you still had to worry about being bushwhacked by bandits.

This was no tragedy. Under the direction of Rockefeller's talented associate John Archbold, Ohio Oil remained a distinct entity. And it grew, reaching dominance in Ohio and Indiana. Even after the Supreme Court broke Standard Oil into pieces in 1911, Ohio Oil kept its momentum, adding rich oil and gas properties. Fueled by new crude, the now-independent company

*T*he Ohio was busy in other states, too— principally in Texas, where its geologists and drill crews found a treasure of an oilfield where it wasn't supposed to be.

One spot where oil was *supposed to be* was east of the Pecos River and east of land owned by a rancher named Ira Yates. Yates thought otherwise. So did Frank Clark, a young geologist who was the subject of eye rolling among veteran drillers because he thought he could find oil from a book, of all things. In the late Twenties, Clark donned fancy lace-up boots and marched around, sizing up the local geology. He told a field manager to drill right over there, on a piece of land west of the Pecos. Ridiculous, thought the field manager, and canceled the order. Clark let go a howl, most unseemly for a young man bred on books. And he got his way.

Crews drilled west of the Pecos, on Yates' land, and were surprised when a gush of crude exploded out of the ground and rained on several hundred yards of surrounding real estate. That well was worth $10 million to $15 million at the time, the time being 1926, and it was just the tip of the reservoir. The Yates Field was born.

Almost 60 years later, when U. S. Steel bought Marathon (the name was changed in 1962), the field was still going strong. It was the country's largest producer. It accounted for a third of Marathon's stateside production, and for U. S. Steel, it was Marathon's richest asset.

*S*oon after the company started up, it began rolling out an ambitious international exploration and production agenda that scattered Ohio Oil people over the globe—Mexico by the Twenties, then Canada, Brazil, Guatemala, Egypt, Tunisia, Indonesia, Libya, Australia, Niger, Colombia, the North Sea.

Alaska, too, at a time most oil companies didn't see that land's potential for oil riches, but only saw a vast wilderness perched on the distant, northerly rim of the continent and topped off by an immense dollop of ice and snow.

But Alaska had always been a petroleum treasure chest waiting to be opened. Ohio Oil was one of the first companies to go there. Its geologists had rubbed elbows with trappers and gold miners in Alaska in the Thirties. They knew oil was hiding somewhere. Oil seeps broke the secret. Alaskan natives even used tar from the seeps to waterproof their sealskin boats. But the land revealed no clues as to where it had cached the oil.

Then, in the Fifties, along came Ohio Oil's Russ Simonson, a highly astute explorationist who liked to work alone. He flew over, drove over or tramped upon most of the state's tempting terrain, making himself an

A production platform in Alaska's Cook Inlet where Ohio Oil-Marathon were trail blazers in opening up Alaska's wealth of oil and natural gas

expert in Alaska's geology. His studies—plus the work of other Ohio Oil geologists—prepared the way for big discoveries, including the state's first major oil strike, in 1959, at Swanson River on the Kenai Peninsula. Those strikes touched off an avalanche of further finds. Other oil companies swooped in. But Marathon, by virtue of the work of its Ohio Oil pioneers, can rightly claim to be one of the first to set free Alaska's wealth of oil and natural gas.

Natural gas became an Ohio Oil–Marathon forte. By the time of its merger with U. S. Steel, the oil company held generous gas reserves. They were tapped by a half-dozen production platforms—steel islands that stood on stilts in the frigid waters of Alaska's Cook Inlet. Shipping that gas was a problem, until the company devised a method of liquefying it, chilling and shrinking it to 1/600th of its original volume so it could be transported in special tankers.

Innovation kept proving to be the most useful drilling tool. The company put to work drilling platforms tailored to Alaska's bone-chilling temperatures, devastating winds and, in its waters, waves that reached 28 feet and creeping pack ice six feet thick. The payoff was more petroleum.

This island of steel was one of many such platforms that Marathon placed in operation off the United Kingdom in the North Sea's Brae Field.

The M in an irregular hexagon replaced the Marathon banjo with the Greek runner in 1962.

*M*arathon wasn't afraid of water. During the Seventies, it helped develop the first U. S. offshore oil port for supertankers. The Louisiana Offshore Oil Port— "Loop"—was built 19 miles out in the Gulf of Mexico, in water deep enough to let huge tankers comfortably unload their cargos of foreign oil. A 48-inch pipeline fed that oil to distribution lines onshore.

Contending with surly elements and nightmare weather must have been in the job description for petroleum hunters and gatherers, because Marathon people had to suffer them off the coast of Great Britain, in the North Sea, on the Brae oilfield.

Brae was a huge success story in the Eighties. Marathon was one of the first oil companies to smell oil in the Brae area, and, in 1964, it became one of the first to buy leases there. Twelve years later, Marathon acquired a U.S.-based operation which held interests in the Brae Field and which had made a very encouraging find of gas and a light grade of oil there. Marathon's drillers rubbed their hands together. Then they drilled four new wells, all dry.

But the gloom lifted in the summer of 1977, when a third well struck oil in an undrilled region of the field. That new oil happened to be more than two miles below the seabed, the deepest oil found under the North Sea up until that time. And the oil was hot, gaseous and highly corrosive. Producing it called for equipment of special steel and a

Starvin' Marvin outlets provided customers the opportunity to gas up and pick up the evening meal at the same time.

monstrous platform that stood twice as high as the Statue of Liberty. Building, installing and fitting out this super-platform was an epic undertaking. Nature made things interesting by stirring up one of the worst winters in history, throwing at the platform winds that topped 100 knots. "We've worked on major projects in different parts of the world," groaned project manager Corky Frank, "but nothing to equal the magnitude, or importance, of this one."

The big reward for the crews came when the oil started to flow in July 1983, four months after drilling began.

The big reward for consumers comes when the fuel derived from Marathon oil gets rid of winter's chill, and other petroleum-based products put jets in the air, cars on the road, keep businesses running and the lights on.

The petroleum product nearest to most peoples' hearts, of course, is gasoline. America's scrapbook is fat with photos

and other mementos of its gas stations—brightly colored, spotted at just about every corner, with flags snapping in the breeze, sharply dressed pump jockeys eager to fill your car's tank and, in the "bay," busy mechanics noodling under car hoods. At least that's the way it was in the gas station's early days. And it is odd that gasoline marketing, the end-of-the-line piece of oil business most visible to most people, could ever be an afterthought to an on-top-of-things company like Marathon. But that was the case.

When Marathon was still Ohio Oil, its managers were all crude-oil producers, born and bred. They admitted they knew almost nothing about the products that came from that crude. Anyway, until the automobile came to stay, oil was refined mainly for its kerosene, for lamps. Gasoline was discarded.

The popularity of the auto turned the market all around, and, in 1924, Ohio Oil Managing Vice President O. D. Donnell looked up from his oilfield production charts and decreed: "We must diversify. We must integrate and develop outlets for the company's crude oil."

Expanding into products—going "downstream"—would give the company an especially reliable customer. Itself. It "sold" its oil to its refineries, then to its service stations—then to the people in the flivvers.

Straightaway, Ohio Oil got into the downstream end of the oil business, purchasing the Lincoln Oil Refining Company, which consisted of one behind-the-times refinery that was lucky to put out 500 barrels of gas a day, and 17 "Linco" service stations in Indiana. The Ohio rebuilt the refinery, which was in Robinson, Illinois, then started adding service stations.

In 1930 came an important purchase: the Transcontinental Oil Company. The big attraction was Transcontinental's Yates Field leases, but the deal also transferred to Ohio Oil a hugely valuable asset—the Marathon name. Transcontinental had emblazoned it, along with the slogan "Best in the Long Run," over a Greek marathon runner. The company got a lot of mileage out of that runner. He became so familiar to motorists that, in 1962, on its 75th anniversary, the company changed its corporate name to Marathon. The runner image reflected the company's extensive operations, which now included another refinery, distribution terminals and service stations acquired from other oil companies.

The Marathon man would give way to the company's big, red M symbol. But Marathon kept running. It sprinkled stations along the new interstates, kept upgrading its refining processes and automated its terminals, where gasoline pipelines met tank trucks. Later, the company retuned its refineries to run the new, environmentally positive, unleaded blends.

The world was a lot different from the one in which refiners dumped gasoline into rivers. But customers' shopping preferences were evolving, too.

Now a service station wasn't just the place to refuel your car or truck, it was a place to refuel yourself and the family by ducking into the building for milk, bread and snacks. It was the age of the convenience store. People gassed up and picked up some deli before driving on. Marathon fit their individual bills for prices and products through a variety of subsidiary brands. There were, of course, Marathon-branded stations—some 2,300 of them by the mid-Eighties. And there were 1,300 other outlets in the Midwest and Southeast: Bonded, Gastown, Port, Ecol, Cheker, Speedway, Value and— the ultimate tag for a bargain-pricer— Starvin' Marvin.

It wasn't Henry Ernst's oil company any longer. It was U. S. Steel's, and it worked.

Chapter 17

Fasten Your Seatbelts

"I have to play by the rules that are there…"

—David Roderick

"The paper shufflers who inhabit executive suites are more damaging than the courtiers of an aristocracy."

—Carl Icahn, *Business Week*, October 27, 1986

The Eighties would prove to be a bumpy ride.

U. S. Steel would endure a recession, steelworker demonstrations (especially in Pittsburgh), the layoff and retirement of thousands of mill workers, management employees and office staff, a failed attempt to import steel slabs from England for processing at Fairless Works, a government-thwarted effort to buy another steel company and a tangle with a notorious takeover artist.

It would acquire about $10 billion in assets, primarily in energy. But it also would close outmoded steel mills, sell close to $7 billion in assets and businesses, and write off some $3.5 billion, most of it in steel.

As a result, the corporation would emerge from the decade leaner and more sharply focused.

The ride wasn't all turbulence. The decade also would bring a corporate name change, the purchase of Marathon Oil Company and Texas Oil & Gas and the creation of three separate corporation stocks.

First came the recession. The nation was slogging through it during 1982, and the steel business was performing poorly. But the oil industry revealed no sign of a slump, and when the corporation's financial results for 1982 were in, they heralded the wisdom of mixing steel and oil. Marathon was performing as advertised.

The year 1982 had been less than shining, and the corporation recorded a net loss of $361 million. The lion's share of that loss was in steel. On the other hand, the new business in the portfolio, energy, was a most encouraging bright spot. Marathon had come through with a $5-billion jump in corporate sales, and had tacked a welcome $1.2 billion dollars onto the corporation's operating income. This in a recession year.

When the bottom line was filled in, however, the corporation had suffered a staggering decline, but the fall would have been far worse had it not been for Marathon. And David Roderick could have been excused for gloating just a little when, during the corporation's annual meeting in May of 1983, he reported the Marathon effect to shareholders:

"The addition of Marathon Oil to the U. S. Steel family was intended to broaden our base and reduce our vulnerability to reverses in any one of our business segments while multiplying our opportunities for growth and profitability. That it did during 1982—in all three respects. Our oil and gas businesses are good investments at present, and they will result in an even greater payoff in future years."

From where the shareholders sat, Marathon was the *head* of the steel family Roderick talked about. There was no denying that this corporate family had undergone an amazing transformation. Now it was an energy company.

Stockholders had reason to cheer the positive financial results of the Marathon Oil acquisition at the corporation's 1983 annual meeting. The oil company's principal developmental work was centered in the North Sea's South Brae Field, where this 21,000-ton steel platform jacket was being towed to its drilling site.

The 1970s were marked by tough and painful decisions that involved the closing and/or demolition of outmoded plants and facilities throughout the corporation.

Anything new and promising would be welcome, because the early Eighties would prove to be difficult for management and employees. U. S. Steel may have bought itself a protective umbrella when it acquired Marathon, as Bruce Thomas, chief financial officer during the period, later suggested. But that didn't mean the corporation had seen nothing but blue skies during the decade's first few years.

For one thing, criticism was raining on the company. In late 1979, for example, a *Business Week* editorial had bemoaned the closings of plants that year by U. S. Steel and other American steel majors.

The editorial writer conceded that, with the damage done, management alone could not rebuild U. S. Steel's strength. "The first step," *Business Week* proposed, "must be to change the law to ease the burden of the huge investments that will be required to modernize the steel industry. With this must go more flexible treatment of depreciation so that in a period of severe inflation investors can recover the full cost of new plants by the time old ones are outmoded." Roderick had been preaching the same message.

Continuous casters, such as this four-strand bloom/billet unit at Torrance Works, accounted for only 20 percent of the company's steelmaking output in the late 1970s. That figure was well below the casting capabilities of German, Japanese and other foreign competitors.

Business Week also focused on U. S. Steel's productivity. It lagged, the magazine claimed, almost all its major competitors. Despite the closings, the magazine pointed out, antiquated open hearths still accounted for almost a third of U. S. Steel's steelmaking capacity. And while the company employed continuous casters to make 20 percent of its steel (the American steel industry's overall rate was 14 percent), it still lagged behind the Germans (38 percent), the Japanese (50 percent) and other foreign competitors.

William R. Roesch

And yet the corporation put on a good front.

"There is no reason that U. S. Steel cannot be a totally competitive company and it will be," the corporation's president and chief operating officer William R. Roesch told *Business Week*.

Readers who knew Roesch (pronounced "rush") were confident they could take that comment to the bank. Before joining U. S. Steel in 1978 as executive vice president of steel and domestic raw materials, he had been CEO of both Jones and Laughlin (later LTV) and Kaiser Steel. And it was there that the tall, graying executive earned a name as a razor-sharp steel manager and a fervent cost cutter. The reputation was one reason Ed Speer hired him away from Kaiser; one of Roesch's jobs at U. S. Steel was to resuscitate plants that could still produce, and prune away the ones that were hopelessly behind the times.

A year after he arrived, Roesch moved into the president's chair, which Roderick had vacated for the chairman's seat. When he checked the records turned in by U. S. Steel's mills, Roesch saw that turning around the aged operations would be like moving the Allegheny Mountains.

Politics complicated the task. Since President Kennedy had blown up at Roger Blough over price hikes in 1962, the steel industry had been under government pressure to keep its prices down. When voluntary restraint by the industry was deemed ineffective, the government simply imposed wage-price controls as a means of fighting inflation.

David Roderick took an unprecedented step in 1983, surprising his allies and critics alike. He confirmed to reporters that, as rumor had it, U. S. Steel was negotiating to buy steel slabs from British Steel Corporation.

The plan was this: U. S. Steel would shut down the outmoded open hearths and blast furnaces at its Fairless Works. No longer would the mill produce its own slabs. Now it would roll finished product from slabs produced at British Steel's plant in Ravenscraig, Scotland. Those slabs would be shipped to Fairless for finishing. And to top it off, British Steel would invest in the finishing end of Fairless Works.

"News of the Fairless talks sent shock waves through labor, government and the industry," wrote George McManus in the May 20, 1983, issue of *Iron Age*. "There were angry protests from the steel union, which had just agreed to pay cuts. Congressmen vowed to bar the Fairless deal through legislation."

The New York Times gasped over the deal, and about Roderick, in a July 10, 1983, follow-up to the news: "No other domestic steelmaker had ever proposed imports on such a grand scale and, more important, no other steel executive previously had been more outspoken in his opposition to steel imports than Mr. Roderick."

Even executives from other steel companies complained. One griped to the *Times* that the deal "hurts our credibility." His argument: As chairman of the American Iron and Steel Institute, Roderick was the chief spokesman in his industry's fight against imports. And he was talking out of both sides of his mouth.

As usual, such comments failed to faze Roderick. Clearly, though, his patience had run out. After years of repeating his anti-dumping sermon to authorities right up to U.S. Presidents, after years of seeing nothing done while dumped steel ate up the American market, after watching his company and industry bleed red ink for almost two years, Roderick had had enough. If no one in authority would act, he would.

"I have to play by the rules that are there," he told McManus, "even though I don't like them." Playing by the rules meant that Roderick intended to import slabs—but in compliance with U.S. trade laws. No dumped steel would be allowed.

Chairman David M. Roderick addressed members of the Congressional Steel Caucus in April 1983 to discuss the proposed business arrangements between the company and British Steel.

Roderick argued his British Steel case before the Congressional Steel Caucus, a group of legislators whose mission was to encourage policy that helped steel.

The chairman explained that rebuilding equipment on Fairless' "hot," steelmaking end, to the tune of almost $2 billion, was out of the question. That left the plant's finishing end with no steel to turn into finished products. Half a steel plant with nothing to do would have to be shut down.

Roderick had in mind an alternative plan: Make affordable investments to upgrade the plant's finishing end—"the best part of Fairless"—and then feed it the "fairly priced," meaning non-dumped, steel from Ravenscraig. That way, he explained, the corporation could keep Fairless running. Instead of wiping out 6,000 jobs by shutting the whole plant, the company could save 5,000 jobs on the finishing end. The hot end would be closed, but the 1,500 jobs there would be phased out gradually, through attrition and transfers to other U. S. Steel plants.

It was a revolutionary plan, but revolution, said Roderick, was required. "The domestic steel business has been suffering the most severe case of unemployment and unprofitability in its history. Collectively, it lost more than $3.5 billion in 1982, and operated at less than 50 percent of capacity during the year."

Breaking from tradition, William R. Roesch, president and chief operating officer, sought help from Japanese experts to help turn the balky plate mill at Texas Works into a moneymaker.

In the end, the deal with British Steel fell apart. Government pressure and public opinion doomed it. It had been the boldest example of the corporation's willingness to jump traditional barriers. But it wasn't the only example.

Like other steelmakers, U. S. Steel had a long history of shushing away technology that was not homegrown. U. S. Steel insiders credit Roesch for breaking down that "not-invented-here" mindset.

Not long after he joined the corporation, Roesch took a hard look at the corporation's Texas plant, and its balky pipe and plate mills. Knowing the Japanese were especially clever at getting the best out of technology, Roesch called in experts from Japan's Sumitomo Metals to increase the mills' yields. Their work, said *Fortune* magazine, "turned a perennially unprofitable plant into a moneymaker."

Then Roesch turned to the Gary plant. It had been losing millions of dollars, a month, and much of the trouble was due to a blast furnace and a slab caster built in the early Seventies that had never performed up to snuff. Roesch called in a team from Nippon Steel to fix the trouble.

Roesch, added *Fortune*, "also borrowed a page from the Japanese and began assigning permanent technical teams to the mills to ensure that things that get fixed stay fixed."

The lesson caught on. Fairless Superintendent Frank Hogan, Jr., sent several of his managers to Japan to study its steel industry's technology and production methods.

The corporation was showing Wall Street and the newspaper crowd it no longer deserved the "stodgy" label. Another example appeared in a May 18, 1981, *Business Week* article headlined "Big Steel has started to think big again." It reviewed the corporation's unique leveraged-lease plan to build a new, 600,000-tons-per-year, seamless-pipe mill at its Fairfield plant and, in effect, pay for the plant with its customers' credit commitment.

William E. Lewellen

The financial wizard here was William E. Lewellen, USX's senior vice president-finance and treasurer. Assisting him was Gretchen Haggerty, a young up-and-comer in the corporation's Finance Department. (By the end of the Nineties, she would rise to the position of corporate treasurer and then to U. S. Steel vice president of accounting and finance.)

The mill was, indeed, built, and tubular customers guaranteed a market by contracting to purchase up to 300,000 tons of pipe annually for 10 years.

Today, such deals are semi-legends in the corporation's financial offices.

Robert M. Hernandez

"These people were extremely sharp," Robert Hernandez, USX's vice chairman and chief financial officer, told the author.

Hernandez had joined the corporation in 1968 as a project associate in the business research group, and later worked with the corporation's financial officers, including Lewellen. Hernandez's favorite deal from those days is one Lewellen worked out to finance one of Gary's casters: "We got the manufacturers of the equipment to agree to get paid based on [the number of] tons cast. We had no real commitment to pay. But we convinced them, through a series of economic studies and presentations, that they had virtually no risk that there was a 100-percent chance that the tons would [be produced] and they would get paid. It was basically a debt-free acquisition like paying rent. And it came at a time when we didn't have much money to purchase equipment."

In the early Eighties, though, Roderick's team didn't need to bring in outside experts to tell them many of their works were outmoded. Those plants were producing more red ink than steel. Upgrading most of them—or most of their individual steelmaking and finishing operations—was out of the question. In most cases that would mean tearing out the old facilities and putting in new ones, and *that* would break the company.

Golden-age technology, accompanied by chronically sluggish production rates, wasn't the only trouble suffocating the corporation. U. S. Steel still felt the familiar stranglehold of high labor rates and those pesky imports. Now, high prices for energy and raw materials were tightening the grip.

U. S. Steel wasn't alone. All the integrated steelmakers were losing money, struggling under high labor costs, hampered by inefficient plants, and watching as the minimills and foreign producers ate up their market. The American producers had numbers that showed the damage the under-priced imports had been doing. As Roger S. Ahlbrandt, Richard J. Fruehan and Frank Giarratani pointed out in their book, *The Renaissance of American Steel* (Oxford University Press, 1996), "The rise of imports and depressed domestic demand reduced U.S. capacity utilization rates to below 50 percent in some cases…," driving producers down into the zone of high money losses.

The industry was in critical condition. *How* critical was made clear in mid-1982, when the industry's collective bargaining group, the Coordinating Committee Steel Companies (CCSC), which included the seven leading integrateds, released the results of an independent, state-of-the-business study.

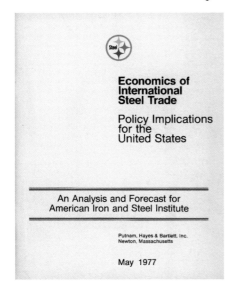

Published in 1977, this state-of-the-business report by the economic firm of Putnam, Hayes & Bartlett predicted that the steel industry would lose 100,000 jobs over an eight-year span unless it overcame the economic, financial and production problems it faced at the time.

It had been prepared by the economic research firm Putnam, Hayes & Bartlett. In its foreword, J. Bruce Johnston, U. S. Steel's senior vice president, employee relations, and the chief negotiator for the CCSC, admitted the findings were "grim." Employment costs in steel were almost twice those in other manufacturing industries; in productivity, foreign producers and even other American industries were leaving American steel in the dust. All this and more even as U.S. steel producers invested almost all their cash flow back into the steel business. If these and other problems weren't taken care of, the American steel industry would lose 100,000 jobs over the next eight years.

The report supported a conclusion that Roderick and Roesch had already reached concerning their company: More U. S. Steel operations would have to be closed sooner or later. The fact that the corporation was losing up to $75 on every ton of steel it shipped said "sooner."

It was time for damage control. And Roderick and Roesch knew one way they could plug the leaks, at least partly: convince the steelworkers that it was in their own interest to agree to a partial give-back of the terms written into the Experimental Negotiation Agreement, or ENA—the no-strike agreement that the producers and unions had signed in 1973.

The producers' intent had been to end strikes—even the threat of strikes—so their customers would end the destructive stockpiling of steel, which would invite in more imports. In exchange for a no-strike pledge, the steelworkers received annual, minimum, 3-percent wage hikes on top of cost-of-living adjustments keyed to inflation.

When they proposed the arrangement, the steelmakers figured the no-strike clause would give them solid ground to grow on. Instead, they got quicksand.

The agreement had governed three rounds of steel talks in 1974, 1977 and 1980, and the bargaining parties managed to settle all the issues at hand. There had been no strikes. But once the agreement's pay-raise machine was cranked up, it had proven to be awesome.

As labor reporter John Hoerr summed it up in *And the Wolf Finally Came*: "The average wage rate at companies covered by the industry-wide agreement, including the 3-percent increases and COLA payments, jumped from $4.27 per hour on August 1, 1972, to $11.91 on August 1, 1982. COLA alone contributed $5.11 of the increase. In that 10-year period, the steel wage rate climbed 179 percent, while inflation rose 132 percent."

Similarly, the machine cranked up vacation, overtime and holiday pay, which were calculated on the base pay rate.

Yes, the agreement had ended hedge buying by steel customers. But it had not ended imports, which, for the producers, had been the point of the entire exercise. In fact, as Hoerr pointed out, it had exacerbated the producers' problems by increasing production costs.

"There was little economic rationale for the steep rise of steel wages in the 1970s," wrote Hoerr in his book. "Output per man-hour had increased by only 1.5 percent per year in the decade before the ENA was signed, and the negotiators were well aware of this."

All that was water over the dam by the time the industry and union began preparing for the 1983 contract negotiations. By then, it was clear to Roderick and the other steel CEOs that the ENA was burying them. It was time for the steelworkers to give up their guaranteed raises. Doing so would be in their interest. If the industry had to go on paying these ballooning wages, soon there would be no industry left.

On April 6, 1982, Bruce Johnston tucked a slide-show version of the Putnam, Hayes & Bartlett report under his arm and marched into Linden Hall, a nineteenth-century Tudor mansion south of Pittsburgh, once the home of a Gilded-Age coal baron. The house and its 785 acres had been converted into a country club and conference center, complete with tennis courts and a golf course. Now it belonged to the United Steelworkers, and Johnston was here to give the members of the USW's executive board a private screening of the worrisome condition their industry was in.

J. Bruce Johnston

Johnston, on behalf of the CCSC, had already asked the union to reopen its existing labor agreement. His main objective was to renegotiate the ENA into oblivion, he hoped. If the report didn't sell his case, nothing would. As Hoerr put it, Johnston's mission was to tell the USW's "assembled officers and district directors that the entire structure, the high wages, middle-class culture, and hundreds of thousands of jobs were in danger of collapsing."

Johnston had earlier unveiled the study's findings at a meeting of the International Iron & Steel Institute, shocking the assembled steel executives there. He got much the same reaction at Linden Hall when he projected the report's bleak picture. Wrote Hoerr:

"As recently as 1960, the U.S. steel industry had had lower costs and better productivity than Japanese, Canadian, and German producers. By 1980 those advantages had been wiped out. It took 7.4 man-hours to produce a ton of steel in Japan and 8.5 in Canada, compared with 9.0 in the United States. It cost U.S. producers $307 to produce a ton of steel, compared with $218 in Canada and $183 in Japan. The study contained other comparisons showing American producers at a disadvantage. Most startling…was a projection of labor costs. If the wage and inflation trend of the 1970s continued, it would cost $66.34 per hour in 1990 to employ one steelworker."

For the union leaders, Johnston's show was the second punch of the day to the stomach. That morning, the union's chief economist, Edmund Ayoub, had given a similar presentation. Ayoub, according to Hoerr, had contended the industry's data "came down too heavily on employment costs as the key problem." His figures played up the steel industry's growing technological lag. "But," Hoerr added, "Ayoub didn't slight the fact that steel's 'real' employment costs (corrected for inflation) rose at a 4.3-percent annual rate through the 1970s, compared with a 2.4-percent growth in productivity. This meant that real unit employment costs rose 1.9 percent per year, choking off profits and investments.

The USW executives digested the figures. One thing was clear. While the union and steel producers differed somewhat on the course the industry was following, both paths led to the same cliff.

Still, the board members had one sore point to go over with Johnston. Why did U. S. Steel have enough money to buy Marathon but not enough to reinvest in its own steel plants?

Johnston explained that the corporation could not afford to borrow the money to modernize its steel plants at the interest rates the banks would have charged for investing in an ailing industry. But, he added, the banks were willing to lend money at market rates for investments in petroleum. (He could have pointed out the urgency to raise cash that was evidenced by the corporation's sale of nonsteel assets. One of them turned out to be the company's own headquarters building in Pittsburgh. U. S. Steel would wind up leasing space in its "home.")

Johnston's borrowing-rates answer seemed to satisfy the board, Hoerr concluded. "The members didn't like U. S. Steel's actions but found it difficult to contest the decision in strictly economic terms."

There followed a series of talks, including a contentious session involving both sides' chief negotiators in U. S. Steel's headquarters.

Although the union's existing contracts with U. S. Steel and six other majors would not expire until August 1, 1983, the producers wanted to replace the pacts immediately with lower-cost agreements. Specifically, they wanted the union to cancel an August 1, 1982, wage hike and accept a pay freeze for the next three years. The deal would include a limit on the current contract's cost-of-living adjustments. Lloyd McBride, USW president, could swallow the wage freeze, but not the COLA limits.

On July 30, 1982, in the ornate Grand Ballroom of the William Penn Hotel in downtown Pittsburgh, McBride presented the industry's proposal to 400 local union presidents, the USW's contract-ratification body.

Meetings Sought with Steelworker Union

.... on May 28 J. Bruce Johnston, chairman of the Coordinating Committee Steel Companies and senior vice president-employee relations for U. S. Steel wrote USWA President Lloyd McBride. The letter was made public on June 18 following a USWA agreement to begin discussions of joint union-industry problems. Following are excerpts of that letter.

Dear Mr. McBride:

The steel industry is in crisis.

In the first quarter of 1982 large operating losses were reported publicly by Bethlehem Steel Corp., National Steel Corp., Republic...

to be in the process of liquidating in one form or another.

In addition to those companies which have disappeared from the steel industry, almost all of the remaining companies have been engaged in permanent and extensive plant shutdowns and discontinuance of operations.

Attached is a list of permanent plant closings which have occurred just since the signing of the 1974 Basic Labor Agreement. There were, of course, many large plants closed permanently in the years preceding 1974 (this list also attached).

Employment in the dom... steel industry is...

of high inflation when replacement costs outpaced original costs by huge margins. Capital recovery times have averaged 12 years for heavy steel mill facilities in the United States versus an average of 5 in Europe, 2 in Canada and 1 in the United Kingdom. Capital formation in Japan has been virtually unlimited by their capital nourishment arrangements for their steel industry. No nation, no industry in any country and certainly no steel industry ever came close to allocating the share of its total GNP that went into the Japanese steel industry in the 15 years following World War II... to the '60s...

It was an angry crowd. After several increasingly lucrative contracts, the union was being asked to give back much of what it had won. Angriest of all, Hoerr pointed out, were the representatives from U. S. Steel. They were still steaming over the corporation's acquisition of Marathon. Why hadn't the corporation put that $6 billion, the deal's total cost, into the mills?

As for the concessions, Hoerr reported, McBride told the presidents that the companies had asked for "more than was reasonable," and called for a vote on a motion to reject the demands.

That was what most of the delegates wanted to hear. Pandemonium broke out as the motion passed.

McBride declined to encourage a spirit of victory. "I say to you, the decision we have made today is not cause for celebration. The problems are mutual [between labor and management], and they have to be solved. This is a mutual failure."

Eventually, reality set in. In November, the ratification committee again voted down a concession package McBride had negotiated. But on March 1, 1983, the committee finally approved a settlement that included an immediate 9-percent cut in wages.

When the math was worked out, the contract shook $3.25 an hour out of the industry's labor rates in 41 months, as reported in the Greensburg (Pennsylvania) *Tribune-Review* in its September 27, 1983, issue.

Not surprisingly, the company-union conflict fed rumors that U. S. Steel was getting ready to close or sell more plants. Certainly, Roderick and Roesch knew they would have to cut steel operations further. As head of steel operations, Roesch owned the task of swinging the axe. He had done a good job of overseeing the corporation's steel business, and had begun to make it more efficient. But he was no longer up to the job.

Roesch was in the clutch of a serious illness and circumstances dictated that he retire. It was a sad end to a brilliant career. His health continued to deteriorate, and he died in 1983.

Thomas C. Graham

Who would pick up where Roesch left off? Roderick knew just the man. He was Thomas C. Graham, president and CEO of Jones & Laughlin Steel Corporation, and, as the authors of *The Renaissance of American Steel* verified, he was known as the most competent operating executive in the steel industry.

Tom Graham was in his mid-fifties, bespectacled and tough. Like Roderick, he had no fear of taking actions that induced wrath, if they were necessary. He had a combative style, and was given to grinning when making hard decisions and delivering bad news, like job cuts. He was soon known around U. S. Steel as the "smiling barracuda."

But he was extremely able, and highly respected. During his decade at the helm of J&L, he had turned the ailing company into a contender. His reputation would grow during his years with U. S. Steel. In a February 25, 1985, review of U. S. Steel, *Business Week* would paint him as "an iconoclast in an industry hardly known for innovators. While most steel executives wailed that megabuck expenditures were the only way to boost productivity, Graham boosted efficiency by motivating managers and workers."

But he'd need more than motivational skills at U. S. Steel.

Shortly after he arrived there in May of 1983, he took a look at the corporation's records. His smile faded. The corporation's market share had recently slipped, as *Business Week* reported, from 20 percent to 15.5 percent. One big reason: U. S. Steel had lost 20 to 30 percent of the business it had been getting from General Motors because competitors were charging lower prices and delivering higher quality.

When Graham studied the corporation's profit and loss statement, as *The Renaissance of American Steel* recounted, he was stunned to see that the steel division had lost $100 million during the month of May.

"With losses like that," he told the book's authors, "you can't meditate for a year on what you have to do. There [was] a certain urgency, because we were bleeding cash by the bucketful. You couldn't shut the money-losing operations down, because everything was losing money."

"No computer program," Graham concluded, "has been devised to solve these problems."

Yet Graham solved them.

One of the first steps he took was to contract out steel-plant jobs that weren't directly related to making steel-maintenance, for example, and machinery repair. Bob Hernandez remembered that Graham even asked Bruce Thomas to figure out an accounting method that gave plant superintendents' profit credit for contracting out support jobs.

Then Graham looked around and retired managers who, as *Business Week* put it, "couldn't adjust to an era in which imports and minimills hold 40 percent of the U.S. market." In their place he installed younger managers, people he defined as "hard chargers, not afraid to speak up and carry the ball." He tightened up the management chain and instructed his managers to draw up challenging but reachable objectives. And he worked with them to make sure the objectives were met.

Then he turned to the advertising and marketing staffs. Insisting that advertising did not sell steel, he cut the staffs from 30 people to five. He also pulled the plug on a 54-person staff whose job—developing a steel export business—was then hopeless. He saw that six management layers separated the vice president of sales from the sales people, wondered whether the word from the top ever got to the bottom and culled four layers.

He also cut links out of the management chain in steel operations, where the bureaucracy was so stifling that, as Fairfield Manager Robert Raybuck later told *Business Week*, even routine decisions "like starting up a blast furnace had to be approved on the 61st floor [in Pittsburgh]."

"There were times," Raybuck added, "you knew there was going to be so much hassle in getting a decision [that] you said, 'Why bother?'"

No longer could the corporation afford a fat, wheel-spinning bureaucracy. Which was why, on September 19, 1983, the company announced it would add 4,000 managers to the 8,000 salaried workers already retired or furloughed in the past year. The white-collar layoffs, *Business Week* offered, were part of Graham's plan to cut administrative expenses in half, to 8 percent of sales. "If he succeeds, he will lop $20 off the cost of producing a ton of steel."

As for the union workers, Graham was still leaving the door open.

On September 26, he was in New York, addressing a group of investment analysts. The Greensburg *Tribune-Review* picked up the story, reporting that Graham had admitted that U. S. Steel was "a high-cost producer," and that Graham was "determined to break even at a shipping rate of only 1 million tons of products going out its mill doors per month and will shrink back, improve yields, boost technology, and hammer down supplier bills to cross that threshold."

But the paper led the article with the fact that Graham "broadly hinted…that labor cooperation on work practices now may yet be able to help save jobs in the corporation's red-ink-drenched Monongahela Valley plants, though their market outlook is grim."

Some of the local plant unions, in fact, had agreed to shaving costs. For example, as Hoerr wrote, Clairton's local had agreed to trim coke-battery crews from 21 to 15. Several other plants made workforce concessions. Either it was far too little, much too late, or the corporation had given a false impression that voluntary cuts of 25 percent to crews here and there would make a difference.

The corporation had cut costs already by merging management staffs at plants that had common products and markets. It wasn't enough.

Management's call for labor's cooperation to help cut costs through workforce concessions was heeded by several plant locals, such as the one at Clairton Works where coke-battery crews were trimmed from 21 to 15.

The older, outmoded plants had been losing too much money. Given the slack demand for steel, the company could not make enough back, not even enough to break even. It had to specialize further.

Roderick had concluded in the late Seventies that U. S. Steel's strategy to survive was to concentrate capital on the most promising products and mills. Now was the time to implement that strategy.

The plan required these steps:

Trim the total mix of steel products, concentrating on the more profitable, less labor-intensive product lines—flat-rolled steels, for example, and seamless pipe and heavy plates and beams.

Let go of the mills which did not produce these products, or could not produce them profitably.

Improve operating efficiencies. Improve product quality to strengthen sales.

Lower costs wherever possible.

And on December 27, 1983, U. S. Steel announced its plans for shutdowns, a process industry had sterilized with the term "rationalization."

It would permanently close its plants in Ensley, Alabama and Cleveland.

It would cut back or eliminate various operations at its plants at Gary, Fairfield, Fairless and Geneva, and at South Works, where it also canceled construction of a rail mill.

The news was especially bad for the Pittsburgh area and the Mon Valley. There, U. S. Steel was going to close facilities at the Clairton, Duquesne, Edgar Thomson, Homestead, National and Irvin-Vandergrift plants.

The second shoe had dropped.

Naturally, U. S. Steel's closing announcement released the cap on frustration, anger, even rage that had been bottled up in the Mon Valley and the other steel towns.

Almost everyone knew a steel worker. Everyone remembered U. S. Steel's plant closings of 1979 and 1980, and the series of layoffs at other producers. Steel was the lifeblood of these towns, and now that lifeblood was being sapped. Adding to the pain was the fact that the corporation had made the dreaded announcement during the holiday season.

There were demonstrations, public meetings and gatherings to lambaste steel, public demands that the corporation reverse its decisions, calls for mayors and other officials to step in and stop the shutdowns. Labor "revolutionaries" arose among the laid-off steelworkers, vowing to make U. S. Steel and the other producers reinstate jobs or raise the benefits for separations.

The most bizarre episodes were organized and staged by the Denominational Ministry Strategy (DMS), a group of Protestant clergy who believed activism would help the unemployed steelworkers.

In 1983, members of DMS staged protests outside branches of Mellon Bank, which they had targeted as an evil agent acting in league with U. S. Steel to drain money from the communities. The militants drove patrons away by spraying them with synthetic skunk oil and stuffing dead fish into safety deposit boxes.

Even more bizarre was a demonstration on Easter Sunday, 1984. Two dozen DMS protestors gathered in the Pittsburgh neighborhood of Shadyside, and, in the middle of Easter services, walked into the Shadyside Presbyterian Church. The church counted among its members some of the city's wealthiest and most powerful people. Tom Graham attended services there. Perhaps the protestors hoped to find him, or Dave Roderick, in one of the pews. In any case, as William Serrin summarized in *Homestead*, the president of the local at U. S. Steel's Irvin Works emerged from the group, strode up to the front of the church and stood next to the pulpit. "As he accused the parishioners of ignoring the plight of the steelworkers, and of maintaining lifestyles that were 'evil and against all biblical example,' the bluebloods sat dumbfounded in their pews."

On December 16, the activists made a return visit to the church. As two dozen demonstrated outside, three men wearing masks burst inside and hurled balloons, said to contain dye and skunk oil, at families of parishioners who were eating a Christmas dinner.

"The incident created a furor," Serrin wrote. "Most people could not understand how the protestors, despite what many regarded as the correctness of their cause, could interrupt a church gathering and target women and children."

It seemed as if civilization in the Mon Valley was starting to crack. U. S. Steel executives were even the subjects of written or phoned death threats. Someone was going to shoot them, or blow up their houses. When the wife of one of the executives answered her phone, a woman on the other end of the line warned her that "we" were going to kill her husband and, perhaps, her, too. Was that the work of DMS? Possibly.

In any case, DMS' ties with the steelworkers and their locals were loose and tenuous, and it was widely agreed that DMS had a bigger agenda: promoting socialism. When the steelworkers realized how radical and hurtful to *their* cause the group had become, they broke off the relationship. One of DMS' chief agitators, The Reverend D. Douglas Roth, served jail time in connection with the demonstrations. Eventually, he was defrocked.

Still, many frustrated steelworkers took part in protests against U. S. Steel and Roderick that were more mainstream. For the most part, these were peaceful demonstrations in which the steelworkers proclaimed their grievances and vented their anger.

Softening the blow of the cuts was what would later be known as a "separation package." It included Supplemental Unemployment Benefits (SUBs) designed to tide the workers over until they managed to find new jobs, or until they reached retirement age. Some employees received SUBs equaling two-thirds or three-fourths of their pay for up to two years. Many older employees retired with the SUBs until their Social Security payments kicked in.

Roderick considered it a good package. But the corporation could not have funded the pensions and benefits of so many laid-off and retired employees had it not been for Enders Voorhees, U. S. Steel's chair of the Finance Committee in the middle of the 1900s.

His involvement goes back to the Fifties, the Korean War years, when corporations were paying excess profits tax. U. S. Steel was "being taxed at 70 to 80 percent," Roderick remembered. While other steelmakers were spending heavily, and being taxed heavily, too, Voorhees opted to protect U. S. Steel cash from the heavy tax rates, and do a good deed for employees in the process, by pouring that money into the employees' pension fund. (In the late Fifties, contributions to the pension fund even exceeded the amount that was currently deductible for income taxes.)

Enders Voorhees

Voorhees' successors, Robert Tyson and Bruce Thomas, kept up the practice. As a result, by the Eighties, U. S. Steel's pension plan was fully funded, adequate to pay pensions and supplemental benefits for the surge of people being retired. In fact, when Roderick became chairman, U. S. Steel had 88,000 employees or survivors on its pension rolls. When he retired, there were nearly 112,000 on the rolls.

The other majors hadn't stashed away enough pension money. "When they wanted to restructure," said Roderick, "they couldn't put thousands and thousands of extra people on their pension rolls. They didn't have the funded pensions to do it."

If only Roderick could have dealt so easily with another chronic problem, the steel that foreign producers kept dumping on the American market.

Lobbying against imports that were heavily subsidized by foreign governments, trying to get the government to take a forceful stand against artificially cheap imports, was becoming a way of life.

In the late Seventies, Roderick told reporters he was gathering and sending enough anti-dumping petitions to Washington to fill a truck. And, in fact, a short while later, he did rent a truck to carry to trade officials in Washington the small mountain of petitions U. S. Steel employees had signed.

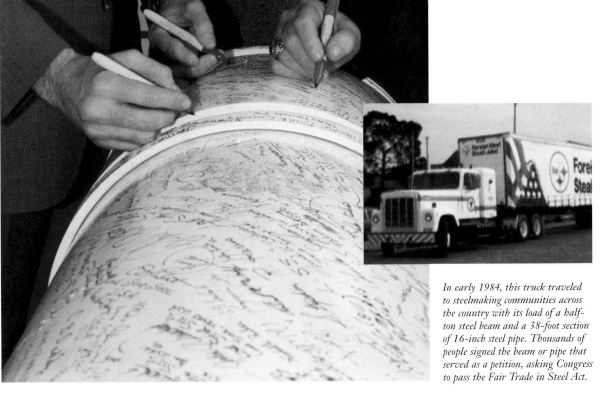

In early 1984, this truck traveled to steelmaking communities across the country with its load of a half-ton steel beam and a 38-foot section of 16-inch steel pipe. Thousands of people signed the beam or pipe that served as a petition, asking Congress to pass the Fair Trade in Steel Act.

There were two other weapons against dumped steel. One was the Voluntary Restraint Agreement, or VRA. These were quotas on U.S. imports that the federal trade officials negotiated with countries that exported steel. The U.S. government had filed documents that were variations on the VRA theme several times since the Sixties. As Christopher Hall explained in *Steel Phoenix*, the VRAs had the advantage of allowing steel prices to be raised without giving up more domestic market share to foreign exports. Critics portrayed American steel as the only industry demanding and winning VRA quotas, but, in fact, the devices were used extensively to protect domestic makers of textiles, footwear, apparel, machine tools, automobiles, even color television sets.

The other anti-import device was the Trigger Price Mechanism (TPM), which the Carter administration had put into effect from 1977 to 1981. TPM set no quotas, but established a threshold price—a price below which imports were officially assumed to be dumped and subject to punitive duties. The drawback was that, unlike the VRAs, the TPM still allowed imported steel into the U.S. market, even though the duties bumped up the price for the steel. Dumping continued. Under pressure from the U.S. steel industry, the U.S. government discontinued trigger prices.

In 1982, the American steel industry returned to VRAs as their favorite shield against unfairly priced imports. At that point, import levels approached 20 percent of the American market. Under pressure from the industry, the U.S. government applied VRAs in October, limiting the market share of European producers to about 5 percent of U.S. consumption. Japan voluntarily restrained its exports to the States.

U. S. Steel never led the industry charge to pressure the government to adopt the agreement. Roderick felt that the VRA wasn't needed if the government would strictly enforce its own trade laws. But he realized that Washington was using trade, not only as an economic tool, but also as one of diplomacy and politics. He, therefore, resigned himself to the imposition of the VRA, something a majority of his peers in the industry wanted, as the best U. S. Steel and the other domestic producers could expect under the circumstances.

For the most part, the VRA scheme was a Band-Aid. When some of the European producers agreed to adhere to the limits, withdrawing imports, nonsignatories such as Spain, Brazil, Mexico, Sweden, Korea and Mexico filled the gap with their own dumped steel. Still, many domestic producers fought through the decade to keep the program going.

And the corporation kept pushing for relief from the imports.

In 1984, a year in which steel imports reached about 26 million tons, thousands of U. S. Steel employees, retirees and shareholders participated in a massive, grass-roots lobbying program aimed at getting the government to enact anti-import legislation.

They were heard, not only by the public, but by Congress, where a bill was introduced in both houses to limit steel imports to 15 percent of the U.S. market for five years. Before the bill could be put to a vote, though, President Reagan announced his own voluntary restraint plan, one designed to limit finished steel imports to 18.5 percent of the domestic market, and to cut off semi-finished foreign steel imports to 1.7 million tons annually.

All in all, 1984 was an encouraging year for the corporation.

After a loss of more than $610 million dollars in 1983, steel operations' income jumped to $142 million, helping the corporation climb from that 1983 loss of more than a billion dollars to a net income of $493 million. The fixes in steel and the Marathon acquisition were paying off.

The company shut more of its uncompetitive or too-costly facilities—the Duquesne blast furnace and bar mills, for example, and Fairless' coke plant. After being idled for 18 months, Fairfield's blast furnace, Q-BOP, slab mill, hot strip mill and other facilities resumed operations under a new local union agreement that eliminated some of the work rule restrictions of the past.

Other investments included $290 million for new slab casters at Fairfield and Gary. Tom Graham called the Gary unit "the most productive caster in the world."

There was more. The corporation and USW worked together to set up nine assistance centers for union employees who had lost their jobs in U. S. Steel shutdowns. In their first strike-free settlement in 20 years, the corporation and the United Mineworkers signed a new contract with wage and benefit increases. And U. S. Steel improved benefits for employees corporate-wide.

Workers drill a well on the platform of the Marathon-operated South Brae Field in the United Kingdom's North Sea. Production of oil from the field lived up to expectations in its first full year of operations.

Marathon, meanwhile, finished the first full year of production at its lucrative South Brae field in the North Sea, and discovered generous deposits of oil off the coasts of Australia and Indonesia.

The icing on the cake: As part of its objective of slashing debt, the corporation reduced long-term debt by $903 million.

Roderick and his team had recreated the company.

"David M. Roderick's controversial strategy for the United States Steel Corporation, heavy layoffs and plant closures in its money-losing steel operations while diversifying into other areas, notably petroleum, is finally beginning to pay off," concluded *The New York Times* on June 5, 1984. Focusing on the corporation's steel operations, the *Times* quoted security analyst Peter F. Marcus: "Looking at their fantastic turnaround, you have to say they're doing a monumental job cutting costs. Their production costs used to be $50 a ton higher than the industry average, but now they're just about $5 higher."

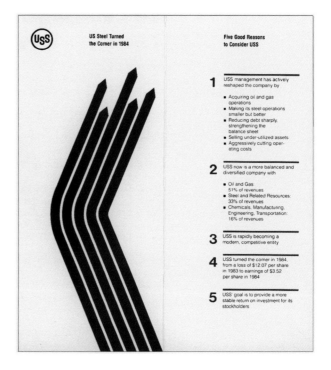

In 1985, the corporation's investor relations staff issued a brochure which, among other facts and conclusions, announced that, after a loss of $12.07 per share in 1983, the corporation had bounced back in 1984 to earnings of $3.52 a share.

The brochure's title: *U. S. Steel Turned the Corner in 1984.*

R oderick was convinced that acquisitions would help the corporation make that turn onto Profitability Street. Steelworkers who thought the corporation was bailing out of steel altogether were encouraged somewhat when, in February 1994, the corporation concluded an agreement in principle to buy National Steel Corporation for $575 million. The purchase was to include iron ore, coal and transportation facilities. But Roderick really had his eye on National Steel's three modern, efficient steel plants, which produced quality, flat-rolled steel. This deal fell through, too, however, when the Department of Justice turned thumbs down on it for antitrust reasons.

The rejected deal was offset by Marathon's successful purchase of Husky Oil Limited of Canada. The $600-million acquisition boosted Marathon's reserves of proven liquids by 44 million barrels, and its natural gas reserves by more than 91 billion cubic feet.

More unusual were two other ventures, one with a customer, the other with a competitor.

In the first, U. S. Steel and Ford Motor Company's Rouge Steel subsidiary created the Double Eagle Steel Coating Company, a joint venture that would produce up to 700,000 tons a year of "electrogalvanized" sheet steel for automobiles. The technology made cars more rust-resistant, and was based on U. S. Steel's method for applying zinc on sheet steel at high speeds, a process used at the Gary Works.

In the second venture, U. S. Steel and Bethlehem Steel joined to pool their research forces on the job of developing "thin-section" continuous castings and to reduce them immediately into steel sheet or strip.

The corporation kicked off 1986 by signing two joint ventures. In one, U. S. Steel and Worthington Industries, Inc. (a Columbus, Ohio-based sheet and strip processor), agreed to build and operate, in Jackson, Michigan, a state-of-the-art plant for processing high-quality steel coils for the auto, appliance and furniture industries.

In the other joint venture, South Korean steel producer Pohang Iron and Steel Company, Ltd. (POSCO) and the corporation became the owner-operators of U. S. Steel's former Pittsburg, California, plant. POSCO acquired half-ownership of the plant and the employees there became POSCO employees. The deal called for the partners to invest more than $300 million over four years to moderinize Pittsburg's finishing facilities, which would process hot-rolled coils into sheet and tin products.

If the deal with the South Koreans was a surprise for anyone who still harbored isolationist views, another joint venture, finalized in 1989, spoke volumes about how much the world had changed in a few decades.

USS/KOBE was born when U. S. Steel and Tokyo-based Kobe Steel, one of the world's largest steel bar producers, established a 50-50 joint venture at Lorain Works in Ohio. Japanese managers from Kobe Steel moved to the States, took offices in the plant and worked with their American counterparts to revive the ailing facility. The secret of the partnership's success was to be the much-admired Japanese management techniques that emphasized the workers' participation in problem-solving and decision-making.

Former President Gerald R. Ford was the keynote speaker for the USS/POSCO joint venture dedication in April 1989. Welcoming him were David Roderick (right), USX chairman, and Thomas Graham (left), USS president.

The irony was as striking as the heat off the glowing steel gliding along the plant's continuous caster. This was the plant whose workers, during World War II, had produced Big Inch, the pipeline that helped fuel America's war machine so it could lick the Axis powers. This plant had produced thousands of tubes for bombs used to defeat the Japanese. Now the Japanese were in Lorain, Ohio. And they were here working with the Americans to turn the plant into a profit-maker.

This was not the old way of doing business. And while Roderick and Graham and the rest of his team had been cooking up these new kinds of partnerships, Roderick was doing homework on nonsteel, nonenergy companies that could serve as the corporation's "third leg."

Roderick had accumulated files on companies from Alcoa to Westinghouse. In 1985 he settled on a company that wouldn't be different enough from steel and oil to be that distinctive, third leg, but that looked like a good encore to the corporation's purchase of Marathon.

It was also an acquisition that, like the Marathon deal, would cause consternation, even anger, among steelworkers and shareholders.

Texas Oil & Gas Corporation—TXO—had been known for some time to Dave Roderick and the rest of his management team.

For one thing, TXO, a Dallas-based driller and producer of oil and natural gas, had for some time purchased pipe from U. S. Steel for its drilling and producing operations. For another, U. S. Steel's pension fund had a considerable amount of money invested in TXO stock. Roderick knew TXO Chairman William L. Hutchison well. Well enough that, in mid-1985, when a TXO financial advisor informed Roderick that TXO "might" be for sale, the chairman wondered why he had not gotten the word from Hutchison himself.

Roderick phoned Hutchison. Was the story true?

"When I called Bill," Roderick recalled for the author, "he said, yes, there was some truth to it. He was sort of tired and wanted to step

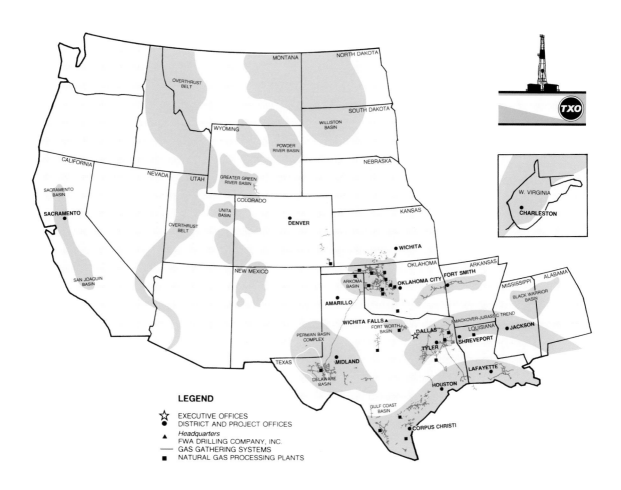

LEGEND

☆ EXECUTIVE OFFICES
● DISTRICT AND PROJECT OFFICES
▲ *Headquarters*
  FWA DRILLING COMPANY, INC.
— GAS GATHERING SYSTEMS
■ NATURAL GAS PROCESSING PLANTS

back a little. In fact, while he was still TXO president, about a year before we talked, he had relinquished the title CEO…of the company." Hutchison's co-founders also wanted quietly to sell their interests in the company.

There was one nagging problem: Natural gas prices had been falling for a couple of years, leaving a glut that would be known, infamously, as the "gas bubble." But the Roderick team saw no reason for prices and the bubble to halt a purchase. "On a long-term basis, [the acquisition] looked like it was going to be attractive."

In October 1985, the deal was announced: Each share of common stock of TXO would be converted into .6333 of a share of U. S. Steel common, and TXO granted an option allowing U. S. Steel to purchase for $1.3 billion all of the capital stock of TXO's gas pipeline business, Delhi Gas Pipeline Corporation and two other companies.

The news release announcing the agreement explained that U. S. Steel would operate TXO as a separate business, and keep TXO's headquarters in Dallas.

Less-encouraging words came from reporters and analysts, even though Roderick and his team launched a road show to convince them that, as *The Wall Street Journal's* J. Ernest Beazley put it, they had "misread the merger."

"Foremost in the minds of many investors," Beazley added, "is the heavy dilution involved in the for-stock buyout. U. S. Steel has estimated that the transaction will result in the issuance of 133.2 million shares, more than doubling the 123.4 million shares the company has outstanding."

Also in the minds of investors was the price that TXO's main product, natural gas, was going for. The *Journal* quoted one investment officer as believing "continuing declines in natural gas prices mean the steelmaker is paying even more than was first thought for Texas Oil."

Still, most U. S. Steel and TXO shareholders saw the glass as half full.

Chairman David M. Roderick addressed U. S. Steel stockholders concerning the proposed merger with Texas Oil & Gas Corporation at a special meeting in Pittsburgh on February 11, 1986. Shareholders of both companies strongly supported the merger.

On February 11, 1986, in Pittsburgh, David Roderick stood at the podium during a special meeting of U. S. Steel shareholders, a meeting called for them to vote on the merger. He listed the deal's merits.

Even as he recognized the stubborn lull in gas prices and the tenacious gas bubble, he promised shareholders the merger would result in "a company which is one of the nation's largest and, probably more importantly, most-efficient competitors in the energy industry while still remaining America's largest and premiere steel producer."

The combined company would be about 13th in the *Fortune* 500 ranking, and would have total corporate revenues of $21 billion.

The final outcome must have silenced the critics.

With a total of 81 percent of the outstanding common shares of U. S. Steel represented, 82 percent of those shares voted for the merger.

At a comparable shareholders' meeting in Dallas, where Texas Oil & Gas shareholders represented a comparable percentage of TXO shares, 87 percent of the votes were cast in favor of the merger.

United States Steel shareholders had approved the merger by more than 4 to 1; TXO shareholders by more than 6 to 1.

Now this multi-industry company needed a new name. A lot of analysts and shareholders would have put oil and gas first in the order.

Renaming the company wasn't a new idea. At every annual meeting after the corporation's acquisition of Marathon, it seemed, shareholders had stood and borrowed the microphone to lobby Chairman Roderick on changing "U. S. Steel" to something that better reflected the corporation's new diversity.

At the February 11, 1986, special meeting for a shareholders' vote on the TXO merger, shareholders suggested the corporation be rechristened "U. S. Steel and Energy Corporation" or "U. S. Steel Industries."

The year before, at the corporation's 1985 annual meeting, shareholder Lewis Gilbert suggested a new name of his own. It included the letter X, U. S. Steel's stock exchange symbol. "U. S. Steel as a division can still keep [the name] U. S. Steel," Gilbert urged, "but I think maybe USX or something like that..."

New flag signaled new era at USX headquarters in Pittsburgh.

"We wouldn't be wanting to be known as the X Corporation," Roderick answered.

By 1986, however, Roderick had changed his mind...with Bruce Thomas' help. Thomas had reconsidered the Gilbert idea, refined it, established a rationale for it and recommended the name to Roderick. Later, the board voted to accept the name. USX Corporation it was.

At a July 8 press briefing, Roderick proudly explained the rationale behind the new name: "The X, which some of you may not recognize, has been our symbol on the New York Stock Exchange since 1924, and that's the trading symbol that we will retain in this changed name."

The new USX name, rendered in a stately logotype, now symbolized a "new" company. Roderick's staff would keep a hand in Big Decisions having to do with investments, strategies, taxes and cash flow. But the businesses would have more freedom to zig or zag as markets demanded. They would have more autonomy.

"We have restructured the company into a parent firm with four operating units," Roderick told reporters. "The parent firm is USX Corporation, taking its name from the U. S. in...U. S. Steel, which is our way of confirming and continuing the leading role we have played over the years as a participant in the industrial life of this country."

The corporation's executive and support staffs would remain in its Pittsburgh headquarters, Roderick added. But now its steel business, one of the four operating groups, would be known as USS. It would operate under Division President Thomas C. Graham.

The second unit, Marathon Oil, would keep its headquarters in Findlay, Ohio, under President William E. Swales, who had been named president when Harold Hoopman retired in 1985.

U. S. Diversified Group, also based in Pittsburgh, encompassed the corporation's chemicals business, its steel service centers, and its engineering, consulting, construction services, real estate, transportation and energy-equipment businesses. Its president: Thomas Marshall.

The fourth group, Texas Oil & Gas, would be headquartered in Dallas under President Forrest E. Hoglund.

As Roderick explained, the new name had been selected from a pool of about 200 rounded up from steel executives and others by a consulting firm. The names included USSA, AMCOR and, rejected as pompous, MAXUS, a play on the first two letters in Marathon, the X symbol, and the "US" in U. S. Steel.

Of course, the corporation was doing much more than playing a name game.

"We are diversifying," Roderick explained, "to give increased balance and stability to our asset base while preserving the basic core businesses that now make up the corporation."

That point prompted a reporter to ask whether the parent corporation would retain responsibility for each business' debt. Roderick explained that the corporation would continue to cover past debt, but, picking steel as an example, he added, "There will be a debt cost assigned to this steel group connected with the past borrowing and so forth for that group."

Another reporter followed up: Wouldn't the business groups be competing for capital allocated by the corporation?

Roderick's answer: "There obviously would be some of that. The allocation of capital will clearly be a prerogative of the parent company. And therefore, [the business groups] would have to justify any projects that they wish to make. They would have to show a reasonable rate of return or reasonable expectation of return."

Stand alone or fall alone. It was not the answer the steelworkers or union wanted to hear, especially now, with negotiations under way for a new contract. The *Pittsburgh Post-Gazette* ran a cartoon showing "USX" in large, red letters, and a steelworker who proclaimed, "I think we're the 'EX'!"

The real steelworkers probably didn't think the cartoon was very funny.

The latest round of tri-yearly talks between the company and union had begun the month before the corporation's name change. But, now, negotiating was a new game. For one thing, the majors had abandoned group bargaining, opting to settle individual contracts with the union. For another, financial distress had led the majors to close mills and merge. A couple had even gone bankrupt.

As spring turned to summer, the union had wrapped up negotiations with the majors that were left—except U. S. Steel. Most of the talks had been peaceful, but some were not. Now the union and Big Steel squared off for what would be, in labor-writer Hoerr's words, the battle of the century.

U. S. Steel came out with big guns. Right after its name change, it distributed to all its employees a slick, color brochure titled *USS Today*, a take-off on the popular daily, national newspaper.

The booklet was loaded with color bar charts and tables that capsulized the woes of the steel industry and USS. It answered its own questions:

"Is USS Putting Money In Or Taking Money Out Of Steel?" one chart asked. The answer: The company had invested almost $3 billion in its steel operations between 1980 and 1985.

"What Did USS Get For All The Cash Invested In Steel?" asked another chart. Answer: A loss of $2.4 billion.

This publication was distributed to all U. S. Steel employees as negotiations between the company and the union approached an August 1 deadline on a new labor contract in 1986.

Another chart reminded readers of the union's insistence that any concessions with the majors would have to be tied to the amount of the majors' losses. A bright red bar revealed that U. S. Steel's $2.4-billion cash drain topped the losses of the other majors.

The union, Hoerr wrote, refused to take any of the company's figures seriously. The reason? It insisted the corporation's $2.4-million loss was artificial because the corporation had not included in its calculations earnings of coal and other operations that were deemed nonsteel. These exclusions, the union argued, had the effect of skimming off some of the profits normally reported for the steel business.

The critical issues for deliberation boiled down to two: the company's practice of contracting out work to nonunion employees, and the high employment rates the steelworkers were accruing as a result of the ENA formula. The union wanted the company to restrict, if not end, contracting out. The company's goal was to convince the union that it had to give back a substantial amount of what it had gained under the ENA-driven contract.

While the company's customers stockpiled steel—and the corporation's top management and white-collar workers got used to salary cuts—the haggling dragged on. Neither side was prepared to give much ground on these two issues, but the clincher was their failure to agree on wage reductions. The union was willing to give back something, but both sides used different formulas, and their final numbers weren't even close. Recognizing that U. S. Steel had begun to shut down its furnaces, and that the two parties stared at each other over an unbridgeable gap, the union opted to cut its losses. It offered to continue working under the old contract. If it decided, later, to go on strike, it would give the company 24 hours notice and help with an orderly shutdown.

The offer gave the union two advantages. If U. S. Steel accepted it, the company would have to pay unemployment compensation to the laid-off steelworkers. If the company rejected the deal, the union could claim the corporation had locked out the workers.

As Hoerr records the incident, the steel industry's chief negotiator Bruce Johnston turned the offer down flat. "Lockout," he told Bernie Klieman, his union opposite, would be a "legal fiction." The right word was "strike." Furthermore, Johnston wanted to know, how could the company attract customers if the union could "pull the trap door" in 48 hours?

Negotiations stopped right there. A few days later, Hoerr noted, union pickets showed up at U. S. Steel plants with signs on which the word "strike" had been replaced with "locked-out."

It was August 1. The strike/lockout of 1986 had begun. It would last six months.

W as it a strike or a lockout? Hoerr, for one, concluded that "strike" best fit the circumstances: The union had "refused to work at the company's offered price." Nevertheless, a few weeks after the strike signs went up, the Pennsylvania Department of Labor and Industry ruled that USX had, indeed, locked out the steelworkers. That meant, as Hoerr explained, some 6,200 workers were eligible for unemployment benefits. This turn of events surely didn't make continued bargaining any more enjoyable for Johnston and his crew.

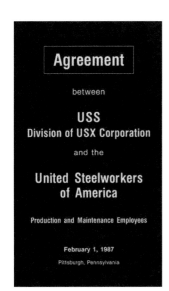

This agreement ended the steel industry's longest strike, with both sides claiming their share of settlement victories.

In any case, the talks ground on, at a cost to USX that various observers estimated at $3 million to $5 million a day. When the disagreements stretched into December, the two sides decided to bring in an arbitrator. Starting December 21, this umpire met with the bargaining parties, every day except Christmas Day, through New Year's Day. On January 3, he delivered his findings and decisions.

When the talks were finally over, both sides claimed some victories.

U. S. Steel won wage and benefit cuts of $2.52 an hour for the contract's first year, $2.20 an hour for the second year and $2.07 for the third and fourth years. Both sides made trade-offs, too, in the disputes over contracting out. The company agreed to a general prohibition against subcontracting work, and the union allowed some exceptions for example, subcontracting the finishing of steel to outside shops to meet customer demands for quality and delivery.

Other compromises were made in the areas of pensions and rehiring of laid-off steelworkers if new jobs opened. The union also agreed to an extension of the labor contract from three to four years, a concession which would afford the company a longer period of labor stability. In return, USX said it would upgrade some of its plants, for example, by building casters at its Fairfield and Edgar Thomson Works and modernizing the Irvin Works' 84-inch strip mill. It also agreed to fund retraining programs for laid-off steelworkers.

The dealing was over. But the stress didn't end.

On February 4, 1987, David Roderick held a news conference to announce it was closing a number of plants in a $1.03-billion write-off. Besides shutting down production units at various plants, the corporation would put its Geneva Works in Utah, its plant in Baytown, Texas, and parts of its National plant near Pittsburgh on "indefinite idled status," what Hoerr called a kind of limbo.

The announcement meant almost 4,000 USX employees had lost their jobs at midnight, December 31, 1986, while they were picketing to save them. Hoerr: "Their jobs had not existed on January 27 when the USX board of directors approved a $1 billion write-off of assets, in the very week that they voted to save their jobs by ratifying the new contract." Furthermore, since the plants were not formally closed, the employees still working there could not claim shut-down benefits.

The USW leaders and the steelworkers felt they had been betrayed. Hoerr concluded the union had been amply warned. "In the summer of 1982," he wrote, "Roderick told reporters that a strike 'would raise a great risk to a number of [U. S. Steel plants] as to whether they will ever open again.'" If the warning was ample, it was also subtle.

U. S. Steel's commitment to build a new continuous caster at its Fairfield Works became a reality in April 1987. Taking part in the official groundbreaking ceremonies were (left to right) Alabama Governor Guy Hunt, USS President Thomas Graham, and Alabama State Treasurer George C. Wallace, Jr.

As if a strike wasn't enough to contend with in an already hectic year, the corporation found itself the target of takeover artists. These were members of a new breed of hit-and-run investment bankers or just plain speculators who snapped up chunks of corporate stocks they deemed to be undervalued, short-changing shareholders. When these pirates saw that their real or feigned bids to take over "ailing" companies had driven up the prices of stock, they scooped up their earnings and dashed off after another target.

In mid-September of 1986, newspapers passed along rumors that Texas oilman T. Boone Pickens, Jr., considered to be of the raider ilk, had accumulated as many as eight million shares of USX stock. An Associated Press item on September 20 noted that Minneapolis "investor" Irwin Jacobs seemed to be dabbling in USX stock, too, and that Australian "businessman" Robert Holmes a Court had said he wanted to buy as much as 15 percent of the corporation. The ensuing market frenzy rocketed

USX's stock to the top of the most-active list—"up 66 percent to 25, on September 22," *Business Week* later reported.

Also on the newspaper lists of phantom investors was Carl C. Icahn, a busy New York City-based "financier" who, as *Business Week* put it, had "amassed a personal fortune by capitalizing on his Darth Vader image to make corporate boards tremble."

Carl Icahn made a run at USX as a prime takeover target in the mid-1980s.

The 50-year-old Icahn had gotten rich by going after companies he insisted were in the bargain basement because of inept management. He sold himself as a hero, sweeping in to rescue impoverished shareholders. His biggest trophy so far had been TWA. He'd taken over the troubled airline in 1985 and, by cutting flights, wages and jobs, had steered the company on a course to profitability. *Business Week* pegged his takings in October 1986 at $200 million or more in trading profits from over a dozen takeover attempts, and another $220 million from his holdings in TWA and USX.

While the movies depicted Wall Street raiders as raptors who operated out of lavish, well-staffed offices, Icahn took care of most of his business from modest Manhattan digs. His operation consisted mainly of himself and a long-time associate, an investment adviser whose brain was as good as a CAT scan when it came to scrutinizing the financial muscle and bone that supported and powered the corporate body. Icahn, no slouch himself at sizing up companies, dismissed the Darth Vader comparison, calling himself the Lone Ranger and his partner Tonto. If the corporate chieftains weren't exactly playing the role of bad guys, they still shivered when Icahn and his sidekick rode into town.

Now Icahn had his sights on USX, and was quietly amassing USX stock. (He'd soon snapped up an 11.4-percent stake.) At the end of the first week, he struck. In a letter to David Roderick, he made a "friendly" offer to buy USX. The tag on the takeover bid: $8 billion, which figured out to $31 a share. If successful, this would be the third-largest acquisition in U.S. history, United Press International said.

The deal was to be sealed through the takeover specialist's favorite method of financing, a leveraged buyout. In a filing with the Securities and Exchange Commission, Icahn declared his affiliates would, as UPI paraphrased him, "put up approximately $1 billion cash with the remainder to be raised by Drexel Burnham Lambert Inc., the largest underwriter of high-yield, low-rated 'junk bonds.'"

Icahn claimed his agenda was to deliver to shareholders a share price that reflected the true value of their company, especially the value of Marathon. The oil company's stock, he argued, was artificially low, despite the USX "stand-on-your-own" doctrine for its businesses. In the competition for capital, oil was not getting its due.

Icahn had a similar grudge against the managers of most of the country's big corporations. They had let their companies get fat and slow. Instead of contributing, the managers interfered. As Icahn was quoted in *Business Week*'s issue for October 27, 1986, America's CEOs were bureaucrats who had "produced a corporate welfare state, an army of nonproductive workers." If he ran the corporation as he ran TWA, he would cut the fat and the costs, freeing up the promising businesses so they could produce for shareholders a return that was commensurate with their real value.

Nonsense, sniffed the executives at U. S. Steel and other corporations. Icahn's game really was to use that kind of talk to drive up the price of stock. Then he would sell his stock and disappear.

If Icahn thought that Roderick was sluggish, he badly misjudged this particular CEO.

Roderick had begun circling his wagons right after picking up early rumors of an impending takeover attempt. As *Time* sized up the situation, Roderick had resolved to save his company: "The chairman knew that Icahn might sell off USX piece by piece, since the breakup value of the firm is estimated to be more than $61 a share, or $15.8 billion … ."

Roderick okayed a study aimed at finding a restructuring and cost-cutting formula that would raise USX's stock and shoo Icahn away. Fine, said Icahn. But if Roderick's plan didn't look potent enough to boost USX's stock, the chairman must submit Icahn's offer to shareholders for a vote—or face the possibility of a hostile takeover, probably at less than $31 a share. Also, in the middle of the Icahn commotion, USX spun off its chemical business. But the corporation denied that this move had anything to do with de-Icahnizing the company. Rather, it was another step in USX's overall strategy for streamlining.

Then Icahn backpeddled. In mid-January of 1987, he abruptly gave up, "outmaneuvered," *Time* claimed, "by Roderick."

The chairman pulled off what the magazine called a "relatively simple ploy that dashed Icahn's hopes...."

"... USX had borrowed $3.4 billion last year under terms that allowed the lenders to call in their loans immediately if the company were taken over. At the end of December, Roderick cleverly decided to use up these funds to pay off other debts. If Icahn had gained control of USX, the banks could have demanded repayment. That in effect raised the cost of taking over the company from about $7.1 billion to $10.5 billion."

Icahn had backed off, but he didn't go away. He kept buying stock. He remained a threat, and he kept circulating in the background, except for the times he sprang to the foreground to advise Roderick what to do to improve the corporation's performance and worth. They got together for these chats for more than two years, in Pittsburgh and on Icahn's turf, New York City.

In fact, Icahn so frequently invited Roderick to join him in posh Manhattan restaurants to dine and talk business that the press began to wonder whether the two had come to enjoy each other's company.

In January of 1989, *The Wall Street Journal* even compared the two to another duo that had moved from combatants to confreres. The paper reminded readers that Roderick and Icahn had been "locked in a high-stakes brawl" a little more than two years before, then observed that "no one would have thought the men would become the corporate world's version of Reagan and Gorbachev.

"But that is just what has happened," the writers suggested. "Last week, the pair dined at a private club in Manhattan. Next month, they are scheduled to meet again at a restaurant near Mr. Icahn's office in Mount Kisco, N.Y. They trade tips on raising thoroughbred horses, a shared interest. They talk about politics, sports, their families and even their upbringings."

They also talked a lot about how to fiddle with and fine-tune the company's operations and structure in order to beef up the stock. Or, rather, Icahn did. Roderick listened and shook his head.

"I'd go up and have dinner with him in restaurants in New York," Roderick recalled after he had retired. "He had all sorts of ideas, about spinning off the steel division, selling assets…all sorts of fancy ideas. I'd say, 'Okay, Carl, I hear you. Interesting thought. I'll think about that.' Constant dialogue, just him talking and talking. It went on for a couple of years."

Icahn, claimed Roderick, was getting desperate. "He needed to get out," meaning Icahn was not making money because he had to service loans for his stock purchases while low gas prices and a lackluster steel market were shortchanging him on his returns from USX stock. He had to find a way to cut his losses.

What the *Journal* didn't know was that, back in 1986, not long after Icahn made his first offer for USX, Roderick had called him up for a secret meeting, one that spilled over into a second secret session. Both meetings were on neutral turf, the offices of investment bankers, with no one in the room but Roderick and Icahn.

Roderick: "I told him, we'll look at what you want to do, but I'm not going to let you come in and look at the books, I'm not going to let you do due diligence. It's just that simple. And if you get your financing, then, fine. Go ahead and buy us."

Icahn abandons takeover bid of USX Corp.

NEW YORK (UPI) — New York investor Carl C. Icahn Thursday said he has abandoned his $31-a-share bid to acquire USX Corp. because the nation's largest steelmaker made his offer "virtually impossible .. to consummate."

But Icahn, who had threatened a takeover of USX unless the company took action to enhance the value of its stock, said in a filing with the Securities and Exchange Commission that he may consider waging a proxy battle to win seats on the board

possibility of our $31 offer," Icahn said.

Last month Roderick told a news briefing in New York that USX was "still trying to get a definition" of Icahn's intentions in amicable discussions between the two parties.

At that time, the USX chairman said the federal investigation involving Wall Street arbitrageur Ivan Boesky, who agreed to pay the SEC a record $100 million penalty for engaging in insider trading on takeovers, had "complicated and prolonged" the USX talks with Icahn.

Icahn, who has staged a number

Excerpted from a UPI news service report

But Roderick knew Icahn was having trouble getting financing. Icahn's handling of TWA had given potential backers chills, and they were getting leery because another takeover artist had just made news by overstepping legal lines, right into jail.

Finally, tired of the talk, Roderick told Icahn he was handing the job of dealing with him over to USX's general counsel, Dominic B. King. "I said, I've got a company to run. You can mess around and come up with these ideas, but I've got a strike on my hands, I'm doing 99 things here. If you have ideas, you [can talk with] King."

But the years of strategizing to fend off Icahn and the sessions with Icahn on the phone and in the restaurants took their toll on Roderick.

"He cost me time, and he stopped me strategically from going forward with some things that I would have liked to have done."

One of those things would have been "to continue growing the company. I wouldn't sit there just selling assets and not making acquisitions. I think we had to get back on a growth curve, and, if I had stayed there for another couple of years without that diversion, I think I could have gotten on that track."

Still, despite his manner of speaking to and about Icahn, Roderick credited him with brains: "He was smart...a very bright idea guy."

Another complement: "He was a good guy to have dinner with."

One of Roderick's tactics with Icahn was to wait him out. Or talk him out. And he maintained the strategy into 1988, when the time came for him to pass the reins to Charles A. Corry, who, with Roderick's recommendations and blessings, had by then become president of USX and chairman-elect. Corry had joined Roderick and Icahn at a couple of their dinners, and by now had come to know the financier fairly well. He even liked him, which was good, because Icahn wasn't going away soon. Corry would spend a lot of time dealing with him, even good-naturedly putting up with his phone calls, numerous and sometimes at odd hours.

Asset sales during the 1980s included American Bridge Division, one of the corporation's best-known and oldest businesses. Among ABD's famed bridge-building projects was the New River Gorge Bridge near Fayette, West Virginia. Dedicated in October 1977, it was, at the time, the world's longest main steel arch span and the highest bridge east of the Mississippi.

B y the time Roderick stood before shareholders at his last annual meeting, on May 1, 1989, in Pittsburgh's beautiful Heinz Hall, he had earned the right to soak in the shareholders' praise for turning their company around, and to brag just a little about his accomplishments.

USX was now a different corporation, and not just in name. In addition to selling chemicals, Roderick and his team had closed parts or all of the company's aging steel plants. But the write-offs and asset sales had also embraced some of the company's best-known businesses, some of them as old as the corporation itself: American Bridge, Universal Atlas Cement, Michigan Limestone, U. S. Steel Supply, U. S. Steel Products, Quebec Cartier Mining Company and USS Alside.

When the cash register stopped clanging, USX had enriched its coffers by more than $7 billion and discarded some of the most celebrated and storied members of the corporate family.

Roderick's reshaping of the corporation had shown results. Net income had bounced around and, in 1986, had bottomed out with a $1.8-billion loss in net income. Then the corporation rebounded, in no small part because of Roderick's reorganizing and trimming away of facilities that would never be anything but dead weight. Net income jumped to $219 million in 1987, then sprang to $756 million in 1988.

Steel operations? Sales had climbed from $3.7 billion in 1987 to $5.8 billion in 1988. Operating income had soared from a $1.4-billion loss in 1986 to a $501-million gain in 1988. It was one of the steel segment's best years.

Actually, the American steel industry was running more efficiently, and riding higher; *World Steel Dynamics* calculated that steel producers now used 6.807 man-hours per shipped ton, versus 6.57 for Britain and 6.84 for Japan. In its June 13, 1989, issue, *Financial World* declared: "If the U.S. steel industry now ranks as the most efficient in the world, ... then USX's steel subsidiary [U. S. Steel], which has slashed its man-hours per shipped ton from 10.8 in 1982 to just 3.8 last year, is probably now the most efficient producer in the world, a stunning accomplishment."

Roderick summed it up this way for the shareholders in Heinz Hall:

"Our steel sector has been rationalized, with unprofitable lines eliminated and redundant capacity pared. Yet, while reducing our dependence on steel, we have certainly not abandoned nor de-emphasized that sector of our business. We remain America's largest steel producer, and we are one of the lowest-cost producers of steel in the world. [Our] productivity has risen in tandem with the quality of our products."

He left the mike with applause ringing in his ears.

GETTING REAL

Business writers liked to call David Roderick "tough." They were right. Tough he was—like the doctor who prescribes bitter medicine because he knows it will save the patient, or the business analyst who cuts jobs because the numbers say it must be done.

The compact, bull-necked Roderick came from the same North Side neighborhood as many of the steelworkers. He won a reputation in the neighborhood as a formidable boxer, and, in the Marine Corps, as a crack shot. After the service, he returned home, clerked for Gulf Oil and marched through ten years of night school, finally earning a degree in economics and finance.

After starting at U. S. Steel as an assistant comptroller, he hopped around Europe as an accountant for the corporation's international projects, then returned home to work his way to the top.

He knew what he'd find there: an array of steelworks on life-support. He could have juggled numbers until he could pass the problem on to a successor, but he opted to act. He closed dead-weight mills, weeded out less-than-critical corporate staffs and trimmed the bloated chain of command. And he took the heat.

Tough? Roderick was a realist. Nothing demonstrated that as well as the coolness he maintained when some of the displaced steelworkers and their allies stepped over the accepted lines of protest, and the respect he maintained for the steelworkers through the conflict.

David M. Roderick had a side that most steelworkers never saw.

*S*ome of the anti-USX rallies wandered onto the U. S. Steel executives' home turf.

Protesting workers marched around Bruce Thomas' home. A few times, they visited Roderick's home, which sat on a hill, at the end of a long, winding driveway.

Sometimes they would announce their presence by using small explosives to blow up his mailbox.

"It would be in the evening, and you could hear them pop," Roderick told the author. "But who cared? I just went out and bought a new mailbox."

The protestors also rallied for marches around Roderick's house.

"They would say they were going to come out and march around my house, picket my house, and the word would leak out. They would want it to leak out because they wanted the media there— that was the whole purpose. They were trying to attract attention. So the police would call me, and they would say, what do you want us to do? Do you want us to stop them from coming up the driveway?

"I said, no, let them come."

And come they did.

"They showed up a couple times. One morning they showed up about 11 o'clock, about 50 of them, and just walked around the house carrying signs. There were a couple of television cameras there. And you just go about your business. I'd be sitting there, reading, and they'd knock on the door."

Roderick and his wife just ignored the commotion. But when the visits became more frequent, the corporation posted security guards, some wearing night-vision goggles. This was not so much because anyone thought the steelworkers, angry as they were, were a real threat to the Rodericks. The problem was, with all the picketing and TV coverage, people now knew where Roderick lived. Who knew whether a troubled person who had nothing to do with the conflicts in steel would wander up Roderick's drive?

As Roderick later insisted, he was unconcerned about danger. He took no steps to stop the steelworkers from voicing their anger, or to limit where they could speak out. They even showed up at U. S. Steel headquarters and were allowed to parade through the lower lobbies.

"Let's face it, steelworkers are hard-working people, people who labored hard all their lives," Roderick said. "They are responsible. Most of them are family men. They don't go around shooting people. And I never felt threatened. I walked everywhere in the city. I walked to meetings at the Hilton, to the Duquesne Club, to the ball games. I never felt threatened."

*H*ere was a side of David Roderick that most of the steelworkers never saw—the Roderick who came from Pittsburgh's streets, who knew the steelworkers and who understood their strengths as well as their frustrations and fears, and who viewed their demonstrations and the anger they directed at him as perfectly understandable. During interviews for

this book, he talked at great length about this subject, often characteristically switching between past and present tense:

"At the time of the shutdowns, the steel sector was under tremendous decline and pressure. We had enough steel capacity, and I was willing to leave the money that was in steel in steel, but I certainly wasn't willing to go out and take nonsteel assets and invest them in the steel sector. I have no regrets about that, absolutely none.

"I'm not shutting down a Homestead because I dislike [the steelworkers]. I'm doing it because Homestead can no longer make it. It can't be competitive in quality or cost. Its facilities are obsolete. It no longer has a productive life.

"Closing a steel plant is a hurtful thing. If you were a steelworker, wouldn't you be mad? If I were a steelworker, I'd be walking around with a sign. Who would be happy about this? So, the steelworkers' behavior wasn't unreasonable.

"I think people misrepresent my attitude toward steelworkers. I've always defended our steelworkers. And I knew

The Gary Memorial Medal, the highest award of the American Iron and Steel Institute, was one of many honors David Roderick received. The presentation was made in 1984 in recognition of his distinguished career in the steel industry.

that our workers, with equipment older than European and Japanese equipment, [turned out more steel per] man-hour than almost all our international competitors. The problem was, we were paying [wages] three and four times as much as our foreign competitors per hour. It was the cost of the steelworker, not his work and abilities, that was the problem.

"Today, our steelworkers are very, very productive compared to their foreign counterparts. But they're still expensive on an hourly basis. Back then, my objective

The David M. Roderick Wildlife Reserve was dedicated by Roderick in 1991. The 3,131 acres of woodlands, wetlands and scenic bluffs, overlooking Lake Erie in northwestern Pennsylvania, are managed by the Pennsylvania Game Commission. The property was originally envisioned by Carnegie as the site of a pipe mill in 1900 and as a new U. S. Steel plant in the 1970s.

was, [because] they were so expensive, you had to have fewer of them."

When Roderick retired as chairman in 1989, he left one major piece of unfinished business—getting Carl Icahn off the company's back. That, Chuck Corry would do in high style, and to the satisfaction of the raider himself.

What a decade Roderick's chairman-ship had been. Most spectacular of his moves was the energy business he brought into the corporate mix, a character change so radical that U. S. Steel would require

a name change. Of his purchase of Marathon, of his downsizing of steelmaking capacity by retiring facilities and workers, of his sale of under-performing assets, of the sum of these efforts, many have said he saved U. S. Steel from the fate of many of its competitors.

Given the long days he devoted to the business of his company, it is surprising that he had time to serve the community, as well. But he did, especially in the area of education: as a trustee and past chairman of the board of trustees of Carnegie Mellon University and as a director of St. Vincent College and the University of Pittsburgh Medical Center. He was also director of the Allegheny Trails Council, Boy Scouts of America.

Roderick's career was capped by many honors, but four must have held special significance for him: the Gary Medal (1984), highest award of the American Iron and Steel Institute, of which he had once been chairman; a similar award (1989) from the International Iron & Steel Institute, which he had also served as chairman; the Americanism Award of the Anti-Defamation League of B'nai B'rith (1984) and the Horatio Alger Award (1988), presented by the Horatio Alger Association of Distinguished Americans.

He could really relate to that last award. The years of his youth had taught him all about bootstraps.

Each of these three men (left to right) B. F. Fairless, E. R. Stettinius, and E.M. Voorhees left their mark on the financial workings of the corporation during their tenures as chairman of the Finance Committee.

THE MONEY MEN

Paper—the cash and securities that are the tools of finance—is as crucial to steel as ore and blast furnaces. Accordingly, strong financial controls have been in place at U. S. Steel since master financier J. P. Morgan created the company in 1901.

The way those controls have been implemented, however, changed over the course of the corporation's life.

From April 9, 1901—a week after the corporation sprang to life—through August 1, 1975, the Finance Committee chairman was the second- or third-most-powerful person in the corporation. In the early years, the finance chairmen even reported to the board, not to the chairman of the board. Over the hundred years of U. S. Steel (USX), the Finance Committee chairmen have included: Elbert H. Gary, himself; Myron C. Taylor; Edward R. Stettinius, Jr.; Benjamin F. Fairless; Enders M. Voorhees; Robert C. Tyson; and David M. Roderick, the last chairman.

All were extremely able, but Voorhees became something of a legend.

A recruit from Johns-Manville Corporation, Voorhees was highly regarded nationally for his financial expertise and creativity. He was highly influential in U. S. Steel's policies and direction. In fact, U. S. Steel owes much to Voorhees for its emergence at the end of the twentieth century as the major U.S. steel producer—possibly its survival. The reason: Voorhees' forethought in funding the corporation's pension plan to the brim.

One of Voorhees' admirers was W. Bruce Thomas, who retired in 1991 as USX's chief financial officer and vice chairman of administration.

Voorhees, Thomas said, was concerned that labor agreements would generate growing pension liabilities. During Voorhees' time, pension funds typically were managed for corporations by banks. Voorhees saw safety in more-direct control, so, in effect, he brought management of the funds in-house.

"In 1950," Thomas explained, "Voorhees hired Harvey Mole from the Bank of New York to recruit and direct a staff that would manage the pension fund for the corporation. Voorhees withdrew the company's pension funds from the banks and directed Mole to invest a major portion of them in equity securities. It was a dramatic departure from the then-standard practice of investing pension funds only in high-quality, low-interest-rate bonds."

The Fifties and Sixties turned out to be an excellent time to invest in common stocks, noted Thomas, and Voorhees' program was a huge success. It continued to be a success right into the next century, as the corporation's pension funds were managed internally by what Thomas considered to be "a talented group of analysts and portfolio managers."

Demonstrating the wisdom of Voorhees' approach, added Thomas, is the fact that, between 1950 and 2000, the corporation paid to pensioners a total of $21.3 billion. Despite this staggering amount, the corporation's pension funds totaled $11.3 billion at the end of 1999, an amount that substantially exceeded the corporation's net worth.

Other groundbreaking ideas credited to Voorhees include what Thomas called an innovative, standard-costs system that allowed corporate managers to assert even stronger control in reducing expenses. Voorhees also brought corporate tax lawyers and accountants together into one group — a move that eliminated professional rivalries and stimulated the staff to find even more ways to reduce corporate tax liabilities.

Voorhees' relationship with U. S. Steel President Ben Fairless was another example of a true partnership. As Thomas recalled, "Over the 20 turbulent years between the mid-Thirties and the mid-Fifties, they worked together as a highly effective team. Although each reported directly to the board of directors, their tenure was characterized by genuinely friendly cooperation, always in the best interest of the corporation, free of any struggles over power."

Voorhees was greatly respected for his adherence to the path laid out by Judge Gary, a path that was ethically correct. Thomas was introduced to that quality when he first met Voorhees. This was back in the early Fifties, when Thomas was a young tax executive in the New York office of U. S. Steel's Orinoco Mining Company. He was preparing to head for Venezuela and a job tending to the corporation's tax interests at the subsidiary's then-new mine and mining town in Venezuela — the enterprise launched under Fairless.

Venezuela was then a recovering dictatorship, but even as a fledgling democracy, its government was not known for moral rectitude. It was a climate in which a young executive might have trouble sticking to the path of righteousness. Figuring that Thomas would benefit by some calibration of his ethical compass, Voorhees called Thomas to come up for a chat at 71 Broadway. Thomas went, wondering why he was being summoned from someone so high on the corporate ladder.

"Voorhees introduced himself," Thomas recalled, "and said, 'I understand you are going to Venezuela and you are going to handle taxes down there.'"

Then Voorhees came to the point, as paraphrased by Thomas:

"You know, some of the countries down there may not be quite as honest as we are up here. There may come a time when one of the people there suggests something that sounds good for the company, but that would not be right, ethically. I wanted to tell you that, if we ever find you're making money for the company by doing something that's not right, you're gone. I don't care how much money you might cost the company by doing what's right. We'll stand behind you and protect you."

The sermon stood Thomas in good stead after he got to Venezuela, and found his corporation caught up in a government scam designed to make it repay taxes it had already paid. Thomas called up the local official charged with auditing the company's tax records and invited him to lunch so they could talk things over. Clearly, U. S. Steel had paid the taxes already, Thomas reminded his guest over lunch. Couldn't the official fix the matter?

The answer: Well, my office doesn't have the furniture it should have and the people who work for me don't have nice desks and air conditioning. If you take care of that problem for me, I'll forget about your tax problem.

Thomas thought about the offer, the potential for further taxes or other trouble if he declined. And he thought about Voorhees. Then Thomas gave his answer. "That wouldn't be right. So go ahead and write up your report and we'll take it to court."

The outcome? "The guy left that afternoon," Thomas said. "He didn't even finish his audit, and never came back.

"But, you know," he added, "if I hadn't had that conversation with Voorhees, I don't know what I would have done."

Future chairmen would take the same care that Voorhees and Fairless had exercised in managing their corporation's fiscal affairs. The era of almost complete autonomy for the corporation's chief of finance technically ended in 1975, when Chairman Ed Speer replaced the Finance Committee with the "Committee on Financial Policy." Speer chaired the new committee, himself, and the committee continued to report to the board. David Roderick chaired the committee as corporate chairman from 1979 to 1984. But when Roderick handed the purse strings to Bruce Thomas in 1984, he revised the reporting procedure again: Thomas now answered to the chairman of the board.

Thomas, though, was the first to hold the title CFO, chief financial officer, acquiring it with his vice chairmanship in 1982. A native of Michigan, he had served in the Air Corps during World War II, done graduate work at New York University Law School, and had been a member of the Michigan State Bar. After joining the Oliver Iron Mining Division in 1952 and serving in Orinoco positions,

Robert M. Hernandez (left) succeeded W. Bruce Thomas, who was the first to hold the title of Chief Financial Officer.

including comptroller, he had become USX's director-taxes and then vice president-taxes in 1967. He had been elected vice president and treasurer in 1971 and vice president and a director in 1975. By the time he retired in 1991, he had been credited with financing $23 billion in corporate projects.

Succeeding Thomas was Robert M. Hernandez, elected by the board to be USX executive vice president, accounting and finance, and CFO. As the corporation pressed into the twenty-first century, Hernandez would prove to be a formidable corporate financier. In the words of Thomas, "he is probably as good a chief financial officer as there is in the country."

Pittsburgh-born, Hernandez earned a bachelor's degree in economics and mathematics from the University of Pittsburgh and an MBA in corporate finance from The Wharton School of the University of Pennsylvania. He joined

USX in 1968 as a project associate in the corporation's business research group in Pittsburgh, and advanced through positions including assistant corporate comptroller, vice president and treasurer, and president of USX Corporation's U. S. Diversified Group. He was elected vice president of finance and treasurer in 1990, joined the USX board in 1991 and, in 1994, became vice chairman.

Hernandez counted among his trophies the plan to break USX stock into separate shares for steel and energy— the arrangement that let Carl Icahn ride off into the sunset.

Chapter 18

Carl Makes His Exit

Chuck Corry's phone rang, and the chairman could have bet who was calling: Carl Icahn.

The financier had been making frequent calls from his New York office to the new USX chairman. He'd even adopted a habit of calling a half hour before the time Corry usually departed for home, keeping the chairman on the phone for a good hour while he offered all kinds of advice about bolstering USX's stock.

On this day, Icahn was calling to tell Corry that he had located someone who would buy Marathon, right now, for $13 billion in cash. Who? asked Corry. The head of French energy giant Elf-Aquataine, answered Icahn. So Corry, not wanting to annoy his corporation's largest shareholder, placed a call to France, and to the French executive.

"I had never laid eyes on this guy," Corry later admitted. "I said, 'I understand you're willing to buy Marathon Oil for $13 billion, cash.' He starts stuttering…'Well, I know Marathon's a fine company with fine assets, but…'"

"Who told you I wanted to buy Marathon?" the Elf chief asked.

"Do you know Carl Icahn?" Corry asked in return.

The answer: "I've not met Mr. Icahn."

That was life with Carl.

Corry had inherited Icahn from Dave Roderick and felt obliged to continue the dialogue. Icahn, after all, could command a considerable number of shareholder votes, and he did have some good ideas about structuring the corporation. Sometimes, though, it seemed he delighted in jerking Corry's chain. Corry had other things to tend to. He had played an important supporting role in getting USX down to fighting weight. Now it was his job to make sure his corporation remained a contender as it entered the Nineties, its tenth decade of life.

For a corporation whose steelmaking unit was nearing its 100th birthday, USX was amazingly youthful.

It was much leaner, faster on its feet, than the giant Judge Gary had led. Its once-necessary but now-burdensome layers of bureaucracy had been stripped away. Part of this was because the company had kept tightening up the management chain. Part was because computers had sent information and decisions galloping up and down the chain at almost the speed of light.

Those ideas were galloping all over the world, too, knocking down cultural and trade barriers in their paths. The "us-and-them" attitude was evaporating. The corporation had done joint ventures in Europe in decades past, but now these deals were easier to pursue in areas where it had been unthinkable—the former Soviet Union, for example. Deals around the world made even more sense now; the economies of the different nations were getting to be a big blur.

As for the steelworkers, they were now no less a source of labor than they were a source of ideas. Some were going off to the auto plants and factories of customers, conferring with managers and with their own counterparts on the lines. They were troubleshooting, solving technical problems, giving customers advice that would let them get the most for their money in the shortest time.

This was a fresh breeze sweeping through U. S. Steel. It would play a big part in the rebound the company experienced at the end of the twentieth century. It was making things a whole lot easier for the managers in charge of USX's steel team, Chuck Corry and Tom Graham.

It would do the same for the duo that would lead the corporation's steel business into its second century. One was Thomas J. Usher, who would advance in 1990 from executive vice president for heavy products to president of U. S. Steel and, in 1995, would be elected chairman of the board and CEO of USX. The other was Paul Wilhelm, who, in 1995, would replace Usher as president of U. S. Steel.

Before that, though, we must go back to Chuck Corry. He had to take care of an important mission—solving the Icahn problem.

Corry wasn't one to let Icahn grind him down. Corry was too cool for that, too amused by the foibles of business. Years later, he would smile about some of his dealings with Icahn, gleefully relating, for example, how he had cured Icahn of his chronic, late-afternoon phone calls: "I knew Carl slept in his office, so I started calling him at six-thirty in the morning. I did that about twice, and he stopped calling me at five in the afternoon."

Corry had come to like Icahn. "We had some stress, but the guy had a sense of humor. He was easy for me to relate to."

Yet Corry saw little humor in what Icahn could have done with the corporation. Icahn had attracted a cadre of investors who had followed his example, taking a stake in USX. He said he was looking into ways to break the corporation's oil and steel businesses apart, make independent companies, the idea being that the parts would be worth more than the whole. His investors were ready to step into board positions.

But Corry and his fellow executives at USX were convinced that Icahn's main agenda was to cash out of USX after hiking its stock prices, leaving behind a limping corporation. "[Icahn] was a threat to our shareholders and employees," Corry said later. "What he did to TWA he could have done to us. And he would have loved to get his hands on our $10-billion pension fund."

In fact, a few years earlier, Icahn had agreed with Roderick that
he would back off on his takeover maneuvers. But in late 1989, as *The
Wall Street Journal* put it, Icahn shattered this "unwritten standstill
agreement." After hiking his stake in USX stock from 11.4 percent to
13.1 percent of the shares, he was back, taking another run at the
corporation. He proposed that USX's energy and steel business be
separated. And not a few retirees liked what he was selling. A proxy fight
was brewing.

Things really got interesting for Corry during the corporation's
annual meeting for 1990.

Corry had set the annual meeting for Findlay, Ohio. It seemed like
a good idea. It was Marathon's hometown. And it was off the beaten track.

"Findlay was hard to get to," Corry conceded later. "We had
2,000 retired steelworkers angry about shutdowns and cutbacks. We'd
come out of an era of concessionary contracts, and they had provoked a
lot of fire at our annual meetings. I thought, why not a nice, quiet
shareholders meeting in Findlay? We'd get low attendance. It would be
a nice first meeting for me."

Wrong. As Corry later admitted between chuckles aimed at himself:

"We got more damn people, and it was because we were in the midst of our first and only proxy fight. The national press was there. I got out of the car and the media descended on me, microphones in my face. We had to change the venue, move from the Elks hall to the high-school auditorium. We had professors from California and the University of Minnesota sounding off about proxy contests and management's responsibilities. The meeting went on for something like two hours and fifty minutes.

"It was the worst annual meeting…completely the opposite of what I had planned."

"It was completely opposite of what I had planned," said Chuck Corry regarding the first annual meeting he presided over in 1990 as USX's new chairman.

Sharing the spotlight with the new chairman was Icahn himself, who rose to encourage shareholders to vote "yes" for Proposal No. 4, his plan for spinning off USX's steel business into an independent, publicly traded steel company to be known as U. S. Steel Corporation. Referring to a fellow shareholder's comments, Icahn said he agreed that steel and oil faced "great needs" for capital. "But it intrigues me," he added, "as to why it is believed that the oil business has to supply the steel business with that capital."

Why, he asked, should USX "jeopardize the future" of its oil business, which he called a jewel, by diverting capital from oil to steel? "It's analogous to taking the smartest child you have, and saying to that child, you have to go out and farm for the rest of your life to bring in capital for the rest of the family, when, instead, perhaps that child… should go to medical school or law school."

Icahn insisted that USX's stock was undervalued, that the steel industry was on the verge of a boom.

"Our urban centers are falling apart. There will be needs for tunnels, bridges…and this demand has to be capitalized. What I believe USX should do is do this spin-off, or something like a spin-off of this nature, and then go out and find equity capital for the steel business—bring in a partner. Bring in a foreign partner."

Then a gentle threat: Five or six "key institutions" had agreed "something must be done"—even if shareholders did not buy Icahn's spin-off.

Icahn already had in his pocket the 22 or so percent of the votes required for his Marathon breakout. But Bill Lewellen, then a senior executive vice president-finance and treasurer, had been busy, too. He'd led a team that went around to major shareholders, explaining why their shares would be more valuable if steel stayed in the family. Near the end of the century, Corry recalled the results: "We identified about $110 million a year in annual savings we got from being two companies, versus one."

When the votes were counted at the meeting, Icahn had lost, but not by an overwhelming percentage. A little more than 75 million shares were cast in favor of his resolution. Almost 100 million were cast against it.

Icahn withdrew. Still, he kept his USX stock, and he kept proposing schemes to Corry. But he was getting nowhere, losing credibility as a takeover king, and hurting for cash for his next deal. He needed an escape hatch, one that would let him walk away from the company after having done something to make it stronger.

A short while later, Corry found one.

During a meeting of the corporation's policy committee, Bob Hernandez had tossed out an idea he thought might give Icahn a graceful out: spinning off an entirely new class of stock for the corporation's steel business.

Hernandez explained the concept during an interview for this book.

"General Motors had used a similar idea when it bought EDS from Ross Perot. Perot didn't want to take General Motors stock for the acquisition." How could the performance of an auto company stock reflect the real worth of its electronics business? GM's solution was to create a separate class of stock that tracked EDS' performance— GM-E stock, the E standing for electronics.

After getting the go-ahead from Corry, Hernandez worked out a variation of the GM theme for USX shareholders—one that would offer them stock for the steel business and a separate stock that would represent the corporation's energy business. But, as *Forbes* later explained, only the equity portion of the corporation's capital would be broken into the two stocks. USX would remain one corporation.

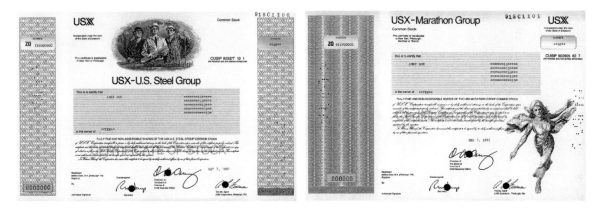

A new stock plan that appeased Carl Icahn and gave USX shareholders the best of two worlds called for the issuance of common stock in the steel business and common stock in the corporation's oil business.

The scheme would give shareholders the best of both worlds. They could receive their normal dividends for their current USX shares, plus 20 cents for each new steel share in the first year. They could invest separately in either the corporation's steel business or its energy operations. Alfred Kingsley, Icahn's partner and senior vice president, explained the deal to the press this way: "If you don't like a mix of vanilla and chocolate and you want a 20-cent dividend, then it's a good deal."

But the two-stock plan had to receive Icahn's blessing before it could be put to shareholders. So Hernandez and USX General Counsel Dominic "Don" King flew to New York to run it by Icahn.

"Don and I negotiated with Icahn," Hernandez later recalled. "We had to redo our corporate charter. And we signed a standstill agreement that would cause Icahn to go away for something like seven years if shareholders approved the new stock plan. Icahn committed to vote his shares for it. Icahn thought the plan was a good idea."

But the deal wasn't sealed yet. Leaving Icahn to think it over further, Hernandez and King returned to headquarters and waited. A while later, in January 1991, while Corry, Hernandez, King and other

USX officials and directors were in Florida for their annual executives' meeting, Icahn phoned Corry. He was ready to sign.

Corry sent Hernandez and King on the mission north. The idea was for them to shoot up to Icahn's office, get his concurrence and fly right back to Florida in time for the annual meeting of USX officials. Hernandez and King commandeered a Marathon jet and flew from sunny Florida to frozen New York wearing only informal, tropical-weight clothes. After they had convinced Icahn to sign, they headed back to the meeting, arriving just in time for the board to talk over the deal and subsequently approve it.

The deal was packaged for a shareholders' vote just in time for the 1991 annual meeting in Houston.

Before shareholders cast their ballots, Corry explained the two-stocks plan: "Stockholders will be given two separate securities with the option to retain or sell either or both.... New investors will now be able to make an investment in either energy or steel. And, while there are no guarantees, we think it will increase the aggregate value of the combined equities of the corporation. Initially, the energy share will pay $1.40 per annum in dividends, and the steel shares will pay a dollar. And that, compared with the old basis of $1.40 per annum in total dividends, will come out to be $1.60 in total for the combined dividends."

The proposal won in a landslide, with more than 96 percent of the shares voted in its favor.

It was a face-saver for Icahn. He could walk away from USX claiming he'd played a role in detaching steel from oil, giving shareholders a "pure play." A week after the shareholders' vote, he sold his USX shares, ending, as the Associated Press put it, "a long and tempestuous relationship with the steel and energy conglomerate."

Icahn was gone. USX could get on with life. And Chuck Corry could focus full attention on managing the corporation.

He saw now the value of trying to merge some of the corporate cultures of Marathon, U. S. Steel and USX. The cultures were so disparate at the time of the acquisition that they seemed to defy integration. Besides, Roderick had initially preferred to keep the cultures segregated:

Delhi Group
A unit of USX Corporation

Image counted, but numbers counted more. That fact of corporate life inspired Corry and his advisors to return to the device of spinning off separate shares of stock, *à la* the issuing of unique shares for Marathon. In fall of 1992, the corporation split off Marathon's Delhi Gas Pipeline Corporation into a separate company, the Delhi Group, with its own stock.

Delhi held natural gas reserves (273 billion cubic feet, according to the new group's first annual review, covering 1992) and operated gas pipelines and processing plants, mainly in Texas and neighboring Oklahoma. It had access to gas transmission lines, comparable to the railroad trunk lines and branches that delivered products to distributors around the country. And USX thought the gas business was about to get really good. "Changes are in the works that could bring accelerated growth for Delhi and other players in the natural gas industry," said Corry and Delhi Group President David Kihneman in a duet in the Delhi employee magazine.

These changes would include the promotion of natural gas as a leading "clean fuel," and deregulation of gas pipelines that would let Delhi add reserves, expand its pipeline network, tap into new markets, and make more money. Shareholders deserved a unique stock for this. It would make an about-to-boom USX business look even better. But the promises never came through, and, in 1997, USX sold Delhi to Koch Industries, Inc.

The corporation took TXO through much the same exercise, one intended to satisfy cynics like the disgruntled diner who almost winged Fred Leuffer with a dinner roll. Back in 1990, USX had insisted that, finally, *finally*, the natural gas business was heading for good times, and had mingled TXO with the rest of the corporation's oil and gas operations in what it called the Marathon Group. Later in the decade, TXO vanished as a stand-alone entity, its operations absorbed by Marathon.

The now-you-see-it, now-you-don't stock machinations kept USX's lawyers busy. So did a major crop of lawsuits they wrapped up during the Nineties at Corry's prodding and with his hands-on involvement.

But there was one suit Corry took directly to the public. It involved the U.S. Occupational Safety and Health Administration—OSHA— which charged his corporation with a list of safety violations at U. S. Steel's Fairless and Clairton Works, in Pennsylvania.

Labor Secretary Elizabeth Dole had announced the charges with great fanfare in November 1989. The allegations went back to June, when OSHA got a warrant for wall-to-wall safety inspections of the steel plants. While the *Philadelphia Inquirer* pointed out that injuries were not uncommon in the steel industry, it quoted Dole as calling Fairless "dilapidated," and the subject of "particularly flagrant" government findings—excessive noise, dim lighting, electrical violations, garbage-strewn floors, improper crane operation, lack of proper machinery guards, sloppy safety records.

It was quite a list, and it inspired OSHA to sock U. S. Steel with a fine of $7.3 million. It was an OSHA record.

U. S. Steel President Tom Graham thought the charges were an outrage. "Let me assure you," he wrote in a letter to employees, "our commitment to you and all the people of USS is to provide a safe and healthy workplace. We think we are doing that."

Statistics backed him up. "During the first six months of 1989," Graham wrote, "[U. S. Steel] ranked as the best among major steel producers in terms of lost workday case frequency, fatality frequency and cases involving days away from work." On November 22, U. S. Steel filed a formal notice that it was contesting the charges. Four days later, in a front page, exposé-style story, the *Philadelphia Inquirer* cataloged U. S. Steel's alleged sins. It trotted out stinging interviews with former Fairless workers and dredged up accidents that had occurred years earlier.

At this point, Corry stepped up to the plate to face Secretary Dole, whom he thought was pitching high and inside.

In a full-page ad, in the November 30 issue of the *Inquirer*, Corry blasted the paper's portrayal of U. S. Steel as indifferent to worker safety, and criticized OSHA's description of Fairless as dilapidated.

Then he sprang a surprise: "Last week, I toured the Fairless plant. My visit was unannounced and unrehearsed.... Frankly, I was

USX Corporation
600 Grant Street
Pittsburgh, PA 15219-4776
412 433 1101

Charles A. Corry
Chairman, Board of Directors
& Chief Executive Officer

This letter from USX CEO Charles Corry was reproduced as a full-page ad in the Philadelphia Inquirer *in response to the paper's cartoon portrayal of U. S. Steel as indifferent to steelworkers' safety.*

November 30, 1989

An Open Letter To The Readers Of The Philadelphia Inquirer:

A prompt response is in order to all readers of the Philadelphia Inquirer concerning the front page story in last Sunday's edition discussing health and safety conditions at the USX Fairless Works in Bucks County. The story described Fairless Works as "dilapidated" and the company as indifferent to worker safety. I take exception to these conclusions.

There is no consideration more important than the health and safety of our employees. We take very seriously our commitment to provide a safe and healthy work place. We are doing just that at Fairless Works. The plant compares favorably with other such facilities in the steel industry in terms of safety and health. The plant management is committed to implementation of an effective, ongoing safety program.

Last week, I toured the Fairless plant. My visit to the plant was unannounced and unrehearsed. My intention was to view things as they are on a daily basis. Frankly, I was encouraged with what I saw—even more so with what I heard from the workers I met. Without exception, they assured me that they regard Fairless as safe and healthy.

While at Fairless, I reviewed their 1989 safety record to determine whether there were any lost time accidents that could be related to the alleged violations cited by OSHA. There were no such accidents during 1989.

An intensive evaluation of the recent OSHA citations is underway at Fairless Works. During my tour, I observed maintenance and repair work in progress to correct several of the alleged deficiencies cited by OSHA. A substantial majority of the alleged violations already has been corrected.

Our evaluation of the citations is continuing. As it progresses, we will be guided by our own record in safety and our determination to meet our obligations to our employees and their families. "Safety First" is a slogan originated by our company long before OSHA was founded. But it is more than a slogan. It is a philosophy of doing what is right in the workplace. We remain committed to that philosophy.

C. A. Corry

encouraged with what I saw—even more so when I heard from various workers I met. Without exception, they assured me that they regard Fairless as safe and healthy."

Corry also revealed in the ad that he had observed maintenance and repairs in progress "to correct several…deficiencies." He reviewed the mill's safety records to check OSHA's charge of lost-time accidents during that year. His findings: "There were no such accidents during 1989." He revealed that several OSHA citations covered sections of the works that had been closed for years, and a frivolous charge which was almost laughable: a missing screw in a two-screw light-switch plate.

After some tough deliberations, U. S. Steel and OSHA negotiated a settlement. OSHA withdrew a number of its citations and agreed to cut the company's $7-million fine in half. Corry had made his stand. And he didn't want to be dragged through further lengthy and costly litigation. So the company paid the $3.5 million.

Other events of the Nineties were a lot more upbeat.

The decade opened with the appointment of Thomas J. Usher as president of the steel division and a member of USX's corporate committee. The following year, 1991, he was elected president of the U. S. Steel Group and to the board of directors. For the next few years, he was to oversee major modernization projects at Gary Works and the Mon Valley's Edgar Thomson plant.

But Usher was on the fast track: In 1994, he was elected president and chief operating officer of USX Corporation.

That same year, a lot of people were pleasantly surprised—especially the steelworkers—when the USX board added a director familiar with the views of labor. He was Ray Marshall, who had been secretary of labor under President Jimmy Carter and now was a professor of economics at the University of Texas at Austin.

Ray Marshall, former secretary of labor under President Jimmy Carter, brought labor's views to the table with his election to USX's board of directors in 1994.

Electing a director who would bring labor's views to the table had always been taboo. But this was the post-'86 contract era. The wall between the corporation and union was shrinking, becoming easier to reach across. In fact, it was United Steelworkers President Lynn Williams who had recommended Marshall to Corry. It was time, Williams thought. The auto industry had put union representatives on its boards.

Corry was a bit skeptical about the idea. It was a tricky balancing act. "I pointed out to Mr. Williams that this was a conflict of interest." Why? Because it would be difficult for a director with ties to the union to view himself or herself as a representative of the constituency the board represented.

Corry also spoke with Marshall. "I gave him the same talk [about] the importance of not seeing himself as just a representative of the steel union, but seeing himself as one of a group of directors who represented all the shareholders. He had to embrace the concept, or I would object to his being nominated."

Obviously, Marshall took the message to heart. He served with distinction on the board until his retirement in August of 2000.

"Ray Marshall worked out splendidly," concluded Corry.

For the record, the corporation's board welcomed its first woman director when Dr. Jeanette G. Brown was picked in 1993. Her election ended a campaign to get women on U. S. Steel's board launched decades earlier by Wilma Soss, well-known shareholder-activist.

This map showed the location of the 54 minimills within the United States in the late 1980s. A rarity two decades earlier, the minimills had since become a potent factor in the production and marketing of steel.

Also cheering to the company was an impressive round of improvements at U. S. Steel plants.

One fact of life in steel was this: You could never stop upgrading and modernizing. A mill was always a work in progress. As the Roderick years dissolved into the Corry era, U. S. Steel was still fighting to improve its machinery, and therefore its productivity and costs.

One motivation here was the minimills. Some of them weren't so "mini" anymore. A better way of identifying the species was "electric-arc furnace users," because all they used were electric furnaces. They melted a lot of scrap steel in them. Whatever you called them, these producers now accounted for more than 20 percent of domestic steel shipments. "The minimill," *U S Steel News* acknowledged, "has penetrated some product areas so effectively that those markets have been all but abandoned by U. S. Steel and other large integrated steel producers."

The foreign producers were still a threat, of course. Dumping had turned into an eternal curse. Still, U. S. Steel and other majors were in much better fighting shape than before. As David Roderick claimed in an August 12, 1987, *Investor's Daily* piece, "There's no question, with the productivity improvements of the past four years, that [the American integrated mills] clearly are the low-cost producers. We haven't been able to say that for 30 years."

USX's steel operations were on the upswing. "The company's [U. S. Steel] unit has bounced back far more quickly than most observers expected," *Investor's Daily* told its readers. "Starting from the ground floor when the steelworker strike ended February 1, [U. S. Steel] already is operating at 78 percent of its raw steel production capability.... By June 30 it had regained a 13.5 percent market share, which compares with a pre-strike share of about 17 percent."

What's more, the publication added, U. S. Steel had required only 3.8 man-hours for each ton of steel shipped during the second quarter of 1987. Five years earlier, the average had been more than 10 man-hours.

Speaking to an audience of more than 400, Vice President Dan Quayle led dedication ceremonies for the Fairfield Works' continuous slab caster by congratulating USS for the $200-million investment in the caster and hot strip mill modernization. At left is Tom Usher, then USS executive vice president— heavy products, who hosted the ceremonies; at right is Steve Bennett, Fairfield Works general manage at the time.

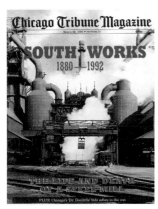

South Works closed up shop after 112 years of existence.

But the company could never be satisfied. Competitors were investing in their works, too. Enough was never enough, and the corporation kept pouring money into its steel unit.

This was good news for the company's employees and neighbors. The memories of the shuttered mills (South Works, in Chicago, with U. S. Steel since the first day of the company's existence, would close in 1992) and the malaise in the industry had stirred up talk in the steel towns that the corporation was bailing out of the steel business. It was an option Corry and his team were forced to consider. What major steelmaker wasn't? But who would buy the cavernous mills and massive machines of a "mature" industry? The more-promising option for USX was to keep investing in what it did best.

The whispers of further company shutdowns faded when, in 1988, U. S. Steel launched a $550-million capital spending program.

Some of that money covered final work on a new, super-efficient slabcaster at the Fairfield Works. The machine boosted the company's caster capacity by 1.5 million tons and made Fairfield a new-age, all-caster plant. When the work was finished, the plant threw a party to dedicate its new caster and its newly modernized hot strip mill. Guest of honor Dan Quayle, Vice President of the United States, addressed the crowd, predicting good times ahead for steel.

After a five-month rebuilding program, Gary Works' No. 13 blast furnace was "blown in" with an upgraded casting capacity of 8,000 tons of hot metal per day.

Some years later came the startup of a $250-million continuous caster at Mon Valley's Edgar Thomson plant. When it became operational in 1992, it produced glowing, 8-inch-thick slabs on two parallel lines, a design that allowed it to run efficiently at a range of production rates. Better yet, it made USS an all-caster steel producer, highly efficient and fit for the future.

The party continued.

Fairfield Works added a $50-million hot-dip galvanizing line that produced light-gauge, galvanized sheet steel mainly for the skin of metal buildings. Mon Valley's Irvin plant cranked up a series of towering, pressure-cooker-like units—annealing furnaces. Their magic ingredient was hydrogen, which slashed from five days to two the time it took to treat rolls of steel so they were softer, more crinkle- and crease-resistant for the auto plants.

This new, single-stack annealing furnace at Mon Valley Works was one of several major projects that resulted from the corporation's $550-million capital spending program, which got under way in 1988.

In fall 1996, Edgar Thomson's workers turned on a $36-million degasser—a monstrous assembly of vessels that gave molten metal a shot of oxygen, scrubbing out almost all the residual carbon and producing steel that was strong yet especially workable in the equipment that formed auto bodies.

Gary Works got a share of the renewal money. Back in 1991, the works had finished a modernization that slashed cooling time for steel from the hot strip mill from 20 hours to two. Gary's No. 4 blast furnace was upgraded to accommodate fluxed pellets, a newer feed prepared by U. S. Steel's Minntac mining operations in Minnesota. Gary's largest blast furnace, No. 13, was rebuilt. Its tinning mill was reworked to make better tin-coated steel—the kind used for food cans—faster. The company invested $40 million to modernize Gary's 160-inch plate mill, and installed a $240-million continuous slab caster, making Gary an all-caster plant.

Gary was unlike the other U. S. Steel plants. As we've seen, U. S. Steel, under the direction of its first chairman, Judge Elbert H. Gary, had built, along with the mill, a town for the steelworkers. It built the city hall, churches, playgrounds and houses. Judge Gary took the town under his wing, channeling corporate money to the school and hospital, and into the town's power and water plants. The corporate kitty covered police and fire protection, road repair and other items, on and on.

It was a wonderful policy for the town, but it became unrealistic. Gary, Indiana, was a dependent of U. S. Steel, so it *became* dependent on U. S. Steel. Papa Steel would provide. That was the mindset. But Gary was a business, even though the local tax policy suggested the local government seemed to think of it as a charity.

In 1999, the taxes levied against Gary Works exceeded $100 million, earning the works the distinction of being the most heavily taxed manufacturing facility in the country. Had the Gary plant been taxed at the same rate as nearby Bethlehem Steel and National Steel in Porter County, the tax liability would have been reduced to $19.5 million.

Paul J. Wilhelm had suceeded Usher as president of the U. S. Steel Group in 1994. He knew the company could not live with such disparities. He told the Gary town fathers so. As the *Indianapolis Star* quoted him, he "would make no investments at Gary or hire any new employees until the tax burden was lessened."

Wilhelm summed up the message for the author: "We intend to continue to rebuild the plant's infrastructure, and keep up with maintenance. But to build new facilities with the tax base we have is impossible. We spent something like $600 million over the last five or six years in facilities that, by rights, should have been located in Gary, and were not. The reason was the tax situation. It's cheaper for us to produce [basic steel] in Gary, ship it to our PRO-TEC plant in Ohio for coating and to Chicago for further processing than it is to deal with the tax base in Gary."

Late in 2000, this tax problem had yet to be resolved. Meanwhile, officials from U. S. Steel and the City of Gary were working to solve it.

USS tin plate held its own against stiff competition from other packaging materials.

Like the corporation's steel operations, research in the Nineties had been downsized. A research group of about 150 scientists and technicians at the Monroeville center was no longer doing pure research. Now they were working on sure things, doing research aimed at making today's steels even better. Customers wanted steels that were even more resistant to weather or road salt. They wanted steels that were lighter and more economical, but stronger, always stronger. They wanted sheets of low-carbon steel that could be easily pressed into curves and angles without a wrinkle or rip. All the time. They were never satisfied. And U. S. Steel's research people couldn't be, either.

One of the ways to make better steel was to improve the equipment that made it. Consider the ironmaking blast furnace. It is lined with refractories, ceramic bricks that are temperamental. When refractories fail before they are due to be replaced, production schedules are wrecked and money is wasted. Lining life has never been predictable. The researchers, however, developed an early-warning system—an array of electrical probes mounted inside the furnace. The probes measured temperatures and temperature changes so precisely that operators could use them to target lining failures. The technique held the promise of lengthening lining life. That could translate into lower operating costs—quality steel for less money.

The researchers also developed a new procedure for introducing iron pellets into furnaces in a manner that distributed them more evenly, promoting more uniform heat.

The research teammates delivered. They reduced the costs of producing tinplate — for cans and other containers — without compromising quality. They designed even better protective coatings for steel. They were satiating Detroit's appetite for ever-more-versatile auto steels.

As USX Chairman Tom Usher said during a 1999 speech: "Eighty percent of the automotive steels in use today were not available five years ago."

He'd likely be able to say the same thing five years down the road.

"Research has a way of raising our sights," a research technician had said. "We don't want merely to be part of a peer group. We want to be first."

"Can do" was back.

THREE-CARD CORRY

Charles A. "Chuck" Corry liked to tell amusing stories, even about himself. Like the one about the young U. S. Steel management trainee (Corry) and the lake freighter captain.

It went like this: Chuck Corry was on his first job with U. S. Steel, as a trainee on American Steel & Wire's tax staff in Cleveland. He didn't know there was another Charles "Corry" working in the same building, Admiral Charles R. Khoury, president of the Pittsburgh Steamship Division. During his third day on the job, trainee Corry got a frantic phone call from a freighter captain: "Sir. I'm up at the Soo locks and I have to offload. My ship needs repairs. Could I extend my schedule a day, maybe a day and a half?"

As Corry picked up the story: "My mind is racing. What kind of tax problem is involved in an iron ore carrier? There's got to be a tax problem somewhere. So I

say that it 'sounds like a good idea to me.'" And as the captain prepared for this "authorized" delay, Charles Corry returned to his tax work, impressed with the "sir," and that his department commanded respect even in matters so far afield.

Eighteen jobs later, Corry was chief executive officer of USX Corporation, a blend of the energy culture of Marathon Oil and the steel culture of U. S. Steel. He was infinitely wiser, but still, candid and accessible. He liked to pop in on staff members, unannounced, to chat about what they were doing. It was un-USX-like, but it was the right touch. USX was entering a less regimented era. Managers no longer sent orders raining down on employees. Now, employees worked together, and with customers, creating decisions in situ. They solved problems and helped shape strategies. Meanwhile, managers up the chain concentrated on policy, got together resources the troops needed, and cheered them on. Corry was good at that.

Corry was a different kind of chairman, soft-spoken, unassuming. While other executives strode to and fro, the press noted, Corry ambled. His human touch was just as powerful. Maybe more.

He was a product of Ohio. As a boy in Cincinnati, he studied piano. At the University of Cincinnati, he played varsity tennis and majored in zoology and geology before earning a degree in political science. He returned to the university to study law. In 1959, after a two-year time-out to serve with the Air Force in Europe, he graduated with a law degree and honors. Then it was on to U. S. Steel's American Steel & Wire in Cleveland, followed by tax and finance jobs in Pittsburgh and New York, and posts at Homestead Works, American Bridge and as the corporation's assistant comptroller.

Upper management's confidence in Corry's range became obvious when he was advanced to vice president of Corporate Planning. In that job, he kept a scrapbook of potential acquisitions. Its contents ranged from the obvious to the unexpected: business magazines had it that the corporation maintained a file on cereal-maker Kellogg. Tony the Tiger on the U. S. Steel team? Corry wouldn't have thought it made that always-sought-after "good fit," but the concept probably tickled him.

One of the companies Corry filed away was a nice little oil concern called Marathon. When Mobil Oil launched a hostile takeover of the smaller competitor from Ohio, Corry shared his Marathon file with Dave Roderick. Marathon looked good, he told Roderick. Wouldn't it rather be part of U. S. Steel Corporation? Roderick is said to have pondered a moment before pronouncing: "Go forth, my son, and acquire." Corry chased down the deal that would make his company three-fourths energy—and keep it afloat.

Corry was tenacious. He waltzed takeover artist Carl Icahn around and around until Icahn—freed by Corry's plan to break apart Marathon and U. S. Steel stock—could break off and find a new partner. When the Occupational Safety and Health Administration charged U. S. Steel with a shocking list of safety and health sins, Corry smelled politics. Instead of issuing protestations and denials from atop the corporate headquarters, he showed up at the plant, unannounced, and inspected it himself—the better to refute the overwrought accusations.

Corry the lawyer saw his chairman's role as that of a risk manager.

"We had this huge risk in the early Eighties," he told the author. "We were almost consumed by costs and liabilities."

At the top of the stack were legacy costs—"costs of all the shutdowns, the situation of having 20,000 people working in steel and 95,000 on the pension roll. The 20,000 had to support the pensions and medical benefits for the other 95,000 [pensioners], and for their spouses, as well. This was a big tiger you had by the tail. I saw it more as a matter of managing risk than of running a business."

*But risks were everywhere, raising
such questions as: What's our exposure?
How can we shrink this exposure?
By selling a business? Through a
joint venture?*

*Nowhere had risk management
been more apparent on Corry's watch
than when USX stepped in to cut its losses
from dragged-out lawsuits. Corry called
them "megabucks" suits.*

*One involved a dispute over how
much the corporation owed a natural
gas supplier. Another, how much
the corporation owed employees at the
closed-down Geneva (Utah) Works.*

*An antitrust case between the
corporation and some Great Lakes
shippers seemed to be immortal. When
USX lost an appeal in Federal District
Court, the case rose to the Supreme Court
for consideration. But the Supreme Court
rarely hears appealed cases, Corry knew.
That fact gave him a good reason to
propose to LTV Corporation, the major
opposing litigant, that the case be settled.*

*"Think of this as a three-card poker
game," Corry told LTV's lawyers. "We've
both been dealt two cards, and you're
ahead. With the next card, you could take
everything. But you might lose everything."*

*Chuck Corry blended a steel culture with an
energy culture. He was also a risk manager.*

*LTV settled for less than 70 percent
of what it had won to that point.*

*For Corry, it was a small victory
grabbed from the jaws of a big defeat.
His instincts had been on target; the
Supreme Court refused to consider the
case, and, if Corry hadn't settled, his
corporation would have paid vastly more.*

*It was a small trophy, a reason for
a lawyer to smile.*

*"I got into that case," Corry said,
"because the lawyers had assured me for
years that we were going to win, and I
wasn't going to wait for another loss."*

Chapter 19

'The right people
at the right time'

Tom Usher felt especially good about the new energy in U. S. Steel, and about the employees' new devotion to being the best. He called it the "New Steel." And he got an opportunity to brag a little about the new steel and the new corporation at USX's 1996 annual meeting.

The meeting was his first as chairman and CEO. Chuck Corry had passed the torch to him the previous year. Now Usher was a step above the activities in his steel division. He would come to regret the distance, to miss the direct interactions with the people from the mills. But his enthusiasm for the steel side of the business was as evident as ever as he filled shareholders in on what was happening there.

In 1996, the annual meeting was in Cincinnati, in the Netherlands Plaza Hotel. Some 4,400 shareholders lived in the area. After saluting Ohio, the employees at the USS/KOBE plant in Lorain and the more than 4,000 Ohio employees of Marathon and its marketing division, Usher turned to the job USX employees around the map had done during 1995.

The U. S. Steel Group had increased sales to almost $6.5 billion in 1995, its best year since the group was established, he proudly reported. The Delhi Group had expanded its gas reserves. Marathon had raised crude oil production in Texas, the Gulf of Mexico and the United Kingdom.

Then Usher, in his first remarks to shareholders, delivered some facts that said even more: "The quality of our products was affirmed in 1995 as all of our steel producing and finishing operations were certified as meeting the stringent ISO 9000 standards." ISO 9000 was an international standard of quality, and much hungered for among corporations.

There was more good news: "U. S. Steel is the number-one supplier of steel to three major U.S. automakers, the nation's appliance manufacturers and other makers of value-added steel products."

There was more yet: "In 1995, U. S. Steel compiled the best safety record among the eight major steel producers…. Environmentally, we are gratified that our efforts were recognized in 1995 by numerous awards from federal, state and local environmental agencies."

Usher being Usher, the "we" he talked about included the employees that hit the targets and captured the trophies.

By 2000, Usher and Wilhelm could be satisfied that they had done their environmental homework very well, indeed. Most of the problems had been solved, and U. S. Steel plants around the country were largely in compliance with EPA, state and local environmental laws. The pesky, final few percentage points of emissions or effluents, however, still eluded the best science and most advanced controls.

On this point, even the United States Supreme Court decided in 2000 to consider the question as it related to air quality. Given the

A strong emphasis on safety in the workplace earned many U. S. Steel plants a variety of safety awards during the 1990s. In this group photo, state representatives presented Clairton Works with the distinguished Pennsylvania Governor's Award for Safety Excellence. On hand to accept the award were headquarters personnel, plant officials, employees and union members.

extraordinary costs to industry and the possible loss of jobs, was the mandate to banish every last trace of pollution constitutional? Should the Clean Air Act, revised in 1990, take into consideration not just the health effects, but the costs of compliance as well?

However the issue might be settled, Usher and Wilhelm were focused on another environmental conundrum—something called the Kyoto Global Climate Change Agreement.

Known in shorthand as the "Kyoto Protocol," the agreement had been adopted in 1997 by a number of United Nations countries to promote a worldwide understanding by 2007 of how to deal with global pollution. If approved, the agreement would require all industrialized nations to reduce their emissions of greenhouse gases—such as carbon dioxide, or CO_2, created when oil, coal and natural gas were burned.

The most likely method for reducing CO_2 emissions would be through a tax. Such a carbon tax, according to an estimate in the January 2000 issue of *U S Steel News*, would raise the cost of fuel and energy—electricity by 33 percent, coal by 275 percent and natural gas by 60 percent.

In the summer of 1997, Usher explained to the readers of *U S Steel News* just how the protocol would impact American industries: "It's not hard to see the outcome of such an agreement. U.S. industrial facilities that burn fossil fuels—85 percent of the energy used in the United States—will be at a serious disadvantage. Companies will be forced to shift many of their operations to exempted developing nations such as Brazil, China, India, Mexico and South Korea," he noted. "Petroleum refining and steel [manufacturing], along with aluminum, cement, chemicals and paper and pulp, would be the six hardest-hit U.S. industries," he added, citing a study by Argonne National Laboratories for the Department of Energy.

Wilhelm felt just as strongly when, in mid-2000, he observed for the author: "I think there's a willingness of [our government] to move basic manufacturing out of this country."

The Threat of Kyoto

Implementation of the Kyoto Protoc~' or Kyoto Global
Climate Change Agreement, would ~~~~~~ ~ ~~~~~ ~ industrial
sector of the United States. Steelma
the hardest hit. That's not an alarm
And, unfortunately, it's a very real
worse yet, the U. S. Steel Group b

The Kyoto Protocol stems from a seemingly well-intentioned effort to protect our
planet by limiting the emission of "greenhouse gases," which some scientists
believe are causing the earth's temperature to rise (*see Global Warming: Fact or
Fiction?*). The 1997 agreement, produced by the United Nations Framework
Convention on Climate Change, requires
developed countries to restrict greenhouse gas emissions, but exempts
developing countries from setting any
limits.

Since greenhouse gases - particularly
carbon dioxide - are emitted largely from
the burning of fossil fuels
such as coal, oil and natural
gas, it would be necessary
to ration or tax the use of
energy to force the reductions necessary to meet
Kyoto-mandated limits in the
United States. If the Administration opts to levy a
"carbon tax," by 2010 the
cost of electricity would
likely escalate by 33 percent, coal by 275 percent
and natural gas by 60
percent. Such increases

**Global Warming:
Fact or Fiction?**

As the world rushes to stop global warming,
respected scientists wage a heated debate
about the degree to which human actions
contribute to climate change. The U. S. Steel
Group believes there are simply not enough
facts to say for sure. As a company, we're
calling for more research. Before corrective
actions as drastic as those called for in the
Kyoto Protocol are implemented, we want to
be certain there is a problem. Is the earth's
temperature really rising, and if it is, does
that present a problem to the earth's inhabit-
ants? Some say the benefits of a warmer
climate would more than offset any down-
sides, which are not likely to be at all catastrophic.

Following are some interesting facts that
have not been widely publicized. They are
included to help put the more frequently
publicized claims about the "reality" of
global warming in perspective. If you would
like to study the issue in more detail, there is
a wealth of information available on the
Internet. The Global Climate Coalition, called

The
Pro
rec
de
*countries to
restrict
greenhouse*

lack the co~~
environmental contro~.
have in the United States,
worldwide emission levels
from steelmaking would not

The Kyoto Protocol wouldn't be resolved until after the corporation's 100th anniversary. But Usher and Wilhelm and their colleagues would continue to monitor what they considered to be politically inspired and off-base formulas for curbing global warming.

Meanwhile, they would also combat another phenomenon undermining the steel industry.

Below-cost, market-saturating waves of cheap, dumped steel from abroad had been a curse for the American steel industry for more than three decades. Now, as the twenty-first century neared, America's economy was hit by a tidal wave of the stuff.

"The American steel industry is under attack," Paul Wilhelm declared in the fall 1998 *U S Steel News*. "Foreign countries with collapsing economies are illegally dumping millions of tons of steel on American soil and selling them at cutthroat prices. Unable to find markets in their own countries, Russia, Japan, Brazil and other steel-producing nations are trying to export their way out of economic crises at our expense." It was a call to action in an across-the-steel-industry campaign called "Stand Up for Steel."

From Labor Day to Election Day, in 26 cities across the country, tens of thousands of Americans rallied in support of the U.S. steel industry, its workers and their communities. "Speaking with one voice," as the *News* put it, "members of the United Steelworkers of America, executives of leading American steel companies and local politicians implored our federal government to stop the unfair—and illegal—dumping of foreign steel on American soil."

Wilhelm spoke at several rallies, calling the imports crisis "a dagger aimed at the backs of [our] people." He admitted that some people thought that, because it made for cheaper products, dumped steel was good for consumers.

His reply: "So is smuggling!"

U. S. Steel President Paul Wilhelm (above) drives home a point at a "Stand Up for Steel" rally at a USX plant site. Steelworkers (left) join the industry-wide campaign, a call to action to alert all Americans of the economic dangers posed by the flood of unfairly traded steel imports.

Usher also weighed in on the steel import issue. In September of 1999, he wrote a Labor Day op-ed piece for the *Pittsburgh Post-Gazette*: "The U.S. steel industry is not opposed to importing fairly traded steel. But we all should be outraged when American steelworkers—the best-trained and most-productive in the world—are forced out of their jobs so that foreign workers in less efficient steel mills can keep their jobs."

He reinforced this view in a 1999 talk at Pittsburgh's Duquesne Club. "We are not against other countries exporting steel. We are against them exporting steel that is unfairly priced, and we are against other countries exporting their unemployment to us.

"They should not be permitted to repair their economies at the expense of ours. Russia, for example, has been the largest exporter of flat-rolled steel to the U.S. market despite inferior technology, productivity and environmental standards."

Meanwhile, steelmakers had filed more than 40 dumping complaints against their overseas rivals in Japan, the United Kingdom, Indonesia, Turkey and other countries, and had won most of the cases. The victories heartened American steel: "We will turn up the political heat," promised USW's chief lobbyist, William Klinefelter. "We're talking about people's livelihoods."

In July 2000, the U.S. Commerce Department released a 240-page report that dissected the 1998 import crisis and that, as the *Pittsburgh Post-Gazette* put it, "backs up many of the contentions of U.S. steelmakers" that foreign nations had been subsidizing their steel companies' production, and that those producers had been dumping under-priced steel in the States.

"In the report," noted the *Post-Gazette*, "the Clinton administration…promised to establish an 'early warning system' for U.S. steelmakers that involves closely monitoring imports, to provide faster relief to affected communities and workers, and to establish an interagency response team to coordinate the response."

Paul Wilhelm had some trouble, however, with the Commerce Department report, and he made them clear during his interview for this book.

"They talk in that report about all the things that are wrong, but they never say, 'Well, here's what we're going to do about it.' So it's up to us to do something about it. It's up to us to field the trade suits. And trade suits are extremely expensive, and it takes a year and a half or two years to get action. In that time, so much damage has been done that companies go out of business."

As the interview unrolled, it became clear that Wilhelm firmly believed the U.S. government and foreign producers had American steel producers in a trap.

To start with, as Wilhelm explained, at the end of the twentieth century, the market for steel in the United States was about 125 million tons annually. "American producers have only enough capacity to supply 100 million tons of steel annually. That means 25 million tons have to come from somewhere to fill the gap. In a fair market, that 25 million tons would be imported. But, in fact, imports into the United States total about 40 million tons of steel a year."

What happened to the difference, the remaining 15 million tons of imported steel?

"It eats into the American producers' share of the market. Which would be fine, if the game was being played with a straight deck. But the game is rigged. Foreign governments, many of whom own their steel companies, use their tax systems to subsidize those steel producers. Or the steel producers take the tail end of their steel production—the cheap-to-produce stream of steel—and dump it in the USA at [ridiculously] low prices—prices American producers couldn't touch."

Wilhelm pointed out that "[t]here is…too much excess capacity around the world. There is something like 850 million tons of capacity and somewhere between 650 million to 700 million tons of consumption. And a lot of this capacity is either extremely inefficient, environmentally unsound, low in quality, or just subsidized like crazy, so that, if you're a foreign producer, you can produce this stuff and ship it anywhere.

"[As a foreign producer], you're not interested in running a profit center. You're interested in running an employment center.

"The United States is the only open market in the world," continued Wilhelm. "So much so that other countries take advantage of us. We're the best steel market in terms of volume and price. So there is a natural attraction to come here."

Topping everything off is the U.S. government's reluctance to intervene—to stand up for steel. This would be inconvenient politics. "There's this belief," noted Wilhelm, "that, 'Well, China's going to open its market to the people here who sell computers, and you guys are a small part of the economy. You're small potatoes.'

"My answer to that is we have to have rules-based trade. It has to be the same for everybody. It has to go in both directions. If that happens, it'll be true competition. Only the strong will survive."

Given environmental uncertainties and steel dumping—what kind of U. S. Steel would emerge in the 2000s? A reflective Tom Usher could only tell the author that the company would be "different." "I think," he said, "that in both our businesses [steel and energy], there will be significant changes over the next four years." Different *how* he would intimate in late 2000 when he talked before a meeting of Wall Street analysts. "Although I believe that our present [corporate] structure has served us well," he told them, "I also believe that it is appropriate at this time to review thoroughly our [steel and energy] stock structure to determine if it continues to be the best structure for optimizing shareholder value.

"Accordingly, at my recommendation, our board of directors… authorized management to retain financial, tax and legal advisors to perform a comprehensive study of our target stock structures and of alternative structures which may be in the best interest of all USX shareholders," Usher said. The panel's study, he added, would take "several months to complete."

Earlier in 2000, U. S. Steel had taken an adventurous step to enhance its position as the country's largest steel producer and the value of its stock. In this world of skewed competition and home-government indifference, it made every sense for a steel producer to go out into the world, find good steelmakers to partner with, to spread their risks by going global.

U. S. Steel had been in partnerships in other countries during the Sixties and Seventies. It had been an interesting experiment, but it hadn't counted for much. Now, as U. S. Steel was looking at its second century, things were different. Now, establishing partnerships "over there" was good insurance. It was the only way to grow.

U. S. Steel took the plunge. In October 2000, it purchased the Slovak steel company Vychodoslovenske zelziarne a.s. (eastern Slovakian ironworks)—or VSZ, headquartered in Kosice. "If nothing else," Usher observed, "the purchase proved how much the world had changed in a decade." Imagine it. VSZ shareholders letting Americans buy their company. In a country that had been an ally of the Soviet Union.

"We decided that we really wanted to do something about growing this company," Wilhelm said in his interview. "We went through the Eighties downsizing from necessity. It was time to grow the business or go out of business. Going out of business wasn't in my vocabulary, so we started looking around to see how to make this company grow."

VSZ was well-known to Wilhelm. He and John Goodish, president of USX Engineers and Consultants, Inc., had checked out the steelmaker in the mid-Nineties. Then they tested the waters in Europe by establishing a small tinning joint venture with VSZ. It succeeded.

VSZ was central Europe's largest flat-rolled steel producer, making just under four million tons of raw steel a year, all continuously cast. One of its main products was tin-mill steel for food packaging—a rich market in eastern Europe.

The new U. S. Steel subsidiary had been named U. S. Steel Kosice, s.r.o., and would represent about 25 percent of U. S. Steel's expanded steel manufacturing capacity. John Goodish was named president.

At a news briefing which followed signing ceremonies in Kosice, Wilhelm noted that U. S. Steel was committed to a 10-year capital improvement plan for the new subsidiary, subject to then-current business conditions and available cash flow of more than $700 million, mainly "to broaden the company's value-added product line."

"This," Wilhelm said, "will enable U. S. Steel Kosice to advance to the front ranks among European steel producers and become the competitive leader in the central European steel market," Wilhelm said.

In recent years, Wilhelm observed, U. S. Steel had been urged by a growing number of its American customers to make such a global move into Europe, where those customer companies had been establishing operations to capitalize on a dramatically increasing demand for consumer goods. Now, it was being done.

Almost simultaneous with the VSZ acquisition, U. S. Steel rounded out its tin operations by buying LTV Corporation's tin-mill products business. Included in the deal were LTV's tin-processing facilities at Indiana Harbor, Indiana, not far from Gary Works.

Commenting on the new venture, Usher spoke of the synergies between Gary Works and the newly acquired tin operations close by. "The possibilities are exciting," he said, "and will benefit both our customers and stockholders."

The blast furnaces and water treatment facility (left) and the cold roll strip mill (right) at U. S. Steel Kosice, s.r.o., located in Kosice, Slovakia. Acquired in late 2000, the new subsidiary will expand U. S. Steel Group's steel manufacturing capacity by about 25 percent.

Over there. As U. S. Steel's Slovakia partnership demonstrated, it was where many of the opportunities were. But there was one thing the corporation could still depend on "over here" in the States. Sharp people. Companies depended more than ever on their people, on their talents, commitment and willingness to work in teams. Quality, performance, partnership—these things had begun to sound like clichés—but, as sharp employees knew, they were absolutely necessary in the new economy. This was what Usher and Wilhelm insisted upon. And you could tell they meant it from the way their eyes brightened when they touched on the subject.

Yet Tom Usher could have turned into a technocrat. He'd been educated as an industrial engineer and held a Ph.D. in systems engineering from the University of Pittsburgh. He'd come up through the corporation's industrial engineering department, then jumped over to South Works to start a climb through administrative jobs. He was elected president of U. S. Steel and to the USX board of directors in 1991. Four years later, he was elected USX chairman and chief executive officer.

Tom Usher, USX chairman and CEO, and Paul Wilhelm, USS president and vice chairman of USX, are leading the way into the new millennium.

In his 1999 Duquesne Club speech, Usher confided that during his first few years as CEO, "We made a lot of bold, innovative moves, our revenues increased some 10 percent, [our] debt was reduced by a half billion dollars, market value increased some 50 percent and net income went up fourfold...and we cleared our financial decks by settling about $700 million worth of litigation against us."

Usher was an up-through-the-ranks guy. His way of operating was to point the way to employees, then get out of their way so they could deliver.

"I like to get good people," he admitted. "I like to give them a chance to get satisfaction out of their job by making an input. I like to make sure we're thinking on the same page as to where we want to go. I think one of the best contributions I've made so far is to get everyone pulling in the same direction, to provide a vision of what is going on and what our objectives are."

For all his affinity with the people from the shop floor, for all his thinking about the future, Usher took care to look back, as well, to principles that formed his corporation. He was a student of history, the history of steel. He wove history's lessons into his perspective on today and tomorrow. And the lessons weren't all about management techniques or the technology of steel. They were human. They touched on the spirit of the company.

"A lot of the company's character was established right at the beginning," he said, "certainly, the air of dominance and strength and power that it had. And a sense of what's right. Judge Gary was a guy who instilled a lot of good principles. Certainly a respect for safety, and integrity and ethics, that I think has carried on to this day."

Usher was a student, as well, of folly.

"One of the worst things that happened to this company was the late '73 to '74 boom. It was a time during which people should have seen what was coming in terms of foreign competition and the need to be world-class in productivity and quality. Nineteen seventy-four was a great year. Things were just booming here, and it created a mindset that this was the norm, that the good times were normal, when, in fact, they were an aberration. When things started to go downhill in '75 and '76, they said, well, *that* was just an aberration.

"They had it 180 degrees wrong. And that mindset precipitated a lot of the conflicts of the Eighties. We weren't ready for reality. Otherwise, we would have downsized in a more orderly way, as opposed to the machete-type approach we had to take in the Eighties, by necessity."

The Nineties, on the other hand, were just the reverse of the Seventies. The last decade of the century would begin with wrenching losses, but end with spectacular gains.

In the first three years—1991-1993—USX hit a rough patch. It gulped down more than $2.6 billion in losses in its energy and steel segments. The hardest to swallow was steel's losses—$2.3 billion, attributed in part to dumped steel imports that washed over the domestic market like a biblical flood. Energy markets were also in a slump, further driving down tubular prices and shipments.

But in 1994, the turnabout began, and from then through the end of 1999, energy and steel performed like a Broadway hit. During that period, the steel segment racked up more than $1.6 billion in net income, and the energy unit raked in more than $2.4 billion in net income. Not a bad way to end the twentieth century.

Wilhelm came from the same mold as Usher.

Another one of U. S. Steel's native Pittsburghers, he too was an engineer—with a bachelor's degree in mechanical engineering from Carnegie Mellon. He came up through plant production and supervisory positions, served as Fairfield's general manager, then moved on to general manager of tubular products. After running USS/Kobe in Lorain, Ohio, he came back to Pittsburgh to rise to the steel group's presidency in 1994. He joined the USX board in 1995 and was elected vice chairman in 2000.

One of Wilhelm's strengths, like Usher's, was the ability to keep in touch with the people on the mill floor as well as the people at the top. This showed when, during his book interview, he turned enthusiastically to the subject of the corporation's employees.

Clearly, this was a subject he liked to talk about. And he gave a little speech, one that was very telling:

"When I first started with this company, the average guy who worked at the plant had started at U. S. Steel in 1931, '32, '33. The second big hiring we had was '49, '50, after World War II. The next was in the early Seventies. They were really a contrast. "The first group, from the Thirties, were extremely hard-working people. A lot were first generation, from the old country. They did what they were told, and they made things happen. The second group was very disciplined, coming out of World War II. The third group had lived through the post-Vietnam, drug culture era.

"And it was funny, when we had meetings—we'd sit down and talk over safety or customer issues, for example—the group from the Thirties would sit there, and, when we asked whether there were any questions, they'd get up and leave. The second group would challenge you on some things. 'Why should we do that?' The third group, the people from the protest era, would be upbeat, enthusiastic.

"The people in that third group—the people we have today— truly care. They want to be environmentally responsible. They want to be safe. They want good product. They take pride in working with customers. You used to send a vice president out to a customer to solve a problem, and he'd have lunch with another vice president and come back and nothing would change. Today, you send one of our workers out and he or she comes back and says to their group, 'Here's what's wrong and here's what we're going to do to fix it.' And they do it. They're just outstanding. They want to do what's right. They want to help. They want this to be a better company. They're concerned about the environment that their kids are being raised in.

"We have the right people at the right time."

The "right people" that Paul Wilhelm was referring to were his steel people, of course. But to Tom Usher, the "right people" also worked at Marathon Oil. They should also be included in the equation.

As this book traces the fortunes of U. S. Steel, it also describes the transformation of the world's first billion-dollar corporation, a steel producer, into an energy company, one that now is only one-third steel. Usher explained the makeup of USX in his Duquesne Club talk. "Our home page on the Internet… will tell you that USX is a major producer of oil and gas, as well as the nation's largest producer of steel products. The emphasis there is correct. USX is primarily an energy company now, and about three-fourths of our revenue comes from our Marathon Group.

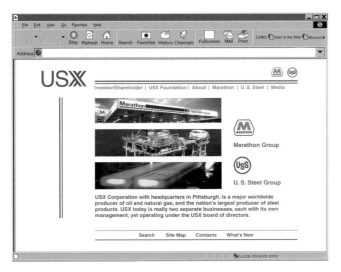

USX's homepage on the Internet: www.usx.com

"And the fact that the income of the nation's ninth-largest oil company is more than twice that of the nation's largest steel company gives you an idea of the relative size of those two industries."

Overseeing the exciting things happening at Marathon is a man Usher recruited from outside the company—Clarence P. Cazalot, Jr. In March 2000, he was named president of the oil company and a vice chairman of USX. He was also elected to the board. Formerly, he had been vice president of Texaco Inc., and president of its production operations.

Clarence P. Cazalot, Jr., president of Marathon Oil Company and a USX vice chairman

The telling of the U. S. Steel story is nearly at an end. The next—and final—chapter focuses on those "right people" who have turned an old steel company into a key component of a revitalized and vibrant steel and energy corporation.

Tom Usher, Paul Wilhelm, Bob Hernandez, Clarence Cazalot— they were a new generation of managers, attuned to the new, global world of commerce. They were erasing old barriers as they took U. S. Steel, Marathon Oil and USX into the 2000s. Everyone was on the same wavelength.

It was the right team at the right time.

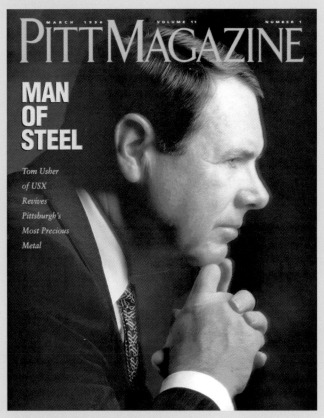

MARCH 1994   VOLUME 11   NUMBER 1

PITTMAGAZINE

MAN OF STEEL

Tom Usher
of USX
Revives
Pittsburgh's
Most Precious
Metal

Photographed by Peter Liepke

THE MAN WITH THE VISION

Early in his tenure as president of U. S. Steel, while on a tour of the company's Gary Works, Tom Usher took time to hop over to the local steelworkers' union hall. He strolled into the local's office, unannounced, and sat down to chat with the union leaders and to hear what they had on their minds.

The officials and workers in the hall were amazed by the visit. "It was very, very unusual," local president Cary Kranz told The New York Times*. "Other heads of U. S. Steel would never have dreamed of being in the same room with the union people. He is bringing in a breath of fresh air."*

Kranz was right. Usher represented a new kind of manager, one who had emerged from a younger generation of employees. He held a doctorate but spoke shop-floor with the rank and file. He was hailed as an excellent manager, inspiring, yet street-smart. And he was taking the art of managing into territory demanded by the times.

"Tom Usher ... seems to be totally committed to getting everyone involved in the process of quality," said Paul T. Sullivan, an executive director for purchasing at Ford Motor Company, a major USX customer. "To me, he is a different breed of fellow."

Sullivan was right, too. Usher was like a lot of other members of the steel breed in that he was a Pennsylvanian. He was born in Reading, his mother's hometown, but from there, his life took a different twist. Usher spent his early years living with his grandfather while his father— a Secret Service agent—was stationed in the Pacific. The young Usher hopped about, living in Washington, D.C., New Jersey, New York, West Virginia and in the Philadelphia area before winding up in Pittsburgh in the late 1950s. He graduated from Wilkinsburg High School. He then attended the University of Pittsburgh, where he earned a bachelor's degree in industrial engineering, a master's in operations research and a doctorate in systems engineering.

VISION:

A profitable steel company that earns an adequate return for its shareholders and provides sufficient capital to assure its long-term success.

An innovative steel company that clearly distinguishes itself as the industry leader in providing superior quality and service to its customers, while continuously reducing costs to achieve a status of low-cost producer.

A company that has respect for all employees, creates an atmosphere which motivates employees to fully utilize their talents, encourages all employees to work together effectively, and promptly recognizes and rewards each employee for contributions to the overall success of the company.

A company that values diversity in its work force, fosters a safe and healthy work place, is environmentally responsible, and at all times conducts itself in an ethical manner.

A company in which each employee takes pride in being an important and contributing member.

To achieve this Vision, we must significantly elevate our performance standards and consistently achieve these new levels.

None of these objectives alone will be sufficient for success; together however they will allow us to maximize and balance the benefits to all of our employees, customers, shareholders and communities.

U. S. Steel Group
A unit of USX Corporation

Introduced by Tom Usher in 1992, this Vision credo presented a blueprint for enhancing the corporation's worldwide competitive position as well as motivating employees to achieve their full potential.

Usher joined U. S. Steel's industrial engineering department in 1966, and held a number of positions before moving through superintendent stints at South Works in Chicago and at Gary. From there it was back to Pittsburgh as director of Corporate Planning, and up through jobs including managing director for facility planning, engineering, research and industrial engineering, president of the U. S. Steel Mining Co., Inc., senior vice president for steel operations and, in 1990, president of the steel division. He was elected president of the U. S. Steel Group and to the USX board in 1991,

president and chief operating officer of USX in 1994 and chairman of the board and CEO in 1995. Along the way he raised three children with his wife Sandy. His membership in a "different breed" became immediately apparent through his management style. He turned the old top-down, command-driven methods upside down. He believed in tapping the knowledge and energies of his people. He operated on the human touch. He routinely sent subordinates birthday cards. He brought people together. Small wonder that Usher is considered the author of U. S. Steel's Vision philosophy, introduced in 1992 to inspire employees to even greater achievements. Usher-esque in its language, the credo declares that, to be successful, the corporation must not only deliver superior quality and profits. It must have respect for its employees, instill pride in them, motivate them to achieve their full potential.

Usher's methods worked. As Business Week *acknowledged in its May 15, 1995, issue, "Usher has led U. S. Steel to an impressive comeback. In the past five years, the company has pushed ahead of German and Japanese rivals in productivity. "At the same time," added* Business Week, *"he has prepared for a down market in common grades of steel by forging high-tech joint ventures with Japan's Kobe Steel Ltd. And last year he even teamed up with minimill nemesis Nucor Corp. in a joint venture to develop new steelmaking technology."*

Usher brought the same roll-up-the-sleeves spirit to the position of chairman. It spilled over into the way he tackled a very chairman-like extracurricular activity: He agreed to head a group of local business leaders in generating support for nearly a billion dollars of downtown Pittsburgh projects aimed at reviving the city, keeping its professional baseball and football franchises and turning the area into a popular "destination center."

Part of the task was to triple almost the size of the city's convention center. Also on the project list were more than $50 million in improvements to the city's riverfront. At the end of the century, Usher could see part of the program's results from the top floor of the USX headquarters: Across the Allegheny River, two neighboring, new stadiums, for the Pirates and the Steelers, were shaping up. How his corporation would shape up wasn't so clear. "I can't really tell you what the company will look like in 10 or 20 years," he told a Greensburg (Pennsylvania) Tribune Review writer in April of 1997. "It's very, very difficult to project things like that.... I guess the best way to look at it is like having a couple of kids," Usher added, referring to his corporation's steel and energy businesses. "We try to do what is best for each of them, but they're totally different."

Then he added a wish: "I'd like to reinforce pride on the part of our employees and retirees that we're no longer a company that is just shutting things down, but a company that is on the move and growing and doing good things."

Management, employees, retirees, shareholders. "We" were all in this together. Usher sent that message to all levels of the corporation and community.

During U. S. Steel's annual Good Fellowship outings at Allegheny Country Club, he stationed himself at a par-three hole, the 15th, where he played every foursome of employees that came through. He kept this up from eight in the morning until six in the evening, competing in friendly games with over 200 golfers during one outing, playing the same hole over and over, and chatting and posing for pictures with each group. It had to be exhausting, but Usher knew the message he was sending to employees about how much he valued them was worth it. "They loved it," said one of his par-three competitors, Bruce Thomas, retired USX chief financial officer and vice chairman-administration. Usher was comfortable with everyone.

Sister Marita Charley, former principal of Good Shepherd School in Braddock, Pennsylvania, recalled for the Pittsburgh Post-Gazette her encounter with Usher when he was working as part of a group of USX employees painting the school's third floor and gymnasium: "He had his painter's hat on and was right in there with them. Looking at him, you just wouldn't know he was an important man. And when he left that day, he came up to me and said, 'Sister, if you ever need anything, don't hesitate to call.'" She did call, and Usher, as a result, provided scholarship money so needy kids in Braddock could attend the school.

This life-size crèche received widespread community acclaim when it was displayed on the plaza of the USX Tower for the first time in 1999. Usher was instrumental in soliciting funding for the project and in making other arrangements for its Pittsburgh debut.

Another time, he received a call from the bishop, himself—Bishop Donald Wuerl of the Catholic Diocese of Pittsburgh. The bishop wanted to find a prominent piece of private downtown real estate on which to construct a crèche. It was to be the only church-authorized replica of the Vatican's original in St. Peter's Square in Rome, the bishop told Usher, and it would be sponsored by the Christian Leaders Fellowship representing the heads of all Christian denominations in Pittsburgh.

Usher agreed to spearhead the project. Business, labor and religious leaders agreed to provide funds and resources.

But how to proceed? This was no simple tabletop crèche. It was to be life-size. The stable would soar atop the 60-foot fountain in the Plaza of the USX Tower. The figures in the nativity would stand at least six feet tall.

In time, all the plans came together: The set designers from Pittsburgh's Civic Light Opera built the crèche from plans provided by the Vatican. Pietro Simonelli,

who had sculpted the figures in St. Peter's Square, replicated them for Pittsburgh.

On December 6, 1999, the crèche was dedicated, and over that holiday season, thousands of visitors—many from out of state—saw and were moved by it. The crèche was rebuilt on the Plaza again in 2000. In all likelihood, it would become an annual tradition.

Then there was the time Usher repeated his surprise visit to a local USW union hall. This time it was the Clairton, Pennsylvania, local. And this time Chairman Usher brought with him U. S. Steel President Paul Wilhelm. "I always thought that was kind of neat," USW District 10 Director Andrew "Lefty" Palm told one of the papers. Then the union official paid the chairman what may have been the greatest compliment he could receive.

He called Usher "a stand-up guy."

Chapter 20

The Best of All Worlds

The best of all worlds. U. S. Steel would achieve that state only when the company consistently produced the highest quality steels *with* processes that were pollution-free *by* employees requiring the fewest number of man-hours to make a ton of steel…when customers were not only satisfied with the steel they received from U. S. Steel but were eager, as well, for the hands-on support of the company's service teams which visited to insure that customers got full measure from their purchase…when the company made a fair and reasonable return on the products it sent into the marketplace.

The Nineties seemed to be the time when most of these conditions came together. The company, and all within, were energized and motivated and upbeat. Employees had found new importance and value, not only in their jobs, but in themselves. They had been empowered by U. S. Steel's management, invited to become true partners, to be part of the decision-making process.

It began in the Eighties with the Apex quality programs, was heightened by Tom Usher's Vision program in the early Nineties. In the final decade of the twentieth century, employees—from top to bottom, from managers to plant workers—had made incredible contributions to the fortunes of U. S. Steel. This last chapter focuses on them and on their road to excellence.

Their story provides a fitting end to a book which is as much a record of the human being and the human spirit as it is a history of stone and mortar, machinery and products.

In early 2000, Tony Pacilio (center), production manager, and Melissa McLaughlin (right), customer technical services manager, traveled to Kosice, Slovakia, in eastern Europe to assume new assignments at U. S. Steel Kosice, s.r.o. Welcoming the newly married couple was Anton Jura, the plant's managing director.

Just after their wedding and just before the calendar flipped to the year 2000, Melissa McLaughlin and Tony Pacilio packed their bags, said goodbye to their friends at U. S. Steel's Gary Works and boarded a plane.

Their destination: Kosice, Slovakia, in eastern Europe.

But this was no honeymoon trip. The young couple was flying eastward to fill jobs at U. S. Steel's new joint-venture company, VSZ U. S. Steel, s.r.o.—Melissa as customer technical service manager, Tony as production director. As reported in the last chapter, U. S. Steel in late 2000 purchased VSZ and changed its name to U. S. Steel Kosice, s.r.o.

Neither McLaughlin nor Pacilio could call this a job hop. For both, this was a *leap*. They would have to settle down in Kosice while they found their way to customers in Slovakia, the Czech Republic, Poland, Hungary, Austria, Ukraine, the Baltic states and other European countries. They would have to learn new languages and feel their way around these new lands so they could take care of business in accordance with habits and customs of cultures that, to them, were entirely new.

More, they would have to introduce Slovak workers to a new style of management, one marked by a freer exchange of ideas and more responsibility for each worker. This new way would replace business practices that had been inefficient, even shady, but shrugged off as the way things were done.

It wasn't long before the couple was making progress. As Melissa reported to fellow employees via the *U S Steel News*, she and Tony were introducing "consistent and fair business practices," which seemed to be working: "I believe we've already started to make a difference."

It was an amazing assignment.

It was an amazing age.

More than ever, the corporation was entrusting sizeable responsibilities to its employees—to young managers like McLaughlin and Pacilio and to hourly workers who knew how steel was made and how it could be made even better.

Back in the States, employees who punched time clocks and belonged to the union were kicking around product and process improvements with their managers, and running off to appliance and auto plants to try those ideas out on the managers there, and on their own counterparts on the lines. They were troubleshooting. They were solving technical problems for customers, advising them on ways to get the most for their money out of steel and its products.

Now they were less a source of labor and more a source of ideas. And, with U. S. Steel workers walking around the lines at a Ford or Chrysler plant, where did Big Steel end and its customers begin? Was the question even relevant?

On the management side of the equation, the old, salute-and-obey model was vanishing. "Managing" no longer meant "Do what I say." It meant giving people the training, resources and encouragement they needed to discover for themselves what had to be done—then getting out of their way.

This was an infectious idea. Its power was evident in the fresh enthusiasm of worker-led teams. They were looking for every possible way to fine-tune what they were doing so they could keep improving quality. They were putting their talents and intelligence to the job of reducing even further the traces of pollution their plants emitted. They were turning areas of their plant grounds into wildlife preserves, places where children came to learn about nature. They were working even harder in the communities, making them better places to live.

They believed in these things. They were part of it. It reflected what was good about *them*.

Something was going on here, something new.

Where had it begun?

A good place to start is the Mon Valley in the mid-Eighties. That's where *Industry Week* magazine took readers when, in 1996, it named U. S. Steel's Mon Valley Works as one of America's best. How did the works earn that rating? In a 1996 *Industry Week* story, writer John H. Sheridan attributed it to attitudes that sprang from an initiative introduced in 1984, the APEX quality program.

"Originally," Sheridan explained, "the acronym stood for 'appliance product excellence,' a campaign to meet the rigorous quality demands of the appliance industry, the plant's major market segment. The program was later expanded to include automotive steels, and today, APEX stands for 'all people, all process, all product excellence.'"

What the acronym *really* stood for was employee spirit. And it wasn't the birth of APEX that made the spirit come alive. Oddly enough, the double dose of energy and dedication seemed to be part of the fallout of the steel strike of 1986—the longest steel strike in history. As one hourly employee told the author, that strike delivered a big dose of reality: "People looked around and saw how few workers were left. They decided that, if they wanted to have a job, they'd better do what they could to keep the works going."

Management looked around, too, and realized the workers, being right on the front lines, working with the steel, had a lot of answers locked up in their heads. The business demanded yet more speed, more efficiency. Why not plug the worker into the idea machine?

They did, and the walls came down. A trickle of ideas from the hourly people grew into a flood.

APEX, the quest for quality's highest peak, was one result.

As Sheridan noted in his article, APEX "quickly evolved into an ongoing, comprehensive effort that stresses continuous improvement in many areas—including initiatives to help customers reduce their production-related costs. In the last two years alone, employee teams have helped customer plants to identify and achieve more than $25 million in cost savings."

When the folks at Whirlpool's Marion, Ohio, plant needed help in cutting their own costs, Mon Valley sent two hourly workers,

Mon Valley Works was the proud recipient of this prestigious Industry Week *magazine award as a quality supplier in 1996.*

In this Whirlpool facility in Tulsa, Oklahoma, a Mon Valley Works team followed a steel coil through the manufacturing process. Team members included (left to right) Nancy Amati, test report clerk; John Borkowski, team captain and APEX representative; Jim Pasquarelli, team captain and utilityman; and Diane Verdish, systems repairman.

Temper-Mill Roller John Prestia and Recoiler Operator Roger Arison, to team up with Whirlpool engineers.

Sheridan wrote what happened: "The two employees followed four coils during shipment to find out what happened to them after they left the U. S. Steel plant wrapped in protective packaging. En route, the steel was diverted to a processing firm for slitting. 'We discovered that this company removed our cardboard packaging at its plant,' Prestia says. 'Then it shipped the coils to Whirlpool without the protection, causing damage along the way.'"

As a result, Mon Valley modified the packaging so it would stay on the coils all through shipping. It was a simple solution to a simple discovery. But no one had thought of it before because no one had checked into the problem.

The workers were rooting out troubles. Typically, they jumped into a company van and took two-day trips to customer plants. As Irvin's APEX Coordinator Mike Buckiso explained to Sheridan, the idea was less to find improvements right away and more to make themselves known to customers' managements and employees.

"Having a better knowledge of the downstream things that go on with our product can be a real awakening," explained former Mon Valley General Manager John F. Kaloski. "If there is an issue at a customer plant, they'll pick up the phone and call the guy at our rolling mill. They

Seven monthly production records were broken in 1996 at the 84-inch pickle line of Mon Valley Works' Irvin Plant through the teamwork of this APEX group: (left to right) Marcie Omasta, laborer; Rich Montgomery, utilityman; Paul Tomcanin, millwright; Joe Bradley, APEX representative; and Pete Janicki, ironworker.

don't call me. They call the guy who can actually do something about it at the moment."

The Mon Valley worker-troubleshooters took turns on the quality teams, serving three-month rotations, then returning to their regular jobs. The turnover generated feedback that kept everyone up on the status at customer plants. The workers also teamed up with managers to scrutinize their own plants during regular audits of process and quality procedures.

"Who would do a better job than the folks who actually do the job?" asked Fred Harnack, then the operations manager at Mon Valley's Edgar Thomson plant.

The same thing was going on at other U. S. Steel plants. But this "thing" was alive. Over time, APEX evolved from quality into team efforts aimed at digging out problems in safety, delivery, environmental protection, productivity, even financial performance.

What a difference. Sheridan listed the results at the Mon Valley plants: a 66-percent reduction over three years in product rejections in the Mon Valley plants themselves. A 65-percent reduction in slab-caster "breakouts"—leaks of molten steel from the cores of castings. And, from customers, a string of awards for making better steel and giving A-plus-plus service.

Rich Holm probably could have told you more ways to raise quality than just about anybody on the corporation's APEX teams. Holm, like a lot of other hourly employees, was right *there* when steel was made. He'd been *there*, too, when customers turned the steel into fenders and auto hoods. He was a veteran steelworker and one of the first members of an APEX committee called the Gary Works Hourly Liaison Team. That was when he was a cold reduction sheet finisher, back in the late Eighties. Ten years later, when he shared his memories and knowledge for this history, his title was customer liaison.

APEX had a life of its own. It short-circuited quality issues and questions that had been wandering up and down the management tiers at Gary, or for that matter, at customer plants. Now questions and problems were settled in a straight line—one that went straight from the workers who made the steel to the workers who turned the steel into cars or steel siding for buildings, or into cans.

And Holm's customer liaison title meant just what it said. He worked with the steelworkers at Gary, and directly with workers and managers at an auto plant that was one of Gary Works' many customers.

At Gary Works' Broadway Avenue entrance, the APEX sign reminded visitors and employees of the plant's APEX total quality system.

He knew how Gary's people made steel. He knew what Ford, Chrysler or GM did with that steel. That meant he could see ways that people on both ends could turn out improved products at less cost by doing their jobs better, or at least differently. If he couldn't, he'd get the details from the workers at the customer plant. Maybe the steel was scratched, or—hell on customers' machinery—speckled with dirt. Or maybe little wrinkles were showing up in a hood.

Holm would run the problems back to his team at Gary. Chances were he would confer with the people on the Ford, Chrysler or GM line. Someone would chase down a solution: Alter the steel's chemistry to get rid of the wrinkles, maybe, or change rolling techniques to improve the way the machinery shaped the steel. Or package the steel differently to eliminate specks of dirt.

Holm and the other liaisons at Gary made the contacts and made things happen. Fast. And they didn't have to find their foremen to get permission. "U. S. Steel gives us hourly people the same authority as managers," Holm, with a clear note of pride in his voice, told the author.

Holm's boss, Jim Banas, a 36-year U. S. Steel veteran and hourly liaison team coordinator, shared the spirit. "Our team," he pointed out, "is involved in every aspect of producing steel—from high-tech tasks like taking samples for metallurgical testing, to saving two feet of steel from a coil in the scrap pile."

"Every aspect" meant the little things, the details and bugs, that, without the right attention, could hide *now* but show up later, much to a customer's irritation.

Customers knew about the spirit.

"Rich and the liaison team come in and participate in line team meetings, and share their knowledge of steel and processing and the associated defects that may be the root cause of a problem for us," Cindy Renault, quality manager for DaimlerChrysler's stamping plant in Warren, Michigan, told the author. "The biggest benefit has been a rise in the level of communications. It has raised our peoples' awareness of issues with our parts."

Trust helped. As Renault added, from the start the Daimler-Chrysler employees "recognized that Rich was like them, and that he would take their issues back to USS and bring them back the answers."

There were two secrets here: getting into the customers' heads and following the trail of details.

On the first: Workers at U. S. Steel and at customer plants reinforced their understanding of what each other did by touring each other's plants. From the steelworkers' end of things, the idea was to see firsthand what machinery and processes customers used to make their products, then discover ways to help those customers improve product and costs. For the autoworkers who toured Gary, it worked the same way, but in reverse. Between visits, both sides viewed occasional videotapes of their opposites' operations.

What came out of this, Banas and Holm could see, was that workers at both plants felt they were part of one process. They *all* worked with steel. They *all* made cars.

But problems waiting for solutions weren't always lurking in the manufacturing end. They could be hiding in shipping or packaging. They were often behind little things, issues that seemed too trivial to worry about. Finding them was the second secret.

Like the time Banas and Holm noticed that the workers at GM's Lansing, Michigan, plant were throwing away the plastic rings that prevented damage to steel coils during shipment. The rings were landfilled. Why couldn't they be recycled—returned to U. S. Steel for reuse?

Holm and Banas asked. The customer said, no, recycling wasn't worth the trouble. But that didn't stop the Gary duo.

"We kept working on it and found out how much money they could save," said Banas. "When Rich and I found they were throwing these things away, we found a guy who was willing to pick the rings up, clean them and send them back to Gary."

The result? Lansing plant was saving almost $50,000 a year in landfill charges. Now it was worth the trouble.

The *coup de grace* for the Gary duo was their design of a protective, plastic sack which is slipped over Gary's steel coils after they are coated at U. S. Steel's joint-venture Double Eagle Plant in Dearborn. Protected by what the steel team dubbed "baggies," the coils could be shipped right to the customer plant and stored on the floor. (Previously, they had been shipped to a safe place, a warehouse, then delivered to the plant when they were needed.)

"It saved 25 bucks in packaging costs per coil," said Holm.

The savings added up. Fast. That was quality, too. Quality caring and quality service.

Technically, "quality" meant product integrity, but it could mean different things, as well.

To the customers that fashioned steel into corrugated sides and roofs of metal buildings, it meant protection for the machinery that did the work. "The edges of struts have to be free from burrs so that when they go through their processing lines, they don't damage their rollers," explained Amy Roberts, a project engineer at U. S. Steel's Fairfield Works. "We don't want to ruin their equipment."

Carmakers needed top-quality materials technology. For one thing, it was a crucial weapon in their fight against weight. They had to meet some tough miles-per-gallon targets mandated by the government. As metallurgical engineer Mike Juddo explained, U. S. Steel was working with the auto industry to meet those targets by producing high-strength steels that could be rolled into lighter gauges, allowing carmakers to reduce the weight of their vehicles without compromising "crashworthiness." Cars had to be engineered to be as strong tomorrow as they were today, for the safety of the passengers.

Juddo, in fact, was director of product technology at U. S. Steel's Automotive Center, an auto-steel research and test center that the company had opened in 1999 in Troy, Michigan, right in the carmakers' backyard. The engineers at the center partnered with automakers in a search for stronger, more formable steels and designs that took full advantage of that lightness and strength.

Steel was in a race against lighter metals, chiefly aluminum and manganese, for the material of choice in vehicles.

Engineers at U. S. Steel's Automotive Center in Troy, Michigan, partnered with automakers in a search for stronger, more formable steels and more creative auto designs.

But steel had an edge: For one thing, it was cheaper. "Aluminum and magnesium are lighter," explained Juddo, "but, for most applications, they cost the automakers a lot more than steel."

Also, studies had shown steel to be superior to aluminum in the category of environmental friendliness: "It turns out that the production of aluminum puts more carbon dioxide emissions into the air than steel. Over the life of a car, you might never make up the difference with aluminum—even though you might get better gas mileage."

The post-'86-strike, roll-up-your-sleeves-and-do-it attitude was evident. The workers and technical and management people at Clairton Works were only too happy to work together to get their plants up to environmental snuff.

*T*his was a Team.

Clairton's people worked up a program called CITE (Continuous Improvement to the Environment), in partnership with the local community college. Under the program, Clairton employees learned more about running the plant's environmental-control equipment— and the importance of cleaning the environment. The program won awards and was exported to Gary Works and other U. S. Steel plants. More importantly, it made the workers part of something bigger than simply making coke. "When employees understand how every facet of the plant interrelates, they realize the importance of their individual job performance," Clairton conveyor-man Wendell Hopkin told a *U S Steel News* reporter.

Nowhere was the new spirit more alive than in the eight-man team of Clairton workers appointed to take another look at the age-old problem of leaking coke-oven doors.

Once before, the company had taken steps that improved the doors' seals, preventing much of the polluting fumes from escaping. But it wasn't enough. The new team took a look at the problem, went out and

Training classes were an integral part of Clairton Works' Continuous Improvement to the Environment (CITE) program. In this photo, Instructor D. McVicker (right) explains the details of coke battery operation to (standing, left to right) M. Sauritch, C. M. Jones, P. Upston, (seated) L. Mandolesi, and D. Hamlin.

tested door designs used at coke ovens all over the world, and came up with their own version. It was thicker, and it had a round-cornered seal. And it flat-out stopped fumes.

Then U. S. Steel's Mon Valley employees proved one good idea leads to another. They rigged up a system that piped Clairton's coke oven gas to the Irvin plant where it was burned in slab-reheating furnaces. This was as far as you could come from the days of the old beehive ovens that issued not only coke, but clouds of poisonous gas, and when no one cared enough to try to fix the trouble.

The "green" doors were only one way to deal with pollution. Since the mid-Seventies, Clairton had operated a plant in which bacteria gobbled up contaminants in the works' wastewater. Now a $40-million installation at Clairton was laying a blanket of inert gas over benzene in storage tanks, stopping the fumes from escaping into the air. (Gary was installing a similar system.) And, now, Clairton was extracting harmful chemicals from the coke-oven gas and turning it into harmless nitrogen and water. In the bargain, it won a bushel of environmental awards.

But Clairton employees weren't satisfied. They kept finding ways to do good by the environment.

The topper came when they teamed up with a local garden club to create, on the plant grounds, a butterfly garden. So now you had coke workers teaming up with suburbanite green thumbs to plant a 1,500-square-foot garden that would beautify the plant grounds and serve as a

CITE
Continuous
Improvement
To Environment

CHOOSING TO BE THE BEST

habitat for colorful monarchs, swallow tails and other butterflies that flitted around laying their eggs. The garden even attracted humming-birds. And it went well with Clairton's 55 park-like acres of woods, fields and hillsides along the Monongahela River. This was some coke works.

Gary added its own butterfly reservation. And tended it very carefully. It even called in a military helicopter to airlift three junk cars from the oak savanna that had become part of one of Gary Works' wildlife habitats. Airlifting the wrecks minimized damage to the turf that was home to the endangered Karner Blue butterfly, due to hatch any day.

But butterflies weren't the only wildlife U. S. Steel employees tended. Minntac's 16-square-mile settling basin for mine residue was a natural home to bald eagles, osprey, great blue heron and Canada geese.

Steel and coke-plant employees worked hard to return their grounds to nature. Fairfield people worked with the State of Alabama to restore a creek near the plant, transforming it into a healthy home for fish and other aquatic life. Clairton had created its 55-acre park. Fairfield and Gary also set aside acreage which the national Wildlife Habitat Council certified as official wildlife habitats, protected homes for fox,

The Wildlife Habitat Council paid special tribute to these members of the YWCA Garden Club of McKeesport, Pennsylvania, for their help in creating and maintaining this butterfly garden at Clairton Works: (left to right) Eloise Vadia, Ann Grouber, Margery Schriber, Patty Funk, Bill Graeser (Wildlife Habitat leader), Roberta Johnson, Rhoda West, Jewel Kelly and Diane Soltis.

deer, hawks, owls and other animals. Employees erected birdhouses for nesters there. Gary's three houses, each 5 feet by 5 feet and 3 feet tall, served as shelters for two rare peregrine falcons that called the works their home.

One of U. S. Steel's most unusual environmental projects also involved the Wildlife Habitat Council. In 1993, the company, employees and the council teamed up to preserve a four-acre wetlands bordering the Irvin plant, turning it into an innovative outdoor learning center for school children in the Pittsburgh area's Baldwin-Whitehall School District.

Two teachers from the District—Joy Kretzler Smith and her husband, Ed—developed a pilot program at the site, and, since then, more than 12,000 students have participated in a variety of hands-on educational programs there. In late 2000, the Smiths received from the council its Community Partner of the Year award, the first individuals (as opposed to an organization) to be so honored.

Representatives from eight countries in central Europe toured the park in 2000 to observe how industry and the community can work together to protect the environment. It seemed likely that the Pittsburgh program would become a model for wildlife habitat projects throughout the world.

The Mon Valley Works' Edgar Thomson and Irvin plants became the first ISO-certified steel facilities in U. S. Steel in the summer of 1994. Displaying the ISO 90021 certification are (left to right) local union members Don Conn, Don Thomas and Phil DeNunzio, all now retired, and John Kaloski, former Mon Valley Works general manager.

There were other dimensions to the corporation's environmental program—invention of other technologies, further environmental training for employees, partnerships with local schools to sponsor student field trips to wildlife areas. When it came to safeguarding nature, the employees and the managers of Big Steel were believers. It showed in the results.

There's an endnote to the Clairton story. In 1998, the plant received the local, Three Rivers Environmental Award for environmental stewardship. It also became the first steel or coke industry plant to achieve ISO 14001 certification, an internationally coveted crown of environmental quality.

Related to the corporation's environmental work was its recycling program. U. S. Steel employees teamed up with other steel companies to promote collection and recycling of steel cans and other steel containers. The company also promoted programs to save refrigerators, stoves and autos from the dump and send them back to the mills to be reincarnated as part of new steel, for new products. The cars Gary had airlifted from its butterfly refuge went straight to the plant's BOP shop, to be born again as part of new automobiles.

Old autos, cans and stoves also could come back as houses. Or at least as substitutes for the wooden two-by-four frames that houses were built on. And U. S. Steel was promoting steel framing, made from recycled steel products, for just that purpose.

It made sense. By the early Nineties, wood framing had a lot more knots, and cost more. Light-gauge, galvanized steel was stronger and a lot cheaper than it had been a decade earlier. Steel didn't warp or rot, and termites couldn't get their teeth into it. Frame a home in steel and it could stand up to hurricanes that flattened houses framed with wood. Add a galvanized steel roof and you had a fortress.

Steel two-by-fours sounded weird, but assembling them wasn't hard. Builders and framers of homes for needy families learned that in a seminar run by employees of U. S. Steel's Fairfield Works. Framers out in the real world must have agreed. In 1994, according to the corporation's annual report, galvanized sheet-steel framing—the *new* two-by-four—was used to build the skeletons for 40,000 homes. Steel roofs were put on 40,000 new homes, and 160,000 older homes were retrofitted with them.

Steel homes multiplied, especially in hurricane zones. According to the National Association of Home Builders, shipments of light-gauge steel for homes grew more than 41 percent between 1998 and 1999.

It was another way steel was changing the way we lived.

Steel framing took on new popularity with contractors as shipments of light-gauge steel for homes grew more than 41 percent between 1998 and 1999, according to the National Association of Home Builders.

Doing the best job for customers, the community and the environment was its own reward for most, if not all, U. S. Steel employees. But recognition added to a job well done.

In U. S. Steel, as in other companies, one of the forms recognition took was awards—awards from other national and local governments, publications and customers from Chrysler to Campbell Soup. Awards for cost-effectiveness, product design, material engineering, grounds beautification, breaking operating records, and in more obvious categories such as safety, environmental control, and for being a top-notch supplier.

In 1991 alone, U. S. Steel employees received no fewer than 16 major quality and supplier-of-the-year awards. They were the first steel employees—domestic or foreign—to win Ford's and Chrysler's top quality awards in the same year.

The next year, a five-person customer-liaison team from the Gary Works won for their plant the first Quality Cup Award ever presented in the manufacturing category. It was a highly esteemed, national recognition by the Rochester Institute of Technology and *USA Today*. Meanwhile, the Fairfield and Fairless works rounded up best-supplier trophies from major suppliers. And by 1993, U. S. Steel employees could say they had made their company the only domestic steel producer to have won product-quality awards from all of the Big Three automakers.

Awards kept coming in from national and local companies and associations. To Mon Valley: "top-operation" and maintenance awards from two trade magazines, plus, two years in a row, *Industry Week*'s Best Plant of the Year trophy.

Fairfield employees displayed Emerson Electric's Distinguished Supplier Award, among others. Clairton employees won for their leakless coke oven doors and butterfly garden.

All U. S. Steel employees shared an EPA corporate award for lighting conservation. And their company was the only steel supplier in the nation to win General Electric's Distinguished Supplier Award.

It did seem that the awards trend tilted upward as the decade progressed. Certainly, one influence was a new campaign to inspire

U. S. Steel employees to break the bank in quality, customer service, cost control—in overall excellence.

This was Tom Usher's Vision program, introduced in the early Nineties when he headed U. S. Steel. He knew that the job of steelmaking could be improved. But he didn't want management to tell employees how. He wanted employees to develop their own set of principles which would guide them in their work. He was empowering workers, and the guidelines they created were formalized in the Vision statement. It sought to elevate performance across the board by giving employees concrete ideals to shoot for. It broke into seven categories where the company should be at its best.

Boiled down, Vision said the ideal corporation was profitable, innovative, respectful of employees, was marked by a diverse workforce and a safe and healthy workplace, was one employees were proud to be part of, kept raising its performance standards, and devoted itself to the good of its employees, customers, shareholders and communities.

But this was not just a list of objectives that someone posted on a wall and left there. This list trickled down to all employees, who, participating in local Vision team meetings, shared their ideas about what the ideals meant to their operations and to them, personally. And they sought ways to translate Vision into on-the-job attitudes and actions.

(Below left) Following almost three years of certification effort, Gary Works earned Ford Motor Company's elite Q1 Quality Award. On hand for the presentation were Alex Trotman (left), executive vice president, Ford North American Automotive Operations and Gary representative George Lukes, manager, Quality Assurance.

(Below right) Kudos from automakers. Jim Carlton (left), Chrysler's director of Raw Materials Purchasing and Stamping, presented the Gold Pentastar Award to Paul Kadlic, then general manager, Sales-Central. The award was Chrysler's highest recognition of superior service, quality and technology by U. S. Steel as a supplier.

The *1993 Annual Review* for the U. S. Steel unit was dedicated to Vision, and introduced the program as a "caldron of ideas, goals and actions."

Tom Usher, U. S. Steel's president then, added his own thoughts:

"The steel business is changing. Customers demand continuously improving steel quality and service. Competition is tougher—new products, minimills and foreign steel keep pecking away at markets we traditionally serve. Therefore we have to change dramatically to mold our company in such a fashion to be our customers' supplier of choice next year, in the year 2000 and in the year 2010."

The Vision ideals would lead the way.

But who knew what the steel business or the energy business would bring in 2010? Or tomorrow?

The world was spinning into a new millennium.

USX was entering a new age. Anyone who doubted that had only to tap into the age's new communications tool, an invisible, global communications medium called the Internet, and log onto e-STEEL. This was an electronic steel center, one that would let customers anywhere order tons of steel simply by striking some keys on their computers.

Big Steel did not operate the same as it once did. Now, instead of handling physical tasks down on the steelworks floors, workers were up in air-conditioned booths, controlling operations with desktop computers. Still, size and technology alone didn't matter.

Spirit did. And U. S. Steel's people had spirit to spare. Their company was still the top steelmaker in America, and the lowest-cost producer. Much, maybe all, the credit for that went to the employees. Salaried or hourly, executive or laborer, it made little difference. They were working together. They were standing shoulder to shoulder.

What *couldn't* they do tomorrow?

Afterword

In 2001, U. S. Steel is a vastly different steelmaker than it was when Judge Gary first presided over it in the early 1900s. Then, we made literally hundreds of steel products at dozens of steel mills across the country, and we aimed to serve all steel markets wherever we found them. In 1901, with 168,127 workers, U. S. Steel shipped 8,197,232 tons of steel. In 1999, on the cusp of our centenary, we shipped 10,629,000 tons of steel product with 19,266 workers.

Today, U. S. Steel is a trimmer company. We are more selective in the steels we offer, producing only those for markets which guarantee us the best return. In late 2000, U. S. Steel added extensively to its world wide capabilities: it bought the steel-producing operations of VSZ a.s. in the Slovak Republic, the largest flat-rolled steel producer in Central Europe, renaming it U. S. Steel Kosice. And to round out its domestic tin-producing operations, U. S. Steel bought the tinmaking business of LTV Corporation.

U. S. Steel, therefore, not only remains America's largest steel company, but it will be one of the premier steelmakers in Europe, as well.

As we move further into the twenty-first century, USX Corporation, no doubt, will be changed significantly. Today, energy represents more than two-thirds of USX business, while steel accounts for the balance. U. S. Steel and Marathon each has its own class of stock. To determine if this structure serves the best interest of our shareholders, our board in late 2000 authorized an analysis by independent financial, legal and tax advisors. Sometime in 2001, U. S. Steel's 100th anniversary year, the board will announce the outcome of its review.

I am optimistic that, in some form, there will be a U. S. Steel a hundred years from now … still honored as the "good trust" … still sought after by investors … still respected for helping customers and the nation meet their challenges across the world … still considered by young people just starting out and veteran employees, alike, as a good place for pursuing careers … still recognized for providing a clean work environment from which employees return home, safely, each and every day.

Thomas J. Usher
February 25, 2001

Bibliography

Ahlbrandt, Roger S., Fruehan, Richard J., Jr., and Giarratani, Frank, *The Renaissance of American Steel*
(Oxford University Press, 1996)

Bain, Edgar C., *Pioneering in Steel Research*, *A Personal Record* (American Society for Metals, 1975)

Barnett, Donald F. and Schorsch, Louis, *Steel: Upheaval in a Basic Industry*
(Ballinger Publishing Company, 1983)

Brands, H. W., *TR: The Last Romantic* (Basic Books, 1997)

Brecher, Jeremy, *Strike!* (South End Press, 1997)

Bridge, James Howard, *The Inside History of the Carnegie Steel Company, 1903*
(Aldine Book Company, 1903; reprinted in 1991 by University of Pittsburgh Press)

Brody, David, *Steelworkers in America* (University of Illinois Press, 1998)

Carson, Rachel, *Silent Spring* (Houghton-Mifflin Company, 1962)

Casson, Herbert N., *The Romance of Steel* (A. S. Barnes & Company, 1907)

Chernow, Ron, *Titan: The Life of John D. Rockefeller, Sr.*
(Random House, 1998)

Churchill, Winston, *Memories of the Second World War* (Houghton-Mifflin Company edition, 1959)

Cotter, Arundel, *The Authentic History of the United States Steel Corporation*
(The Moody Magazine and Book Company, 1916)

Cotter, Arundel, *United States Steel: A Corporation With a Soul* (1921)

Cotter, Arundel, *The Gary I Knew* (Stratford Company, 1928)

Evans, Harold, *The American Century* (Knopf, 1998)

Flink, James, *The Reader's Companion to American History* (Houghton-Mifflin, 1991)

Garraty, John, *The Great Depression* (Harcourt Brace and Company, 1986)

Gossel, Peter and Leuthauser, Gabriele, *Architecture in the Twentieth Century*
(Benedikt Taschen Verlag, 1991)

Halberstam, David, *The Fifties* (Villard Books, 1993)

Hall, Christopher G. L., *Steel Phoenix: The Fall and Rise of the U. S. Steel Industry* (St. Martin's Press, 1997)

Hessen, Robert, *Steel Titan: The Life of Charles M. Schwab* (University of Pittsburgh Press, 1975)

Heyman, Neil, *World War I* (Greenwood Press, 1997)

Hoerr, John P., *And the Wolf Finally Came* (University of Pittsburgh Press, 1988)

Johnson, Paul, *Modern Times: The World from the Twenties to the Nineties* (Harper Collins, 1991)

Johnson, Paul, *A History of the American People* (Harper Collins, 1997)

Kennedy, David M., *Freedom From Fear: The American People in Depression and War, 1929-1945* (Oxford University Press, 1999)

Klingaman, William K., *1929, The Year of the Great Crash* (Harper & Row, 1989)

LePell, Fred, *Irving S. Olds: The Nicest Man I Ever Met* (Lind Brothers, 1980)

Lorant, Stefan, *Pittsburgh, The Story of an American City* (Doubleday and Co., Inc., 1964)

Mason, Alpheus Thomas, *Brandeis, A Free Man's Life* (Vikings Press, 1956)

McCullough, David, *The Path Between the Seas* (Simon and Schuster, 1977)

McCullough, David, *Truman* (Simon and Schuster, 1992)

McDonald, David, *Union Man* (Dutton, 1969)

Miller, Lonnie, *Robena: A Chronological History of Robena Mine in Greene County, Pennsylvania* (self-published, 1997)

Musselman, Moris, *Get a Horse!* (J. P. Lippincott Co., 1950)

O'Toole, Thomas, *The Economic History of the United States* (Lerner Publications Company, 1990)

Patterson, James T., *Grand Expectations* (Oxford University Press, 1996)

Preston, Richard, *American Steel* (Prentice Hall, 1991)

Reeves, Richard, *President Kennedy: Profile of Power* (Touchstone, 1994)

Reich, Robert, *The Work of Nations* (Random House, 1991)

Schreiner, Samuel A., *Henry Clay Frick* (St. Martin's Press, 1995)

Serrin, William, *Homestead: The Glory and Tragedy of an American Steel Town* (Times Book Division of Random House, 1992)

Sidey, Hugh, *John F. Kennedy, President* (Atheneum, 1963)

Smith, Page, *America Enters the World* (McGraw-Hill, 1985)

Strouse, Jean, *Morgan: American Financier* (Random House, 1999)

Tarbell, Ida M., *The Life of Elbert H. Gary* (D. Appleton and Company, 1925)

Wall, Joseph Frazier, *Andrew Carnegie* (Oxford University Press, 1970)

Warren, Kenneth, *The American Steel Industry: 1850-1970*
(University of Pittsburgh Press reprint, 1988)

Wasserstein, Bruce, *Big Deal* (Warner Books, 1998)

Yergin, Daniel, *The Prize: The Epic Quest for Oil, Money and Power*
(Simon and Schuster, 1991)

Archives of U. S. Steel/USX Corporation, Annandale, Pennsylvania

Selected Historical Archives of Carnegie Steel Corporation donated by USX
Corporation to the John Heinz Regional History Center, Pittsburgh, Pennsylvania

Position Papers prepared especially for this book in 1999 by the Law Department,
USX Corporation:

Hilton, Robert E., *The Acquisition of Marathon Oil Company by U. S. Steel,
Corporate Structure, From Holding Company to Operating Company*

Lerach, Richard E., *President Truman's Seizure of the Steel Industry,
U. S. Steel in World War II—The Truman Committee's Investigation
Relating to Steel Plate Products*

Lynch, David A., *Summary of the U. S. Steel Dissolution Case, 1910-1920*

McKim, William J., *U. S. Steel and the Environment*

Stanton, Robert M., *The Reformation of U. S. Steel*

White, William L., Jr., *A Chronological Summary of Labor Relations at U. S. Steel*

Wilson, John F., *Role of U. S. Steel in International Trade Policy and Litigation*

These texts published by U. S. Steel or its subsidiaries were also used in the writing
of this book.

Steel Serves the Nation, The Fifty Year Story of United States Steel, 1901-1951
(1951)

*The Radio Story of the Industrial Family that Serves the Nation...
United States Steel* (1946)

Steel Making in America (1949)

Steel: A Pictorial Presentation of United States Steel Corporation (1941)

Steel in the War (1946)

One Hundred Years On the Frontier (Marathon Oil Company, 1988)

Acknowledgments

*T**he Corporation* flickered into life more than five years ago. It was then that James L. Hamilton III, general manager, public affairs for USX Corporation, first approached then-Chairman Charles A. Corry and soon-to-be Chairman Thomas J. Usher to discuss possible projects in 2001 to help U. S. Steel observe its 100th birthday. The centerpiece, they decided, would be a permanent record of those years, a centennial biography.

Hamilton turned to Warren Hull, former director of corporate communications, asking him to come out of retirement to edit the book. Norman V. Richards, who succeeded Hull, joined his colleagues, and the triumvirate created a general concept for the history and picked a writer, Brian Apelt.

Throughout the creative process, Hamilton and Richards offered insightful suggestions regarding content, read hundreds of pages of manuscript and reviewed page proofs. To them, the author and editor are both indebted and grateful. The book is better for their involvement.

A narrative comes to life only when it succeeds in bringing *life* to its characters. In this book, you will meet many past, recently retired and current officers and executives. Many of them are historical characters whose early service to U. S. Steel helped to shape the corporation of today. Others are contemporary, and their firsthand reminiscences and observations are recorded in the last chapters of the book. To these latter folk, we express our appreciation for their interest in the project and for their candor during interviews.

Other USX employees—retired and active—also contributed mightily to the project: Dan D. Sandman, USX's general counsel and secretary, who provided advice on numerous points of corporate law; Charles G. Carson III, U. S. Steel Group's vice president-environmental affairs, who ensured accuracy in matters concerning U. S. Steel's pollution-control programs; Thomas W. Sterling, president, Transtar and former vice president-employee relations for U. S. Steel Group, who offered insights into the company's labor relations history; Vincent L. DiRicco, former editor of *U S Steel News*, who served as photo editor, researching corporate archives and libraries for photographs and art work; Robert L. Iland, manager, creative services, and his associate, Paul Klauss, commercial artist, who evaluated hundreds of photos and scanned the best for this book.

As word of the project spread, other employees, active and retired, came forward to offer a hand. They were valuable sources of background and memories: D. John Armstrong, Lynn D. Bell, John T. Bird, Betty Lou Bommer, Linda K. Boswell, Donald Clay, Doris J. Duncan, Thomas R. Ferrall, Joseph E. Furey, Grace M. Gawaldo, John Gregurich, Don Herring, Robert E. Hilton, William E. Keslar, Keith Kolb, Cary Kranz, Richard F. Lerach, David A. Lynch, Timothy P. McKay, William J. McKim, Lois B. Miller, William J. Muldoon (intern), Dr. William Murphy, Kris L. Price, Robert M. Stanton, Audrey Tietel, August M. "Buddy" Vann, Vicki Walker, William L. White, Jr. and John Wilson.

Every book demands an accurate and willing coordinator who will process chapter drafts into the computer, keep track of hundreds—if not thousands—of changes and corrections and who is prepared at a moment's notice to provide a clean, updated manuscript. Carlee J. Taylor performed this function tirelessly for **The Corporation**, and with laudable efficiency.

People outside USX also assisted: Michael Ellis, editor, Uniontown (Pennsylvania) *Herald Standard*; Mrs. Blaine Fairless; Jack Graham, Washington (Pennsylvania) *Observer Reporter*; Dr. Carolyn Schumacher, former director of Library and Archives, The Senator John Heinz Regional History Center, Pittsburgh; Lonnie Miller, coal industry historian, western Pennsylvania; and Kenneth R. Utz, former city editor, *Illinois State Journal*.

The design and print production of this book were entrusted to an all-Pittsburgh team: Janusz Einhorn, Jenifer Schweitzer and Carol Pickerine of Einhorn Design; and Stephanie Firtko of Hoechstetter Printing.

Dr. James Maher, provost, University of Pittsburgh, and Cynthia Miller, director, University of Pittsburgh Press, guided us safely through the mysteries of publishing—especially Ms. Miller, who joined the project in its first days. She was always ready with encouragement and solid advice.

We appreciate the efforts of all these individuals. As the corporation has always been defined in large measure by its employees, **The Corporation** is defined by those who helped in its creation.

The Author
The Editor
February 25, 2000

Index

Making continuously cast steel at U. S. Steel's Mon Valley Works in Pittsburgh, 2001.